Also by Wallace Stegner

FICTION

Remembering Laughter (1937)

The Potter's House (1938)

On a Darkling Plain (1940)

Fire and Ice (1941)

The Big Rock Candy Mountain (1943)

Second Growth (1947)

The Women on the Wall (short stories, 1950)

The Preacher and the Slave (1950; reprinted as *Joe Hill:
A Biographical Novel*, 1969)

The City of the Living (short stories, 1956)

A Shooting Star (1961)

All the Little Live Things (1967)

Angle of Repose (1971)

The Spectator Bird (1976)

Recapitulation (1979)

Crossing to Safety (1987)

Collected Stories (1990)

NONFICTION

Mormon Country (1942)

One Nation (with the editors of *Look*, 1945)

*Beyond the Hundredth Meridian: John Wesley Powell and the
Second Opening of the West* (1954)

*Wolf Willow: A History, a Story, and a Memory of the Last
Plains Frontier* (1962)

The Gathering of Zion: The Story of the Mormon Trail (1964)

The Sound of Mountain Water (essays, 1969)

The Uneasy Chair: A Biography of Bernard DeVoto (1974)

The Letters of Bernard DeVoto (editor, 1975)

American Places (with Page Stegner and Eliot Porter, 1981)

One Way to Spell Man (essays, 1982)

The American West as Living Space (1987)

Where the Bluebird Sings to the Lemonade Springs (1992)

MARKING THE SPARROW'S FALL

MARKING THE SPARROW'S FALL

The Making of the American West

Edited and with a Preface by

PAGE STEGNER

A JOHN MACRAE / OWL BOOK

Henry Holt and Company / New York

Henry Holt and Company, LLC
Publishers since 1866
115 West 18th Street
New York, New York 10011

Henry Holt® is a registered trademark
of Henry Holt and Company, LLC

Published in Canada by Fitzhenry & Whiteside Ltd.,
195 Allstate Parkway, Markham, Ontario L3R 4T8.

Library of Congress Cataloging-in-Publication Data
Stegner, Wallace Earle, 1909–1993.
Marking the sparrow's fall: the making of the American West /
edited and with a preface by Page Stegner.
p.   cm.
"A John Macrae book."
ISBN 0-8050-6296-3
1. West (U.S.)—Description and travel.   2. Stegner,
Wallace Earle, 1909–1993.   I. Stegner, Page.   II. Title.
F591.S8235   1998   97-49281
978—dc21   CIP

First published in hardcover in 1998 by
Henry Holt and Company, Inc.

A John Macrae / Owl Book

Designed by Michelle McMillian
Frontispiece by David O'Conner/Graphicstock

Printed in the United States of America

3   5   7   9   10   8   6   4   2

For Allison, Rachel, and Page

It is a country to breed mystical people, egocentric people, perhaps poetic people. But not humble ones. At noon the total sun pours on your single head; at sunrise or sunset you throw a shadow a hundred yards long. It was not prairie dwellers who invented the indifferent universe or impotent man. Puny you may feel there, and vulnerable, but not unnoticed. This is a land to mark the sparrow's fall.

from *Wolf Willow: A History, a Story, and a Memory of the Last Plains Frontier*

CONTENTS

Foreword: I Sing of America   xi

Preface   xv

HOME GROUND

Child of the Far Frontier   5

The Making of Paths   11

That Great Falls Year   16

At Home in the Fields of the Lord   29

Xanadu by the Salt Flats   38

The World's Strangest Sea   46

Lake Powell   57

Back Roads River   68

Back Roads of the American West   82

Why I Like the West   96

Contents

TESTIMONY

Wilderness Letter   *111*

It All Began with Conservation   *121*

The Best Idea We Ever Had   *135*

Qualified Homage to Thoreau   *143*

Living on Our Principal   *149*

Bernard DeVoto   *161*

Conservation Equals Survival   *174*

Now, If I Ruled the World . . .   *182*

INHERITANCE

The Twilight of Self-Reliance   *189*

Living Dry   *213*

The Rocky Mountain West   *230*

Land: America's History Teacher   *260*

GENESIS

Genesis   *281*

Foreword: I Sing of America

All my life I have been going away east and coming home west.

The first short story I ever published was about a young man driving his Model A from Kansas City across the plains and mountains and into the plateaus, until after thirty-six hours in the saddle he arrived at a Mormon cow town in Castle Valley, under the San Rafael Swell, to discover that the girl he was hurrying home to had found other consolations in his absence.

Not much of a story. The best thing in it was the exhilaration of driving west after a period of exile. The trip it reported took place forty-three years ago, the $25 that *Story* magazine paid me for the story did not last, and I've recovered from the girl long since. But in spite of the things that have happened to the West since 1932, things as drastic in their way as what happened to the girl, I have never recovered from the country.

Phoenix may be wreathed in smog and ringed with suburban sprawl, the air from Mexican Water to Grand Junction may be so glucky with particulates from the Four Corners power plant that you can't get a good picture of the most photogenic region on earth, the roads may have become superhighways leading from tourist trap to tourist trap, where they sell back to the white man the cheap gewgaws with which he subverted the red man a hundred years ago. The forest reserves and even some of the national parks may have half surrendered to the ski resorts, some of the loveliest canyons may be drowned under dubious draw-down reservoirs, some of the wildest rivers "tamed" (read "killed"). The only visible civilization the traveler sees may be the plastic roadside culture. We have spoiled a lot of the West as we have spoiled other parts of America, and it is a country that does not quickly heal. Nevertheless, every time I drive into it, any part of it, by any road, there comes some moment, generally in the early morning when the flat light reaches and reaches to pick out mountains or mesas half hidden beyond the rounding edge of the world, when I think, My God! There it is! There it still is!

And what is "it"? Is it anything more than the "landscape constantly increasing in scale" that Howard Mumford Jones says Americans have escaped into on their way west? I think so. Driving from rainy Washington or Oregon toward Idaho and Montana, you don't drive into any grander landscape, but you do drive into the West. Eastward.

All of the Wests, whether shortgrass plains, alpine mountains, slickrock plateaus and canyons, sagebrush or alkali deserts, are big. But the real West, the authentic West, must also be arid. From the hundredth meridian to the crest of the Sierra/Cascades, something abides that is different, separate, uniquely itself. What creates that uniqueness is the fact that except on the mountains, where much of it falls as snow, the annual rainfall is less than twenty inches.

Aridity makes all the difference. As Walter Webb made clear in *The Great Plains*, it is aridity that discourages the growth of turf and substitutes bunchgrass, sage, creosote bush, and bare ground. Aridity clarifies the air and electrifies distances. It dictates the very landscape—the erosional shapes of mesas, buttes, and cliffs; the profiles of canyons; the habits of rivers. It begets a new flora and a new fauna. Aridity inspired barbed wire and the windmill, altered laws and social organization, profoundly affected men, myths, and moralities.

It is probably a combination of a different landscape and an abiding human freedom-dream that tourists respond to in the West, and that accounts not only for careers like that of Billy the Kid but also for the whanged buckskins and picaresque lifestyles of transient hippies. But what a native recognizes and responds to, what tells him he is home, is the effect of aridity, apparent to all his senses. And if he has the freedom-dream, as he probably does, he also feels the tug of its opposite: sanctuary.

Escape into freedom exposes one to the dangers of a country not noticeably friendly to human occupation: one feels the empty spaces between the stars. That makes the oases where water has made a tentative abiding place all the more precious. There is no green so tender and welcoming as the irrigated green of a Nevada valley or a pocket among the red Utah cliffs. Nothing so stirs the spirit of someone who is really out submitting to the West's freedom as the trees of a town. A few cottonwoods, the guggle of water in a creek or ditch, can have as profound an effect on me as the grandest view. The grandest view somehow *includes* it, even if unseen. The equation is not complete without it.

And in spite of much human destruction, in spite of the huckstering of scenery and the commercializing of beauty and grandeur and awe, there is a lot of the West where both illimitable freedom and perfect sanctuary may be found. Aridity has done that, too. There is an awful lot of the West that hasn't enough water to endanger it, and there are oases (off the main highways) where a simpler, safer, more reverential relationship with a hard country is still maintained.

I know a lot of them, and they comfort my soul. But they should be discovered, not advertised.

Wallace Stegner

Preface

In the four years following my father's death a number of people have approached me with various projects related to his life and work, but with one or two exceptions I have declined. However worthy the contemplated activity, however great my personal affection for its subject and respectful of the body of work he produced, I have had no desire to become the docent for my father's literary legacy.

But the proposal to gather together his major writings on the American West tempered my reservations because, for one thing, it spoke to particular interests of my own, and for another, it seemed a reasonable extension of the intermittent collaboration we began back in 1978 with the co-authoring of *Rocky Mountain Country*, continued in 1981 with *American Places* also edited by this book's editor, and sustained along the way with a joint public appearance or two—events that we referred to as the Stegner dog and pony show.

There was a third, more important, incentive. When I began to consider what might be included in such an anthology I assumed I would necessarily rely heavily on work previously published in the five well-known (and still available) volumes of nonfiction, *The Sound of Mountain Water*, *One Way to Spell Man*, *Wolf Willow*, *American Places*, and *Where the*

Bluebird Sings to the Lemonade Springs. The purpose served by reprinting Wallace Stegner's reflections on the West as living space would be their concentration in a single volume.

But what I uncovered, as I thumbed my way through his colossal output (an oeuvre that spanned some fifty-five years), was a considerable body of material that had never appeared in *any* book, in some cases articles and essays that only a devoted scavenger of magazine and journal publications might reasonably know or possess. Even I was unaware of their existence. And since, as everybody knows, yesterday's newspaper or magazine is today's fish wrapping, there suddenly seemed an opportunity to preserve something valuable that would otherwise be lost.

If, of course, any of this stuff was worth preserving. "I have written reams of grocery-buying junk during my lifetime," my old man once told an interviewer, "and [my] bibliography shows it." The obvious question was whether these "discoveries" were of anything important, or just the unearthing of a prolific artist's kitchen midden.

There are about forty such pieces in all, some clearly dated in time, some of a strictly travelog nature, a few concerned with nonwestern regions of the country. But most are as relevant to issues that still confront the American West as any of his better-known works, and all of them are written with the same stylistic grace and intellectual rigor that earned him, over the years, his enormous readership. So far as my literary sensibilities can detect, none of it qualifies as "grocery-buying junk." Certainly not the wisdom of "The Twilight of Self-Reliance," which his biographer, Jack Benson, calls "the most complete exposition of Stegner's political-social beliefs" that he ever wrote; not "Land: America's History Teacher," a compact account of states' rights and public land policy and a powerful argument for continued federal control of the public domain; not "The Rocky Mountain West," as exceptional a survey of the "land of little rain and big consequences" (for those who remain in denial about aridity) as one can find.

Certainly not the humor of "Why I Like the West," wherein he insists that as a wild man from the West "I have always done my honest best to live up to what tradition says I should be. I have always tried to look like Gary Cooper and talk like the Virginian. I have endeavored to be morally upright, courteous to women; with an innate sense of right and wrong but without the polish that Yale College or European travel might have put upon me. I have consented to be forgiven my frontier gaucheries, and I did not hold it against the waiter in the Parker House bar when he removed my feet from the upholstery."

Certainly not the equally hilarious "Xanadu by the Salt Flats," wherein he recalls his days as a hot-dog vendor at Saltair, a pleasure dome on the shores of the Great Salt Lake. "Now and again, on a picnic hill, when the incense of hamburgers and hot dogs grows thick and stupefying, I am moved to rise on my hind legs with a spatula in one hand and a bun in the other and give voice to an atavistic howl, a nasal, high, drawn-out ululation like that of a muezzin from a minaret or a coyote from a river bluff.

" 'Wellllll, they're all hot, they're all ready-uh! Faaaamous Coney Island red-hots! It's a loaf-a-bread-a-pound-a-meat and all the mustard you can eat for a thin skinny little dime, folks! Step oooooovah!' "

All this may have bought the groceries, but none of it was junk.

The second obvious question was why he didn't preserve these essays himself in some collection of his own making. I think quite simply he *forgot* about a lot of the things he had written—forgot because there was so much of it, and because both his themes and his personal convictions were often repeated and continuously expanded, whether his medium was fiction, nonfiction, address, lecture, interview, or just "a conversation with."

It is useful to remember that Wallace Stegner was a writer whose *incomplete* bibliography, compiled in 1990 by Nancy Colberg, lists 35 published books (including 15 novels, 5 works of history, and 2 biographies), 57 short stories, 242 articles, 164 first-appearance contributions and books edited (including forewords, afterwords, introductions, essay chapters, and critical prefaces). He was, moreover, a novelist, historian, biographer, and essayist who for four decades of his adult life was also a full-time professor of American literature and director of the Stanford Writing Program. There just was not a whole lot of time in his day to sit around annotating a curriculum vitae and organizing old files.

In selecting appropriate texts I was initially reluctant to put aside major essays like "Striking the Rock," "Variations on a Theme by Crèvecoeur," "The Gift of Wilderness," "Dead Heart of the West," and "Inheritance." In the end I included almost nothing of his previously collected nonfiction—in fact, there are only two abridged chapters from *Wolf Willow*, as they originally appeared in *The New Yorker* and *Horizon* magazine, two essays from *Where the Bluebird Sings to the Lemonade Springs*, and the "Wilderness Letter" from *The Sound of Mountain Water*. The latter has had greater exposure than practically anything he ever wrote, but I could not bear to leave it out. Without it the modern conservation movement would still be trying to mine quotable nuggets from Henry David Thoreau and Aldo Leopold, and it is certainly one of the greatest statements of an environmental ethic ever written.

Finally it seemed both to me and my editor, Jack Macrae, that to include in this literary gathering only the eloquence of Stegner the essayist, historian, and environmental advocate was to ignore what his career had first and foremost been about—i.e., the writing of fiction. We wanted a dramatized work (or works), but *which* of the many choices might best fit with the general conception of the book was not immediately clear. Happily my mother, Mary Stegner, pointed to the obvious—the novella "Genesis" from the hybrid history/story/memoir of the last plains frontier, *Wolf Willow*. Not only is "Genesis" the best story he ever wrote, in my opinion, but it is a narrative of rugged individualism subsumed by and sublimated to the need for cooperative enterprise, and this, as any reader of Stegner's work quickly understands, is what the demythologized West was *absolutely* all about.

Memory, history, story, defense of the earth—what began as a kind of congeries of my father's major writings on civility and the American West became, I believe, something altogether more consequential. It became an addition to the general account rather than a summation of previously acknowledged parts. As such it is as complete and comprehensive a statement as we are ever likely to have about what it means to be a westerner, about what it means to know ourselves as "a part of the natural world and competent to belong in it." Long ago, when Archibald MacLeish wrote "the West is a country in the mind, and so eternal," he was speaking of a geography of the imagination, of an artistic identification with the wild, arid domain beyond the Rocky Mountains from which our most important stories arise. He might well have been speaking of the country in Wallace Stegner's mind.

Page Stegner
Santa Cruz, California

Part One

HOME GROUND

Editor's Note

The essays in the section that follows were written over a thirty-year period and are among the most candidly autobiographical of Wallace Stegner's uncollected writings. Novelists publish their lives "piecemeal and in disguised form, all the time," he once wrote. "They use up their autobiographical capital in fictions." But not all of it, obviously. There was enough left over for seventeen or eighteen personal pieces in *Where the Bluebird Sings to the Lemonade Springs, American Places,* and *The Sound of Mountain Water* and for nine more that are gathered in this edition. Although the focus is always on place (rather than on the "I" of the beholder), one gets a clear autobiographical line that extends from childhood in Saskatchewan and Great Falls to adolescence and early adulthood in Salt Lake, thence outward into plateau country, the arid home ground of wind and rock and sky that played such a major role in the shaping of Stegner's artistic sensibility.

"Child of the Far Frontier" first appeared in *Horizon* magazine in 1962 and is an abridged version of a chapter in *Wolf Willow.* "The Making of Paths" is also an abridged version of a *Wolf Willow* chapter, and first appeared in *The New Yorker* in 1958. "That Great Falls Year" appeared in *Montana Spaces: Essays and Photographs in Celebration of Montana,* edited by William Kittredge, 1988. "At Home in the Fields of the Lord" appeared in *The Sound of Mountain Water*, 1969; "The World's Strangest Sea," in *Holiday* magazine in 1957. The earliest of these pieces, "Back Roads River," appeared in the *Atlantic Monthly* in 1948; the latest, "Xanadu by the Salt Flats," in *American Heritage* in 1981. "Lake Powell" was written for *Holiday* magazine in 1966. "Back Roads of the American West" and "Why I Like the West" were both written for *Tomorrow* magazine in 1950.

Child of the Far Frontier

Unless everything in a man's memory of childhood is misleading, there is a time somewhere between the ages of five and twelve that corresponds to the phase ethologists have isolated in the development of birds, when an impression lasting only a few seconds may be imprinted on the young bird for life. Expose a just-hatched duckling to an alarm clock, or a wooden decoy on rollers, or a man, or any other object that moves and makes a noise, and it will react to that object for life as if it were its mother. Expose a child to a particular environment at his susceptible time and he will perceive in the shapes of that environment until he dies.

The smell of the gray-leafed shrub called wolf willow brings back my childhood as infallibly as if it were Proust's tea, but other things than smells will do it. I can sing an old Presbyterian Sunday-school hymn, "The Fight Is On, Oh Christian Soldiers," and instantly I am seven or eight years old, it is a June day on the old Saskatchewan homestead, the coulee is full of buttercups, and a flickertail's close-eared head is emerging in jerks from a burrow, the unblinking almond eye watching to see if I move. Only because I must have sung it to myself in that spot, a few bars of that tune can immerse me in the old sun and space, return me to the big geometry of the prairie and the tension of the prairie wind.

I still sometimes dream, occasionally in the most intense and brilliant shades of green, of a jungly dead bend of the Whitemud River below Martin's dam. Each time I am haunted, on awaking, by a sense of meanings just withheld, and by a profound nostalgic melancholy. Yet why should this dead loop of river, known only for a few years, be so charged with potency in my unconscious? Why should there be around it so many other images that constantly recur in dreams or in the phrases I bring up off the typewriter onto the page? They lie in me like underground water; every well I put down taps them.

I suppose I know, actually, why that river dream is so potent. As the summer prairie of the homestead taught me identity by exposing me, the Whitemud River valley where we wintered taught me about safety. In a jumpy and insecure childhood where all masculine elements are painful or dangerous, sanctuary matters. That sunken bottom sheltered from the total sky and the untrammeled wind was my hibernating ground, my place of snugness; and in a country often blistered and crisped, green became the color of safety.

I do not mean to indulge in psychological narcissism. There is something else here, a nature-nurture problem of a more general bearing. For the processes of deculturation, isolation, and intellectual schizophrenia that I underwent as a result of being brought up on a belated, almost symbolic frontier were until recently a most common American experience. Like other Americans uncertain of who they are, I take a firm hold on the certainties of where I am from. I can say to myself that a good part of my private and social character, the kinds of scenery and weather and people and humor I respond to, the prejudices I wear like dishonorable scars, the affections that sometimes waken me from middle-aged sleep with a rush of undiminished love, the virtues I respect and the weaknesses I condemn, the code I try to live by, the special ways I fail at it and the kinds of shame I feel when I do, the models and heroes I follow, the colors and shapes that evoke my deepest pleasure, the way I adjudicate between personal desire and personal responsibility, have been in good part scored into me by that little womb-village and the lovely, lonely, exposed prairie of the homestead.

However anachronistic I may be, I am a product of the American earth, and in nothing quite so much as in the contrast between what I knew through the pores and what I was officially taught. For education tried, inadequately and hopelessly, against all odds, to make a European of me. I was charged with getting in a single lifetime, from scratch, what some people inherit as naturally as they breathe air. And not merely cultural matters. I was nearly twelve before I saw either a bathtub or a water closet; and when I walked past my first lawn, in Great Falls, Montana, I stooped down and touched its cool nap in awe and unbelief. I think I held my breath—I had not known that people anywhere lived with such grace. Also I had not known until then how much ugliness I myself had lived with. Our homestead yard was as bare as an alkali flat, because my father, observing some folklore fire precaution, insisted on throwing out the soapy wash water until he had killed off every blade of grass or cluster of false mallow inside the fireguard.

Still, there are some advantages to growing up a savage, and to tell the truth I am not sure I would trade my childhood of freedom and the outdoors and the senses for a childhood of being led by the hand past all the Turners in the National Gallery. Anyone starting from deprivation is spared getting bored. You may not get a good start, but you may get up a considerable head of steam. I am reminded of Willa Cather, that bright girl from Nebraska who memorized long passages from the *Aeneid* and hunted down whatever Old World culture was available to her in Red Cloud or Lincoln. She tried, and her education encouraged her, to be a good European. And yet she was a first-rate novelist only when she dealt with what she knew from Red Cloud and the big grasslands. They were what she was born to write; the rest of it was got up. Eventually, when education had won and nurture had conquered nature and she had recognized Red Cloud as a vulgar little hole, she embraced totally the traditions of strangers, and ended neither quite a good American nor quite a true European nor quite a whole artist.

Her career is a parable. If there is truth in D. H. Lawrence's assertion that America's unconscious wish has always been to destroy Europe, there is equal truth in the assertion that every American is an incipient expatriate tempted toward apostasy and reconciliation with the Old World parent. It is a painful division, and the farther you are from Europe—that is, the farther you are out in the hinterlands of America—the more painful it is. Contradictory voices tell you who you are and who you ought to be. You grow up speaking one dialect and reading and writing another. During twenty-odd years of education and another thirty of literary practice you may learn to be nimble in the King's English; yet in moments of relaxation, crisis, or surprise you fall back into the corrupted lingo that is your native tongue. But you can hardly write that lingo if you try: all the forces of Culture and snobbery are against your *writing* by ear, for your most native audience. For one thing, your most native audience doesn't read—it *isn't* an audience. You grow out of touch with your dialect because education and association lead the other way. Only an occasional Mark Twain or Robert Frost speaks with the country tongue. The deculturation of the frontier leads not on to something new but back to an indifferent copy of the abandoned old.

In practice, frontier deculturation means a falling-back on mainly oral traditions, on the things that can be communicated without books: on folklore, on the music and poetry and story easily memorized, on the cookery that comes not from cookbooks but from habit and laziness, on the medicine that is old wives' tales. Before it was more than half assembled from its random parts, the folklore of Whitemud was mine. But I also read whatever books I could lay hands on, and almost everything I got from books was at odds with what I knew from experience or irrelevant to it or remote from it.

Our house contained some novels, mainly by George Barr McCutcheon and Gene Stratton Porter, a set of Shakespeare in marbled bindings with red leather spines and corners, and a massive set of Ridpath's *History of the World*. I handled them all, and I suppose read in them some, uncomprehendingly, from the time I was five. It was my mother's inaccurate boast that I had read clear through Ridpath's eight or nine volumes by the time I was eight.

Let us say that I had looked at the pictures, and learned a few names, and could parrot a few captions. Much of that random rubbish is still in my head like an impression in wax, and comes out of me now as if memory were a phonograph record. What strikes me about this in recollection is not my precocious or fictitious reading capacity, and not the durability of memory, but the fact that the information I was gaining had not the slightest relevance to the geography, history, or life of the place where I lived. Living in the Cypress Hills, I did not even know I lived there, and hadn't the faintest notion of who had lived there before me. But I could have drawn you a crudely approximate map of the Baltic or the Mediterranean, recited you Tom Moore songs or Joaquin Miller's poem about Columbus, and given you a rudimentary notion of the virtues of the Gracchi or the misfortunes of the Sabine women.

Though my friends and I sometimes planned gaudy canoe expeditions down the Whitemud, we had no notion where such a trip might bring us out, and no notion that there were maps which would tell us. The willow-fringed stream, after it left the Hills, might as well have been on its way to join the Alpheus. The Hills of which I was an unknowing resident were only a few fixed points: North Bench, South Bench, the sandhills, Chimney Coulee. I did not relate them, for knowledge of place, like knowledge of the past, meant to me something far and foreign.

In general the assumption of all of us, child or adult, was that this was a new country and that a new country had no history. History was something that applied to other places. It would not have seemed reasonable to any of the town's founders to consider their activities history, or to look back very far in search of what had preceded them. Time reached back only a few years, to the pre-homestead period of the big cattle ranches. Some ranches had weathered the terrible winter of 1906, and to a child these survivors seemed to have been there forever, floating in an enduring present like the town. For that matter, I never heard of the terrible winter of 1906 until many years later, though it had affected my life for me before I was born.

Under the circumstances it might sound fanciful to suggest that either the geography of the history of the Cypress Hills could have had any substantial part in making the minds and characters of children reared there. Certainly they could have no strong and immediate effect, as they might have upon a child who passes every day the rude bridge where the embattled farmers of Concord precipitated a new age with a volley of musketry; or upon a child who flies his kite in the Saratoga meadow where the bronze boot commemorates the nameless heroism of a traitor. The past becomes a thing made palpable in monuments, buildings, historical sites, museums, attics, old trunks, relics of a hundred kinds; and in the legends of grandfathers and great-grandfathers; and in the incised marble and granite and weathered wood of graveyards; and in the murmurings of ghosts. We knew no such history, no such past, no such tradition, no such ghosts. And yet it would be a double error to assume that my childhood had no history, and that I was not influenced by it.

For history is a pontoon bridge. Every man walks and works at its building end, and has come as far as he has over the pontoons laid by others he may never have heard of. Events have a way of making other events inevitable; the actions of men are consecutive and indivisible. The history of the Cypress Hills had almost as definite effects on me as did their geography and weather, though I never knew a scrap of that history until a quarter century after I left the place. However it may have seemed to the people who founded it in 1914, Whitemud was not a beginning, not a new thing, but a stage in a long historical process.

History? Seldom, anywhere, have historical changes occurred so fast. From grizzlies, buffaloes, and Indians still only half-possessed of the horse and gun, the historical parabola to Dust Bowl and near depopulation covered only about sixty years. Here was the Plains frontier in a capsule, condensed into the life of a reasonably long-lived man.

And even though unwritten, it is not lost. Experience enlarges and illuminates it, it continues as remembered faces, it echoes in the head in half-forgotten names, it exists as a part of folklore. Without having been taught, it is to some degree understood. Like the sensuous images persistent from childhood, like the ineradicable attitudes and prejudices, the history of one's truly native place may be comprehended in the bone and the blood, and one may build a life forward from it as surely as if his past had been learned under savants and memorialized in monuments and ruins.

The Making of Paths

On the Saskatchewan homestead that we located in 1915 there was at first absolutely nothing. I remember it as it originally was, for my brother and I, aged eight and six, accompanied my father when he went out to make the first "improvements." Our land lay exactly on the international border; the four-foot iron post jutting from the prairie just where our wagon track met the section-line trail to Hydro, Montana, marked not only the otherwise invisible distinction between Canada and the United States but the division between our land and all other, anywhere.

There were few other marks to show which three hundred and twenty acres of that empty plain were ours. The land spread as flat as if it had been graded, except where, halfway to our western line, a shallow, nearly imperceptible coulee began, feeling its way, turning and turning again, baffled and blocked, a watercourse so nearly a slough that the spring runoff had hardly any flow at all, its water not so much flowing as pushed by the thaw behind it and having to go somewhere, until it passed our land and turned south, and near the line found another lost coulee, which carried in most seasons some water—not enough to run but enough to seep, and with holes that gave sanctuary to a few minnows and suckers. That was Coteau Creek, a part of the Milk-Missouri watershed. In good seasons we sometimes got a swim of sorts in its holes; in dry years we hauled water from it in barrels, stealing from the minnows to serve ourselves and our stock. Between it and our house we wore, during the four or five summers we spent vainly trying to make a wheat farm there, one of our private wagon tracks.

Coteau Creek was a landmark and sometimes a hazard. Once my father, gunning our old Model T across one of its fords, hit something and broke an axle. Next day he walked forty miles into Chinook, Montana, leaving me with a homesteader family, and the day after that he brought back the axle on his back and installed it himself after the homesteader's team had hauled the Ford out of the creek bed. I remember that square, high car, with its yellow spoke wheels and its brass bracing rods from windshield to mudguards and its four-eared brass radiator cap. It stuck up black and foreign, a wanderer from another planet, on the flats by Coteau Creek, while my father, red-faced and sweating, crawled in and out under the jacked-up rear end and I squatted in the car's shade and played what games I could with pebbles and a blue robin's egg. We sat there on the plain, something the earth refused to swallow, right in the middle of every-thing and with the prairie as empty as nightmare clear to the line where hot earth met hot sky. I saw the sun flash off brass, a heliograph winking off a message into space, calling attention to us, saying "Look, look!"

Because that was the essential feeling of the country for me—the sense of being foreign and noticeable, of sticking out—I did not at first feel even safe, much less that I was taking charge of and making my own a parcel of the world. I moped for the town on the Whitemud River, forty miles north, where we lived in winter, where all my friends were, where my mother was waiting until we got a shelter built on the homestead. Out here we did not belong to the earth as the prairie dogs and burrowing owls and picket-pin gophers and weasels and badgers and coyotes did, or to the sky as the hawks did, or to any combination as meadow larks and robins and sparrows did. Our shack, covered with tar paper, was an ugly rectangle on the face of the prairie, and not even the low roof, rounded like the roof of a railroad car to give the wind less grip on it, could bind it into the horizontal world.

Before we got the shack built, we lived in a tent, which the night wind constantly threatened to blow away, flapping the canvas and straining the ropes and pulling the pegs from the gravel. And when, just as we were unloading the lumber for the shack, a funnel-shaped cloud appeared in the south, moving against a background of gray-black shot with lightning-forks, and even while the sun still shone on us, the air grew tense and metallic to breathe, and a light like a reflection from brass glowed around us, and high above, pure and untroubled, the zenith was blue—then indeed exposure was like paralysis or panic, and we looked at the strangely still tent, bronzed in the yellow air, and felt the air shiver and saw a dart of wind move like a lizard across the dust and vanish again. My father rushed us to the three shallow square holes, arranged in a triangle, with the iron section stake at their apex, that marked the corner of our land, and with ropes he lashed us to the stake and made us cower down in the holes. They were no more than a foot deep; they could in no sense be called shelter. Over their edge our eyes, level with the plain, looked southward and saw nothing between us and the ominous funnel except gopher mounds, the still unshaken grass. Across the coulee a gopher sat up, erect as the picket pin from which he took his name.

Then the grass stirred; it was as if gooseflesh prickled suddenly on the prairie's skin. The gopher disappeared as if some friend below had reached up and yanked him into his burrow. Even while we were realizing it, the yellow air darkened, and then all the brown and yellow went out of it and it was blue-black. The wind began to pluck at the shirts on our backs, the hair on our heads was wrenched, the air was full of dust. From the third hole my father, glaring over the shallow rim, yelled to my brother and to me to keep down, and with a fierce rush rain trampled our backs, and the curly buffalo grass at the level of my squinted eyes was strained out straight and whistling. I popped my head into my arms and fitted my body to the earth. To give the wind more than my flat back, I felt, would be sure destruction, for that was a wind, and that was a country, that hated a foreign and vertical thing.

The cyclone missed us; we got only its lashing edge. We came up cautiously from our muddy burrows and saw the clearing world and smelled the air, washed and rinsed of all its sultry oppressiveness. I for one felt better about being who I was, but for a good many weeks I watched the sky with suspicion; exposed as we were, it could jump on us like a leopard from a tree. And I know I was disappointed in the shack

13

my father swiftly put together on our arid flat. A soddy that poked its low
brow no higher than the tailings of a gopher's burrow would have suited
me better. The bond with the earth that all the footed and winged creatures felt in that country was quite as valid for me.

And that was why I so loved the trails and paths we made; they were
ceremonial, an insistence not only that we had a right to be in sight on
those prairies but that we owned a piece of them and controlled it. In a
country practically without landmarks, as that part of Saskatchewan was,
it might have been assumed that any road would comfort the soul. But I
don't recall feeling anything special about the graded road that led us
three-quarters of the forty miles of our annual June pilgrimage from town
to homestead, or for the wiggling tracks that turned off it to the homesteads of others. It was our own trail, lightly worn, its ruts a slightly
fresher green where old cured grass had been rubbed away, that lifted
my heart; it took off across the prairie like an extension of myself. Our
own wheels had made it; broad, iron-shod wagon wheels first, then
narrow democrat wheels that cut through the mat of grass and scored the
earth until it blew and washed and started a rut, then finally the wheels of
the Ford.

By the time we turned off it, the road we had followed from town had
itself dwindled to a pair of ruts, but it never quite disappeared; it simply
divided into branches like ours. I do not know why the last miles, across
buffalo grass and burnouts, past a shack or two abandoned by the homesteaders who had built them, across Coteau Creek, and on westward
until the ruts passed through our gate in our fence and stopped before
our house, should always have excited me so, unless it was that the trail
was a thing we had exclusively created and that it led to a place we had
exclusively built. Those tracks demonstrated our existence as tri-
umphantly as an Indian is demonstrated by his handprint painted in
ochre on a cliff wall. Not so idiotically as the stranded Ford, this trail and
the shack and chicken house and privy at its end said, "See? We are
here." Thus, in a sense, was "located" a homestead.

More satisfying than the wagon trail, even, because more intimately
and privately made, were the paths that our daily living wore in the
prairie. I loved the horses for poking along the pasture fence looking for a

way out, because that habit very soon wore a plain path all around inside the barbed wire. Whenever I had to go and catch them for something, I went out of my way to walk in it, partly because the path was easier on my bare feet but more because I wanted to contribute my feet to the wearing process. I scuffed and kicked at clods and persistent grass clumps, and twisted my weight on incipient weeds and flowers, willing that the trail around the inside of our pasture should be beaten dusty and plain, a worn border to our inheritance.

It was the same with the path to the woodpile and the privy. In June, when we reached the homestead, that would be nearly overgrown, the faintest sort of radius line within the fireguard. But our feet quickly wore it anew, though there were only the four of us, and though other members of the family, less addicted to paths than I, often frustrated and irritated me by cutting across from the wrong corner of the house, or detouring past the fence-post pile to get a handful of cedar bark for kindling, and so neglecting their plain duty to the highway. It was an unspeakable satisfaction to me when after a few weeks I could rise in the flat morning light that came across the prairie in one thrust, like a train rushing down a track, and see the beaten footpath, leading gray and dusty between grass and cactus and the little orange flowers of the false mallow that we called wild geranium, until it ended, its purpose served, at the hooked privy door.

Wearing any such path in the earth's rind is an intimate act, an act like love, and it is denied to the dweller in cities. He lacks the proper mana for it, he is out of touch. Once, on Fifty-eighth Street in New York, I saw an apartment dweller walking his captive deer on a leash. They had not the pleasure of leaving a single footprint, and the sound of the thin little hoofs on concrete seemed as melancholy to me as, at the moment, the sound of my own.

That Great Falls Year

When my family came down out of Saskatchewan to Great Falls, Montana, in the fall of 1920 I was eleven years old. For most of my conscious life I had known only our scruffy little village in the valley of the Whitemud River, a village five years younger than I was, and in the summers a homestead as lost out on the prairie as a rowboat in an empty ocean.

I had always been sickly, with croups and coughs and pneumonias, and in winter lived on Scott's Emulsion, a repulsive form of cod liver oil. But I had also lived a life so free and unsupervised that it astonishes me now to remember it. I was much outdoors, both summer and winter. I had owned and used guns since the age of seven or eight, and like frontier boys in general I had grown up killing things—gophers, rabbits, small fur-bearers, even the occasional feral cat whose pelt was worth fifty cents in the St. Louis fur market. And I had secrets darker than I would ever have turned loose. My father's erratic and sometimes unlawful activities had taught me to keep my mouth shut, and given me, along with some private shame, a wariness older than my years. In other ways I was younger, even infantile. And I was studious, a reader, in love with words. When under strain, or when things weren't going well, I sometimes reverted to baby talk that drove my father crazy.

In short, an uncouth sensitive little savage with terminal sniffles, a cry-baby with an extensive history of dealing death, a pint-sized loner with big daydreams, clammy self-doubts, and an ego out of proportion to the rest of him.

And ignorant—utterly, wonderfully ignorant. I knew nothing of the world outside my own experience except what I had picked up from books and from the Sears Roebuck and T. Eaton catalogs, and none of that was real. It belonged to the world of school, which was as different from my daily life as summer is from winter. What I remember from school is mainly the poetry we read—Tennyson, Longfellow, Joaquin Miller, Tom Moore. I can turn them on yet, hundreds of lines, like indelible neon in my head. But what I remember from recess is something else: fist fights (daily, but not involving me because I was too little and too timid), and times when the whole unlicked horde of us ran yelling along the cutbank trying to stone to death some unlucky muskrat that had set off upriver with a shining stick of water in his teeth.

Briefly, at the age of three, I had lived in Seattle, and before that in North Dakota and Iowa, and so the outside world must have left some marks on me, but at eleven I retained none of that experience. When our green Essex pulled up in front of our rented house in Great Falls, I was as green as the car, incomparably uninstructed in the arts of civilization, as vulnerable to amazement, wonder, perplexity, apprehension, and delight as if I had been a fifteenth-century Carib brought from his island to the court of Castile.

The court of Castile could not have impressed a Carib any more than our new house impressed me. Though in the year that I lived there I came to know Great Falls pretty intimately; from the Giant Spring to Third Island and from Little Chicago to Black Eagle Park, it was not the big city with its paved streets and streetcars, but the household details that impressed me first. I knew about a lot of these details from pictures in the mail-order catalogs, but, like the places and events of books, they were insubstantial, things heard about, never seen. Seeing them, experiencing them, was a series of cultural shocks.

Lawns, for instance, those marvelous green naps so lovely to roll on, so cool to bare feet, so sweet-smelling when just mown. I associate them still with Charlie Russell, who lived near us and whose lawn I mowed a couple of times, that summer or the next. But when we arrived, I had never seen a lawn, or imagined one. Front yards in my experience had been weeds and bare dirt and perhaps some dead nasturtiums clinging to strings against the house. On the farm the yard had been an alkali flat. As for back yards, which here seemed to have laundry lines and fruit trees and garden patches, in Saskatchewan they had been littered with bones, kindling piles, feathers, and sometimes, near the chopping block, chicken heads. Here, the miracle of turf impressed me for the first time with the sheer *comfort* of the earth.

Up the middle of our front lawn, like the part in a bartender's hair, a cement sidewalk ran from street to porch steps. I had never seen a sidewalk, either, except the plank ones that had made passable one block on each side of Main Street. I could imagine how clean this would be on muddy days, how easily shoveled in winter, how much of an improvement on our village paths, muddy or dusty depending on the weather, and in winter only trampled troughs through the snow.

On the riser of the top porch step were brass numbers—448 as I remember. They meant that our address, ours alone, recognizable to postman, milkman, iceman, or anyone, was 448 Fourth Avenue North. I had never known anybody with a street address (or, for that matter, a postman, milkman, or iceman). Those numbers promoted me into heightened identity in the midst of all the strangeness, and it was not until I saw that other houses up and down the street had them too that I lost my awe at our new status. But how *ingenious!* said my respectful mind to me. How orderly! How right!

On every side, at every moment, I found household marvels. Electric lights came on at the flip of a switch. No more trimming of wicks and wiping out of smoked lamp chimneys with crumpled newspapers. No more carrying of an inadequate glow from room to room. (But no more tranced moments of staring into a cross in the lamp chimney, either, and wondering who was going to die. Modern technology ignored the omens of folklore.)

The living and dining rooms in our Great Falls house had hardwood floors whose smoothness absolutely delighted me, and whose unfaded rectangles where other people's rugs had lain spoke of mysterious unknown lives. Until my mother spoiled the floors with our own rugs, I spent a lot of time skating around in my stocking feet in a state of Byzantine exaltation, imagining that I had been transported into an enchanted place and liberated from gravity and friction into a condition known only to birds and fishes.

Before my translation to the advanced civilization of Montana, I had never taken a bath except in a tin washtub in front of the kitchen range, in water warmed on the stove. I was the youngest in the family, and our water came the hard way, by bucket and grunt, up a cutbank from the river and across fifty yards of rough ground, so that I generally got my bath in water that had already cleansed somebody else. But here, in a little room upstairs, were all the things I had seen pictured in the catalogs but had never seen in the porcelain.

Here was a claw-footed long tub into which water poured lavishly, hot or cold, at a turn of a tap. It didn't have to be carried out and dumped later, either, but ran swirling down a hole when you pulled the rubber stopper.

Here was a washbowl, white and gleaming and serviced by similar hot and cold taps. No more tin washbasin on a stand by the kitchen door, no more slop bucket behind a curtain underneath.

And here was the real thriller, a water closet, something I had speculated about, wondering how it worked. It turned out that it was a sort of chair or chamberpot half full of water, that accepted bodily wastes as a chamberpot would, but then at the yank of a chain gulped them down and vanished them. It made the old privy, smelly and fly-blown in summer, icy in winter, with no amenities except an out-of-date Sears Roebuck catalog, so primitive and incompetent in retrospect that I could hardly believe how we had lived only days before.

I was not so dumb that, like Steinbeck's Okies, I thought I had broken the thing the first time I pulled the chain and all that water came down, but I did have to practice on it some to discover that it would not repeat its act at once, that you had to wait a few minutes for it to renew itself before it would gush again. And it did take me a couple of visits before I found that it had a little folding saddle, and did not have to be ridden bareback.

Marvels, sybaritic comforts that within a day I could not have done without. They so fascinated me that for several days I hardly ventured out into the strange streets of town, but contented myself with exploring and experimenting with what I found in the house. I got my monkey fingers into everything, and shortly I got a monkey's comeuppance.

In the baseboard of the living room there were little brass sockets with two holes in them into which could be plugged the cords of lamps. One of these had had its insides unscrewed, leaving a hole about an inch deep and as big around as a quarter. It struck me as a fine secret place to keep my little hoard of nickels and pennies, for it had a brass cover that closed down over it, sealing it away from other eyes. When no one was around, I opened the little door and shoved some coins in against the back wall of the hole.

The world exploded in my face, paralysis flashed through me, I was knocked silly. When I got myself together I felt as if all my hair had been singed off. There was a smell of brimstone. My coins, dented and scorched, were scattered across the floor. Shocked and shamed, but not as ignorant as I had been a minute before, I gathered them up and sneaked away.

It may be that all that episode taught me was not to put fingers or coins into hot electric outlets. But I think it taught me a somewhat larger truth too: nothing potent and attractive is without danger. Civilization is built of thunderbolts.

Shortly I learned some more lessons.

We had arrived so close to the beginning of school, and my mother had been so busy getting us settled, that Sunday came upon us before she could get me down to Strain's Department Store for some new school clothes. Apologetic at having failed me, she wondered if, just for the first day or so, I would mind going in what I had.

I had no problem with that: I think I *wanted* to go in what I had worn up in Canada, for I could see how different Montana was, and it seemed to me that in my Canadian clothes I might look foreign, exotic, and interesting, a hardy frontiersman. And I was not afraid of starting school in a strange place: I looked forward to the opportunity. School was where I shone. In our village I had been the bright boy, had skipped the third grade, and had a letter from my old teacher to my new ones saying that I should be allowed to skip the seventh too, that I was ready for eighth-grade work.

On Monday morning my mother put my brown bag of lunch into my hand and looked me over uncertainly. "Can you do it all right? Would you like me to go with you?"

Have my mother lead me by the *hand* to the *eighth grade?* "Heck no!"

"Have you got your letter?"

I patted my buttoned-down hip pocket.

"Miss Merryman said take it to the principal."

"Sure, sure."

"All right." She stood looking at me a minute, stooped to give me a hug. Her eyes were shiny and her voice a little shaky. "Do well, now. Have a good time. Learn a lot. Come right home after. I'll want to hear all about it."

I can see that little runt setting off down the street, and I want to call him back. My imagination, operating from a base nearly seventy years later in time, cringes. The storyteller in me sees this as the beginning of an Ugly Duckling story, and the Ugly Duckling story requires multiple humiliations before it reaches its triumphant fairy-tale ending in the beauty of white feathers.

Come back, I want to advise him. Put it off a day. Wait until your mother can get you some shoes, at least. Those elk-hide moccasins were O.K. for a jerk town on the Whitemud, but they look pretty funny on pavement, in combination with short pants and long black stockings. While she's at it, have her get you something besides that orange sweater with the turtleneck up under your ears, and the white stripe around the chest that makes you look like a Hampshire shoat. And for God's sake quit stalking pigeon-toed as if you were a six-foot-three Daniel Boone on the track of a bear. Come on back home. Tell your mother you have a headache.

Futile, of course. He left sixty-seven years ago.

On the way to school, if I found myself catching up with other kids, I walked slower. If any showed signs of catching up with me, I walked faster. If confrontations and meetings looked inevitable, I crossed over and walked on the other side of the street. I elected to be remote, mysterious, interesting, aloof, and self-sufficient like Lassiter in *Riders of the Purple Sage.* I regretted that I had had to sell my .22 before we left Canada: it would have completed my character and costume.

Cocooned in self-consciousness and fantasy, I walked through the stares of kids crowding the lawn and the front doors of the junior high school. I found the principal's office. By a girl whose eyebrows went up in astonished circumflexes, I was told to wait. I waited. Eventually I was called.

The principal, a tall lady with braids around her head and glasses on a black ribbon pinned to her breast, put on her glasses and looked across her desk at me. She seemed inclined to smile. She had big teeth.

"Well! What's your problem?"

I dug my letter out of my hip pocket and handed it over. She took off her glasses to read it. Then she put them on to read me. She said, "How old are you, Wallace?"

"Eleven." My squeaky voice made eleven sound so inadequate that I hurried to add, "I'll be twelve in February."

She was already shaking her head. "And you think you belong in the eighth grade?"

"Miss Merryman said I should."

"I know. She says very nice things about you. But do you know how old most eighth graders are? Thirteen or fourteen."

"I've always been the youngest!"

"I expect you have. But that may not have been the best for you. I don't believe in pushing pupils, even very bright pupils as I'm sure you are, so far ahead. Even in Grade Seven, which is where I think you belong, you'll be younger than everyone else."

I had not been prepared for any such rejection. Catastrophic tears rushed to my eyes, my woe bubbled up and overflowed. "Oh, come," the principal said. "If you're big enough to think you belong in the eighth grade you're big enough not to cry over a little disappointment."

Obviously I was not too big to cry. Obviously it was not a little disappointment. Crushed, ashamed, and accusing, I smeared a wrist across my wet eyes, looking as lugubrious and wronged as I knew how. For though I could not help bawling, and hated myself for my weakness, I hoped to gain something by it. Stubbornness plus tears were a formula that had worked for me before, and something told me this principal with the Teddy Roosevelt teeth was a softy like my mother.

She said, almost coaxingly, "You wouldn't want to be placed too high and have to go back. You wouldn't want to fail."

"I won't fail!"

With my letter in her hand, she stood up. She came around the desk. For the first time she got a full view of me, all four feet ten of me, in my Hampshire-shoat sweater and my elk-hide moccasins. "Well, my goodness!" she said. "Aren't you something!" She snorted something like a laugh. She studied me with her knuckles against her teeth. "You really think you can do it, don't you?"

"I know I can," I said, and bravely checked my tears, watching her for the final weakening.

It came. "Oh, why not?" she said suddenly. She leaned and wrote something on a piece of paper and folded the paper into the envelope with Miss Merryman's letter. But she still did not put it in my hands. "You understand that if you can't do it, you'll have to be set back a grade."

"Yes, ma'am. I can do it."

Shaking her head, shrugging, surprised at herself, she handed me the envelope. "Take this to Miss Temby, third room up the hall on the right. That will be your home room."

I felt her hand on the top of my head, my neck was twisted back and forth as if it were threaded and she was trying to start it straight. I looked up into her toothy smile, which at once became a laugh. "Now get," she said. "You're already late, and Miss Temby hates tardiness." A bell rang. I got.

Shaken, relieved, and triumphant, I scuttled into the hall and down it past two rooms crowded with students. I was saying over to myself the name, Miss Temby, so that I wouldn't forget it. I suppose I had visions of conning Miss Temby as I had conned the principal.

I found out, that morning and later, that there were plenty of things besides tardiness that Miss Temby hated, and that she was about as easy to con as the Angel Gabriel. She hated tardiness mainly for the interruptions it caused, but also for the character flaw it revealed. She hated interruptions of all kinds, and character flaws of all kinds. She hated breaches of order and discipline and those who created them. She hated carelessness, forgetfulness, playfulness, and inattention, which she lumped together as signs of irresponsibility. Years later, in troubled sleep, I have seen Miss Temby bending over me stiff with indignation, her eyes like burning coals, and heard through the fading mists of the dream her hissing voice: "Irre*spons*ible, Wallace!"

Two things Miss Temby liked, absolute attention and the right answer, and she could speak grudging approval when she got them. But the only thing she ever outright praised was perfection, and that was rare. It was certainly not what I suggested when I stood in her doorway, tardy, delinquent, and clearly lost.

"What room are you looking for?"

"Is this Miss Temby's room?"

"Yes, but I can tell you it's not yours. What grade are you in? Fifth? Sixth? They're in the other wing."

"The principal sent me here. I'm supposed to be in the eighth grade."

Laughter puffed out of the watching class. It hit me in the face like a wind. I don't know if I saw myself then as they saw me, but I do now: a scrawny runt in a sweater that engulfs his ears, his skinny legs in black stockings, his feet in stained moccasins. It is too bad I came before Disney. I held up my letter as proof that I was what I said I was. Miss Temby knocked twice on her desk to silence the laughter, and motioned me in. I stood before her, before them all, with my ears in flames while she read Miss Merryman's letter and the principal's note.

Long pause. Exasperated sigh. Tightened lips. "Good Lord," Miss Temby said. "What next? Well, put your lunch in the cloakroom—we don't allow them in desks. While you're at it, leave that sweater in there too. It's a provocation."

More laughter. This time Miss Temby did not silence it by knocking on her desk. Though I could not then have formulated the lesson I was learning, which was that autocrats find scapegoats necessary as lightning-rods to divert away from themselves the hostility their autocracy inspires, I understood with cold clarity that Miss Temby had deliberately humili-ated me and invited the class to join her in laughing at me. Hating her, I found a place for my lunch. Hating her, I tore off the hateful sweater that I had myself picked out of the T. Eaton catalog the Christmas before. Hating them all, I slunk back in and found an empty desk, where I sat through an hour of roll call, study cards, and textbook distribution, feeling the eyes slanted at me, the appraising looks, the incredulous smiles. There was not a pupil there, even among the girls, that I would have dared challenge. The boy behind me was as big as a man, and could have used a shave. What I could not deal with physically I dealt with in words, and those unuttered.

Yeah, laugh. Go on, laugh. You're so big, did any of you ever win a prize for killing more gophers than any kid in Saskatchewan? Did any of you ever shoot yourself through the big toe with a .22 long? How many muskrats did you trap last winter, hey? I got fourteen. How many ermines? I got two. How many mink? I got one. And I shot a beaver but he sank and I didn't get him. How much did you make last winter, trapping? I made eighty dollars. Go ahead, laugh. You'll find out. You'll find out I'm smarter than you, too.

Careful, I want to tell him as he seethes and shrinks and tries to hide his moccasins among the iron legs of his desk and tries to fix his face so that it will register alertness to Miss Temby and aloof indifference to the kids around him. Careful. Because I remember, as he cannot yet know, that in a moment Miss Temby will announce a review test in algebra, to see how much of last year's work has lasted over the summer. And I know, and so does he, that he never heard of algebra. I know that by the frantic exercise of guesswork and common sense he will get a grade of 12 out of a possible 100, and that Miss Temby the rest of the morning will look at him every now and then with gloomy implacable eyes.

By the time Miss Temby had whipped through our algebra quizzes and announced that most of us had retained nothing, *nothing,* and that we would have to have two weeks of review before we could go on to geometry, it was noon. The bell rang, the pupils swarmed out. I did not. Miss Temby, locking her desk, said to me, "Go outside and get some fresh air. Don't eat your lunch at your desk." My soul said to her, in bitterness, I know more about fresh air than you'll ever know. I'm from *Saskatchewan.* But when I went into the cloakroom to get my lunch, intending to eat it in the hall, both my lunch and my sweater were gone.

I knew what would happen if I went outside. Some kid would be strutting around in my sweater, with the turtleneck up to his eyes, groping blindly, saying, "Where's the eighth grade? I belong in Miss Temby's room." Some other kid would ask if I'd lost my lunch, and produce it, and pretend to hand it to me, and at the last minute pass it over my head to somebody else. Then we would have a nice game of keep-away. The hell with it. I sat gloomily at my desk the whole noon hour.

• • •

Somehow I survived that first day. I even, before the year was out, managed to get Miss Temby's grudging approval on several occasions, and at least twice her enthusiastic praise: once when she asked us to recite six lines of any poem we knew, and I recited her the whole of Joaquin Miller's "Columbus," "without"—Miss Temby cried in consternation and pleasure—"without a *single* mistake!" and the second time when I wrote her a theme about getting half-buried in a cave-in in the coyote-dug foothills above the Whitemud River. I really believe she was the first person who ever indicated that I might have a literary career.

But I never forgave her, even when she praised me, for when it most mattered, she had laughed, and invited the class to laugh; and laughter is the bitterest of all disparagements, unarguable, irresistible, not to be countered or palliated.

When the three-twenty bell finally rang, light-years after I had come so happily out of the principal's office, I waited until the room had cleared, and then went outside. But I hadn't waited long enough. There was the kid in the sweater, the other kid with the lunch. I started to walk past them, they started to encircle me to have some fun. But right out of the blue, a rough, hoarse, just-changed voice said, "Lay off! Let him alone." I turned around, and there was the big kid who sat behind me, the one as big as a man and in need of a shave. He held out his hand, and after a minute the kid with the sweater pulled it off and handed it over. The one with the lunch passed it like a football. Jeering, but not very sure of themselves, they let us walk away together.

"Where you live?" this man-sized kid said to me.

"Fourth Avenue North."

"You're on my way. Come on."

He walked me home, saying next to nothing. He lived in Little Chicago, across the river; his father worked at the smelter. I realize now, though I didn't then, that his natural way home was a long streetcar ride, and that by walking with me, he was giving himself a three-mile hike. Humble, grateful, proud to be seen with him, I went along with him to our street and our house, and there at the beginning of our sidewalk told him so long, see you tomorrow. I did not thank him, though I was fully aware of what he had done for me. I had a feeling thanks would make him uncomfortable. And I did not tell my mother about him. I didn't tell her much about the day, though she was curious, and kept inquiring. I went into the dining room and sat at the table and did my homework, hating the thought of tomorrow but determined that, since I had to go back to that place, I was going to be prepared for anything Miss Temby might ask.

That big boy, six feet tall and outweighing me by at least a hundred pounds, is the thing I most want to retain out of that year's school. Without knowing much of anything, I sensed that, coming from Little Chicago, he was second-class, like me. Maybe he too understood that we had inferiority in common, maybe he just accepted, out of pure good nature and decency, the role of protecting a runt. Even on days when he walked home with me, he rarely said much, but he listened while I told him about my gopher-killing prize, and about my trapping, and about the homestead, and about the Whitemud River. I was grateful for his friendship; he was my first friend in Great Falls.

Like everything else that I encountered in that Great Falls year, he taught me a lesson. He taught me that friendships, whether they should do so or not, change with circumstances, and that they involve obligations that we don't always live up to.

By the time I began to feel confident in the eighth-grade room, and got my hand to flapping to beat others in answering Miss Temby's questions, it had begun to dawn on me that my friend, whose name was Joe Something, something Polish or Bohemian—Sedlacek? Sokolski?—was not only the biggest boy in the class but the slowest. He had been kept back about as much as I had been pushed ahead.

Sometimes I helped him with his homework, though generally he just shrugged, indicating either that he didn't intend to do it, or couldn't do it even with help. When anyone bothered me, I looked for him; and I was not above using his name as a threat. But I confess that before very long I felt superior to him. I knew a mixture of shame and impatience when he was paralyzed by one of Miss Temby's questions. Sometimes I whispered answers to him, or passed him the answer on a note, and once I got caught. "Irres*pons*ible, Wallace!" Sometimes, even with the answer in his hand or still echoing in his ear, he still managed to fumble it. Sometimes the class laughed at his dumbness. Sometimes I did, too, incredulous that he could not see what was so plain, or remember what had just been said to him.

Nevertheless, my friend, my protector, my Fidus Achates. Our symbiosis lasted until about Thanksgiving, when he simply stopped coming to school. Perhaps he was dragged off by his migrant family, perhaps he was simply hopeless of ever making it. From where I now sit, I know that there were plenty of boys like him, and plenty of families like his, in the mines and smelters of Montana at the beginning of the twenties. They had linguistic problems, or they had had only the most irregular schooling, or they had to drop out to work. But of all the lessons that I learned, one on top of another, in my first year in civilization, the one Joe taught me—the lesson of kindness and human decency, unmotivated by anything but good nature and goodwill—is the one I most value.

It shames me now that I can't remember that decent, humble, suffering fellow's name.

At Home in the Fields of the Lord

I have always envied people with a hometown. They always seem to have an attic, and in the attic albums of pictures, spellers used in the third grade, go-carts and Irish mails with the scars of young heels and teeth on them. In the houses of these fortunate ones there is always some casual friend of thirty or forty years' standing, someone who grew up next door, some childhood sweetheart, some inseparable companion from primary days. Some people even live in the houses their fathers and grandfathers used; and no matter how wide they may scatter from the hometown, always behind them is a solid backstop of cousins and grandmothers and relatives once or twice removed, maintaining the solidarity and permanence of the clan.

None of these forms of moss clings to a rolling stone, and I was born rolling. If I met a playmate of forty years ago we would not recognize each other even as names. Since I left them (or they me) to move elsewhere, I have never again encountered a single one of the children I knew in any of my various dwelling places. The things that accumulate in others' attics and in their memories, to turn up again in their futures, have been cleaned out of mine five dozen times to simplify moves. Since I was born in Iowa in 1909 (my hometown held me six weeks) I have lived in twenty places in eight different states, besides a couple of places in

Canada, and in some of these places we lived in anywhere from two to ten different houses and neighborhoods. This is not quite the same thing as traveling extensively; it involves having no permanent base whatever. Until my wife and I built a house I am sure no member of my family had ever owned one.

The absence of roots has always seemed to me a deprivation both personally and professionally. Personally, I was condemned to friendships that were always being sharply cut off and rarely renewed, so that for a time they tried to live by mail and then lamely dwindled out. Professionally, as a writer, I considered myself unequipped with the enduring relationships from which the deepest understanding of people might have come. I have always thought of myself as a sort of social and literary air plant, without the sustaining roots that luckier people have. And I am always embarrassed when well-meaning people ask where I am from.

That is why I have been astonished, on a couple of recent trips through Salt Lake City, to find a conviction growing in me that I am not as homeless as I had thought. At worst, I had thought myself an Ishmael; at best, a half stranger in the city where I had lived the longest, a Gentile in the New Jerusalem. But a dozen years of absence from Zion, broken only by two or three short revisitings, have taught me different. I am as rich in a hometown as anyone, though I adopted my home as an adolescent and abandoned it as a young man.

A Gentile in the New Jerusalem: certainly I was. Salt Lake City is a divided concept, a complex idea. To the devout it is more than a place; it is a way of life, a corner of the materially realizable heaven; its soil is held together by the roots of the family and the cornerstones of the temple. In this sense Salt Lake City is forever foreign to me, as to any non-Mormon. But in spite of being a Gentile I discover that much of my youth is there, and a surprising lot of my heart. Having blown tumbleweed-fashion around the continent so that I am forced to *select* a hometown, I find myself selecting the City of the Saints, and for what seems to me cause.

It has such a comfortable, old-clothes feel that it is a shock to see again how beautiful this town really is, quite as beautiful as the Chamber of Commerce says it is; how it lies under a bright clarity of light and how its outlines are clean and spacious, how it is dignified with monuments and steeped in sun tempered with shade, and how it lies protected behind its rampart mountains, insulated from the stormy physical and intellectual weather of both coasts. Serenely concerned with itself, it is probably open to criticism as an ostrich city; its serenity may be possible only in a fool's paradise of isolationism and provincialism and smugness. But what is a hometown if it is not a place you feel secure in? I feel secure in Salt Lake City, and I know why. Because I keep meeting so many things I know, so many things that have not changed since I first saw the city in 1921.

True, it has grown by at least fifty thousand people since then, new roads have been built and new industries imported, new streets of houses are strung out from the old city limits. But there were people and roads and industries and houses there before; these new ones have not changed the town too much, and seem hardly to have affected its essential feel at all.

It was an amazement to me, returning, to realize how much I know about this city until I remembered that I had lived there off and on for nearly fifteen years; that as a Boy Scout I had made an elaborate and detailed map of its streets in order to pass some test or other; that as a high school student I had solicited advertisements among all its business houses; that while I was in college I had worked afternoons in a store that was always in need of somebody to double as a truck driver, so that I delivered parcels lengthwise and endwise over the city. There is no better way to learn a place; I have known no place in that way since.

Moreover, Salt Lake is an easy town to know. You can see it all. Lying in a great bowl valley, it can be surmounted and comprehended and possessed wholly as few cities can. You can't possibly get lost in it. The Wasatch comes with such noble certitude up from the south and curves so snugly around the "Avenues" that from anywhere in the city you can get your directions and find your way. And man has collaborated with Nature to make sure that you can't get lost. The streets are marked by a system so logical that you can instantly tell not merely where you are but exactly how far you are from anywhere else. And when your mind contains, as I found recently that mine did, not merely this broad plat but a great many of the little lost half streets with names like Elm and Barbara and Pierpont, then you have blocked off one of the great sources of nightmare.

You can't get lost. That is much. And you can always see where you are. That is even more. And you can get clear up above the city and look all the way around and over it, and that is most. Looking into the blank walls of cities or staring up at them from dirty canyon sidewalks breeds things in people that eventually have to be lanced.

Sure and comfortable knowledge is reinforced by association, which often amounts to love and always involves some emotional relationship. Mere familiarity, I suppose, generates an emotional attachment of a kind, but when years of the most emotionally active time of one's life have been spent among certain streets and houses and schools and people and countrysides, the associational emotion is so pervasive that it may be entirely overlooked for years, and comprehended only in retrospect. Nostalgia, the recognition of old familiarity, is the surest way to recognize a hometown.

In a way, my family's very mobility helped to make this town peculiarly mine, for we lived in many neighborhoods. We lived at Fifth South and Fifth East under old cottonwoods behind a mangy lawn; we lived on Seventh East across from Liberty Park so that I knew intimately the rats in the open surplus canal; we lived in a bungalow on Eighth East, an old brick ruin on Twenty-first South and State, a pleasant house on Fifteenth East above the high school I attended. We lived on Ninth East and Fourth South, on Seventh South and Eleventh East, in an apartment on First Avenue, in an ancient adobe down near the heart of town by the post office. I beat my way to school across lots from many different directions, and my memory is tangled in the trees on certain old streets and involved in the paths across many vacant lots and impromptu baseball fields.

The mere act of writing them down amplifies and extends the things that remain with me from having lived deeply and widely in Salt Lake City. I suppose I played tennis on almost every public and private court in town, and I know I hiked over every golf course. For three or four winters, with a club basketball team, I ran myself ragged in the frigid amusement halls of a hundred Mormon ward houses and took icy showers and went home blown and rubber-legged late at night. With a team in the commercial league, or with the freshman squad at the university, I hit all the high school gyms, as well as the old rickety Deseret Gymnasium next door to the Utah Hotel, where cockroaches as big and dangerous as roller skates might be stepped on behind the dark lockers. From games and parties I ran home under dark trees, imagining myself as swift and tireless as

Paavo Nurmi, and the smell and taste of that cold, smoky, autumnal air and the way the arc lights blurred in rounded golden blobs at the corners is with me yet. It makes those streets of twenty and twenty-five years ago as real as any I walk now; those are the streets I judge all other city streets by, and perhaps always will.

This, I discover belatedly, is the city of many firsts: the first car, the first dates, the first jobs. No moon has ever swum so beguilingly up over mountains as it used to swim up over the Wasatch; none has ever declined so serenely as it used to decline sometimes when we came home at two or three after a date and a twenty-mile drive out to Taylorsville or Riverton to take our girls home. No friends have ever so closely and effortlessly touched the heart. No sandwiches have ever since had the wonderful smoky flavor that the barbecued beef used to have at the old Night Owl on Ninth South, by the ball park. No heroes have ever walked so tall as Willie Kamm and Tony Lazzeri and Lefty O'Doul and Duffy Lewis and Paul Strand and Fritz Coumbe of the old Salt Lake Bees in the Pacific Coast League. The year Tony Lazzeri hit sixty home runs over the short left field fence at Bonneville Park I haunted State Street, outside that fence, and risked death in traffic a hundred times to chase batting-practice balls and get a free seat in the left field bleachers. And when Coumbe, who had pitched (I believe) for the Athletics and played against Babe Ruth (Ruth hit the first ball he threw him over the centerfield fence) came to live in the other half of a duplex from us, and brought other heroes home with him, and gave me a left-handed first base mitt that had belonged to George Sisler, I grew twelve inches overnight.

Here for the first time I can remember triumphs, or what seemed triumphs then. In Salt Lake I wrote my first short story and my first novel. In Salt Lake I fell in love for the first time and was rudely jilted for the first time and recovered for the first time. In Salt Lake I took my first drink and acquired a delightful familiarity with certain speakeasies that I could find now blindfolded if there were any necessity. I experimented with ether beer and peach brandy and bathtub gin and survived them all, as I survived the experience of driving an automobile at sixteen or seventeen, by hairbreadth but satisfactory margins.

It seems to me now that in the course of one activity or another, driven by that furious and incomprehensible adolescent energy which lies dead somewhere in Salt Lake and which I wish I could bring back as readily as I bring back its memory, I surged up and down and across the New Jerusalem from Murray to Beck's Hot Springs, and from Saltair to Brighton and Pinecrest. And how it was, its weathers and its lights, is very clear to me.

So is the country that surrounds the city and that gives the city so much of its spaciousness and charm and a large part of its nostalgic tug.

Salt Lake lies in the lap of mountains. East of it, within easy reach of any boy, seven canyons lead directly up into another climate, to fishing and hunting and camping and climbing and winter skiing. Those canyons opened out of my back yard, no matter what house I happened to be living in. City Creek and Dry Canyon were immediate and walkable. Parley's could be penetrated by the judicious who hung around on the tracks behind the state penitentiary and hooked onto D&RG freights as they began to labor on the grade. Sometimes we rode a boxcar or a gondola; sometimes an indulgent fireman let us ride on the coal in the tender. Up in the canyon we could drop off anywhere, because even with two engines on, the train would only be going ten or fifteen miles an hour. South of Parley's was Mill Creek, and this we reached on more elaborate expeditions with knapsacks. In spring there were lucerne fields and orchards to go through toward the canyon's mouth, and the lucerne patches could always be counted on to provide a racer snake or two, and the orchards a pocketful of cherries or apricots. On a hot day, after a climb, cherries chilled in the cold water of Mill Creek and cherished, one by one, past teeth and palate and throat, were such cherries as the world has not produced since.

And the other canyons: the little swale of Hughes, where in late April the dogtooth violets were a blanket under the oakbrush; Big Cottonwood, up which ore trucks used to give us a lift to the Maxwell or the Cardiff mine, and where the peaks went in a granite whorl around the lakes and cottages of Brighton; Little Cottonwood, with the ghost town of Alta at its head, since famous for ski slopes; and Bell's, a glacial U with waterfalls and hanging glacial meadows lifting in a long steep southward curve toward Long Peak and the point of the mountain, from which we could look down on the narrows where the Jordan River slipped between alluvial gravel slopes toward the dead sea.

Knowing Salt Lake City means knowing its canyons, too, for no city of my acquaintance except possibly Reno breaks off so naturally and easily into fine free country. The line between city and mountains is as clean as the line between a port city and salt water. Up in the Wasatch is another world, distinct and yet contributory, and a Salt Lake boyhood is inevitably colored by it.

There is a limit to the indulgence of recollection, for fear nostalgia should be overcome by total recall. But it is clear to me, now that I have chosen a hometown, that I do not believe unqualifiedly in a "most impressionable age" between five and ten. The lag between experience and the kind of assimilation that can produce nostalgia is considerable, I suppose. In our early maturity we have just come to realize how much our tender minds absorbed in early childhood. But later we may have other realizations. Other recollections brighten as the first ones fade, and the recognition that now makes me all but skinless as I drive down Thirteenth East Street in Salt Lake City is every bit as sharp and indelible as the impressions my blank-page senses took as a child. Not all experience, not even all romantic and nostalgic experience, is equivalent to Wordsworth's.

Any place deeply lived in, any place where the vitality has been high and the emotions freely involved, can fill the sensory attic with images enough for a lifetime of nostalgia. Because I believe in the influence of places on personalities, I think it somehow important that certain songs we sang as high school or college students in the twenties still mean particular and personal things. "I'm Looking over a Four Leaf Clover" is all tied up with the late-dusk smell of October on Second South and Twelfth East, and the shine of the arc light on the split street tipping up the Second South hill. "When Day Is Done" has the linseed oil smell of yellow slickers in it, and the feel of the soft corduroy cuffs those slickers had, and the colors of John Held pictures painted on the backs. "Exactly Like You" means the carpet, the mezzanine, the very look and texture and smell, of the Temple Square Hotel.

Salt Lake is not my hometown because my dead are buried there, or because I lived certain years of my youth and the first years of my marriage there, or because my son was born there. Duration alone does not do it. I have since spent half as many years in Cambridge, Massachusetts, without bringing from that residence more than a pitiful handful of associations. I was not living in Cambridge at the pace and with the complete uncritical participation that swept me along in Salt Lake. To recall anything about Cambridge is an effort, almost an act of will—though time may teach me I took more from there, too, than I thought I did. But Salt Lake City, revisited either in fact or in imagination, drowns me in acute recognitions, as if I had not merely sipped from but been doused with Proust's cup of reminding tea.

From its founding, Salt Lake City has been sanctuary: that has been its justification and its function. And it is as sanctuary that it persists even in my Gentile mind and insinuates itself as my veritable hometown. Yet there are darker and more ambiguous associations attached to it, and it is strange to me, returning, to find myself looking upon Salt Lake as the place of my security. It never was at the time I lived there. I suppose no age of a man is less secure than adolescence, and more subject to anguishes, and I think I do not exaggerate in believing that my own adolescence had most of the usual anguishes and some rather special ones besides. Certainly some of the years I lived in Salt Lake City were the most miserable years of my life, with their share of death and violence and more than their share of fear, and I am sure now that off and on and for considerable periods I can hardly have been completely sane.

There are houses and neighborhoods in Salt Lake whose associations are black and unhappy, places where we lived which I thought of at the time as prisons. Yet revisiting the city I am warmed by this flood of recollection, the unhappiness dwindles into proportion or perspective, even unimportance. Or perhaps the unhappiness takes on a glow in retrospect, and perhaps the feeling of security and well-being which Salt Lake gives me now is partly satisfaction at having survived here things that might have destroyed me. Or perhaps it arises from the pure brute satisfaction of having experienced anything, even misery, with that much depth and sharpness. Or perhaps, like the discomforts of a camping trip that become hilarious in the telling, the verbal formulation of distress has the capacity to cure it. So Emerson, after flunking a mathematics examination in college, could go home and triumph over all the arts of numbers by writing a destructive essay on the subject.

I suppose that may come close to the core of my feeling about Salt Lake. Returning is a satisfactory literary experience; the present has power to evoke a more orderly version of the past. And what is evoked, though it may be made of unpleasant or unhappy elements, is satisfactory because it *is* a kind of vicarious thing, a literary product.

Whether it says with the Anglo-Saxon poet, "That have I borne, this can I bear also," or whether it says, "There, for a while, I lived life to the hilt, and so let come what may," my hometown, late discovered, is not a deprivation or a loss or a yearning backward. I recently had the experience of recognizing, and with pleasure, what the city meant to me, but I was not heartbroken to leave either it or that youth of mine that it embalms, and I do not necessarily yearn to return to either. It does not destroy me with a sense of lost green childhood or of any intimation of immortality long gone and irrecoverable. There is only this solid sense of having had or having been or having lived something real and good and satisfying, and the knowledge that having had or been or lived these things I can never lose them again. Home is what you can take away with you.

Xanadu by the Salt Flats

Memories of a Pleasure Dome

Now and again, on a picnic hill, when the incense of hamburgers and hot dogs grows thick and stupefying, I am moved to rise on my hind legs with a spatula in one hand and a bun in the other and give voice to an atavistic howl, a nasal, high, drawn-out ululation like that of a muezzin from a minaret or a coyote from a river bluff.

"Wellllll, they're all hot, they're all ready-uh! Faaaamous Coney Island red-hots! It's a loaf-a-bread-a-pound-a-meat and all the mustard you can eat for a thin skinny little dime, folks! Step ooooooovah!"

My grandchildren, embarrassed, interest themselves in ants and other small objects in the grass.

"Wellllll, it's hot hamburgers, hot coffee! Ice-cold sweet milk, buttermilk, and nice fresh homemade pies! Step right up, folks, get yours!"

Nobody responds to my call to prayer. They sneak looks at each other—Has he gone nuts? With dignity I lay down my spatula and remove my apron and let the little monsters serve up their own. They have lost the old-time religion. No elders have instructed them in the mysteries. They have no more idea how you prepare hot dogs for hundreds than they would have how to make loaves and fishes go around. I could tell them: Lay a napkin in the left hand, slap a bun into the napkin, split the bun with one slash of a razor-sharp knife, fork a wiener into the split, slash the wiener open, drop the knife, and with one sweep of a wooden spoon bathe the cleft wiener from end to end in mustard, just as the left hand closes bun and napkin around the oozing and succulent contents and thrusts it into some importunate hand, while the right hand accepts the dime. With that method, you can serve up a hot dog every six seconds, all the time rolling new wieners onto the grill, shifting buns, ringing up dimes, and keeping your mouth going on the supplicatory incantations. Watching these uninstructed modern kids drop their wieners in the ashes, set their buns afire, and spill the mustard, I am just as glad they don't try the professional procedures. They would probably cut through wiener, bun, and napkin into their palms. I have seen it done, and perhaps done it.

What forever separates my grandchildren from me is that they never had a glorious summer job, at the age of fifteen, at Saltair, the stately pleasure dome that used to rise out of the waters of Great Salt Lake, eighteen miles west of Salt Lake City. And they are never going to, for the Coney Island of the West is as dead as the dime hamburger, and all its folksy magic with it. It lasted sixty-five years, from 1893 to 1958, and then it died of change. I am one of the few remaining members of its cult, one of the last depositories of a fragment of its liturgy.

They do not know what they have missed, but I am sorry for them anyway. They will never know the thrill of working in an enchanted palace whose onion domes float on the desert afternoon, and whose halo of light at night pales the stars. They know not the sound of gritty salt underfoot, or the sight of potted palms glittering with salt like tinsel. The smell of the humble hot dog cooking will never arouse them, as it does me, to uncontrollable glossolalia. Their ears will never prick, as mine do, to the spectral chanting of barkers, the thunder and screams from the roller coaster, the sob of saxophones from the dance floor. Nor will they ever hear, in intervals of quiet, the slap of heavy waves down under, down in the caverns measureless to man among the pilings. I went down there once, wading chin deep, and found the place shadowy, lit by flashes and reflections like a sea cave, and haunted by spiders as big as walnuts. The upper-world sounds of public pleasure were muted and far away. The down-under smells were not those of cooking and confections and orange peel and pop, but those of wet salt and brine flies—the same wild smells that had offended Captain Howard Stansbury when he surveyed this desolate dead sea in 1850. If I had been a thinking or prescient creature, I might have felt the shadowy quiet under the pavilion as a threat or omen. Something there was that didn't love pleasure domes, that wanted them down. Having no history, and hence no feel for time, I took Saltair as I found it in the summer of 1924. So far as I knew, it had been there since the Creation, and would be there till Kingdom Come.

Great Salt Lake, though the biggest lake west of the Mississippi, is only the salty remnant of the fresh-water sea called Lake Bonneville that in Pleistocene times stretched from Idaho to Arizona and from the canyons of the Wasatch Range (then fjords) far out into the Nevada desert. We know from layers of hard salt under the mud of its bottom that it has several times dried up entirely, only to be rejuvenated by a wet cycle. In his monograph on Lake Bonneville, G. K. Gilbert predicted that as Mormon irrigators took more and more water out of tributary streams, Great Salt Lake would shrink and perhaps disappear. After a rise in the 1870s, perhaps because of increased runoff following settlement, it fell steadily, as he had predicted, until it reached an all-time low in 1905.

But even while it was falling, the Mormon Church gambled on its future and built Saltair. The church has always encouraged singing, dancing, picnics, family reunions, and other social good times of a decorous kind, and it felt the need of a place of public resort. Brighton, in its glacial cirque twenty-five miles up in the Wasatch, was hard to get to. The beaches on the east and south sides of Great Salt Lake had drawbacks, the former being muddy and the latter being harshly exposed, without a tree or any shade, and being, moreover, a four-hour haul in a wagon. On a blazing Fourth of July or Pioneer Day, the drive out could prepare people for water-based recreation better than the lake could satisfy their need.

For though many people find brine bathing exhilarating, it is a long way from comfortable. You have to learn not to dive, not only because the brine eats at eyes and nostrils like sulphuric acid, but also because the water is so heavy with salt that it can break a diver's neck. You have to learn not to rub your eyes, or if you do, to suck your finger first. And when you emerge into the drying sun and wind you find yourself, unless there is a fresh-water shower handy, coated with salt like a codfish. There is no pleasure quite equal to a hard, salt-coated sunburn. Not even the similarity to the Dead Sea, in a society that delighted in biblical parallels, could make Garfield Beach and the other beaches places of pure pleasure.

The great Moorish pavilion that rose on pilings out in the lake, at the end of a four-thousand-foot causeway, changed all that. From its opening in June, 1893, it was an instant success. The crescent of bathhouses along the pavilion's north edge provided showers of fresh water brought by tank cars from the Wasatch. You did not need to wade through drifts of smelly brine flies to reach the water, but went down steps from a board-walk into water breast deep. You had all that well-advertised fun of bob-bing around like a cork and having your picture taken with your feet out of the water and a newspaper spread before your face, next to a sign that said, "Try to Sink." And when you came out and showered, tingly from the medicinal soaking and with all your cuts and scratches itching miracu-lously toward healing, you could go out onto the midway and be swept up, as I was swept up every day of my summer there, by magic.

You could eat all that junk food and junk drink sold by such mis-sionary priests as I, or you could dine in the Leviathan, the enormous open-sided restaurant through which the lake breeze blew in the daytime and the land breeze blew at night. You could ride the roller coaster or win Kewpie dolls or stagger through the Fun House. You could watch sunsets as spectacular as any in the world, and almost as predictable as daylight and dark.

And you could dance. How you could dance. The floor, as big as the Mormon Tabernacle and domed over by the same sort of turtle-back roof, was locally believed to be the largest in the world, and may have been. Nine thousand people, on at least one occasion, danced on it at the same time to the music of R. Owen Sweeten's band. Or bands. On special occa-sions, dancing was continuous, with a band at each end of the floor, one picking up as the other stopped. I remember the time when they forbade the Charleston for fear all those people coming down hard on the down-beat would shake the whole pavilion into the lake.

When the hippodrome wasn't being used for dancing, it was used for other things: statehood celebrations, Tabernacle Choir concerts, band concerts, political rallies, even prize-fights. In 1910 Jack Johnson and Jim Jeffries were scheduled to fight forty-five rounds there for the heavy-weight championship, but Mormon scruples got in the way and the fight was moved. No Mormon scruples stood in the way when Rudolph Valentino and his dancing partner paid a visit, in the twenties, but so many Mormons and Mormon cars stood in the way that he couldn't get out to the lake and had to be rescued and delivered, an hour and a half late, by a special train.

Actually, there were fairly constant clashes between the recreational principle and Mormon scruples. Compared with the ordinary midway, Saltair was almost squeaky clean, but no one who worked out there could fail to learn which concessions people who wanted a drink or a bottle should be sent to, and there were girls who were around so frequently that we thought them employees. My brother, who worked at the bath-houses, had a lot of stories to tell, most of which I could not believe but would have liked to. And there were enough difficulties about illegal sales of beer, and disregard of the Sunday closing hours, so that eventually the church unloaded Saltair, taking pains to sell it to a syndicate of hierarchs whose standards were as high as the church's own.

During the summer of 1924 we knew Saltair at its absolute peak. From its low in 1905 the lake had begun inexplicably to rise, and in 1910 was up eight feet. By 1924 it was at its highest measured level. The Jordan River sewage, brine flies, and other tourist attractions were all washed far inshore, and the pavilion rose out of clean water. The air was dry, keen, bracing, a combination of sea and desert. The view was, and is, one of the great views of the world, whether one was coming out across white flats toward chemical-blue lake and brown islands, with Saltair's painted domes bellying over the water like the spinnakers of a fantastic fleet, or whether one was going back toward the city and the noble curve of the Wasatch, touched even in August by high snow. Tourists were enrap-tured, locals complacent, money easy, the twenties in full flower. I re-member it like lost Eden. And they actually paid me twenty-five cents an hour, $2.50 for a ten-hour day, just to work there. I would have paid *them*.

As good as any part of the Saltair experience was the going out and the coming home, especially the coming home, on the open excursion cars of the electrified Utah and Nevada Railroad, whose directors were snugly synonymous with those of Saltair. Since the stand where I worked stayed open till the last dog was hung, I always took the last train, the eleven o'clock, perching in my ice cream pants and my straw skimmer where I could watch the city's lights and the dark loom of the mountains rush toward me across the flats. We were buffeted by the night wind and the salt-flat smells. Necking couples sat on the steps, eyed with disapproval by matrons in charge of large families. Boys worked their way fore and aft along the cars, risking their necks and interrupting the neckers. Whole cars sometimes burst spontaneously into song. If we were lucky, a moon would have floated free of the Wasatch and would be washing the broad valley with silver. Sometimes we came in like an old-fashioned hayride, the little kids asleep, the lovers quiet, the singers all sung out. It was too good; we should have known it wouldn't last.

All through its history Saltair suffered from the forces that wanted it down. Every winter the salt-laden wind ate its paint off. Waves heavy with salt washed away bathhouses and tore out stretches of causeway. There was a succession of fires. Then in April, 1925, just about the time I was beginning to dream of another summer out there, I stood on the lawn of my high school, on the eastern edge of the city, and watched smoke and flames erupt at the edge of the lake. Smoke on the water, fire on the flood. It made a spectacular blaze, visible from every point in the valley.

There was immediate talk of rebuilding it; so indispensable a public facility couldn't be allowed to sit out there on its charred stumps. But there were cautionary circumstances. The insurance had covered less than half the rebuilding cost. Any potential operator was looking at replacement costs of at least $185,000, as well as at the high expense of maintenance. The short season of only a hundred days, from Memorial Day to Labor Day, was made even shorter by early-spring or late-fall cold spells and by violent summer thunderstorms. And there was the growing ubiquity of the automobile, which released people from the need for public transportation to public places of resort, and freed them to hunt up private places in the mountains, and other resorts such as Lagoon, where there were trees, coolness, and swimming "in water fit to drink."

Those considerations delayed the rebuilding until 1929, and 1929 was too late. For one thing, the lake had begun to fall again in 1925. For every foot it fell, it shrank drastically in size, leaving its exposed flats littered and smelly. People who always had assumed that the lake water, 26 percent salt, would kill anything, now began to wonder if that polluted shore was safe. The beaches on the south end, clean and with newly installed fresh-water facilities and even a little carefully nourished shade, were more attractive. Through the declining years of the Depression nobody much but tourists came to my old place of magic. The lake shrank until the pavilion stood high and dry, and swimmers had to be taken out to water, a half mile or so, in cars. Automobiles parked down under, among the salt-crusted pilings where I had once waded chin-deep inspecting spiders and mysteries. The giant roller coaster, half rebuilt in 1931, was again destroyed by fire, and as soon as they started rebuilding it again, a windstorm blew it down, killing two workmen.

It is like the story of a glamorous woman growing old and stooping to ever more embarrassing pretenses. With face lifts and paint jobs, the Coney Island of the West limped through the 1930s and into the 1940s, until it was closed during World War II and the rolling stock of its railroad turned over to Hill Air Force Base. After the war all that rolling stock was converted into scrap, and the old excursion-car experience was over.

But the resort itself was not dead. Stubbornly (someone must have loved it as I did, as people love the San Francisco cable cars), the Ashby Snow family that then owned it renovated it for a third incarnation. In 1954 they re-roofed the hippodrome and refinished the dance floor, created parking space, restored old concessions and added new ones, diked a six-acre area around the pavilion, and pumped in lake water to set the place once more in the salt sea.

Nothing availed. Personal wheels gave the public too many desirable alternatives. Reopening on May 27, 1955, Saltair held its own for two years only. Then another fire destroyed the bathhouses and pier, and in August, 1957, a freak windstorm tore through and blew down the roller coaster yet once more. Despite the engaging of such big attractions as Stan Kenton, Frankie Laine, and Nat King Cole, public response was unenthusiastic, and on Labor Day, 1958, the gates were closed for good. Since then, fires and winds and corrosive salt have swept the place, and salvagers have picked its bones.

And yet the something that wants a pleasure dome to rise out of the dead sea, at the edge of the sterile salt flats, is nearly as persistent as the something that wants it down. Saltair lingers in memories other than mine, a mirage, a fairyland that promises, at least to fifteen year olds of all ages, perpetual glamour. Let the lake level begin to rise in a new wet cycle, and another plan for rejuvenating Saltair will rise with it. Though I would not invest money in its resurrection, I would bet on the inevitability of the attempt.

Early in 1980 a Salt Lake City photographer, John Telford, produced a portfolio of ten Great Salt Lake prints that capture miraculously the moody light and startling contrasts of a lake that belongs on the moon. There is not a human being in any of the photographs, nothing but sand, salt, water as shining and heavy as mercury, islands like jutting bones. As an introduction to his own splendid images, Mr. Telford has inserted a print made from a glass-plate negative by C. R. Savage. It is a print of superb quality, from a superb negative, and it shows the Saltair pavilion as it looked around 1905. Savage caught the place out of season. No bathers clutter the water in front of the crescent of bathhouses, only a few human figures corrupt the perfection of the pavilion crowned by its domes and minarets. The carpenters' Gothic gingerbread is as delicate as lace; everything about the pavilion is precise, cleanly defined, exposed luminously on a gray day without glare. It looks very much like the Saltair that I knew in 1924; if there are differences, I don't want to know about them. Because this is a picture of perfection, in its way. This pleasure dome was never built. It was decreed, it rose like an exhalation.

The World's Strangest Sea

On the face of the Wasatch Mountains, in Utah, and on the faces of the tormented desert ranges westward, there are lines of terraces like the grades of abandoned roads. The highest is a thousand feet above the floor of the valley. Up there the soil is underlaid with flattened, polished stones: the beach of a great lake that in glacial times pushed against this eastern wall of the Great Basin. It made fjords of the Wasatch canyons and a great bay of Cache Valley, where the city of Logan now lies. Westward it spread more than a hundred miles, submerging low mountains and making islands of high ones. Northward it reached four arms into what is now Idaho; southward, a long bay almost touched present Arizona.

This was Lake Bonneville, a fresh-water sea as big as Lake Michigan. Stand on its highest terrace and count the ledges, in places only a few, in places several dozen, that the receding waters cut in the mountainous shore. Some are so faint that a heavy growth of grass obscures them; some so broad and deep they indicate a stable level over thousands of years. And away westward twenty-five miles or more, against the foot of brown mountains and islands, you can see what is left of that inland sea—a thin line of quicksilver, of lead, of improbable turquoise, of deep-sea cobalt, or of molten metal, depending on the condition of the sky: Great Salt Lake.

It is a remnant only, one tenth the area and one sixtieth the depth of its parent, which first reduced itself by cutting a high-water overflow channel through Red Rock Pass in Cache Valley, and then dried up spasmodically and irregularly over thousands of years. More than once, we know from layers of hard salt under the clay of its bottom, it has dried up completely, only to be given new life by a rainier cycle. The country around it, once rich with vegetation, has been for many centuries a barren desert. The once-sweet lake, having no outlet except evaporation, is, at low water, saltier than the Dead Sea.

Fly over it and see it as the residual puddle it is, set in borders of white salt or putty-colored mud from which rise worn and half-buried mountains. Drive toward it, say along Highway 40 from Wendover on the Nevada line, and you cross for scores of miles the ancient lake bottom, the concrete-hard Bonneville Salt Flats, where Ab Jenkins, Sir Malcolm Campbell, John Cobb and others have set so many automobile speed records.

All approaches except that from the mountainous east must brave a desert bleaker than Arabia. The Western Pacific comes east across the salt desert and circles the lake's south shore. The Southern Pacific offers the best of all the approaches—straight across the desert to Lakeside and from there across the Northern Arm and Bear River Bay by the combined trestle and fill of the Lucin Cutoff.

Everything about Great Salt Lake is bizarre and contradictory. Remnant though it is, it is still the biggest lake west of the Mississippi. In a land where water is more precious than diamonds, this lake seventy-five miles long and fifty wide provides not a single oasis; it offers little recreation or refreshment, and though it has been on the map as long as America has been a nation, it remains almost unknown.

It is a desert of water in a desert of salt and mud and rock, one of the most desolate, and desolately beautiful, of regions. Its sunsets, seen across water that reflects like polished metal, are absolutely unrivaled. Its colors are of a staring, chemical purity. The senses are rubbed raw by its moonlike horizons, its mirages, its parching air, its moody and changeful face.

Unknown as it is, its name is familiar the world over, and millions have sampled the two things it offers the tourist—sunsets and nonsink swimming. This last is possible only at the lake's south end, where Sunset Beach, Black Rock and Saltair are clustered. It is less recreation than an "experience." A hundred and ten years of it have created a body of lore, passed on to the uninitiated.

It is impossible to sink, as advertised. But it is difficult to swim because the buoyancy lifts your feet higher than your head. You can drown while floating like a cork. If you want a life preserver, tie a ten-pound weight to your ankle to keep you upright.

Unless you are fond of a sensation like sulphuric acid in your eyes and lye in your throat, keep your eyes and mouth shut and out of water. If you have to rub your eyes, suck your finger clean of salt first.

Swimming in the brine is exhilarating but you will be uncomfortable later unless you shower in fresh water. Otherwise, you end up crusted with salt like a herring.

Don't dive. In 1924 I saw a high-school boy disregard the signs and take a running dive off the Saltair pier. When we fished him out, his neck was broken. He had not hit the bottom—only the water, more than one fourth of which, as of last year, was solid matter.

G. K. Gilbert, when he studied old Lake Bonneville for the Geological Survey in the 1880s, predicted that Great Salt Lake would dry up as irrigation took more and more of the water from the Jordan, the Weber and the Bear rivers, and from the smaller mountain streams. But the lake's level, though down from the all-time high of 1873, has been fluctuating, with peaks of high water in 1885, 1910 and 1924. Since the all-time low of 1940 it has started stubbornly to climb again, and has risen six feet. But even if it should rise to the 1924 level, Great Salt Lake is never likely to become a casual resort. At best it is glaring hot in summer, mosquito-haunted in late autumn when unused irrigation water fills the sloughs along the eastern edge, and bleak in winter. In spring the larvae of the brine flies, one of the few forms of life that breed in the lake water, wash up on shore in a layer that Captain Stansbury, who surveyed the lake in 1850, described as looking like dried cow dung, and of a "sulphureous smell." Boating can be dangerous. There is not a tree or picnic spot. If you tried to water-ski, and took a spill, you could break bones.

When I was fourteen I sold hot dogs and hamburgers at Saltair, the resort built on pilings in the lake's south end. It was the old Saltair—since burned down and rebuilt. In those years the water was six feet higher than at present, and swimmers who now must chase the receding waters in little cars could step from their bathing houses into breast-deep brine.

In daytime the lake air was hot, rich with popcorn and spun candy and the smoke of frying. The whole pavilion, even the potted palms, glittered with an air-borne deposit of salt; salt gritted underfoot; the pilings, pink below the water line, were crusted white above. At night, because the water cooled more slowly than the land, the air stirred with a land breeze that strengthened as darkness came on, bringing hints of the mountains to the east, and more than a hint of the salt flats along the water's edge. Everything was louder and brighter at night: the roar of the roller coaster and squeals of girls, the glitter of thousands of lights, the barbaric noises of what we proudly called the Coney Island of the West.

Sometimes we slipped away from the stand for an after-dark swim, moving quietly among the reflected green and blue and lemon yellow of lights on the water's metallic surface. Cradled in water warm as milk, we felt the sting of brine in every cut, and over us washed the secret, half-tainted shore breeze with its smell of the flats. To me it was an enchanted place.

It is natural that a desolation as forbidding as Great Salt Lake should have come slowly into knowledge. Father Escalante heard about it from the Utes in 1776 but did not visit it; for half a century afterward it changed shape, size and position at the whim of creative map makers. Then, toward the end of 1824, young Jim Bridger floated down Bear River in a bullboat and unsuspectingly dipped his hand for a drink in the brackish water of Bear River Bay. He was the discoverer, but he thought he had found the Pacific.

Other mountain men had a hand in its exploration. Jim Clyman, hunting for beaver streams that he might have hunted more profitably in hell, led a party that circumnavigated the lake in a bullboat in 1826—a feat so heroic that few have tried it since. In 1827 Jed Smith and two companions crossed the desert from California and barely made it to water near the lake's southwest corner. In 1833 Joe Walker took forty trappers around the Northern Arm and onto the Humboldt, and demonstrated that there was no outlet. And in 1843 and again in 1845 John Charles Frémont, with Kit Carson, Basil Lajeunesse and others, visited the two largest islands and explored the route across the salt desert that would become known as Hastings' Cutoff—one of the tragic roads of the West.

The Mormons who in 1847 began building a society along the lake's eastern edge have their own rich history. Great Salt Lake itself has little except the frail lore of its islands and the record of the wagon trains and railroads that tried to break through or around its terrible deserts. It was neither resting place nor water transportation, but a deadly barrier. The Bartleson wagons that made the first wheel tracks in this country fought their way across the Promontory Mountains, around the Northern Arm, and southwest across the desert until they gave up at the foot of the Pequop Mountains like a desert river dying in an alkali sink. Later wagons learned to go roundabout northward, from Fort Hall past the Raft River Mountains and onto the Humboldt. But Frémont's route across the salt desert from the lake's south end was urged upon the Donner-Reed party in 1846 by the fast-talking promoter Lansford Hastings. Worn out from laboring through the Wasatch, the party lost so many oxen and mules on the seventy-five-mile waterless march to Pilot Peak that they never recovered the strength or heart that would have taken them over the Sierra before the snows came. Those who died prepared their death here.

In many ways the north end of Great Salt Lake is more interesting than the south. There both history and high ground come close to the water's edge. From there is the best access to most of the islands. And there in Bear River Bay, at the mouth of the lake's principal tributary, is one of the two concentrations of life the bitter sea can show. It is so swarming with wildfowl that it makes all the more notable the desolation out beyond.

As you go west from Brigham City out onto the delta of Bear River the hayfields give way to marshland and tules. In a ditch beside the road a black-and-white western grebe dives. A white egret watches you pass. A great blue heron flaps off with his crest feathers flattened backward, his neck folded tight, his legs trailing: he looks as big as a Navy trainer.

You go past the Bear River Migratory Bird Refuge and onto the dikes that divide the marshes into five great fresh-water ponds. At every yard the birds thicken. A wedge of geese honks over; the sky is darkened by a driving flurry of teal. Clear to the horizon the lead-colored water is flickering with the white, tipping tails of feeding pintail. White islands in the distance turn out to be massed hundreds of pelicans or swans. The canals are alive with grebes, avocets, snowy egrets, glossy ibises, black-necked stilts, night herons; the air vibrates with the swift zigzag flight of snipe, phalaropes, sandpipers; the shallows are almost obscured by teal, canvasback, spoonbill, gadwalls, Canada and Ross' and snow geese, California gulls, black-crested cormorants. Among the tules flit yellow-headed blackbirds—birds I have known only in Saskatchewan, where many of these autumnal ducks were born. It is a place to set a bird watcher wild. Where else could you see 15,000 whistling swan in one flock? Greenwinged teal or pintail a half million at a time? Canvasback by the hundred thousand?

Jim Bridger, in 1824, reported seeing millions of ducks here. So did Frémont, who visited the Bear River delta in September, 1843. So did Capt. Howard Stansbury, coming through with his division of the Pacific Railroad Surveys in 1849. But gunners, the diversion of Bear River water to irrigation, the drying up of the marshes, and botulism threatened to leave this bird heaven as barren as the salt lake outside. Only the establishment of the Bear River Migratory Bird Refuge in 1928 saved it. Every year thousands of sick ducks are picked up, cured, banded and released. One pintail saved from death at Bear River Bay in 1942 turned up less than three months later on Palmyra Island, 3,600 miles away in the Pacific.

This is a wonderful place; it deafens and cheers us with the whistle of wings and the squawks of an extravagant overflow of life. And it is one of the few areas around Great Salt Lake that is easily accessible, open to the public and sure to please. Six thousand duck hunters shoot there every fall. On occasion licensed trappers thin its muskrat population, and licensed fishermen seine its carp. But mostly it is sanctuary, a feeding and resting ground for millions of birds.

When I was younger I used to shoot in these marshes. From here on I shall only watch. Better than shooting is the close sight of a western grebe swimming up a canal with her babies on her back, or a thousand Canada geese waddling like barnyard fowls along a dike, or a flock of unwieldy pelicans fighting to take off.

It is hardly Great Salt Lake at all, for the ponds within the dikes are fresh. But there is a seasonal interdependence with the lake. Thousands of gulls, pelicans, and cormorants nest on Gunnison, Hat, Egg, Whiterocks and other Great Salt Lake islands, and in spring swarm on those barren rocks as in other seasons they swarm here. The gulls sometimes feed on the brine-fly larvae, but for cormorants and pelicans there is not a scrap to eat in all the lake's expanse. They nest there only for safety. They fly to Bear River or into the fields and ditches eastward to feed. Students eating lunches on the high-school lawns of Salt Lake City are visited every spring noon by hungry gulls, and gulls follow the plowing farmers as cowbirds follow a herd. These are the gulls to whom the Mormons erected the monument in Temple Square, the birds that appeared like a host from heaven to gobble up the 1848 plague of crickets.

Let us work closer to the lake and the islands. We can take a historic route and examine a couple of ghosts on the way.

Highway 191 leads out of Brigham City north of west. At Corinne, among green farms, we meet the first ghost—a sleepy village that was from 1869 to 1903 one of the most important towns in Utah, a division point on the railroad, the hub of a freighting network to the Montana and Idaho mines, the site of a big smelter, the home port of a short and unlucky series of ore-carrying steamboats, the stronghold of the anti-Mormon population, a boom town with big ambitions and thirty saloons.

Quietly it lies on the banks of shrunken Bear River. What it fought has taken it over. When it wore itself out, Mormon farmers bought it up and leached the alkali and sin out of its soil and made it, in that phrase that is like a leitmotif in Mormon thinking, "blossom as the rose."

Pass by Corinne, turn off on Highway 83 along the north shore of Bear River Bay. This is a fine paved road leading only to a point in history. We are paralleling old railroad grades—two of them. For dozens of miles the Central Pacific and Union Pacific built side by side, refusing to meet because there was a prize of land that went with each completed mile. Ruins of an old competition, the grades are both without ties or rails now.

A highway without destination leads us up a dry pass to a saddle where the road ends at a stucco monument. We let the motor die and listen to the wind blowing through this gap in the yellow hills, a dry sound as melancholy as the ruined shacks, broken fences, scattered boards and snarls of rusted wire that are all the remains of the town of Promontory. This is a real ghost, as dead as Baalbek.

This was where Leland Stanford swung his hammer on the golden spike (and missed it the first time, irreverent eyewitnesses said). Here, on May 10, 1869, America became a continental nation, and men waved bottles of champagne from the cowcatchers of facing locomotives while Chinese, Irishmen, politicians, railroad officials, Mormon dignitaries, gamblers and sinful ladies from Corinne cheered. Here happened the single most symbolic hour in the West's history.

Disappointed visitors have scribbled caustic remarks on the monument's register, but for me Promontory is an impressive place. You can hear echoes of history in this saddle of the Promontory Mountains.

Down the east side of the Promontory Mountains, which thrust thirty-five miles into the lake, there is a road—not a good road, but good enough. Eastward, Bear River Bay is a glaring salt flat except where a tongue of pale turquoise curves up toward the Bird Refuge and the river mouth. An orange-headed worm of train creeps toward Ogden along the straight line of the fill across the bay. Beyond it and the low hump of Little Mountain surges up the Wasatch, violet and rose, one of the most beautiful of ranges.

As we curve around the tip of Promontory Point to parallel the railroad, the lake is there, vast, blue as vitriol. It is a color that only desert lakes and seas have, the color of the Persian Gulf. Its shallowness, the light bottom, the glazed desert sky, the border of snowy salt, give Great Salt Lake its light, pure, mineral brightness.

Across a five-mile channel is the turret-crowned hill of Frémont Island, and beyond that the higher and more rugged hump of Antelope Island. Around the Point at Little Valley is the latest of the transportation boom camps that have made much of the lake's history.

In the next four years, tourists willing to drive the gravel road down the Promontory, and passengers on Southern Pacific trains crossing the Lucin Cutoff, will have a close-up view of one of the biggest railroad-engineering jobs since the Central Pacific crossed the Sierra Nevada. North of the present railroad trestle a solid fill will be built up, thirteen miles long, sixty to seventy feet deep, four hundred feet wide at the

bottom and forty feet at the top. To supply rock for the fill whole mountains will be brought down to lake level on conveyor belts. The benefits of
replacing the old trestle, itself an engineering marvel, will be double-
track, full-speed operation and elimination of such dangers as fire (which
destroyed part of the trestle last May) and ice. The ice is not a joke.
Though the brine never freezes, it sometimes gets so cold that fresh
water, flowing in on top of it, freezes instantly, and piles up as icebergs
and floes, sometimes thirty feet high.

Only in a boat do you realize how big Great Salt Lake is. The scale of
everything around it is so vast that the real dimensions are lost. But stand
beside the end of the trestle at Saline and look west, and you can see it
dipping to the curve of the earth, and if you can arrange a boat ride to one
of the farther islands, say Gunnison, you can prepare for two hours of
steady cruising at just about eight knots.

Notice the wake. The water cuts like gelatin, stiffly, and the wake does
not widen and roll, but falls in nearly parallel folds. Streaks of bubbles
scum the turquoise surface like the suds of a detergent. The pinkish
specks in the water are brine shrimp, smaller than a housefly but said to
be edible if one takes the trouble of seining up a cupful or so. Nobody
does, though a company in Ogden seines them for fish food.

The launch plods on, the great sky flaws a moment with cloud, the
water changes instantly from turquoise to vitriol, to lead, back to
turquoise. Ahead, Gunnison Island has lifted its northward-facing
cliff higher out of the water. Alfred Lambourne, who in the 1890s tried to
turn this island into a vineyard, thought the profile was like that of a
crouching lion.

No need to land on Gunnison Island. Its barrenness is amply visible
from the lake, and its history is all contained in that bizarre adventure of
Lambourne's and in the story of the guano diggers whose enterprise
balked his plans. The ruins of two stone huts are still there. The vines have
been dead for fifty years and more. The guano has proved unprofitable.
All that surely remains is the huts and a book, *Our Inland Sea* (originally
Pictures of an Inland Sea), in which Lambourne recorded in impressionistic
prose-poetry his fourteen months of isolation. He claimed to have been

the only man ever to live for love on one of Great Salt Lake's islands. It is an odd distinction, but he is entitled to it.

As we go back along the trestle we face the boomerang curve of Frémont Island and, farther south, the islanded mountain which is called Antelope.

The water glares like aluminum. A train pokes along the trestle and passengers stare down curiously; we wish we had the stuffed carp that former trestle tender Bob Goodnow used to tow behind his boat to astonish the rubbernecks.

The train and the boat are the only life. We see not a single one of the fabled herd of Great Salt Lake whales, not a whisker of the Great Salt Lake Monster, not even a bird cutting the bright air or riding the metallic water. Instead, there is a dreamlike quality in the stillness of the water, in the emptiness of life in lake and sky.

Yet we have hardly landed before three black squalls spring up between Frémont and Carrington islands. Lightning licks out of them, the south grumbles with thunder. Before we have the launch swung into its cradle under the trestle, the wind is hammering against us and the waves are pounding heavy as lead against the fill. It is a lesson in why small boating is a touchy pastime here. The wind can spring as suddenly as an animal, and the brine waves hit a boat with considerably more than the weight of ordinary water.

It is five miles from Promontory Point to Frémont Island, which may be visited with the permission of Charles Stoddard, who leases it as a sheep range.

Three quarters of an hour by boat, an eight-hundred-foot climb, and you are on the turret that led Frémont to call this Castle Island. Here the past has left its mark: a seven-inch cross scratched in the rock by Kit Carson when he came here with Frémont in 1843.

Look around at 360° of bright aquamarine, glittering salt, brown mountains. Between dark outcroppings of slate, the treeless island slopes are gray, old gold, sage green. In this autumn season it is ineffably still—not a bird's cry, not a sheep's baa, not the chirr of a grasshopper, not a rustle of wind in grass.

• • •

At the present stage of water, Antelope is not an island; a causeway connects it to the mainland. The blooded horses that the Mormon Church used to run out here are gone. So are the sheep that once were pastured on Antelope. But the buffalo that were planted here in the 1890s have multiplied and made the place their happy home.

There is not much on any of Great Salt Lake's islands for the casual tourist; they offer nothing but solitude and a desolate beauty. But the desolation becomes a kind of good in itself that is worth preserving. The desert lake and its desert islands are assured to us as a permanent wilderness.

We drive back along the causeway and the flats, and from the highway look back at Antelope's bulk. Now it is as I remember it and as it ought to be kept: distant, tawny and amethyst in the late afternoon, with the west foaming into a sunset beyond it, and the lake glittering like a sword blade along its foot. It is there to be looked at but not disturbed.

Lake Powell

Glen Canyon, once the most serenely beautiful of all the canyons of the Colorado River, is now Lake Powell, impounded by the Glen Canyon Dam at Page, Arizona. The lake, most of which is in the state of Utah, is called a great recreational resource. The Bureau of Reclamation promotes its beauty in an attempt to counter continuing criticisms of the dam itself, and the National Park Service, which manages the Recreation Area, is installing or planning facilities for all the boating, water-skiing, fishing, camping, swimming, and plain sight-seeing that should now ensue.

But I come back to Lake Powell reluctantly and skeptically, for I remember Glen Canyon as it used to be.

Once the river ran through Glen's 200 miles in a twisting, many-branched stone trough 800 to 1,200 feet deep. That was not deep, as the Colorado's canyons go, just deep enough to be impressive without being overwhelming. Awe was never Glen Canyon's province. That is for the Grand Canyon. Glen Canyon was for delight. The river that used to run here cooperated with the scenery by flowing swift and smooth, without a major rapid. Any ordinary boatman could take anyone through it. I went through once with a party that contained an old lady of seventy and a girl of eleven. There was superlative camping anywhere, on sandbars furred with tamarisk and willow, under cliffs that whispered with the sound of flowing water.

Through many of those 200 idyllic miles the view one saw was shut in by red walls, but down straight reaches or up side canyons there would be glimpses of noble towers and buttes lifting high beyond the canyon rims, and somewhat more than halfway down, the Kaiparowits Plateau, 7,500 feet high, thrust its knife-blade cliff above the north rim to face the dome of Navajo Mountain, more than 10,000 feet high, on the south side. Those two uplifts, as strikingly different as if designed to dominate some gigantic world's fair, added magnificence to the intimate, colored trough of the river.

Seen from the air, the Glen Canyon country reveals itself as a bare-stone, salmon-pink tableland whose surface is a chaos of domes, knobs, beehives, baldheads, hollows, and potholes, dissected by the deep cork-screw channels of streams. Out of the platform northwest of the main river rise the gray-green peaks of the Henry Mountains, the last-discovered mountains in the contiguous United States. West of them is the bloody welt of the Waterpocket Fold, whose creeks flow into the Escalante, the last-discovered river. Northward rise the cliffs of Utah's high plateaus. South of Glen Canyon, like a great period at the foot of the fifty-mile exclamation point of the Kaiparowits, is Navajo Mountain, whose slopes apron off on every side into the stone and sand of the Navajo Indian Reservation.

When cut by streams, the Navajo sandstone—which is the country rock—forms monolithic cliffs with rounded rims. In straight stretches the cliffs tend to be sheer; on the curves, undercut, especially in the narrow side canyons. I have measured a 600-foot wall that was undercut a good 500 feet—not a cliff at all, but a musical shell for the multiplication of echoes. Into these deep-scoured amphitheaters on the outside of bends, the promontories on the inside fit like thigh-bones into hip sockets. Often, straightening bends, creeks have cut through promontories to form bridges, as at Rainbow Bridge National Monument and Gregory Natural Bridge in Fiftymile Canyon. And when a river cleft has exposed the rock to the vertical thrust of its own weight, fracturing begins to peel great slabs from the cliff faces. The slabs are thinner at top than at bottom, and curve together so that great alcoves form in the walls. If they are near the rim, they may break through to let a window-wink of sky down on a canyon traveler, and always they make panels of fresh pink in weathered and stained and darkened red walls.

Floating down the river one passed, every mile or two on right or left, the mouth of some side canyon, narrow, shadowed, releasing a secret stream into the taffy-colored, whirlpooled Colorado. Between the mouth of the Dirty Devil and the dam, which is a few miles above the actual foot of Glen Canyon, there are at least three dozen such gulches on the north side, including the major canyon of the Escalante; and on the south nearly that many more, including the major canyon of the San Juan. Every such gulch used to be a little wonder, each with its multiplying branches, each as deep at the mouth as its parent canyon. Hundreds of feet deep, sometimes only a few yards wide, they wove into the rock so sinuously that all sky was shut off. The floors were smooth sand or rounded stone pavement or stone pools linked by stone gutters, and nearly every gulch ran, except in flood season, a thin clear stream. Silt pockets out of reach of floods were gardens of fern and redbud; every talus and rockslide gave footing to cottonwood and willow and single-leafed ash; ponded places were solid with watercress; maidenhair hung from seepage cracks in the cliffs.

Often these side canyons, pursued upward, ended in falls, and sometimes the fall came down through a slot or skylight in the roof of a domed chamber, to trickle down the wall into a plunge pool that made a lyrical dunk bath on a hot day. In such chambers the light was dim, reflected, richly colored. The red rock was stained with the dark manganese exudations called desert varnish, striped black to green to yellow to white along horizontal lines of seepage, patched with the chemical, sunless green of moss. One such grotto was named Music Temple by Maj. John Wesley Powell on his first exploration, in 1869; another is the so-called Cathedral in the Desert, at the head of Clear Water Canyon off the Escalante.

That was what Glen Canyon was like before the closing of the dam in 1963. What was flooded here was potentially a superb national park. It had its history, too, sparse but significant. Exploring the gulches, one came upon ancient chiseled footholds leading up the slickrock to the mortared dwellings or storage cysts of the Basket Makers and Pueblos who once inhabited these canyons. At the mouth of Padre Creek a line of chipped steps marked where Fathers Escalante and Dominguez, groping back toward Santa Fe in 1776, got their animals down to the ford that was known afterward as the Crossing of the Fathers. In Music Temple men from Powell's two river expeditions scratched their names. Here and there on the walls near the river were names and initials of men from Robert Brewster Stanton's party, which surveyed a water-level railroad down the canyon in 1889–1890, and of miners from the abortive gold rush of the 1890s. There were Mormon echoes at Lee's Ferry, below the dam, and at the slot canyon called Hole in the Rock, where in 1880 a Mormon colonizing party got their wagons down the cliffs on their way to the San Juan.

Some of this is now under Lake Powell. Because I don't much like the thought of powerboats and water-skiers in these canyons, I come in March, before the season has properly begun, and at the time when the lake is as high as it has ever been, but still more than 200 feet below its capacity level of 3,700 feet. Not everything that may eventually be drowned is drowned yet, and there are none of the stained walls and exposed mudflats that make a reservoir ugly at low water.

One thing is comfortingly clear from the moment we back away from the dock at Wahweap and start out between the low walls toward the main channel of what used to be Wahweap Creek. Though they have diminished it, they haven't ruined it. Though these walls are lower and tamer than they used to be, Lake Powell *is* beautiful. It isn't Glen Canyon, but it is something in itself. The contact of deep blue water and uncompromising stone is bizarre and somehow exciting. Enough of the canyon feeling is left so that traveling uplake one watches with a sense of discovery as every bend rotates new colors, new forms, new vistas into sight: a great glowing wall with the sun on it, a slot side canyon buried to the eyes in water and inviting exploration, a half-drowned cave on whose roof the reflections of ripples dance like little flames or fireflies.

Moreover, since we float three hundred feet or more above the old river, the views are much wider, and where the lake broadens, as at Padre Creek, they are superb. From the river, Navajo Mountain used to be seen only in brief, distant glimpses. From the lake it is often visible for minutes, even an hour at a time—gray-green, snow-streaked, a high mysterious bubble rising above the red world, incontrovertibly the holy mountain. The broken country around the Crossing of the Fathers was always as wild and strange as a moon landscape, but you had to climb out of the canyon to see it well. Now, from the bay that covers the crossing and spreads into the mouths of tributary creeks, we see Gunsight Butte, Tower Butte and the other fantastic pinnacles of the Entrada formation surging up a sheer thousand feet above the rounding platform of the Navajo. The horizon reels with surrealistic forms, dark red at the base, gray from there to rimrock, the profiles rigid and angular and carved, as different as possible from the Navajo's filigreed, ripple-marked dune surface shapes and monolithic cliffs.

We find the larger side canyons, as well as the deeper reaches of the main canyon, almost as impressive as they used to be, especially after we get far enough uplake so that the water is shallower and the cliffs less reduced in height. Navajo Canyon is splendid despite the flooding of its green floor, which used to provide pasture for the stolen horses of raiders. Forbidding Canyon, which leads to Rainbow Bridge, is lessened, but still marvelous. Rainbow Bridge itself is still the place of magic that it used to be back when we walked the six miles up from the river and turned a corner to see the great arch framing the dome of Navajo Mountain. The canyon of the Escalante, with all its tortuous side canyons, is one of the stunning scenic experiences of a lifetime, and far easier to reach by lake than it used to be by foot or horseback. And all up and down these canyons, big or little, is the constantly changing, nobly repetitive spectacle of the cliffs.

And there is God's plenty of it. This lake is already 150 miles long, with scores of tributaries. If it ever fills—which its critics hope it will not—it will have 1,800 miles of shoreline. Its fishing is good and apparently getting better, not only catfish and perch but rainbow trout and largemouth black bass, sown broadcast periodically from planes. At present its supply and access points are few and far apart—at Wahweap, Hall's Crossing and Hite—but floating facilities are being anchored in the narrows below Rainbow Bridge, and when boat ramps and supply stations are developed at Warm Creek, Hole in the Rock and Bullfrog Basin, Lake Powell will draw people. The prediction of a million visitors in 1965 was wildly enthusiastic, but there is no question that as new facilities extend the range of boats and multiply the places of access, this will become one of the great water playgrounds. The 865,000 expected in 1966 will probably be there.

And yet, vast and beautiful as it is, open now to anyone with a boat or the money to rent one, available soon (one supposes) to the quickie tour by air and hydrofoil, its most secret beauties captured on color transparencies at infallible exposures—it strikes me, even in my exhilaration, that in gaining the lovely and the usable, we have given up the incomparable.

Much of the archaeology and most of the history, both of which were concentrated at the river's edge or near it, are as drowned as Lyonesse. We chug 200 feet above the top of the square masonry tower that used to guard the mouth of Forbidding Canyon. The one small ruin that we see up Navajo Canyon must once have been nearly inaccessible, high in the cliff. Somehow we think it ought to have a line of footholds leading down into and under the water toward the bottom, where the squash and corn gardens used to grow.

The wildlife that used to live comfortably in Glen Canyon is not there on the main lake. Except at the extreme reach of the water up side canyons, and at infrequent places where the platform of the Navajo sandstone dips down, so that the lake spreads in among its hollows and baldheads, this reservoir leaves no home for beaver or waterbird. The beaver have been driven up the side canyons, and have toppled whole groves of cottonwoods ahead of the rising water. While the water remains stable, they have a home; if it rises, they move upward; if it falls, the Lord knows what they will do, for falling water will leave long mudflats between their water and their food. In the side canyons we see a few mergansers and redheads, and up the Escalante Arm the blue herons are now nesting on the cliffs, but as a future habitat, Lake Powell is as unpromising for any of them as for the beaver.

And what has made things difficult for the wildlife makes things difficult for tourists as well. The tamarisk and willow bars are gone, and finding a campsite, or even a safe place to land a boat, is not easy. When the stiff afternoon winds sweep up the lake, small boats stay in shelter, for a swamping could leave a man clawing at a vertical cliff, a mile from a crawling-out place.

Worst of all is the loss of places I remember. Surging uplake on the second day, I look over my shoulder and recognize the swamped and truncated entrance to Hidden Passage Canyon, on whose bar we camped eighteen years ago, when we first came down this canyon on one of Norman Nevills's river trips. The old masked entrance is swallowed up, the water rises almost over the shoulder of the inner cliffs. Once that canyon was a pure delight to walk in; now it is only another slot with water in it, a thing to poke a motorboat into for five minutes and then roar out again. And if that is Hidden Passage, and we are this far out in the channel, then Music Temple is straight down.

The magnificent confrontation of the Kaiparowits and Navajo Mountain is still there, more magnificent because the lake has lifted us into a wider view. The splendid sweep of stained wall just below the mouth of the San Juan is there, only a little diminished. And Hole in the Rock still notches the north rim, though the cove at the bottom—where the Mormons camped before rafting the river and starting across the bare rock-chaos of Wilson Mesa—is now a bay, with sunfish swimming among the tops of drowned trees. The last time I was here, four years ago, the river ran its course in a gorge 300 feet below, where our boat ties up for the night, and the descent from rim to water was a longer, harder way. The lake makes the feat of those Mormons look easier than it was, but even now, no one climbing the thousand feet of cliff to the slot will ever understand how they got their wagons down there.

A mixture of losses, diminishments, occasional gains, precariously maintained by the temporary stabilization of the lake. There are plenty of people willing to bet that there will never be enough water in the Colorado to fill both Lake Mead, now drawn far down, and Lake Powell, still 165 feet below its planned top level, much less the two additional lakes proposed for Marble and Bridge Canyons, between these two. If there ever is—even if there is enough to raise Lake Powell another fifty or hundred feet—there will be drastic losses of beauty. Walls now low, but high enough to maintain the canyon feeling, will go under. The wider the lake spreads, the less character it will have. Another ten feet of water would rise to the top of the arch of the Gregory Natural Bridge and flood the floor of the Cathedral in the Desert; 100 feet would put both where Music Temple is; 200 feet would bring water and silt to the very foot of Rainbow Bridge. The promontories that are now the most feasible camping places would go, as the taluses and sandbars have already gone. Then the lake would be a vertical-walled fjord widening in places to a vertical-walled lake, neither as beautiful nor usable as now. And when there is even twenty or thirty feet of drawdown, the head of every side canyon is a stinking mudflat, and every cliff is defaced at the foot by a band of mud and minerals.

By all odds the best thing that could happen, so far as the recreational charm of Lake Powell is concerned, would be a permanently stabilized lake, but nobody really expects that. People who want to see it in its diminished but still remarkable beauty should go soon. And people who, as we do, remember this country before the canyons were flooded, are driven to dream of ways by which some parts of it may still be saved, or half saved.

The dream comes on us one evening when we are camped up the Escalante. For three days we have been deafened by the noise of our diesel engines, and even when those have been cut off, there has been the steady puttering of the generator that supplies our boat with heat, light and running water. Though we weakly submit to the comforts, we dislike the smell and noise: we hate to import into this rock-and-water wilderness the very things we have been most eager to escape from. A wilderness that must be approached by powerboat is no wilderness anymore, it has lost its mana. Now, with the engines cut and the generator happily broken down, we sit around a campfire's more primitive light and heat and reflect that the best moments of this trip have been those in which the lake and its powerboat necessities were least dominant—eating a quiet lunch on a rock in Navajo Canyon; walking the 1.3 miles of sandy trail to the Rainbow Bridge, or the half mile of creek bottom to the Cathedral in the Desert; climbing up the cliff to Hole in the Rock. Sitting on our promontory in the Escalante Canyon without sign or sound of the mechanical gadgetry of our civilization, we feel descending on us, as gentle as evening on a blazing day, the remembered canyon silence. It is a stillness like no other I have experienced, for at the very instant of bouncing and echoing every slight noise off cliffs and around bends, the canyons swallow them. It is as if they accentuated them, briefly and with a smile; as if they said, "Wait!" and then suddenly all sound has vanished, and there is only a hollow ringing in the ears.

We find that whatever others may want, we would hate to come here in the full summer season and be affronted by the constant roar and wake of powerboats. We are not, it seems, water-based in our pleasures; we can't get a thrill out of doing in these marvelous canyons what one can do on any other resort lake. What we have most liked on this trip have been those times when ears and muscles were involved, when the foot felt sand or stone, when we could talk in low voices or sit so still that a brilliant or collared lizard came out of a crack to look us over. For us, it is clear, Lake Powell is only a means of access; it is the canyons themselves, or what is left of them, that we respond to.

Six or seven hundred feet above us, spreading grandly from the rim, is the Escalante Desert, a basin of unmitigated stone furrowed by branching canyons as a carving platter is furrowed by gravy channels. It is, as a subsidiary drainage basin, very like the greater basin in whose trough lay Glen Canyon, now the lake. On the north this desert drains from the Circle Cliffs and the Aquarius Plateau, on the east from the Waterpocket Fold, on the west from the Kaiparowits. In all that waste of stone fifty miles long and twenty to thirty wide, there is not a resident human being, not a building except a couple of cowboy shelter shacks, not a road except the washed-out trail that the Mormons of 1880 established from the town of Escalante to Hole in the Rock. The cattle and sheep that used to run on this desert range have ruined it and gone.

That ringing stillness around us is a total absence of industrial or civilized decibels, and it blankets a wilderness such as the prophets once went into.

Why not, we say, sitting in chilly, fire-flushed darkness under mica stars, why not throw a boom across the mouth of the Escalante Canyon and hold this one precious arm of Lake Powell for the experiencing of silence? Why not, giving the rest of that enormous water to the motorboats and the water-skiers, keep one limited tributary as a canoe or rowboat wilderness? There is nothing in the way of law or regulation to prevent the National Park Service from managing the Recreation Area in any way it thinks best, nothing that forbids a wilderness or primitive or limited-access area within the larger recreational unit. The Escalante Desert is already federal land, virtually unused. It and its canyons are accessible by packtrain from the town of Escalante, and will be accessible by boat from Hole in the Rock. All down the foot of the Kaiparowits, locally called Fiftymile Mountain, the old Mormon road offers stupendous views to those who from choice or necessity want only to drive to the edge of the silence and look in.

I have been in most of the side gulches off the Escalante—Coyote Gulch, Hurricane Wash, Davis Canyon and others. All of them have bridges, windows, amphitheaters, grottoes, sudden pockets of green. And some of them, including the superlative Coyote Gulch, down which even now it is possible to take a packtrain to the river, will never be drowned even if Lake Powell rises to its planned 3,700-foot level. What might have been done for Glen Canyon as a whole may still be done for the higher tributaries of the Escalante. Why not? In the name of scenery, silence, sanity, why not?

For awe pervades that desert of slashed and channeled stone overlooked by the cliffs of the Kaiparowits and the Aquarius and the distant peaks of the Henrys; and history, effaced through much of the canyons, still shows us its earmarks here: a crude mano discarded at an ancient campsite, a mortared wall in a cave, petroglyphs picked into a cliff face, a broken flint point glittering on its tee of sand on some blown mesa, the great rock where the Mormons danced on their way to people Desolation. This is country that does not challenge our identity as creatures, but it shows us our true size.

Exploring the Escalante basin on a trip in 1961, we probed for the main river through a half dozen quicksand gulches and never reached it, and never much cared, because the side gulches and the rims gave us all we could hold. We saw not a soul outside our own party, encountered not a vehicle, saw no animals except a handful of cows and one mule that we scared up in Davis Gulch when we rolled a rock over the rim. From every evening camp, when the sun was gone behind the Kaiparowits, and the wind hung in suspension like a held breath, and the Henrys northeastward and Navajo Mountain southward floated light as bubbles on the distance, we watched the eastern sky flush a pure, cloudless rose, darker at the horizon, paler above; and minute by minute the horizon's darkness defined itself as the blue, domed shadow of the earth cast on the sky, thinning at its upward arc to violet, lavender, pale lilac, but clearly defined, steadily darkening upward until it swallowed all the sky's light, and the stars pierced through it. Every night we watched the earth-shadow climb the hollow sky, and every dawn we watched the same blue shadow sink down toward the Kaiparowits, to disappear at the instant when the sun splintered sparks off the rim.

In that country you cannot raise your eyes—unless you're in a canyon—without looking a hundred miles. You can hear coyotes that have somehow escaped the air-dropped poison baits designed to exterminate them. You can see in every sandy pocket the pug tracks of mousing wildcats, and every waterpocket in the rock will give you a look backward into geological time, for every such hole swarms with triangular, crablike creatures, locally called tadpoles but really cousins to the trilobites that left fossil imprints in the Paleozoic rocks.

In the canyons you do not have the sweep of sky, the long views, the freedom of movement on foot, but you do have the protection of cliffs, the secret places, cool water, arches and bridges and caves, and the sunken canyon stillness into which, musical as water falling into a plunge pool, the canyon wrens pour their showers of notes in the mornings.

Set the Escalante Arm aside for the silence, and the boatmen and the water-skiers can have the rest of that marvelous lake, which on the serene, warm, sun-smitten trip back seems even more beautiful than when we were coming up. Save this tributary and the desert back from it as wilderness, and there will be something at Lake Powell for everybody. Then it may still be possible to make expeditions as rewarding as the old motor-less river trips through Glen Canyon, and a man can make his choice between forking a horse and riding down Coyote Gulch, or renting a houseboat and chugging it up somewhere near the mouth of the Escalante, to be anchored and used as a base for excursions into beauty, wonder, and the sort of silence in which you can hear the swish of falling stars.

Back Roads River

1

To start a trip at Mexican Hat, Utah, is to start off into empty space from the end of the world. The space that surrounds Mexican Hat is filled only with what the natives describe as "a lot of rocks, a lot of sand, more rocks, more sand, and wind enough to blow it away." The nearest rail point is at Thompsons, up north on the Denver and Rio Grande, 175 miles away by road.

This road, the only real road in the area, has an advantage which some of this country's roads do not: it can be traveled both ways. You can come down Highway 160, which links Salt Lake with Mesa Verde and Santa Fe, and follow the diminishing trail through Blanding and Bluff to Mexican Hat. Or you can come up from Grand Canyon across the Hopi and western Navajo reservations by way of Moenkopi, Tonalea, Kayenta, and Monument Valley. Or if you have no mercy on your car, you can come up from Gallup to Shiprock and then take out over the axle-breaking trail to Kayenta by way of Dennehotso. Or you can fight your way up from the southern Navajo country over wagon tracks deep in sand. When you reach Mexican Hat you are at the end of the world and the beginning of the San Juan country.

It is useful to know where you are. On a map of Utah notice how the Colorado River cuts across the state from northeast to southwest, blocking off a great triangle in Utah's southeast corner. All but the tip of this triangle is San Juan County. Just a trifle smaller than Massachusetts, a little bigger than Rhode Island, Connecticut, and Delaware combined, the county was formed in 1880 before it had any white population. At the last census its population was still under 5,000, and a third of that number were Navajos and Paiutes.

The first automobile crossed the sandy fifty-five miles across Monument Valley between Kayenta and Mexican Hat in 1921. There has been more traffic since, but not too much. This is not real tourist country, irrigated by foreign dollars. This is a scenic dry-farm, the biggest and almost the last. The wilderness stretches out on every side from the San Juan country, a primitive area at least a hundred miles square. But the San Juan country proper, between the Abajo Mountains and Monument Valley, and between the Colorado boundary and Glen Canyon of the Colorado, is the heart of the last great wilderness. Through the middle of it, flowing in a continuous canyon to its junction with the Colorado 133 miles westward, runs the San Juan River, as little known and as little celebrated as the country it drains.

The dozen of us who gather in Mexican Hat Lodge on the evening of June 5 have a date with the river. We are a motley crowd: a movie photographer and his wife, a pair of engineers, a dentist's assistant, a physical education instructor, a radio technician, a few plain tourists, an old lady of seventy-two, and a little girl of ten. In the morning we will start down the San Juan by boat to Lee's Ferry.

We are not pioneers, explorers, or even adventurers, but simply backroads tourists who have put ourselves in the hands of Norman Nevills, probably the best-known river boatman in the world. Norman has been down the full length of the Green and Colorado more than once; he has run the Grand Canyon more times than any man alive or dead, and will run it again this summer. He has run the Salmon and the Snake in Idaho, and he nurses a secret dream of some day running the Brahmaputra, in India. He is like a broncobuster who cannot bear to leave any horse unridden. The trip he will take us on starting tomorrow is a milk run for Norman; he has made it two dozen times. But as he gives us a genial briefing with pictures, it does not look like any milk run to us. Even if it isn't dangerous, even if a spry old lady and Norman's ten-year-old daughter can go along, it looks like excitement and it looks like fun. And even the milk run has been made by only a few hundred people at most.

At Mexican Hat the canyon walls are low, but they rise rapidly downstream. When we gather on the beach after breakfast we see the river bowling along, gray-brown with silt, its middle marcelled with two-foot waves. Yesterday two young men put their homemade boat in the river a little above here to try it out. They managed to struggle ashore at the bridge, but they have decided to take Norman's advice and not attempt the river in that boat. We help them put it back on the roof of their car, and they stand a little disconsolately with the rest of Mexican Hat's slim population as the four square-ended semi-cataract boats of Norman's party shove off. Four of us miss the launching, because we are going overland to the Goosenecks to get pictures as the boats swing into the deep hairpins of the meander. We will join the others about noon at the foot of the Honaker Trail.

One after another the boats pull into swift water, swing sideways to take the waves, and are rushed downstream. They seem to shrink to half their size as soon as they are afloat, and they look tiny and frail as they speed down under the bridge and the cable-hung bucket of the Geological Survey gauging station and disappear around the first bend.

We are at the Goosenecks a good while before the boats, which have to travel sixteen miles in the canyon to reach here. Below us the gray-brown river has sunk itself 1,300 feet into the rock in a perfect double hairpin— what geologists call an "entrenched meander." The San Juan used to be a sluggish river running on a level plain, and meandering like any old-age stream. Then a great plateau was slowly lifted across its path, so slowly that the river could cling to its old course and simply dig in. So it still has the crooked course of a slow river, though it is actually the fastest major stream in the United States, with a gradient of almost eight feet to the mile. Just for comparison, the Mississippi's gradient is eight *inches* to the mile; that of the Colorado in the Grand Canyon, the most furious water on the continent, is 7.56 feet to the mile. The San Juan below us is not furious, but it is undeniably fast; we can see the speed of it in the glasses, looking down on the throat of the middle bend, where the canyon comes within a hundred yards of cutting through the ridge before it turns and makes a three-mile loop westward, to come back barely a stone's throw from where it started.

For nearly an hour we sit on the hot, barren rim with the towers of Monument Valley—Agathla's Needle and the spiry monuments on the Utah side—breaking the southern horizon. Then the first tiny boat comes in sight down below, and we hear Norm's "river voice" bellowing. We bellow back, though we know the river noise will prevent our being heard. The four white twigs rotate in almost military formation through a little rapid and disappear under the wall at the turn. Then they emerge again going away from us, on their way around the tedious three-mile hairpin. After a wait, here they come again. Through the glasses I can see them buck and leap in the waves, and I see a combing wave break clear over the bow of the first boat where Mary sits. I can almost see the expression on her face, and I envy her the coolness of that ducking.

The four of us on the rim are all of one mind: pictures or no pictures, we want to get down and get in on the fun. As soon as the last boat has disappeared we pile in the truck and are taken by a wretched mesa-top trail out to another part of the rim, where a rock cairn marks the top of the Honaker Trail. From here it is 1,300 feet to the river; the way we have to walk, it is three miles.

2

The Honaker Trail has been specially recommended to me by Norm because I am gathering material for a biography of John Wesley Powell, the first navigator of the Colorado. This trail, Norm says, will show me what it means to try to climb out of one of these canyons in case of shipwreck or loss of supplies. It shows me that, certainly, switching along the outcropping ledges, sliding down shaly talus full of fossils, going far out of its way to find a way down to the next ledge. It shows me also, if I needed to be shown, what lengths men will go to for a chance to strike it rich. This trail was built by the Honakers at the turn of the century, and for several years they slaved and sweated trying to get a fortune out of the San Juan gravel bars. Altogether they got about $1,500, perhaps a tenth of what it was worth to build the trail. There is nothing on the trail now but a collared lizard with a canary-yellow collar and a marvelous emerald belly, who obligingly poses for color photographs. He is the one lizard in this country, outside the rare and poisonous Gila monster, who will bite you if you fuss with him.

We meet the boats on a sandbar, and after lunch we get our taste of river travel. The river falls two hundred feet in the next twenty-three miles, shooting us through the Honaker Point, Eyemo, John's Canyon, Government, and Slickhorn Rapids, all of them small, with a fall of about four feet apiece, but all exciting enough to amateurs, and good for enough wettings to cool us off.

There is a feeling of continuous rapids on the San Juan, not only because the current boosts us along at an average speed of seven miles an hour but because of the river's peculiar and characteristic "sand waves." These are formed by the piling up of waves of sand on the bottom, which as they accumulate start a series of water waves moving slowly upstream against the current. The waves appear quite suddenly, move upstream growing deeper and more violent, and crest with a roaring noise for a minute or two before they disappear. At this stage of water they average three feet in height, though occasionally we catch one four or even five feet high. They have been measured up to six. Even in their middle sizes, they toss and pound a boat spectacularly, especially if taken head on. Norm takes them the easy way, sideways, and they afford endless fun with their rocking-horse pitching and the occasional boatload of water they dump on us if we hit them combing.

We are wet and dry all day. At the foot of Slickhorn Rapid, where we pull in to camp after a day's run of forty miles, Paul, our aviation engineer, caps the day by falling off into the rapid's tail wave, clothes, camera, and all. Our camp is among willows and tamarisks on the bar—the tamarisks that not too many years ago were imported from India to combat erosion in desert washes and have now been blown and spread by birds through every gulch in the Southwest. After dinner (steak) all the ladies go off with Norm to be initiated into the order of Driftwood Burners. They build piles of kindling all around an immense tangled pile of driftwood at least an acre in extent, and at a signal touch them off. Within minutes the inferno drives us clear to the water's edge. The hot glow creeps up the cliffs, gradually revealing the rims a quarter mile above; it throws leaping red light up Slickhorn Gulch and touches the abandoned oil rig below the toilsome trail where prospectors at the turn of the century fought their way down here to drill among the oil seeps.

Norm tells us stories of the river, Powell, the ill-fated Brown-Stanton expedition, while the flames eat into the driftwood and the whole gorge glows with red light. Full of energy as a grasshopper, he leads an impromptu squaw dance as close to the fire as skin will stand it, and then abruptly heads for bed. The party breaks up and follows him. Hours afterward I wake in the night and feel at two hundred yards the heat of the embers, and see the steady glow on the cliffs. It is pleasant to think that so big and satisfactory a bonfire has only good results: there is no danger from it, and it helps keep Lake Mead from filling up with drift and debris. Through the night the Big Dipper moves down the slot until its handle rests on the rim where the canyon curves left below camp. At the other end of the reach the moon is coming up, shining pale silver on Slickhorn Rapid.

Kent Frost, the boatman-cook, beats on his frying pan at 5:30. During breakfast the sun touches the rims and begins to creep down, but it still has not reached the water when we stop, after an hour's run, to get pictures at the mouth of Grand Gulch. In this red-walled wash, which caused enormous trouble to the Mormon pioneers coming across from Hole in the Rock in 1880, the archaeologist Prudden first clearly isolated the Basket Maker culture as separate from and earlier than the Pueblo. It has, we know, considerable ruins, but we do not stop to explore. Between walls that rise sheer from the water, but lessen in height downstream, we run down to the open valley called Paiute Farms, beyond the quicksand-sown ford known as Clay Hills Crossing. Here the river spreads out like the Platte over a channel half a mile wide. We hunt cautiously for channels, and several times we go overboard to push. The second boat grounds so definitively that we do not see it again until just before we stop for the night. But in this open stretch we see the only human beings we are to see, besides ourselves, between Mexican Hat and Lee's Ferry. They are four Navajos tending sheep among the tamarisks on the reservation side of the river. On the north bank Norm shows us the bar where he crash-landed his Piper Cub last February and was marooned for two days before another plane located him.

All through the shallows, in a blazing hot afternoon, we cool ourselves off by going overboard to tow or swim behind the boat. Even here on the flats the current is much too strong to swim against; it can barely be walked against. At noon Mary discovered that she could sit down in the shallow water and be pushed along like a kiddy car. But it is a little disconcerting to go overboard with a yell in sand waves four feet high, with the boat standing on its beam-ends, and find the water only knee-deep. We spend half our time throwing each other overboard until the canyon walls begin to narrow again and the river gathers itself.

3

The canyon of the San Juan is geologically a highly instructive place. In any part of this country one learns to recognize the rock strata and know their profiles and coloring and the peculiarities of their bedding and weathering as one knows the faces of his friends. The San Juan gives us a one-way tour of all the strata we have ever known before, but with characteristic perversity starts in the oldest and flows downward into the highest and youngest.

The gray Hermosa and Rico formations in which we started form terraced cliffs with banded horizontal ledges of harder strata. Below the Honaker Trail these beds disappear under the covering layer of the Cedar Mesa sandstone, red and massive, which forms sheer cliffs like those under which we slept last night. At Clay Hills Crossing and along through Paiute Farms we meet the gray-blue Chinle, which breaks down into badlands slopes, and the thin-bedded red-brown Organrock, which in exposed faces erodes into irregular columns and statuary. And finally these are overtaken by the two most impressive layers of all, the Wingate and Navajo sandstones, both very massive and both very beautiful.

The Wingate, which crops out in bold cliffs clear down into New Mexico, is rich red. It forms marvelously sheer cliffs, straight and hewn as the wall of a building, which often rise straight from the water, though where we first meet this stratum it shows talus slopes of great blocks that cover the Chinle and Organrock underneath. The great planes of cliffs are filigreed with delicate tracery and stained with the shiny, black-brown "desert varnish." We float between great blackboards scrawled with the doodlings of giant children. Once we put in to replenish our water at Nevills Canyon, an alcove full of snake-grass and cane and with a clear sweet spring. The hot run through Paiute Farms has emptied our canteens, and though most of us have sampled river water "just to see what water with real *body* to it tastes like," we prefer our drink without quite so much grit.

As we drift on we see, above the cloven front of the Wingate cliffs, the domes and "baldheads" of the salmon-colored Navajo sandstone which forms the roof of the world here. As the Wingate is a cliff-forming, the Navajo is an arch-forming member. High in the walls amphitheaters a quarter of a mile across open up. Their bottoms are green and lush, and high across their upward curve, just below where the arching roofs begin to overhang, there is a level line of seepage at a joint in the rock. From the seepline, water-stain and fringes of maidenhair fern make a scalloped necklace of green and black and white against the salmon-colored wall.

All around the Great Bend we are in the Wingate capped by Navajo, and caves and alcoves and arched windows appear high in the upper wall, with blackboard cliffs below. At one point where the current sweeps close under an overhanging wall, we catch a glimpse of crosshatched petroglyphs. Across the river from here, on his last trip down, Norm surprised a mountain lion at the water's edge.

4

This second night there is no fire or squaw dance. We have run forty-nine miles and pushed and swum, and we hit the sleeping bags early in a camp among great boulders covered with petroglyphic animals and symbols. The last thing I see as I roll in is Annie and Joan, the oldest and the youngest, braiding each other's hair for bed. The first thing I see in the morning is Al, the movie cameraman, somewhat agitatedly shaking two scorpions out of his sleeping bag.

In quick succession this morning we shoot Express Train and Paiute Rapids, both pleasantly exciting, but nothing alarming the way Norm runs them. He is at once so careful and so nonchalant that he makes even bad water look easy. I have tried my hand at the oars several times by now, and I know enough to discount Norm when he says that running these rivers depends 90 percent on the boats, 5 percent on luck, and 5 percent on skill. There is much more skill in it than that, though the boats are amazing—clumsy and hard to row, wide in the beam and square at both ends, but they ride rapids like ducks on a pond.

Where the river swings in another northward bend, Norm takes Al up a cliff and over the ridge so he can get pictures of us coming around. For two or three miles I am the boatman, and without Norm in the boat to point out rocks I am a little edgy as I steer down through the riffles around the bend, trying to keep facing my danger but not quite sure what single rock or cliff is most dangerous. We are to land on a short bar above a big rock, and I pull into the eddy with great brilliance, making the tricky landing so professionally that I am goofily proud of myself and eager to be of assistance to lesser men. George is coming in too low down, obviously bound for a collision with the big rock. I jump overboard to grab his line, and disappear. In the scouring eddy the water is six feet instead of six inches deep. As I come up I hear cheers from the cliff, and see Al and Norm waving. In my first piece of movie acting I have stolen the scene.

Being already sodden, I am the natural goat for a rigged quicksand sequence. I am to step off into a patch of quicksand and be rescued in the nick of time. I step off all right, and the quicksand sucks me in all right, and the ropes and rescuers come flying and I am pulled out all right, but George, one of the boatmen, who used to be an all-conference halfback at Brigham Young, forgets in his enthusiasm that I am locked in to the waist and that my legs bend only one way. From this time until the end of the trip I walk with a cane, but the service we have rendered to cinematographic art gives us all a deep satisfaction.

Now the next-to-worst rapid on the San Juan, Syncline, where the boats are lightened and where some of the passengers have to walk around. Mary and I get to ride it down, thanks to Powell, but it is disappointingly tame, and we think Norman guilty of building up these riffles to something worse than they are. But at Thirteen-Foot Rapid, further along, we see what he means by white water. All the boatmen call this one nasty to run because of its structure, though it is not in a class with the bad ones on the Colorado and Green, with Lodore and Disaster Falls and Badger Creek and the Sockdologer.

Norm wants to stunt this one for the camera. Again thanks to Powell, I get to go along. We row out into the broken rock-filled channel and all in an instant the current grabs us. I have had the oars in my hands enough to know how this would feel if I were rowing. But Norm half stands, watching the white water ahead, picking his way between rocks, driving stern-first toward the end of the chute where the water roars up on a great rock and then falls away to the left in a white cascade. A push with one oar, a pull with the other, a little tense adjustment, a quick pull away, a swing back to duck a water-covered rock, and we drive into the roar of the rapids. Norm has mentioned the express-train, earth-shaking thunder of bad water; we almost get it here. We are deliberately bow-light for the stunting, and at the last minute Norm swings so that our bow climbs the big rock and then falls left down what seems ten sheer feet into a boiling hole, shipping a little water and a lot of spray, and bouncing down into the diminishing tail waves.

The other boats are run through one at a time, two of them smacking solidly into a rock in the deep hole at the rapid's foot, but bouncing off unharmed. We stop for lunch a little below, in Redbud Canyon where there is a sweet-water spring, and after lunch Al and Alma and I go on ahead with Kent, rowing hard to get out in front of the others so we can shoot pictures at the junction with the Colorado.

The last few miles of the San Juan canyon are deep and narrow, beautifully sheer in the Navajo sandstone; the Wingate has slid underneath us. At the junction we float out into a wide, deep, quiet river, moving fast but not as fast as the San Juan, that rounds into a turn to the west. When we land and climb the cliff across the Colorado we can look up Glen Canyon between the salmon-pink walls to a high butte; on every side, across on Wilson's Mesa between the rivers and north and south of us on both sides, the Navajo sandstone is eroded in knobs and domes. Back of us is the knife-edged profile of the Kaiparowits Plateau, high and gloomy, locally called Wild Horse Mesa; and to the south the cool, gray-green mound of Navajo Mountain overlooking the meeting place of the rivers. We are not explorers or pioneers, but we feel a little like explorers here. Not too many people have visited this spot. The distances in every direction are barren of man, the great mountain south of us is a holy place where no Navajo will be caught after dark, there is no sound on our slick-rock ridge except the rustle of a small dry wind.

When we hear Norm's river voice, and photograph the boats stringing out into the big river, and Kent scares the boat party by rolling a tub-sized boulder off the cliff with a heart-stopping roar, we turn our backs on the San Juan. But we do it regretfully. It is a fine, friendly, and very beautiful little river, a marvelous roadway into wonder, and we allow ourselves, in this remote spot, to grow exasperated with the Rivers of America series for not including so colorful a stream. Basket Maker, Pueblo, Navajo, Paiute, Spaniard, Mormon, gold-seeker, and oil prospector have left their scratches on its walls and their quickly erased footprints at its few passable fords. Curiously, the Indian has changed this river more than the white man. There is every evidence that in Pueblo times the San Juan country supported a larger population than it does now, and that the town-dwelling Indians grew gardens where now there are barren boulder-strewn washes. With the coming of the herdsman tribes the desert cover was gradually grazed off, the floods grew more disastrous, and the land that used to line the canyons went down the river.

5

In Glen Canyon we are again in the stream of history, on a main road. Near the upper end, at Hole in the Rock, the Mormon pioneers of the San Juan country blasted their way down the cliffs and struggled across on their way to Bluff and the completion of the most appalling wagon trip ever taken anywhere. Down below us, at Padre Creek, Father Escalante lowered his supplies over the wall and swam his mules across to the south bank on his adventurous way back to Santa Fe in 1776. This part of the Colorado canyon has been a blessed interlude of rest for every river expedition since Powell's first one in 1869. In all the miles of Glen Canyon there is not a rapid, hardly a rock, nothing more dangerous than whirlpools and sucks. Regular boat trips come down from Hite and up from Lee's Ferry through scenery that is at once awesome and charming. The sheer cliffs of Navajo sandstone, stained in vertical stripes like a roman-striped ribbon and intricately cross-bedded and etched, lift straight out of the great river. This is the same stone, though here pinker in color, that forms the domes and thrones and temples of Zion and the Capitol Reef. It is surely the handsomest of all the rock strata in this country. The pockets and alcoves and glens and caves which irregular erosion has worn in the walls are lined with incredible greenery, redbud and tamarisk and willow and the hanging delicacy of maidenhair around springs and seeps. Our real voyaging stopped with the San Juan; from here on we loaf, pulling ashore to explore something every mile or two.

Our first camp in Glen Canyon, just below the junction, is almost unimaginably beautiful—a sandstone ledge below two arched caves, with clean cliffs soaring up behind and a long green sandbar across the river. Just below us is the masked entrance of Hidden Passage Canyon, which at sunup glows softly red, its outthrust masking wall throwing a strong shadow against the cliff. Behind this masking wall is the kind of canyon that is almost commonplace here, but that anywhere else would be a wonder. Music Temple, Hidden Passage, Mystery Canyon, Twilight Canyon, Forbidden Canyon, Labyrinth Canyon, we explore a dozen, and there are dozens that we pass by. The most innocent opening, apparently a mere keyhole of an alcove, may be the door to a gorge a quarter of a mile deep and heaven knows how long, sometimes rods wide, sometimes less than a yard. Often the water has cut down irregularly, so that the walls waver and overhang and cut off the sky. Sometimes one has to ascend wading waist-deep in rock-floored pools; sometimes the canyon will jump suddenly up narrow waterfalls, generally dry at this season, or seeping a thin wetness down the discolored rock.

Follow one of these canyons in far enough, and it usually ends either at a fall or in one of the echoing caves and chambers the Navajo sandstone is fond of forming. Music Temple, for instance, is a domed chamber five hundred feet long and two hundred high, with a little eavespout of a creek coming out of a slot in the roof and dropping into a clear pool. Powell, who camped here on both of his river expeditions, and whose men left their names and initials carved into a rock face here, described the creek-slot as a skylight. It is actually more like the slot in an observatory roof. The shadows in a chamber like this, the patterns of light and shadow, are miraculous and utterly unphotographable, and the walls re-echo the slightest sound.

Mystery Canyon ends in the same sort of domed cave, with an even larger pool. Echo Cave Camp, maintained by Rainbow Lodge just above the Rainbow Bridge, is another such chamber. The walls of Twilight

Canyon are undercut, first on one side and then on the other, with huge caves, one so immense that the whole Hollywood Bowl could be set back into it, and so perfect acoustically that six and seven word echoes pursue us as we walk through. Most bizarre of all the canyons, the spookiest concession in this rock fun-house, is Labyrinth Canyon, which narrows down to less than two feet, and whose walls waver and twist so that anyone groping up this dark, crooked, nightmare cranny in the deep rock has to bend over and twist his body sideways to get through. Floor and walls are pocked with perfectly round pockets like nests, full of the pebbles and rocks that have scoured them. Though we cannot see the sky, we know that the walls go up several hundred feet, and though we scramble back in at least a mile and a half, scaling one dry waterfall, we see no sign of an end. The thought of what it would be like to be caught in here in a rain gives us the fantods, and we come out fast.

The high water tempts us into a number of canyons, for overnight the river has risen from what Norm estimated at 40,000 cubic feet per second to what he is sure is over 60,000, and the doorways of many canyons are flooded so that we can row in as into fjords, winding in and out and once poling through a watery tunnel formed by a fallen slab. Every sandbar is green with tamarisk and redbud; wherever there is an accumulation of soil, cottonwoods have taken hold, to hang on until the next big flood scours the channel clean and the cycle starts over.

Many years ago, reading Powell's account of his explorations, I got the notion that I wanted to come down into Glen Canyon and hole up in an alcove where there was water and a little soil. "Nine bean rows would I have there, and a hive for the honey bee. . . ." Now as I think of what we are likely to see in the papers when we end this river trip in a day or two, I suggest to Norm that I'd still like to hide out here for a while. He is full of enthusiasm at once; he will lend me a boat and help me get in supplies, either by river or by plane. I can sit in my green alcove and watch the river whirl by and write a book.

He doesn't know how close he is to being taken up. I reflect on those scientific friends of mine at M.I.T. and Harvard who are quite seriously stocking their Vermont farms against Armageddon, and it is a temptation to imagine that there might be sanctuary in this remote and beautiful canyon. But that lasts only thirty seconds. Out in the flood-swollen stream, snags and logs and drift go by, rocking in the swift water, circling with corpse-like dignity in eddies and whirlpools, and as we watch we see a dead deer or sheep, its four stiff hoofs in the air, go floating by in mid-river. We abandon the notion of sanctuary: even here, the world would drive its dead sheep and driftwood by the door.

But we can forget that at least another day, until we hit Lee's Ferry. At the mouth of Forbidden Canyon, after we return from the fourteen-mile hike to the Rainbow Bridge and back, we discover that the catfish will bite on anything or nothing, they will rise and gobble cigarette butts, or eat empty hooks as fast as we can drop them in. This is the way things were when the world was young; we had better enjoy them while we can.

Back Roads of the American West

SATURDAY, EARLY JUNE:

The first day of any trip eastward from California does not count, especially if you are hunting back roads. There are back roads left in California, but they are likely these days to be crowded with people hunting chicken houses to live in. Moreover, the Sierras funnel traffic through a few channels, so that until full summer clears the passes you practically have to go past Lake Tahoe, whether you want to or not. And Lake Tahoe now is about as back-roadish as Hollywood and Vine.

But from Carson City on, late in the afternoon, we are on Highway 50, a paved through road which has all the effect of a back road because there is practically nothing on it from Carson City to Ely. Along these 322 miles of the old Pony Express route there are two living towns and one dead one, and those are all. North of us on Highway 40 the towns are only twenty or thirty miles apart, and there along the old California Trail the traffic is fairly dense, but here we do not meet one car an hour. We set the hand throttle at sixty and put our hot feet out the windows.

At seven-thirty, when the sun is dropping over the Stillwater Mountains to the west, we pull off the road, cook supper, and roll into our sleeping bags. The waxing moon that by some unplanned miracle always seems to accompany us into the wilderness swims up over the Clan Alpine range to silver the greasewood and trouble our dreams with strange ecstasies. When I wake for the last time just before dawn it is a bloody disk far down the western sky, and it is a haunting thing to think that it has coasted through all that empty sky and looked down upon all that empty desert without one human interruption.

SUNDAY:

As always in the Nevada desert, we wake to find ourselves ringed with brown, twisted, unfamiliar ranges. Everything except the horizon is empty. There is not a house, a windmill, a cow, a sheep, a hurrying car, a smoke, or a sound.

Our scenery today is the scenery that most tourists, especially grass-loving eastern tourists, deplore. There is a fairly widespread folk belief in America that, next to Nebraska and Kansas, Nevada is the dullest and most desolate state in the Union. Consequently, most summer travelers drive this desert at night, and the scenery they get is what they deserve— the running ribbon of road, the uneasy field of radiance of their own headlights, the movement of scared jackrabbits and sprinting lizards. They miss the gray and green spaciousness, the flats blooming with white flowers of alkali, the twisting passes through the ranges, the brown, baked, barren, heat-disturbed earth, the valleys crawling with mirages.

Austin, still a producing silver camp after three generations of dig-ging, seems very sleepy and dead this early Sunday morning, without an Indian or a miner lounging outside saloon or pool hall. I remember a Saturday night fourteen or fifteen years ago when it was livelier. That night a meteor fell, roaring down over the dark hills as big as a Quonset hut, and everybody in town, Indians and miners and a handful of stranded tourists, rushed out convinced that it had landed just over the hill. None of us ever found it, but we had all had a good close look at the end of the world, anyway. I even seem to remember *hearing* that thing, though like Mark Twain I have caught myself remembering some things that never happened.

At Ely, just beyond the big copper pits and the smelters, we break off Highway 50 and swing south past the Lehman Caves, one of the most remote and unvisited national monuments. We are on back roads now, for fair. Because we have a date tonight away over in Utah, at least two hundred miles farther on, we do not stop at the caves, which are several miles off the road up on the slope of Wheeler Peak.

On southeastward through forbidding and beautiful country, on washboard gravel and dirt roads choked with powder dust. The Wah-Wah Mountains on our left are remote, unpeopled, unwatered, and untreed, and the road crawls from dry pass to dry pass. Yet we know when we have crossed a boundary, not by map or road signs, but by the look and quality of the little ranch settlement on Preuss Lake, an irrigation reservoir. The squared-log house, the pole corrals, the red dust in the bark of the cottonwoods, somehow say "Utah," not "Nevada."

So do the solid, square, New England–looking houses of Milford, and so, even more strongly, do the alfalfa fields and the lines of Lombardy poplars at Minersville. There is a quality to little southern Utah towns that is partly geographical, partly cultural. Some of it undoubtedly comes from the predominantly red soil, and from the startling contrast between red fields and the lush green of irrigated crops. Some of it comes from the trees, the cottonwoods and poplars, and from the way the seldom-stirred dust settles on bark and leaves, and from the way the trees cast shade across red roads and leaking ditches make dark patches in the dust. Some of it comes from the sturdy durability of the houses, from the quiet of the people themselves, from the absence of flash and neon, the lack of taverns and beer joints. Whatever it comes from, the quality is there, and it is like coming home to pull into a street walled by tall poplars and watch a Mormon kid trotting his horse up a lane snowed white with cottonwood fluff.

By the time we reach Beaver, on the Salt Lake–Los Angeles main line, it is clear that we shall be late for our date in Fruita, down in the Capitol Reef. Crossing Utah from west to east, against the grain of the mountains and plateaus, is a slow job. Still, we do not want to stop short and so we grab a quick malted and pull up into the sheer conglomerate canyon leading to Puffer Lake. A gas station attendant has told us that cars came over that summit yesterday for the first time this season. If we can get over, we will save seventy-five miles. And we will get a look at a chunk of back road I have heard of all my life and never driven.

The road is narrow, crooked, and steep, and fairly full of Sunday-fishing Mormons on their way home. In low, with our little one-wheeled trailer bouncing between the ruts, we climb and climb and climb up the slope of Beaver Mountain, known on the maps as the Tushar Range. Maples and alders give way to ponderosa pine, the pine to aspen and spruce. Snow appears in patches, and the air takes on such a bite that we reluctantly run up the top. But it smells so fine and new that we lean out the windows and freeze anyway.

When we break out on the top of the plateau we must be above ten thousand feet. It is near sunset. We run on a good forest road over the lovely, timbered, just-leafing roof of the world. This is another very special feeling, a peculiarly Utah feeling, being this high and yet on level or slightly-rolling land whose forest swings into bays and parks patterned with Forest Service snake fence.

I had almost forgotten—I am always forgetting the important things—how lovely these plateaus are, the Tushar and the Awapa and the Fish Lake and the Sevier, the Wasatch and the Aquarius and Thousand-Lake and the Pahvant, the fingers of lofty tableland that run down through Utah for hundreds of miles, separated by green irrigated valleys. Except at national parks like Zion and Bryce they see few tourists but quite a few hunters and fishermen. As for us, though both car and trailer have taken a beating on this forty-mile cutoff, we are sorry when just at dusk the road coils down a steep dugway and down and down and down into another valley and the town of Kingston. . . .

It is past ten o'clock, and we are starving, tired, eye- and back-weary, when after six hundred miles of medium and bad back road we nose between pole fences and see orchard trees, and next a fence made of great slabs of ripple-marked red sandstone set on edge, and then an immense Fremont poplar with a mailbox nailed to it. We are in Fruita—have almost run through it—and voices halloo from the Chesnutt place and out of a cabin yellow with lamplight come the friends from Salt Lake and Washington, D.C., we have come here to meet. We sit up long enough for a drink and a snack and a talk, but in our bones we feel the unevenness of the road as the continent we have been running over makes itself felt.

Monday:

Everything about this little lost village of Fruita is charming. The cherries are just ripe, and for half the morning we sit with our bare feet in an irrigation ditch and eat hatfuls of Bings and Royal Annes. In the afternoon we dunk in the Dirty Devil's cold roily water under the hot sun between the hot red cliffs. Above us the formations that one comes to recognize like old friends rise one above the other; the cocoa-colored Moencopi, eroding into goblets and statuary; above that the greenish Chinle, salted with petrified trees; above that the massive Wingate Sandstone, red and sheer, stained brown with "desert varnish"; and above that, back in the hinterlands above the gorge of the Fremont, the equally massive white layer called the Navajo, whose domes and "baldheads" made early settlers liken the towers to the Capitol at Washington, and so gave the name to Capitol Wash. These are the same sedimentary layers from which the towers of Zion Park have been carved. They wind and they twist, appear and reappear, through hundreds of miles of cliff and canyon, their qualities and profiles remarkably uniform, though their colors may change. In Glen Canyon, on the Colorado, the Navajo is salmon-colored; in Zion it is almost sugar-white. But wherever it appears it is beautiful.

All around us, in every direction, is country that so far has never taken its pay or paid its penalty for being beautiful. But we are told that a super-highway has already been surveyed down this wash and through this village, and that plans are afoot to "open up" this Wayne County region to the tourist trade. God knows it is worth any tourist's time. But we are all a little sad to think that the oasis of Fruita, whose charm is less durable than that of the red ledges, may be gutted and spoiled. A highway down that wash cannot avoid bringing entrepreneurs with gas stations and lodges and sad little fly-blown cafes. The great poplar which shades half the village would have to come down, as would some of the orchards. There is hardly room enough in the whole pocket to accommodate a three-lane road. The quiet and the far mutter of the Dirty Devil foaming through its gorge would be blotted out by the blast of horns and radios echoing off the cliffs. Nearby towns like Torrey, the nearest source of supplies, where now horses droop at the tie rails and the street is drifted inches deep with cottonwood down, would have to go too.

Much would go—too much. In the shadow of the cottonwoods beside the secret guggle of the ditch we sit and talk until after midnight, but we can agree on nothing except that here is a chance for the Park Service to demonstrate once again that it is one of the few government services with a real interest in preserving and protecting what is left of the continent. Indiscriminate development would ruin this little paradise. The rocks and canyons are pretty well beyond harm barring people with paint cans, but the village of Fruita could be made unrecognizable in a few years. It is worthy of protection; in its way it is as much an archaeological treasure as Mesa Verde, for here is preserved in one tiny green pocket in the sandrock a perfect example of the primitive Mormon frontier village, next door to Heaven and almost as remote as it is possible to get from the populated centers of the nation.

TUESDAY:

Hanksville, Utah, used to be the very end of the world, the jumping off place. Go in any direction from it and you will find more empty space than in most places in America. Northward it is seventy-five miles by beeline, and many more by road, to the coal camps of Emery County. Eastward it is just as far to Moab and Highway 450, which links Utah's San Juan County with the more populous San Juan country of Colorado and New Mexico. Southward across a hundred waste miles is the Arizona border, and beyond that are miles and miles of desert and mesa, the homeland of the Navajo. Westward, fifty miles back up the racking, rock-toothed, wash-cut road we have come, lies Fruita.

In all this desolate beautiful region there are virtually no people: a handful of ranchers in isolated watered pockets, a few nomadic Indians, an occasional sweating tourist. Between the Waterpocket Fold and the Colorado River, between the Navajo reservation and the northern edge of the San Rafael Swell, is an immense, flamboyant, rock-lipped wilderness slashed with canyons and pregnant with distance and overlooked by the rims of the great plateaus and the gray-green lonely peaks of the Henry

Mountains. By this time I have broken the trailer's inadequate hitch twice on the road through Capitol Wash. I have begun to lose the immediacy of my feeling that Fruita and the Wayne Wonderland must be protected and preserved. Its roads, it appears, are ample protection.

Yet there has recently been completed at Hanksville an airport capable of accommodating the biggest planes aloft. Drillers have pierced the deep sandrock and brought in artesian wells, and a crew of CAA men is in residence, operating the control tower for Western Air and United Airlines. Yesterday two airliners and a private plane sat down at this desert landing place, which is squarely on the beam between Los Angeles and Denver. And men are busy just west of here digging uranium and vanadium out of the rock. From the innocent-looking crumbly yellow ore comes the fissionable stuff which might yet make bare-rock wildernesses out of other places than Hanksville.

We are tempted to stop a while in Hanksville and let the ruminant mind browse. But we have a trailer that needs care. On roads like these the linkpins, fragile enough under any conditions, are simply chewed up. About every twenty miles a cotter key wears through, and one side or another of the trailer breaks loose. I am psychologically ready for Green River, where there are mechanics.

Between Hanksville and Green River we throw the trailer once more. But since it is, as old man Chesnutt at Fruita said, nothing but a spur with a box on it, it does not quite put us in the ditch. Still, I have replaced the cotter keys four times now, twice under difficulties, and my patience and my supply of cotter keys are wearing somewhat thin.

But in Green River there is no mechanic available. We roll wearily on to Moab, on the Colorado. Nobody there either, though I am able to lay in a pocket full of new and heavier cotter keys. Nobody at Monticello either, at least nobody who can drill a bolt. Nobody at Blanding. But on paving the cotter keys do not get eaten, so that we are finally at the brink of the northern Navajo reservation with a cranky hitch and only the pocketful of cotter keys for insurance. We chance it.

At Bluff, the lonely dwindling little Mormon town on the San Juan which was settled at such an unbelievable cost in labor and anguish sixty years ago, we camp between an alfalfa field and the river, near a camp of

Navajos. We are too run down by heat and trailer trouble to be very sociable; after the briefest of greetings we make camp, eat a watermelon we have bought at the Bluff trading post, and roll in.

WEDNESDAY:

More birds than I ever heard in one place give us a morning chorus. At the edge of the brush a Navajo woman in a purple skirt and scarlet velvet blouse is picking squaw berries, and we can hear kids yelling over on the river bank. It is cool and peaceful under the great trees. On my back, fixing the hitch for the fifth time before we start, I can even whistle. It is fairly late in the morning before we climb up out of the river bottom and crawl along bare rock ledges and through washes on our way to Mexican Hat and Kayenta.

The road is very bad, but that out to the Goosenecks of the San Juan, which turns off a few miles short of Mexican Hat, is worse. And just as I am looking at the speedometer, wondering that the hitch has not given way under this kind of punishment, the right side of the trailer drops down and I get out to fix it for the sixth time.

The Goosenecks, undeniably a natural wonder, somehow do not excite us, and we ask ourselves why. They are exciting enough from below, from a boat on the river, but sitting here on the rim placidly eating lunch and swinging our legs over the edge we watch the San Juan coil like a convulsive boa through the rock and find that fifteen minutes is all we feel like spending here. The river comes in from the south, swift and foam-tipped in a canyon 1,300 feet deep with gray, evenly ledged walls. The stream swings back upon itself in a perfect hairpin a couple of miles in extent, and then does the same thing all over again. The result is two goosenecks as perfect as if they had been surveyed. Miles around by the way the river travels, it is hardly a half mile across the open ends of the two bows. Amazing, bizarre—but we sit on the rim eating sandwiches and wish there was something to do besides *look*. The forms are not varied enough to keep one's interest; there is little color. And just looking isn't enough. We can sympathize with our child, who is beginning to wish the scenery could be turned off like a radio.

At Mexican Hat I toggle up the hitch with baling wire, and as we cross the San Juan by the high bridge, the USGS man is hanging out over the river in his aerial bucket, taking a stream-flow measurement. The San Juan is swift, coffee-colored, creased with deep sandwaves. It is hard to believe that on occasion it has been almost dry at the bridge.

The moment we climb out of the canyon, Monument Valley begins to open up ahead. The great isolated red and purple spires rise as if out of a mythical sea, very grand and lonely. Even in midafternoon the valley and Monument Pass are bluish with refined haze. Looking is quite enough here; this is no Goosenecks, no simple freak of nature. There are colors and forms here that are hauntingly beautiful. Every time we go through here we think quite soberly that perhaps this is the most beautiful stretch of country we have ever seen, anywhere.

Beautiful as it is, grand and bold and delicate and blasted as a lunar landscape, Monument Pass has not much better to offer in the way of a road than the country we have just come through. Twice we are slowed down by our trailer and stick in deep sand. With our hitch balled up in baling wire, it is a mercy we don't have to unload; eventually we bull our way through. Near Goulding's post we pass the movie set representing Tombstone, Arizona, which was used for the shooting of *My Darling Clementine*. It is all there, from Birdcage Theater to Valley Bank, out in the blasted valley, and a little farther on a crew of long-haired Navajos is dismantling the bunkhouses and messhalls that once housed an extension of Hollywood.

About roads in general the Navajo clerk at Kayenta is discouraging. About the road we have been planning to take, across to Shiprock by way of Dennehotso and the Four Corners, he is emphatic. We could not get the trailer through. Our best bet is to turn off southward a little short of Dennehotso and go on down to Chinle, thence on the main reservation road to Canado, thence over past Window Rock and almost down to Gallup, until we hit Highway 666. This is several hundred miles out of our way, but with the trailer and its infirmities on our minds we think it better to follow his advice. Fairly late in the afternoon we head for Dennehotso, find the fork at a cluster of summer hogans and a water tank, and turn south.

Within two miles we are digging out of the sand. Within another two, an hour later, we are in over the running boards, the universal submerged, the gas tank on the ground, the trailer lying on its belly with its wheel out of sight.

It is after five in the afternoon, and I am not as fresh as I might be. But I get out the shovel. After a half hour we try. No luck. We dig some more and brush the ruts with sagebrush and unload the trailer to lighten the pull. Not an inch. We dig again and lay grain bags and tarps under the wheels and scrape at the loose sand snuggling up under the car. Still no go. Our mood is not made happier to see our young galloping with his dog around through the sagebrush just at the hour when sidewinders like to come out and look around.

At the moment of our bleakest perplexity a car comes from the direction of Chinle, and out of it get a woman and two young men—well-muscled young men, obviously fresh. I relinquish shovel and responsibility to them without a qualm. One of those Navajos who always appear out of the ground when you think you are farthest from man and his habitations appears on a skinny horse and offers advice, jokes, and an occasional push. While the boys dig I find that the lady is Mrs. Bollin, who operates curio shops in Gallup and elsewhere. She has been out buying rugs and jewelry in the reservation.

No mortal would work for money as we all worked on that stuck car. If each of us who passed that way for a month would have put that amount of labor on the road in advance, we would have made a highway of it. But like other mortals we know how to cooperate only after the damage is done. We cooperate now like anything, but it is two sweating hours of digging, rocking, shoving, and digging again before the car finally, with chattering wheels and with everybody pushing and with Hosteen the Navajo falling on his face in the sand, inches up over the crest of the dune and down the other side to hard gravel. We turn around, gun our way back over the dune and get through it, wait for one of the boys to take the Chrysler up and over like a B-24 taking off, and then we shake hands around and go on back to the fork near Dennehotso, where we camp.

For an hour we groggily expect to see the Bollins come along after us, but they do not appear. It is dark before it finally enters our heads that anything could go wrong for these superior people who know the reservation cold, speak Navajo, and have just come over the trail across the Lukaichukai Mountains. Eventually we drive back to see what has become of them. They are sitting with a dead motor exactly where we left them, where they dug us out.

So we can return the favor. We push them out and they camp next to us, making their impromptu beds out of many layers of Navajo rugs and eating breakfast with us in the morning.

The Chrysler has decided to run again. We leave the Bollins—fine people, noble diggers and pushers, and excellent companions—at Dennehotso. Ahead of us are eighteen miles of bare roadless ledgerock before we hit graded road again. The trader's wife at Dennehotso advises us to allow three hours for the eighteen miles. . . .

In the Indian post at Mexican Water, as in all the posts at this time of year, are large signs saying that Fatty Yellowman and Joe Goat and Mrs. Joe Goat and numerous other people had better redeem their pawned jewelry before July 4 or it will be sold for costs. The trader seldom means these threats and seldom carries them out. The jewelry comes out of hock when the owner sells some fleeces or a few lambs, and goes back again as soon as the cash runs short. It is a really hungry Navajo who will let a prized piece of jewelry get away from him for good; and we note again, as we have noted before, that the best looking silver and turquoise we see is being worn by Indians.

FRIDAY:

After a stretch in the bald desert, digging out of sand dunes and creaking over ledgerock and drinking stale water out of a keg, the camp at Mesa Verde is like a clubhouse. As confirmed back-roaders we have on occasion made fun of the dude fixings and the regimentation in the campgrounds of the national parks and monuments, but we make no fun of this.

We come in late, delayed by our repairs at Shiprock and by a side trip over to the ruins at Aztec, in New Mexico. It is almost nine o'clock when we grope into the campground, which is big and spacious and sheltered by thick piñons. For a wonder it is only about half full. Before we roll in we wander over and listen to a talk—a surprisingly good one—by a lady ranger-naturalist, and watch a group of Navajo boys from the lodge put on a sample squaw dance around the campfire. They sing their wild, wavering, high-pitched chants, pleasing our child inordinately and driving a half-dozen leashed dogs into dismayed howling. Then back to camp and the luxury of a long, soaking, delirious shower in good clean shower rooms. Our skins are hungry for water; before sleeping we dump the stale water butt and have a long drink of cold mountain water from the camp tap.

SATURDAY:

A citizen of these United States gets a big dollar's worth for his entrance fee to any national park. This morning we take advantage of the things provided by the pleasantest and most respected of all the government services: a tour of Spruce Tree house, excursions into kivas and around the surface ruins, an hour or two in the park museum before the extremely good dioramas dramatizing the development of the Mesa Verde people from Early Basket Maker to Pueblo II. We get a good, solid, pleasant morning of instruction, and at lunch we reflect almost with awe that in all our camping excursions we have never had an unpleasant word or a surly look from a single member of the Park Service. That service either attracts first-class people, or it and the life it offers breeds them, and I thank it for many things. For a clean campground and the camp stove and table and benches, for that sybaritic shower room and the good handy water and the free wood, for the garbage disposal and the courtesy and the unfailing willingness to be helpful in the face of unreasonable demands. There is not a single thing about the park that I can possibly cavil at except our immediate neighbors in the campground, three young men from Nebraska on their way to make the circuit of the seventeen national parks. One of them I meet in the shower early this morning. He tells me that he has been studying English and philosophy at Columbia, but it is clear that nobody at Columbia has ever instructed this young man how to act in a campground at 5 A.M. He and his pals have banged pans, whistled, yelled, slammed car doors, and made avoidably loud noises ever since they woke up. Maybe someone will teach them manners to match the facilities they enjoy before they finish with the seventeenth national park.

MONDAY:

On the Arkansas we have an object lesson in another kind of "public service" from that practiced at Mesa Verde. We achieve this enlightenment by visiting the Royal Gorge, which advertising has made as well known as the Grand Canyon. We do not stay long—ten minutes takes care of us—and on the way out we compose a little travel note, thus:

The Royal Gorge, more properly known as the Royal Gouge, is a gully cut into the rock by the Arkansas River. Its purpose is to support in comfort the gentlemen who own and operate the Royal Gouge Bridge and Amusement Company of Cañon City, Colorado. It is a fair-sized groove in the ground, though not so impressive as advertised, and not so deep or so sheer or so spectacular that it cannot be matched in a dozen places in the West.

Across this pretty little canyon the Royal Gouge Bridge and Amusement Company has slung a suspension bridge, advertised as the highest in the world, and beyond doubt the shakiest. Anyone can test this statement by paying seventy-five cents to walk out and look over. There is no extra charge for automobiles, probably for the reason that no one who was fully witted would drive a car out on that rickety thing for a Rajah's salary. We conclude (nothing we see during our visit serves to contradict this speculation) that the Royal Gouge Bridge and Amusement Company is trying to get every cent it can out of the bridge before it falls into the Arkansas and drowns numbers of tourists who have paid up their seventy-five cents and whose relatives might sue. . . .

Having vented our venom, we feel better. We wheel on through Colorado Springs, populous with Texas cars, and out onto the flat edge of the high plains. Now we are past what the maps and guidebooks call the exciting country, past all the grand scenery, past all the mannerly and heart-warming Mesa Verdes and the greedy-guts Royal Gouges, yet it does not seem to us that the best of the trip is over and only the monotonous miles remain. There are back roads across the plains as well as across the desert and the mountains, and an eye that is looking can find enough and to spare to interest it. As we make camp under the cottonwoods by an abandoned farmhouse, buttoning ourselves into waterproofs in deference to the blue-black horizon and the forks of lightning in the east, we see Pike's Peak cleanly outlined in the west, seventy-five miles away. In every other direction the sky fits clear down to the ground, with no such prodigious landmarks to break its even line, but we are full of something else that only the plains give; the horizontal feeling, the disc and bowl feeling, the exposure-to-the-weather feeling, the clean true knowledge of the directions, the smell of grassy wind.

In the morning, unless we wash away during the night, I know we shall awake to meadowlarks, and then there will be Kansas and Nebraska and the plains rivers running beside us away from the mountains; and beyond these will be the Missouri choked with brown mud, and beyond that Iowa's narrow upturned concrete roads and towns with great elms and brick-paved streets. Beyond those again will be Wisconsin, breaking in steep bluffs down to its rivers, and beyond that Lake Michigan's oceanic blue.

We do not regret leaving the desert and the mountains, though we will always love and return to both. What impresses us and fills our imagination as we lie in the sleeping bags with the rainy wind whipping leaves and twigs from the cottonwoods over our heads is the way America goes on, and with what infinite variety, in every direction. And when we hit the eastern edge, we can always turn around and come back, and that will be as good as going.

Why I Like the West

It has always been my belief and contention that if the Mayflower had happened to land somewhere on Puget Sound or in San Francisco Bay instead of at Plymouth Rock, men in coonskin hats would now be cautiously exploring the Berkshires and shooting carrier pigeons for their suppers, and the burghers of Brooklyn would still be speaking Dutch. I would go further: like those Francophile scholars who date English literature from the Norman Conquest and shove all the crude Anglo-Saxon beginnings back into a predawn twilight, I would be content to date American literature by its Americanism (that is, by its westernism), and start it not with John Smith or the Plymouth Compact but with Augustus Longstreet or Sut Lovingood or the Big Bear of the Arkansaw.

It is all very well to have Melvilles and Hawthornes, and even Emersons and Thoreaus, and certainly it is more than salutary to have Mark Twains, but to have to go for our first colonial cheepings to the sickly legend of Pocahontas or the dismal Providences of Increase Mather, this is a hard fate. By changing our dating procedure we might at a stroke eliminate the necessity of sending our young back to personages like John Cotton, who liked to "sweeten his mouth with a bit of Calvin" before closing out his eighteen hours of daily study and prayer. We might instead indoctrinate young Americans by contact with such true forefathers as John Phoenix, who once dashed out of a San Francisco saloon to accost the Eagle Baker's wagon and demand a baked eagle.

Cotton Mather would not have done that, nor Jonathan Edwards, nor even the Simple Cobbler of Agawam. They became what they became, and remained what they remained, by the accident of a New England landing, and not ten generations of western rebellion has succeeded in eradicating the provincial and hard-mouthed habits that might have melted away in a year in some climate farther from endurance and closer to indulgence. If this be ingratitude to our Mother East, then it is ingratitude, and that same John Phoenix has written the text: "How sharper than a serpent's thanks it is to have a toothless child."

A wild man from the West, I have always done my honest best to live up to what tradition says I should be. I have always tried to look like Gary Cooper and talk like the Virginian. I have endeavored to be morally upright, courteous to women; with an innate sense of right and wrong but without the polish that Yale College or European travel might have put upon me. I have consented to be forgiven my frontier gaucheries, and I did not hold it against the waiter in the Parker House bar when he removed my feet from the upholstery.

I have been breezy, frank, healthy, relaxed, with a drawling soul and an open heart and a friendly smile. I have obediently liked my beef well done and my r's hard and have let it be known that I eat fried potatoes with my scrambled eggs for breakfast. Without actually wilting when the population was more than ten to the square mile, I have expressed a sense of crowding; and I have publicly honored a friend of mine who moved on from his ranch when it got so crowded he had to put a door on his privy. I have done all this in obedience to the myth of the West; and while doing it I have served as a self-appointed evangelist to rescue unfortunate eastern heathens from the climate, topography, theology, prejudices, literature, railroads, traditions, narrowness, and geographical ignorance that are their heritage. I have not always been thanked, but I have been earnest.

Any conversation which has permitted me to discuss redwood trees, Sierra forests, western rivers, canyons, or plateaus, Pacific surf, Utah trout fishing, or long-distance views has been a honeyhead in which I could happily drown. I have been full of comparative statistics on areas, altitudes, distances; the fact that my favorite county in Utah is somewhat larger than the state of Massachusetts is something I cannot keep to myself. Under the hesitant, skeptical, and envious questioning of easterners I confess to the same sense of well-being that I once felt in Devon while trying to convince a mule-headed young Britisher that in the United States bread came ready-sliced. The paltry eastern landscape I have given my patronizing scorn; I have never been able to refrain from telling easterners that Mount Washington, their pride, could be set down in the Grand Canyon—in a *ditch*—and never show above the rim. They try to greet these revelations with well-bred astonishment, or to laugh them off, but I have seen their souls warp under the strain. Anything they can cite, I can cite bigger.

But it is time to admit that during a long career of western chauvinism I have been trading on the general ignorance of my hearers. Friend or adversary, they have proposed a myth of the West that I have subscribed to, and I have even imposed it upon them sometimes. I have carefully concealed from them what I thought they should have known in the first place—that there is no such thing as the West. There are only Wests, as different from one another as New Hampshire from South Carolina or Brooklyn from Brookline. A few things they have in common, and some of them are important not only to boosters and evangelists but to historians and scholars, but in other ways they resemble each other about as much as Senator Glen Taylor resembles Will Rogers. The West, be it known to all those I have misled, is neither a region nor a way of life nor a state of mind. It is many regions, many states of mind, many ways of life.

When I went "back east" to school in Iowa I took with me the belligerent thesis that all virtue, all good country, all pleasant people, and all pretty girls lay back of me, west of the Missouri if not west of the Rockies. But later, when I found myself an odd sparrow among the polite rustling of the Ivy League, I cheerfully acceded to local custom and included in the West the Iowa and Wisconsin and Illinois I had once fiercely attacked as effete, colorless, and insipid. One glance at the New Yorker's or the Bostonian's map of the United States will make it clear how I could get away with this, and also how great an advantage any Westerner has in a regional argument. Whatever he may *not* know, a Westerner is bound to know geography, and among the heathen he can claim anything for his province and get away with it. If he wants to, he can start the West at the Alleghenies, or the eastern edge of Indiana, and if he is challenged he can conduct a defense in depth. Ohio, Illinois, Iowa, Nebraska, eastern Colorado—he can retreat all the way to the Rockies, and by that time he will have his opponent extended and can whip around and cut his supply lines. And if he is still pressed there are Montana and Wyoming and Idaho and Utah and Nevada and California, New Mexico and Arizona and Texas, to wage a war of movement in. The Easterner who once lets it get established that there is such a thing as the West hasn't got a chance in a quarrel of regional patriotism. He is Napoleon in Russia.

If we admitted its existence, the West would have to be almost as big as Russia. By the test of dialect, which is a reasonable and fair test as far as it goes, there is veritably a West, and it extends from the Alleghenies to the Pacific, from Ohio and Missouri to the Canadian line, with only unimportant islands to interrupt its triumphant oneness. By comparison the dialects of the eastern seaboard are confined and provincial, and even the several variations on southern speech, widespread as they are, reveal themselves as a regional aberration. The speech of the various Wests is the authentic speech of America, purified of the *r* which soundeth not and the *r* which belongeth not and the squat *a* and the other blemishes.

But the Mid-West, which shares this normalized speech with the other Wests, doesn't share all the essentials. From the Alleghenies to the 98th meridian of longitude—roughly to the line of the Red and the Missouri Rivers—and from the Canadian line south to Missouri and Ohio, is one great region, a noble part of America, and worthy of honor. I was born in it and have gone to school in it and worked in it and traveled across it endlessly, and I respect it highly and speak its native tongue, but it is not part of the West, or one of the Wests, unless one is speaking with Bostonians or New Yorkers. It is Mid-West; it stops at the 98th meridian because at about that line the rainfall ceases to be adequate for unassisted agriculture and an entirely new set of conditions is imposed upon the inhabitants.

By this test of aridity, there are few sections west of the 98th meridian which do not qualify as part of the West. Only certain high mountain regions, the coastal parts of Washington, Oregon, and northern California, and the gulf of Texas can properly be exempted. And the aridity test is more meaningful than it might seem, much more meaningful than the test of language, for upon the lack of sufficient rain depends practically all the things that make the Wests western.

Aridity, for one thing, means an unmisted atmosphere, a low relative humidity; and low humidity means bluer skies, longer views, subtler effects of distance, better photography. Aridity means dust, and upon dust are built the much-advertised western sunsets. Aridity means a new set of animals—coyotes, antelope, jackrabbits, flickertails, lizards, road-runners, desert tortoises—and a new set of plants, from sagebrush and shadscale to datura and tumbleweed. It means a changed landscape and bizarre topography, since erosion works very much differently in the absence of a protective mat of ground cover and persistent rains. In a dry land the brinks of hills will be clifflike, not rounded; valleys will often be canyons; hills are likely to be buttes and mesas and barerock movements; the coloration will be not the toned greens of wetter regions but the red and ochre and tan and gray and black of raw rock, the gray of sagebrush, the yellow of dry grass. The whole effect is harsher, bonier, farther, bigger, the difference between a weather-beaten face and one that is well-padded and protected.

Aridity changes the agriculture of the West, turns a farmer's values upside down. In watered country, land is valuable, and water running through it is owned, according to the English precedents of riparian law, by the man who owns the land along the banks. But dry land is worthless without water, and riparian law has given way before changed conditions. In the Wests, most of them, water is life. No ownership of a strip of shore entitles any farmer to empty the stream upon his fields and deprive the man below. Through a water company, private or public, he shares ownership and responsibility, and takes his share at specified periods for specified lengths of time. Out of the conditions arising from dryness have come all the irrigation laws of the American books, all the cooperative systems of water use, and a whole battery of government agencies, especially the Reclamation Service, concerned with the public responsibility to impound and distribute the water that is too expensive and difficult for one man or a group of men to handle alone. That governmental responsibility has dotted the West with reclamation and power dams, public works on an enormous scale, which not only give the western landscape some of its quality, but provide the footings for an entirely new sort of civilization. Charge all this "socialism" to lack of rain.

That same blessed drought prevents, except in sections where water from mountain sources is available, the rabbit-hutch crowding, the intense and greedy occupation and transformation of the earth by numberless hives of people. The population center of the United States is still away back in Sullivan County, Indiana, less than a quarter of the way across the continent, where it can abide for all of me. And though by the 1940 census more people in the western states lived in cities than in the country, only California, Texas, Washington, Utah, and Colorado made that proportion possible. The rest of the West is rural; there is still a lot of space open, and there will continue to be for lack of water. Even the range will not be very heavily populated, because it takes many acres to support one whiteface or Shropshire. Arid and semiarid plains, inaccessible mountains and plateaus, uninhabitable desert, comprise the great bulk of the western landscape. The arable land in Utah, for an example, does not exceed 3 percent of the total acreage of the state.

Wyoming Plateau, sagebrush and jackrabbits and gray plain, where it is sixty miles between towns. Nevada desert, miles of empty alluvial slope and alkali bottom swung between the ranges, and beyond the next range another valley, and the horizons scrawling with mountain crests and heat. The big open spaces of the Utah plateaus, the Idaho lava beds, the "scablands" below Spokane, the Mojave and Colorado deserts, the all but roadless Navajo reservation, bigger than some of the states—the spaces are still open, and the cities are a long way apart.

It is open country and great distances that compel the western railroads to pamper their long-haul passengers with better roadbeds, faster schedules, more and fancier gadgets such as the Vistadome. In an open country everyone is a traveler; most Westerners develop that habit of covering ground in gargantuan chunks. I suspect that the man who contemplates empty landscape while he drives his own car has something of a spiritual advantage on the one who, boxed in a subway or bus, contemplates tomorrow's news in the five o'clock final of some tabloid. I have no statistics on ulcers, but I have convictions and some evidence. I also have duodenal scars, but those are another matter, and from another source.

Beyond dialect and aridity, the Wests have not too much in common. Local developments, local economics, have produced even in the arid regions very different societies. The plains are one kind, cow country is another, mining country is another, Indian country, Mormon country, the Northwest lumber empire, the industrialized agriculture of California's central valley and the lower Rio Grande and parts of Arizona, are all economically distinct. The sub-Wests differ in climate, topography, racial composition, history, orientation. That is why, when an old Harvard friend wrote from Santa Fe that he knew now what I had used to blow off about, I held my peace and withheld judgment. Because Santa Fe is only one of many Wests; my friend may have seen them all, but I suspect he had hold of the elephant's tail and was yelling for dear life that the elephant was very like a rope.

It may be like a rope in New Mexico—or rather in the upper Rio Grande valley—where the combination of ancient Spanish villages and even more ancient Pueblo towns has withstood much of the transforming push of the Anglo-American frontier. New Mexico is bilingual, for one thing, and bi- or tri-cultural; nowhere else in America, perhaps, can you see such contrasts. Sleep out on a piney promontory above the seventeenth-century village of Peñasco, where in the afternoon you have seen peasants threshing oats by trampling the sheaves with horses and winnowing the grain by hand, and after dark look across the great valley and see the multiplex lights, the high, hanging glow like a city among the stars, far over westward on the Jemez Mountains. There is no better view of Los Alamos.

In New Mexico, the elephant is like a rope. In the high border country of Montana and Wyoming, cow country and dude country, the old hunting ground of Crow and Blackfoot, it may be like a wall. Out in Nebraska and Kansas and the Dakotas, out in the great staring exposed plains on the wheel of earth under the belljar of sky, blown on by every wind and torn at by dramatic and tormented weather, it is maybe like a tree. In the sleepy little Mormon towns under the Lombardy poplars, in the red-dirt streets snowed with cottonwood fluff, before the local ward house after Sunday meeting or Mutual, it is something else, perhaps a spear.

In Texas, a world in itself, the most provincial and fiercely local of all the Wests, it is again something different. On the Columbia and the Willamette it is new, in the California coast towns from Santa Barbara south it is like nothing else. And all of these sections and subsections bleed imperceptibly into one another: cow country stretches from Texas to Saskatchewan, from Nebraska and Colorado to William Randolph Hearst's duchy of San Simeon. Copper and gold and silver and lead, molybdenum and antimony, must be mined where they are found; so must the extrusions of soft yellow vanadium and uranium ore that crop out of canyon walls in western Colorado and southern Utah. Every section is a combination of ways of life and states of mind as it is likely to be a combination of topographies.

Just for a sample, try Arizona. It's West, it's arid, it talks American, it can show cowboys and Indians. More specifically, it is part of what, with Texas and New Mexico, is called the Great Southwest. But look at it: The Indians who give Arizona its characteristic color are not the town Indians, though the Hopi reservation lies within the borders of the Painted Desert. The characteristic Indians of Arizona are the nomadic Navajo, and they make an entirely different world from the settled world of Pueblo and Spaniard on the upper Rio Grande. But a good part of Arizona is Mormon, and another kind of life and people revolve around the Temple in Mesa. And in Arizona has grown up a segment of that industrial-agriculture economy dependent on conservation dams, floods of cheap migrant labor, and expensive Washington lobbies, and that is still a third world. Outside all these are the worlds of the tourists and the lungers. Admittedly these elements fuse somewhat, admittedly they are all recognizably western and recognizably American. One may go into the Hopi country and see a bunch of longhairs hanging around the post at Oraibi listening to a World Series broadcast, and in Monument Valley a traveler will encounter Navajo girls wearing saddle shoes and dark glasses, and chewing bubble gum. But the amalgamation is very imperfect, and in some areas the differences increase rather than decrease with time. Change is one constant condition of the West, as of any new country. One of the portentous changes comes with the spread of that industrial agriculture which the West invented. It is not an aspect of the West, of any of the Wests, that I brag of, but no one who has gone among pickers' camps in California, or watched Navajos loading at little remote Arizona posts to be hauled up into Idaho to pick potatoes, will underestimate it as a fact.

The elephant is a complex beast, and the Wests are everything one is looking for. Historically raw-material states, a colonial empire exploited from the first by eastern capital at high interest rates, victimized by short-haul rail tariffs and absentee ownership, they inherit now a new industrialism, and with it every backbreaking problem known to industry anywhere. Neither one people, one topography, one economic structure, nor one climate, the Wests are like a litter of pups, with nothing grown up about them but their feet, who have discovered some time since how to make a big noise with their mouths. This is what I have been helping in, and it is always a satisfaction. But now comes the growing up, and growing up is no particular fun; the "big power" feeling that California has shown with the counting of the 1950 census that will put her next to New York in Congressional representation is a most un-western feeling, up to now. It will become increasingly familiar.

The last time I looked, Colorado, Utah, Wyoming, Arizona, and New Mexico contained exactly half of our national parks and monuments, and the states around them contained twenty-two more. Like aridity, and to a degree *because* of aridity, scenery is a bond among all the Wests, and "development," in most areas, has meant most of all hard roads and accommodations for tourists. Because scenery is one finished product that all the Wests can market, development will continue to mean roads, at least until men succeed in pumping passing clouds for extra rain, and transform the landscape. That tapping of clouds, by dry ice or otherwise, is not so fantastic as it sounds; there has already been a serio-comic exchange between Utah and Nevada over who owns water rights in those potential waters driving eastward across the mountains. If and when those clouds are tapped, I want to be in on the court sessions; the rhubarb that will ensue between California and all states eastward to the Rockies will make the controversies over the Colorado River's water seem pallid by comparison.

Meantime, I want to go on living in some one or another of the Wests, perhaps because they *are* new, perhaps because they are still in the stage of development, not of repair, possibly because of the excitement that accompanies the coming of age of an active and promising adolescent. The Wests are waxing rather than waning countries. I do not think they contain more hospitality than other regions, or more liberalism, or more good sense. Politically they are fairly often conservative and sometimes they are reactionary, and they are as capable of being run by political gangs as other places. But believing to some extent in the effect of place upon people, I think I can see somewhat more openness and frankness, somewhat less repression and inhibition, than is apparent in some other places where I have lived, and maybe I can see also more buoyancy and hopefulness.

Sitting here a few miles from the last sunsets on the continent I find myself as contented as I am likely to be anywhere in 1950, and the meadowlarks in the pasture next door remind me that for better or worse I am not far from my spiritual headquarters. For the meadowlark is another thing that all the Wests have in common. In California he sings more tunes, and sings them a little differently, than he sings in Montana or Saskatchewan, but California or Montana, it is the purest and sweetest birdsong I know, purer and sweeter even than the tune of Vermont's white-throated sparrow, which is saying much. Anywhere where meadowlarks sing any of their many tunes, that will be a satisfactory place for this evangelist. And that will be somewhere west of the Missouri.

Part Two

TESTIMONY

Editor's Note

Although a love of wilderness was clearly bred in Wallace Stegner's bones, his first writings on conservation issues did not occur until 1953 with an article for the *Reporter* called "One-Fourth of a Nation: Public Lands and Itching Fingers." That was followed in 1954 with a piece for *New Republic* called "Battle for Wilderness," and another for *Sports Illustrated* in 1955 called "We Are Destroying Our National Parks." Their effectiveness led Dave Brower at the Sierra Club to lean on Stegner to edit and write a foreword and chapter in a book called *This Is Dinosaur*, which, in turn, led to the defeat of reclamation dams proposed for Echo Park and Split Mountain and saved the monument from disappearing beneath the waters of a man-made lake. It was the first major environmental battle since John Muir and the Sierra Club fought the city of San Francisco over Hetch Hetchy (and lost), and it established Stegner, somewhat reluctantly and somewhat to his surprise, as a principal player in the politics of preservation. Years later, when Tom Watkins accused him of being "one of the most important figures in the modern conservation movement" he deflected the compliment, saying, "I am a paper tiger, Watkins, type-written on both sides."

Sporadic conservation journalism continued after the Dinosaur book, and then in 1960 Stegner was solicited by David Pesonen to help strengthen the argument for wilderness preservation in a report by the Outdoor Recreation Resources Review Commission. In reply he wrote what is now known by every environmentally conscious soul on the planet as the "Wilderness Letter," an argument for the restorative value of wilderness that, like Aldo Leopold's "The Land Ethic" and Henry David Thoreau's "Walking," has become one of the central documents of the conservation movement.

Eight of the "paper tiger's" environmental essays are collected in the following section, including "It All Began with Conservation," the often reprinted "Wilderness Letter," which was first published by *The Living Wilderness Magazine* and later collected in *The Sound of Mountain Water*. *Wilderness* also published "The Best Idea We Ever Had" in 1983 and "Aldo Leopold" (originally called "Living on Our Principal") in 1985. "Conservation Equals Survival" appeared in *American Heritage*, 1969; "Bernard DeVoto" in *Western American Literature*, 1985; and "Now, If I Ruled the World . . ." in *Sierra Magazine* in 1992. "Qualified Homage to Thoreau" was written for a collection entitled *Heaven Is under Our Feet: A Book for Walden Woods*.

Wilderness Letter

Los Altos, Calif.
Dec. 3, 1960

David E. Pesonen
Wildland Research Center
Agricultural Experiment Station
243 Mulford Hall
University of California
Berkeley 4, Calif.

Dear Mr. Pesonen:

I believe that you are working on the wilderness portion of the Outdoor Recreation Resources Review Commission's report. If I may, I should like to urge some arguments for wilderness preservation that involve recreation, as it is ordinarily conceived, hardly at all. Hunting, fishing, hiking, mountain-climbing, camping, photography, and the enjoyment of natural scenery will all, surely, figure in your report. So will the wilderness as a genetic reserve, a scientific yardstick by which we may measure the world in its natural balance against the world in its man-made imbalance. What I want to speak for is not so much the wilderness uses, valuable as those are, but the wilderness *idea*, which is a resource in itself. Being an intangible and spiritual resource, it will seem mystical to the practical-minded—but then anything that cannot be moved by a bulldozer is likely to seem mystical to them.

I want to speak for the wilderness idea as something that has helped form our character and that has certainly shaped our history as a people. It has no more to do with recreation than churches have to do with recreation, or than the strenuousness and optimism and expansiveness of what historians call the "American Dream" have to do with recreation. Nevertheless, since it is only in this recreation survey that the values of wilderness are being compiled, I hope you will permit me to insert this idea between the leaves, as it were, of the recreation report.

Something will have gone out of us as a people if we ever let the remaining wilderness be destroyed; if we permit the last virgin forests to be turned into comic books and plastic cigarette cases; if we drive the few remaining members of the wild species into zoos or to extinction; if we pollute the last clear air and dirty the last clean streams and push our paved roads through the last of the silence, so that never again will Americans be free in their own country from the noise, the exhausts, the stinks of human and automotive waste. And so that never again can we have the chance to see ourselves single, separate, vertical, and individual in the world, part of the environment of trees and rocks and soil, brother to the other animals, part of the natural world and competent to belong in it. Without any remaining wilderness we are committed wholly, without chance for even momentary reflection and rest, to a headlong drive into our technological termite-life, the Brave New World of a completely man-controlled environment. We need wilderness preserved—as much of it as is still left, and as many kinds—because it was the challenge against which our character as a people was formed. The reminder and the reassurance that it is still there is good for our spiritual health even if we never once in ten years set foot in it. It is good for us when we are young, because of the incomparable sanity it can bring briefly, as vacation and rest, into our insane lives. It is important to us when we are old simply because it is there—important, that is, simply as idea.

We are a wild species, as Darwin pointed out. Nobody ever tamed or domesticated or scientifically bred us. But for at least three millennia we have been engaged in a cumulative and ambitious race to modify and gain control of our environment, and in the process we have come close to domesticating ourselves. Not many people are likely, any more, to look upon what we call "progress" as an unmixed blessing. Just as surely as it has brought us increased comfort and more material goods, it has brought us spiritual losses, and it threatens now to become the Frankenstein that will destroy us. One means of sanity is to retain a hold on the natural world, to remain, insofar as we can, good animals. Americans still have that chance, more than many peoples; for while we were demonstrating ourselves the most efficient and ruthless environment-busters in history, and slashing and burning and cutting our way through a wilderness continent, the wilderness was working on us. It remains in us as surely as Indian names remain on the land. If the abstract dream of human liberty and human dignity became, in America, something more than an abstract dream, mark it down at least partially to the fact that we were in subtle ways subdued by what we conquered.

The Connecticut Yankee, sending likely candidates from King Arthur's unjust kingdom to his Man Factory for rehabilitation, was over-optimistic, as he later admitted. These things cannot be forced, they have to grow. To make such a man, such a democrat, such a believer in human individual dignity, as Mark Twain himself, the frontier was necessary, Hannibal and the Mississippi and Virginia City, and reaching out from those the wilderness; the wilderness as opportunity and as idea, the thing that has helped to make an American different from and, until we forget it in the roar of our industrial cities, more fortunate than other men. For an American, insofar as he is new and different at all, is a civilized man who has renewed himself in the wild. The American experience has been the confrontation by old peoples and cultures of a world as new as if it had just risen from the sea. That gave us our hope and our excitement, and the hope and excitement can be passed on to newer Americans, Americans who never saw any phase of the frontier. But only so long as we keep the remainder of our wild as a reserve and a promise—a sort of wilderness bank.

As a novelist, I may perhaps be forgiven for taking literature as a reflection, indirect but profoundly true, of our national consciouness. And our literature, as perhaps you are aware, is sick, embittered, losing its mind, losing its faith. Our novelists are the declared enemies of their society. There has hardly been a serious or important novel in this century that did not repudiate in part or in whole American technological culture for its commercialism, its vulgarity, and the way in which it has dirtied a clean continent and a clean dream. I do not expect that the preservation of our remaining wilderness is going to cure this condition. But the mere example that we can as a nation apply some other criteria than commercial and exploitative considerations would be heartening to many Americans, novelists or otherwise. We need to demonstrate our acceptance of the natural world, including ourselves; we need the spiritual refreshment that being natural can produce. And one of the best places for us to get that is in the wilderness where the fun houses, the bulldozers, and the pavements of our civilization are shut out.

Sherwood Anderson, in a letter to Waldo Frank in the 1920s, said it better than I can. "Is it not likely that when the country was new and men were often alone in the fields and the forest they got a sense of bigness outside themselves that has now in some way been lost. . . . Mystery whispered in the grass, played in the branches of trees overhead, was caught up and blown across the American line in clouds of dust at evening on the prairies. . . . I am old enough to remember tales that strengthen my belief in a deep semi-religious influence that was formerly at work among our people. The flavor of it hangs over the best work of Mark Twain. . . . I can remember old fellows in my home town speaking feelingly of an evening spent on the big empty plains. It had taken the shrillness out of them. They had learned the trick of quiet. . . ."

We could learn it too, even yet; even our children and grandchildren could learn it. But only if we save, for just such absolutely nonrecreational, impractical, and mystical uses as this, all the wild that still remains to us.

It seems to me significant that the distinct downturn in our literature from hope to bitterness took place almost at the precise time when the frontier officially came to an end, in 1890, and when the American way of life had begun to turn strongly urban and industrial. The more urban it has become, and the more frantic with technological change, the sicker and more embittered our literature, and I believe our people, have become. For myself, I grew up on the empty plains of Saskatchewan and Montana and in the mountains of Utah, and I put a very high valuation on what those places gave me. And if I had not been able periodically to renew myself in the mountains and deserts of western America I would be very nearly bughouse. Even when I can't get to the back country, the thought of the colored deserts of southern Utah, or the reassurance that there are still stretches of prairie where the world can be instantaneously perceived as disk and bowl, and where the little but intensely

114

important human being is exposed to the five directions and the thirty-six winds, is a positive consolation. The idea alone can sustain me. But as the wilderness areas are progressively exploited or "improved," as the jeeps and bulldozers of uranium prospectors scar up the deserts and the roads are cut into the alpine timberlands, and as the remnants of the unspoiled and natural world are progressively eroded, every such loss is a little death in me. In us.

I am not moved by the argument that those wilderness areas which have already been exposed to grazing or mining are already deflowered, and so might as well be "harvested." For mining I cannot say much good except that its operations are generally short-lived. The extractable wealth is taken and the shafts, the tailings, and the ruins left, and in a dry country such as the American West the wounds men make in the earth do not quickly heal. Still, they are only wounds; they aren't absolutely mortal. Better a wounded wilderness than none at all. And as for grazing, if it is strictly controlled so that it does not destroy the ground cover, damage the ecology, or compete with the wildlife it is in itself nothing that need conflict with the wilderness feeling or the validity of the wilderness experience. I have known enough range cattle to recognize them as wild animals; and the people who herd them have, in the wilderness context, the dignity of rareness; they belong on the frontier, moreover, and have a look of rightness. The invasion they make on the virgin country is a sort of invasion that is as old as Neolithic man, and they can, in moderation, even emphasize a man's feeling of belonging to the natural world. Under surveillance, they can belong; under control, they need not deface or mar. I do not believe that in wilderness areas where grazing has never been permitted, it should be permitted; but I do not believe either that an otherwise untouched wilderness should be eliminated from the preservation plan because of limited existing uses such as grazing which are in consonance with the frontier condition and image.

Let me say something on the subject of the kinds of wilderness worth preserving. Most of those areas contemplated are in the national forests and in high mountain country. For all the usual recreational purposes, the alpine and forest wildernesses are obviously the most important, both as genetic banks and as beauty spots. But for the spiritual renewal, the recognition of identity, the birth of awe, other kinds will serve every bit as well. Perhaps, because they are less friendly to life, more abstractly nonhuman, they will serve even better. On our Saskatchewan prairie, the nearest neighbor was four miles away, and at night we saw only two lights on all the dark rounding earth. The earth was full of animals—field mice, ground squirrels, weasels, ferrets, badgers, coyotes, burrowing owls, snakes. I knew them as my little brothers, as fellow creatures, and I have never been able to look upon animals in any other way since. The sky in that country came clear down to the ground on every side, and it was full of great weathers, and clouds, and winds, and hawks. I hope I learned something from knowing intimately the creatures of the earth; I hope I learned something from looking a long way, from looking up, from being much alone. A prairie like that, one big enough to carry the eye clear to the sinking, rounding horizon, can be as lonely and grand and simple in its forms as the sea. It is as good a place as any for the wilderness experience to happen; the vanishing prairie is as worth preserving for the wilderness idea as the alpine forests.

So are great reaches of our western deserts, scarred somewhat by prospectors but otherwise open, beautiful, waiting, close to whatever God you want to see in them. Just as a sample, let me suggest the Robbers' Roost country in Wayne County, Utah, near the Capitol Reef National Monument. In that desert climate the dozer and jeep tracks will not soon melt back into the earth, but the country has a way of making the scars insignificant. It is a lovely and terrible wilderness, such a wilderness as Christ and the prophets went out into: harshly and beautifully colored, broken and worn until its bones are exposed, its great sky without a smudge of taint from Technocracy, and in hidden corners and pockets under its cliffs the sudden poetry of springs. Save a piece of country like that intact, and it does not matter in the slightest that only a few people every year will go into it. That is precisely its value. Roads would be a desecration, crowds would ruin it. But those who haven't the strength or youth to go into it and live can simply sit and look. They can look two hundred miles, clear into Colorado: and looking down over the cliffs and canyons of the San Rafael Swell and the Robbers' Roost they can also look as deeply into themselves as anywhere I know. And if they can't even get to the places on the Aquarius Plateau where the present roads will carry them, they can simply contemplate the *idea*, take pleasure in the fact that such a timeless and uncontrolled part of earth is still there.

These are some of the things wilderness can do for us. That is the reason we need to put into effect, for its preservation, some other principle than the principles of exploitation or "usefulness" or even recreation. We simply need that wild country available to us, even if we never do more than drive to its edge and look in. For it can be a means of reassuring ourselves of our sanity as creatures, a part of the geography of hope.

Very sincerely yours,

Wallace Stegner

When I wrote my "wilderness letter" to David Pesonen 20 years ago, I had probably been prompted to do so by David Brower. He was usually the cattleprod that woke me from other preoccupations and from my workaholism and directed my attention to something important. In this case what he woke me to was close to my heart. I had been lucky enough to grow up next to wilderness, or quasi-wilderness, of several kinds, and I was prepared to argue for the preservation of wilderness not simply as a scientific reserve, or a land-bank, or a playground, but as a spiritual resource, a leftover from our frontier origins that could reassure us of our identity as a nation and a people. The Wilderness Bill, already debated for years and the subject of hundreds of official pages, had not yet passed. The ORRRC report,* with its inventory of what remained of our outdoors and its promise of reorganization of the bureaus managing it, seemed a good place to put in a word.

By luck or accident or the mysterious focusing by which ideas whose time has come reach many minds at the same time, my letter struck a chord. Before it had time to appear in the ORRRC report, Secretary of the Interior Stewart Udall had picked it up and used it as the basis of a speech before a wilderness conference in San Francisco, and the Sierra Club had published it as a document of that conference. It was published in the *Washington Post* and the ORRRC report, and I included it in my

---

*Outdoor Recreation for America: A Report to the President and to the Congress by the Outdoor Recreation Resources Review Commission, U.S. Government Printing Office, January, 1962.

collection of essays, *The Sound of Mountain Water*. Before long, some friend of mine saw it posted on the wall in a Kenya game park. From there, someone in South Africa or Rhodesia carried it home and had an artist named C. B. Cunningham surround it with drawings of African animals and birds, and turned it into a poster which the Natal Park Board, a Rhodesian kindness-to-animals organization, and perhaps other groups have distributed all over south and east Africa. A quotation from it captions a Canadian poster, with a magnificent George Calef photograph of caribou crossing river ice; and I have heard of, but not seen, a similar Australian poster issued with the same intent. The Sierra Club borrowed its last four words, "the geography of hope," as the title for Eliot Porter's book of photographs of Baja California. Altogether, this letter, the labor of an afternoon, has gone farther around the world than other writings on which I have spent years.

I take this as evidence not of special literary worth, but of an earnest, worldwide belief in the idea it expresses. There are millions of people on every continent who feel the need of what Sherwood Anderson called "a sense of bigness outside ourselves"; we all need something to take the shrillness out of us.

Returning to the letter after twenty years, I find that my opinions have not changed. They have actually been sharpened by an increased urgency. We are twenty years closer to showdown. Though the Wilderness Bill in which we all placed our hopes was passed, and though many millions of acres have been permanently protected—the magnificent Salmon River wilderness only a few weeks ago—preservation has not moved as fast as it should have, and the Forest Service, in particular, has shown by its reluctance and foot-dragging that it often puts resource use above preservation. Its proposed wilderness areas have consistently been minimal, and RARE II was a travesty.

Nevertheless, something saved. And something still to fight for.

And also, since the BLM Organic Act, another plus-minus development. It is now possible that out of the deserts and dry grasslands managed by the BLM there may be primitive areas set aside as wilderness, as I suggested in my letter to Pesonen and as some of us proposed to Secretary Udall as early as 1961. Unhappily, the Organic Act was contemporary with the energy crisis and the growing awareness that the undeveloped country in the Rocky Mountain states is one of the greatest energy mines on earth. That discovery, at a time of national anxiety about energy sources, has brought forward individuals, corporations, and conglomerates all eager to serve their country by strip mining the BLM wasteland, or drilling it for oil and gas. Economic temptation begets politicians willing to serve special economic interests, and they in turn bring on a new wave of states'-rights agitation, this time nicknamed the Sagebrush Rebellion. Its purpose, as in the 1940s when Bernard DeVoto headed the resistance to it (it was then called Landgrab), is to force the transfer of public lands from federal control to the control of the states, which will know how to make their resources available to those who will know what to do with them. After that they can be returned to the public for expensive rehabilitation

The Sagebrush Rebellion is the worst enemy not only of long-range management of the public lands, but of wilderness. If its counterpart in the 1940s had won, we would have no wilderness areas at all, and deteriorated national forests. If it wins in the 1980s we will have only such wilderness as is already formally set aside. Federal bureaus are imperfect human institutions, and have sins to answer for, and are not above being influenced by powerful interests. Nevertheless they represent the public interest, by and large, and not corporate interests anxious to exploit public resources at the public's expense.

In my letter to David Pesonen twenty years ago I spoke with some feeling about the deserts of southern Utah—Capitol Reef, the San Rafael Swell, the Escalante Desert, the Aquarius Plateau. That whole area has been under threat for nearly a decade, and though the Kaiparowits Complex was defeated and the Intermountain Power Project forced to relocate northward into the Sevier Desert near Lynndyl, the Union Pacific and thirteen other companies are still pushing to mine the coal in the Kaiparowits Plateau, surrounded by national parks; and a group of utilities wants to open a big strip mine at Alton, four miles from Bryce, and a 500-megawatt power plant in Warner Valley, seventeen miles from Zion, and a 2,000-megawatt plant north of Las Vegas, and two slurry pipelines to serve them. The old forest road over the Aquarius is being paved in from both ends, the equally beautiful trail over the Hightop from Salina to Fish Lake is being widened and improved. Our numbers and our energy demands inexorably press upon this country as beautiful as any on earth, country of an Old Testament harshness and serenity.*

It is in danger of being made—of helping to make itself—into a sacrifice area. Its air is already less clear, its distances less sharp. Its water table, if these mines and plants and pipelines are created, will sink out of sight, its springs will dry up, its streams will shrink and go intermittent. But there will be more blazing illumination along the Las Vegas Strip, and the little Mormon towns of Wayne and Garfield and Kane Counties will acquire some interesting modern problems.

What impresses me after twenty years is how far the spoiling of that superb country has already gone, and how few are the local supporters of the federal agencies which are the only protection against it. They would do well to consider how long the best thing in their lives has been preserved for them by federal management, and how much they will locally lose if the Sagebrush Rebellion wins. Furthermore, the land that the Sagebrush Rebellion wants transferred, the chickenhouse that it wants to put under the guard of the foxes, belongs as much to me, or to a grocer in Des Moines, or a taxi driver in Newark, as to anyone else. And I am not willing to see it wrecked just to increase corporate profits and light Las Vegas.

*On September 18, 1996, President Clinton protected 1.7 million acres of southern Utah by the creation of the Grand Staircase–Escalante National Monument.

It All Began with Conservation

Values, both those that we approve and those that we don't, have roots as deep as creosote rings, and live as long, and grow as slowly. Every action is an idea before it is an action, and perhaps a feeling before it is an idea, and every idea rests upon other ideas that have preceded it in time. The modern environmental movement, though it has shifted its emphasis from preservation of precious resources to the control of pollution caused by our industrial and agricultural practices, declares our dependence on the Earth and our responsibility to it, and thus derives pretty directly from the nineteenth-century travelers, philosophers, artists, writers, divines, natural historians and what *Time* has called "upper-class bird-watchers" whose purpose was to know it, celebrate it, and savor its beauty and rightness.

Yes, Virginia, there was an environmental movement before Earth Day, a long, slow revolution in values of which contemporary environmentalism is a consequence and a continuation. We are still in transition from the notion of Man as master of Earth to the notion of Man as a part of it.

Our sanction to be a weed species living at the expense of every other species and of Earth itself can be found in the injunction God gave to newly created Adam and Eve in Genesis 1:28: "Be fruitful, and multiply, and replenish the earth, and subdue it." But what we are working toward, what with luck we may eventually attain to, is an outlook that was frequently and sometimes eloquently expressed by the first inhabitants of this continent. The Indians stressed the web of life, the interconnectedness of land and man and creature. Chief Luther Standing Bear of the Oglala Sioux put it this way: "Only to the white man was nature a wilderness and only to him was the land 'infested' with 'wild' animals and 'savage' people. To us it was tame. Earth was bountiful and we were surrounded with the blessings of the Great Mystery."

The New World was such a blinding opportunity to Europeans, and lay there so temptingly, like an unlocked treasure house with the watchman sleeping, that nobody thought of limits, nobody thought of preservation, until generations of living in America and "breaking" its wilderness had taught us to know it, and knowing it had taught us to love it, and loving it had taught us to question what we were doing to it. All of that is the background of the environmental movement.

It took us 200 years from Jamestown and Plymouth Rock to Americanize our perceptions, loyalties, vocabulary and palette so that we could see America clearly, and take pride in it. New ideas from Europe, especially the interest in nature that came with the Romantic movement, helped that pride along. But what made America the natural garden of those ideas, what most metamorphosed Europeans into something new, was what Europe had long lost and what America was made of: wilderness.

The seventeenth-century settlers did not look on wilderness with the eyes of a 1990 Sierra Club backpacker. Our wilderness is safe, theirs was not. Ours is islands in a tamed continent, theirs was one vast wild, totally unknown, prowled by God-knew-what wild beasts and wild men. In New England they also feared it as the trysting place of witches and devils. Even without devils, the struggle to survive fully occupied the first generation or two, and survival meant, in God's word, "subduing" the wild Earth. Nobody questioned the value of that effort. Civilization was a good; wilderness was what had to be subdued to create the human habitations that looked like progress and triumph even when they were only huts in a stump field.

To the boosters, America was always "prosperous" farms, "smiling" villages, "bustling" towns. But life on the frontier was more often crude and brutal and deprived. Crèvecoeur, in his *Letters from an American Farmer* (1782), painted a rosy picture of the established farm and the self-reliant industrious farmer; but he had to admit that out on the edge, beyond the settlements, were surly, verminous men who lived in dirt-floored cabins with slattern wives and broods of dirty children, sustaining themselves by constant killing of animals and growing ever gloomier and more antisocial by the eating of wild meat. Crèvecoeur thought that as settlement caught up with them they would gradually grow out of their barbarous stage and join the ranks of the happy, prosperous and civilized.

Maybe some of them did. Maybe some just went farther west when the settlements caught up. No matter which they did, the frontiersman was being built by the popular imagination into an idealized archetypal figure, divorced from Europe, divorced from history, homegrown, a demigod in buckskin. His real-life prototype was Daniel Boone. His larger-than-life fictional version was James Fenimore Cooper's Natty Bumppo, "Leatherstocking," who appeared in the novel *The Pioneers* in 1823 and whose story continued on in other novels into the 1840s.

Leatherstocking is everything that any American boy ever dreamed of being. Far from handsome (looks went with the effete and civilized), he is nevertheless fearless, self-reliant, omnicompetent, a keen tracker and a dead shot, a mortal enemy and the most loyal of friends. He is also the soul of chivalry, protecting and saving Cooper's females when they go implausibly astray in the wild woods. An orphan, untutored, Natty has kept the innocence of the natural man. From his brief contact with the Moravians, or from the woods themselves, he has imbibed a noble magnanimity, a sensitivity to beauty and a deep if unorthodox piety. Homeless in the civilized sense, he has made the wilderness his home, and no witches, devils or fears assail him there: he feels the presence of God in every leaf. There is not a trace in him of the overcivilized fastidiousness that in the eighteenth century could lead the French novelist Mme. de Staël to draw the curtains of her carriage, so as not to see the unkempt scenery. Natty glories in the scenery of his woods and mountains, the wilder the better.

But what makes the Leatherstocking Tales significant for this review is that Cooper reveals an ambivalence that will become more common as the nineteenth century careens on, and that is basic to much later environmental thinking. Civilization, on whose side Cooper felt obliged to be, was at war with the wilderness, which he loved. The carriers of civilization in Cooper's novels, the settlers, are often as uncouth and repulsive as they were to Crèvecoeur, and they destroy the beauty and liberty and bounty of the woods.

The same townsmen who throw Natty Bumppo into jail for shooting a deer out of season fire into a passing flock of passenger pigeons with every weapon in town, even cannon, and strew the earth with mutilated flesh and feathers. Wilderness man cannot live with settlement man. Like Daniel Boone when he felt too many people nearby, Natty goes on west, and Cooper's sympathy as well as the reader's goes with him. The destructive practices of settlement, which Cooper was among the first to lament ("What will the axemen do, when they have cut their way from sea to sea?"), are only a step behind.

Emerson, like Natty Bumppo, saw God in every manifestation of nature, but he was hardly a forerunner of environmental thinking. He declared America's intellectual independence of Europe, and he cheered the rocky, gritty American character that he saw forming on the frontiers, but he was too much enamored of American self-reliance and energy to fear any consequences; and though he professed a liking for the wild, it was for the wild of the Hudson River School paintings, in which wilderness is the backdrop for a foreground of homely husbandry—a farmer's cottage, a fisherman, a herd wading a stream, a rude mill. The Philosophers' Camp in the Adirondacks where he and fellow spirits gathered to take walks and hone the art of conversation was wild enough. It was otherwise with his somewhat prickly protégé, Thoreau.

From Walden the Compass Pointed West

For Thoreau, wildness was a passion. "In wildness is the preservation of the world," he wrote, and meant it. Repudiating his countrymen's concerns—progress, betterment, accumulation—and their predatory habits in the wild, he made his most characteristic gesture by building a shack on Walden Pond and living in it in most spartan circumstances for two years. One cannot imagine him as a hunter; he thought every creature was better alive than dead. He loved and studied, not always accurately but devotedly, the creatures of the woods and rivers and ponds around Concord, Massachusetts. From a rustic American base, he strove to look to the edges of the known world, and beyond. Though his life could have been illustrated by the half-tamed, half-wild landscapes of the Hudson River painters, his imagination could not. It demanded the utterly wild, free scenes of a Bierstadt or a Moran.

Thoreau never personally sought the wilderness. His only excursions into really wild country were his expeditions into the northern woods. As he said, he had traveled extensively in Concord. Nevertheless Thoreau was at one with Emerson in turning his back on the Old World. Even in an afternoon ramble, he said, the needle always settled west. He must walk toward Oregon, not Europe.

In Thoreau there is virtually every idea that later became gospel to the environmental movement, but it is there only as idea, not as action or call to action—unless withdrawal is action. He was not much of a believer in government, and he was the total opposite of a joiner. American as he was, wilderness-lover as he was, he was not a conservationist or environmentalist in our sense. Nevertheless, as the painter George Catlin had anticipated the national park idea by suggesting a wild prairie reservation, so Thoreau anticipated the more modest urban-open-space idea by suggesting that every community should have its patch of woods where people could refresh themselves. His notion of nature as having healing powers has now the force of revealed truth. And the form of Thoreau's essays—rumination hung upon the framework of an outdoor excursion—has influenced virtually every nature writer since, from Burroughs and Muir to Wendell Berry, Edward Abbey and Barry Lopez.

Unlike Emerson, Thoreau was not one to search for God or the Oversoul in every natural object, but one senses that he was feeling his way toward an identification with nature not too far from that of the Indians. Yet Thoreau did not develop the concept of the web, the connectedness of all life. The man who did that was George Perkins Marsh.

Marsh was an extraordinary polymath, an architect, linguist, politician, diplomat and the first man to work backward, by the aid of history and science and observation, to the point of view that primitives know simply by participation. He was an authority on the Icelandic sagas and on Norse explorations. He served as congressman from Vermont and in this capacity was one of the main proponents of using James Smithson's bequest to create the institution that bears his name. He was Minister to Turkey, and for twenty-one years Minister Plenipotentiary to Italy. All of those real distinctions are now forgotten. What remains is a single book, first published in 1864 as *Man and Nature,* and reissued in revised form in 1874 as *The Earth as Modified by Human Action.* It was the rudest kick in the face that American initiative, optimism and carelessness had yet received.

MARSH AND "THE DANGERS OF IMPRUDENCE"

Growing up in cutover Vermont, Marsh had observed what deforestation did to streams, fish, birds, animals, the land; and serving for many years in the Mediterranean basin and the Fertile Crescent, he had studied man-made deserts, the barren mountains of Greece, the ruins of once-great civilizations. He saw calamity coming to America, and wrote his book "to point out the dangers of imprudence and the necessity of caution in all operations which, on a large scale, interfere with the spontaneous arrangements of the organic or the inorganic world."

Deforestation meant far more than a future shortage of lumber; it meant potentially irrevocable damage to what we now call the ecosystem. "Man," Marsh wrote, "is everywhere a disturbing agent. Wherever he plants his foot, the harmonies of nature are turned to discords." The process was the more dangerous because its results were not always immediately apparent. In the last year of a destructive civil war that made any expenditure of resources seem justifiable, and on the brink of the rampant exploitation that would follow, Marsh spoke out against every ingrained American faith, including the faith in an inexhaustible continent. "It is certain that a desolation, like that which has overwhelmed many once beautiful and fertile regions of Europe, awaits an important part of the territory of the United States . . . unless prompt measures are taken to check the action of destructive causes already in operation."

The destructive causes were indeed in operation. Having skinned New England, the loggers were now skinning the Midwest at appalling speed. Within a single lifetime they deforested an area the size of Europe. The pineries of Minnesota and Wisconsin were going down the Mississippi as huge lumber rafts. By 1897 the sawmills of Michigan would have processed 160 billion board feet of white pine, and left no more than 6 billion standing in the whole state.

It was like a feeding frenzy of sharks. There has been nothing like it since except the current destruction of the Amazon rain forest. Predictably, Marsh's warnings went unheeded except by a concerned few, upper-class bird-watchers probably, the kind who are generally well ahead of the mass public in these matters. Concerned about the destruction of the forests before reading Marsh, they were doubly concerned afterward, and in 1875 a group of them formed the American Forestry Association with the hope of influencing public opinion and perhaps legislation. Sixteen long years later, when the Michigan pineries were obviously nearing the end of their road, the public indignation that had inspired the formation of the AFA got a rider added to the General Revision Act, authorizing the President to establish "forest reserves on the Public Domain." Benjamin Harrison, and after him Grover Cleveland, and after him Theodore Roosevelt, took advantage of the law, and among them they put 43 million acres of forests, mainly in the West, out of the reach of the loggers. Then in 1907 angry northwestern congressmen pushed through a bill rescinding the President's power to create forest reserves. With the help of his Chief Forester, Gifford Pinchot, Roosevelt named twenty-one new forests totaling 16 million acres, and *then* signed the bill that would have stopped him.

The tracing of ideas is a guessing game. We can't tell who first had an idea; we can only tell who first had it influentially, who formulated it in a striking way and left it in some form, poem or equation or picture, that others could stumble upon with the shock of recognition. The radical ideas that have been changing our attitudes toward our Earth habitat have been around forever. Only if they begin to win substantial public approval and give visible effects do they achieve a plain and even predictable curve of development. But once they reach that stage, they are as easy to trace as a gopher in a spring lawn.

Nearly every aspect of environmentalism since the founding of the

AFA has demonstrated the same pattern: a charismatic and influential individual who discerns a problem and formulates a public concern; a group that forms itself around him or around his ideas, and exerts educational pressure on the public and political pressure on Congress; legislation that creates some new kind of reserve—national park, national forest, national monument, national wildlife sanctuary or wilderness area; and finally, an increasingly specific body of regulatory law for the protection of what has been set aside.

THE IMPASSIONED CAMPAIGN FOR WILDLIFE

Virtually all conservation activity up to the mid-twentieth century was concerned with saving something precious in our national heritage. Thus, as Marsh, and later and more narrowly Gifford Pinchot, galvanized the impulse to protect what remained of our forests, so George Bird Grinnell, a hunting companion and boyhood friend of Theodore Roosevelt's, devoted his time and his magazine, *Forest and Stream*, to the protection of wildlife. He carried on an impassioned campaign against market hunters, poachers and women who wore feathers on their hats; and he and the Audubon societies (he founded the first one in 1886) can be credited not only with the Park Protection Act of 1894, forbidding hunting within the national parks, but also with the first wildlife sanctuary, Pelican Island, which Roosevelt established in 1903. Wildlife protection came lamely and late—the passenger pigeon, Carolina parakeet and other species were gone, the buffalo and antelope were down to remnants, mainly in Yellowstone—but it did come, and those who made it come, by publicity and persistence, were an unlikely combination of bleeding hearts and gunners.

The creation of the first national park happened before this pattern of volunteer organizations working upon politicians had been perfected. It came about in 1872 because a party of Montana explorers had been so struck by the wonders of Yellowstone that they carried to Washington the demand that it be set aside as a public playground. F. V. Hayden's U.S. Geological and Geographical Survey of the Territories helped by laying before a dazzled Congress the paintings of Thomas Moran and Henry W.

Elliott, and the photographs of William Henry Jackson, its expedition artists. Later it published, with fifteen Moran chromoliths, a book that might have served as a model for the Sierra Club's coffee-table books, the first scenic art book with a political purpose.

That first national park was a spontaneous overflow of public enthusiasm. The following ones owed a great deal to a single man, John Muir, and to the organization he founded, the Sierra Club. Yosemite, Sequoia and General Grant national parks (the latter ultimately fused with Sequoia) were largely Muir's doing, as was the Petrified Forest. As John of the Mountains, the grizzled genius of Yosemite, he had entertained the great, among them Emerson and Theodore Roosevelt, on sublime hikes and long campfire talks, and because he knew the Sierra better than anyone, and was even more persuasive as a talker than as a writer, he got himself listened to. In 1892, two years after the Sierra parks were created, he formed the Sierra Club to look after their interests and enjoy their beauty. In 1905 he and the club finally persuaded California to cede back to the federal government Yosemite Valley itself, which had badly deteriorated under state control, so that it could become the heart of the park it belonged in.

"USE WITHOUT IMPAIRMENT"

No story of the national park system would be complete without some mention of the Antiquities Act of 1906, passed because of the depredations of pothunters in archaeological sites in the Southwest. It authorized the President to set aside by proclamation sites that were especially precious or threatened. By 1916 there were twenty such national monuments, many of them scheduled to become national parks by later Congressional action. A quarter of all our present national parks owe their first reservation to the Antiquities Act.

By 1916 there were thirteen national parks, crown jewels without an adequately stated purpose or an adequate keeper. Those that were managed at all were managed by the Army. But in that year the National Park Act gave these reserves their stated purpose, public enjoyment, public use *without impairment*, and created the National Park Service to carry it out.

Muir had a hand in the National Park Act, too, but only posthumously and as a result of his greatest failure. For years he and the Sierra Club had fought San Francisco's effort to dam the Hetch Hetchy Valley, which lay within Yosemite National Park and which Muir thought second in beauty only to Yosemite Valley itself. The effort enlisted public and newspaper support throughout the country. It also revealed a mortal split between conservationists of Pinchot's variety, who believed in "wise use" of resources, and preservationists like Muir, who believed that some natural things were too sacred to be exploited for profit, water, power or any other purpose.

In 1913 Congress voted to approve the dam. Within a year, Muir was dead. But the feelings stirred up by the struggle did not subside, and perhaps there was even some guilt felt by people who had fought on the winning side. Three years after it voted for the Hetch Hetchy dam, Congress passed the National Park Act, with its guarantee that parks should indeed be what Muir and the Sierra Club had insisted they were: sacrosanct, to be enjoyed but not impaired.

That "use without impairment" clause was there when next the Sierra Club and its allies, this time under the leadership of David Brower, found themselves in a battle with dam builders. In the 1950s, as part of the Colorado River Storage Project, the Bureau of Reclamation proposed to build a dam within the section of Dinosaur National Monument in northeastern Utah. The case against the dam was not as strong as that against Hetch Hetchy, for Dinosaur was only a national monument, not a national park, and there had been damsite withholdings. Nevertheless, Dinosaur was part of the national park system, and that system was to be managed for use without impairment; nobody could deny that to drown a canyon under 400 feet of water would impair it. Ultimately it was the "use without impairment" clause that gave the conservation forces total victory. The Colorado River Storage Project was stalled unless that dam was removed from it, and it was.

Historians have concluded that the Dinosaur controversy marked the coming-of-age of conservation, the first time the diverse single-interest organizations joined together for strength, and proved they had a lot of it. But Dinosaur is not understandable without Hetch Hetchy. The tactics, the publicity campaigns, the political skirmishing, were similar in these instances. The difference between defeat in the first instance and victory in the second is that Muir did not have the National Park Act and the "use without impairment" clause to fight from, while Brower and his alliance did. And the precedent has been instructive in later struggles. Other laws, notably the Endangered Species Act, have similarly been used as barricades, and the snail darter and desert pupfish have been enlisted on the side of the environment.

The Movement to Save the Last Wilderness

If the national park idea is, as Lord Bryce suggested, the best idea America ever had, wilderness preservation is the highest refinement of that idea. Parks are designed for careful human use—they could be justified by a Pinchot. But wildernesses are something else. Preservation of wilderness implies agreement with Marsh's observation that wherever Man plants his foot, nature's harmonies are turned to discords. As the culminating aspect of the preservation sentiment, the wilderness movement differs from the park and forest and wildlife movements in its total repudiation of most kinds of human use. What it wants is the continuation of that healthy, natural web of life that Chief Standing Bear and others revered; and if there are human uses implicit in this long-range continuation—watershed protection, protection of genetic variety, the preservation of natural laboratories by which the deteriorating Man-managed world can be judged and perhaps saved—the *sentiment* for wilderness, our creature-love for the natural world, is probably as important. Like the other forms of land preservation, wilderness areas are doomed to be islands surrounded by what constantly threatens to invade and damage them, but that is what we get for learning slowly.

Wilderness has had its prophets, early and late; of the late ones, Aldo Leopold seems to me the greatest. It has developed its organization, the Wilderness Society, one of the most effective of the environmental groups. It has had its landmark legislation, the Wilderness Act of 1964, which authorized hands-off protection for areas carved out of the national forest, national park and Bureau of Land Management lands.

One thing wilderness has not lacked is enemies, for its nonutilitarian reserves are said to "lock up" resources and frustrate our fabled American initiative. Not only resource interests but also incompatible recreationists and both the U.S. Forest Service and the BLM have dragged their heels in the process of wilderness designation. Some people learn late, some never do.

Ironically, wilderness preservation was born in that most utilitarian of organizations, Pinchot's Forest Service. It cropped up here and there like an ineradicable weed. In 1919 Arthur Carhart, a Forest Service architect in Denver, talked his employers out of civilizing Trappers Lake, in Colorado, with summer cottages. He later did the same thing in the boundary waters area of northern Minnesota. In 1924 Aldo Leopold, from the Albuquerque office of the Forest Service, got 900 roadless square miles of the Gila National Forest set aside as a primitive area. (He defined a "wilderness" as something big enough to absorb a two-week pack trip.) In a 1930 issue of *Scientific Monthly*, Robert Marshall, a plant physiologist working in Wyoming's Wind River Range, issued a ringing manifesto calling for identification and rescue of whatever wilderness areas remained. In 1934, after a conference in Knoxville, Tennessee, Marshall, Benton MacKaye and several other foresters determined that an organization should be formed to promote wilderness, and the following January, with Leopold and Robert Sterling Yard among the charter members, they formed it.

Their purpose was to replace the unreliable administrative designations of wilderness with wildernesses that were established by law, and hence impregnable.

Much of the program, as it developed, was the work of Marshall. The philosophical justifications, the statement of first principles, appeared in 1949 in Aldo Leopold's posthumous *A Sand County Almanac*.

In the forty-one years since its publication, *A Sand County Almanac* has become a kind of holy book in environmental circles. It is a superb distillation of what many Americans had been groping toward for more than a century. Leopold loved land, all kinds, but the wilder the better, and over his lifetime of experience with land and its creatures he had come to look upon land as a community, not a commodity. Blessed with a poet's gift of words, trained in forestry, he brought as much sensitivity as Thoreau to his study of nature, and more science. His book comes to its climax in the essay called "The Land Ethic," in which he argues for the kind of responsibility in our land relations that civilized people are supposed to show in their human relations.

Without denying the human need to use natural resources—cut trees, plow prairies, shoot game, whatever—he wanted a portion of the land left wild, for ultimately all human endeavor has to come back to the wilderness for its justification and its new beginnings. He said he would hate to be young again without wild country to grow up in. And he was no lover of public recreation as usually practiced. Recreation could be as dangerous as logging or any extractive use. "Recreational development," he wrote, "is a job not of building roads into lovely country, but of building receptivity into the still unlovely human mind." Knowing how persistent the unloveliness of the human mind could be, he did not expect his land ethic to arrive soon. He perfectly understood that what he described would have its flowering far off, the product of a long, slow and almost total revolution of American values.

Fifteen years after the publication of *A Sand County Almanac*, and after the extraordinary effort of many people, politicians as well as environmentalists, and especially of Howard Zahniser, executive director of the Wilderness Society, Congress passed the Wilderness Bill. Tired of fighting brushfire wars after the Dinosaur struggle, Zahniser had drafted a bill in 1956. During the next eight years he revised it sixty-six times. When, after innumerable hearings and thousands of pages of testimony, it was finally passed, it still contained Zahniser's definition of wilderness as "an area where the earth and its community of life are untrammeled by man, where man himself is a visitor who does not remain."

The passage of the Wilderness Bill, and its immediate designation of 9.1 million acres of wilderness in national park, national forest and wildlife refuge land, marked the climax of preservationist environmentalism. The wilderness designation process, clogged with controversy and sullen with turf battles among the bureaus, and shrilly resisted by resource interests, would go on—still goes on. But a corner had already been turned. Rachel Carson's *Silent Spring*, in 1962, had already made it plain that pollution, not preservation, was to be the principal concern of the future.

And so this is the long road the nation traveled to get to Earth Day

1970. Those who led us down it, the countless individuals and scores of organizations who resisted the lunchbucket and "American initiative" arguments of resource exploiters, did not leave us a bad legacy. Considering the mood in which the continent was settled, and the amount we had to learn, we can be grateful that those battles do not have to be fought, at least not on the same fields, again. We can be just as certain that others will have to be. Environmentalism or conservation or preservation, or whatever it should be called, is not a fact, and never has been. It is a job.

The Best Idea We Ever Had

Let me bear my testimony, as the Mormons say, and acknowledge the debt I owe to a federal bureau for more than sixty years of physical and spiritual refreshment, and for the reassurance it gives me that despite all its faults, democracy is still the worst form of government except all the others.

I have never been an uncritical admirer of the great American public. I came from there, I know its limitations, carelessness, wastefulness, and greed. I have spent years studying the history of our disorderly subjugation of this most splendid of continents and estimating the consequences of an exploitation that ignored consequences. Especially on issues involving public lands, I have often seen voters making almost criminally irresponsible choices, and their representatives pushing bills that sadly confuse private (read "corporate") interests with the public interest.

But ever since I was old enough to be cynical I have been visiting national parks, and they are a cure for cynicism, an exhilarating rest from the competitive avarice we call the American Way. They were cooked in the same alembic as other land laws—the Homestead Act, Preemption Act, Timber and Stone Act, Mining Act of 1872—but they came out as something different. Absolutely American, absolutely democratic, they reflect us at our best rather than our worst. Without them, millions of

American lives, including mine, would have been poorer. The *world* would have been poorer.

I became a national park addict in 1920, when my family toured Yellowstone in a Hudson Super Six. The roads were rough and dusty, the facilities primitive, and the people so few that we waved at every car we met and hobnobbed with every other family in the campgrounds. Around us the great park spread its more than 2 million acres of virtual or actual wilderness, its miles of naturalness and silence. It was an uncomfortable, unsanitary, absolutely thrilling experience.

In 1925 we first saw the southern Utah and Arizona parks. All were young, some were in their infancy, several were still unborn. At Zion, Mormon farms still extended to the mouth of the canyon. We picked grapes off the roadside fences in Rockville, and walked clear to the Narrows without seeing more than forty people. On the Kaibab the mule deer browsed and grazed in African numbers, only months away from the catastrophic die-off that taught the nation one of its first lessons in ecology. The North Rim of the Grand Canyon dreamed barely peopled above the great gulf, its blue air owned by hawks. Bryce, still called Utah National Park, was only a year old; Capitol Reef was neither park nor monument, only a little Mormon oasis of alfalfa fields and fruit trees tucked among the red cliffs along the Fremont River. Arches and Canyonlands were not even conceived. Rainbow Bridge and Natural Bridges national monuments had both been set aside by 1910, but to us they were vague, inaccessible wonders, lost at the end of trails too difficult for us then. Even in 1948, when we finally did reach Rainbow Bridge (by way of the San Juan and Glen Canyon and a six-mile hike up the marvelous stone slot of Rainbow Canyon), there were only a few hundred names on the register ahead of ours.

Checking the Index of the National Park System, I find that I have visited more than a hundred of its areas, some of them dozens of times, and I feel qualified to be an interpreter. I have watched with interest, hope, and dismay what the processes of growth and change have done in sixty-two years. I understand that a great natural *area* is brute luck, a great *system* of such areas saved from exploitation is a national achievement. The health of the system should be a national concern.

. . .

Begin with some history. The national park idea, the best idea we ever had, was inevitable as soon as Americans learned to confront the wild continent not with fear and cupidity but with delight, wonder, and awe. The artist George Catlin suggested it as early as 1830. It had its prophets and ancestors among the nature-philosophers of the Concord school. It went a long way toward articulation when the federal government ceded Yosemite to the state of California for perpetual use as a park in 1864. It reached the threshold of realization in 1870, when a group of tourists in Yellowstone took a vote and by a bare majority decided not to file private claims on those wonders, but to press for their preservation as a public pleasuring ground. It attained formal legal status when Congress created Yellowstone National Park in 1872.

Once started, it grew like the backfire it truly was, burning back upwind against the current of claim and grab and raid. Sequoia and General Grant (later to become part of Kings Canyon) and Yosemite (minus the Valley, which was not receded until 1906) joined Yellowstone in 1890. Mount Rainier was set aside in 1899, Crater Lake in 1902, Mesa Verde, Glacier, Rocky Mountain, and Lassen in the ten years between 1906 and 1916. By then we had clearly proved that our rapacious society could hold its hand, at least in the presence of stupendous scenery, and learn to respect the earth for something besides its economic value.

But the machinery of protection, operated mainly by the Army, was hit-or-miss, and there were people (there are still) who tried to use the parks for their own profit, who cut trees, killed animals, grazed livestock, and otherwise acted as if the national parks were like any other part of the Public Domain. In 1916 the National Park System Organic Act created the National Park Service and gave it responsibility for the eighteen parks then in the system. The service was directed to use methods that conformed to "the fundamental purpose of said parks . . . which purpose is to conserve the scenery and the natural and historic objects and the wildlife therein and to provide for the enjoyment of the same in such manner and by such means as will leave them unimpaired for the enjoyment of future generations."

Enjoyment without impairment was an impossible assignment, but it was not so visibly impossible in 1916 as it is now. In 1916 it seemed necessary to persuade the public to enjoy what had been set aside for it. Thus Stephen Mather and Horace Albright, the shapers of the National Park Service and its first and second directors, felt obliged to play public relations games, urging and advertising people into the parks and then using the visitation figures to justify their budget requests to Congress. There has not been a director since who has not made use of the same figures for the same purpose, but later directors have been less happy about the crowds. Nevertheless, sensitive to political realities, most have felt that their first bureaucratic duty is to serve the public. Most have had to spend a good part of their rarely adequate budgets to build and maintain roads, trails, sewer systems, visitor centers, and other public facilities. All have had to watch the basic resources, natural, archaeological, and historical, suffer impairment.

The system has grown large and complex—unfriendly critics say "unwieldy," which, considering that it has grown faster than the appropriations for its management, may not be too misleading a word. Not only have the national parks themselves increased from the eighteen of 1916 to the forty-eight of 1982, but new categories have been added, some for the purpose of preserving them, some to serve the expanding appetite for outdoor recreation, some for merely administrative reasons.

In 1933 Franklin Roosevelt, restructuring the bureaucracy, turned over to the Park Service nearly fifty national monuments, military parks, battlefields, and cemeteries previously managed by the Departments of War and Agriculture. In the past fifty years many other kinds of reservations have been put under the national park umbrella—National Recreation Areas, National Preserves, National Seashores and Lakeshores, National Wild and Scenic Rivers, National Memorials, National Parkways, National Historic Sites, National Scenic Trails, and the National Capital Parks of Washington, D.C. The White House and the Washington Monument are as much Park Service obligations as Glacier or Grand Canyon, and the National Capital Police who put down riots and rescue plane-crash survivors from the Potomac are an arm of the National Park Service.

But for all the complication of its duties, the Park Service is still primarily a land-preserving, land-managing bureau. It administers 334 areas that add up to 79 million acres, about 1 percent of the land base of the lower forty-eight states and 14 percent of Alaska. It attracted, in 1981, 327 million visitors.

No need to advertise now. So enthusiastically have Americans taken to their parks that in the past three decades, while the population grew by 50 percent, visits to the parks have grown by 800 percent. Also, now that we have built this mousetrap, the world beats a path to our door. What we have salvaged of natural America proves as interesting to foreign visitors as the New Yorks, San Franciscos, and Disneylands. A surprising number of the visitors who crowd the "golden circle" of southwestern parks have stepped off planes that originated in Frankfurt and Tokyo. You may hear as much Japanese as Navajo in the Canyon de Chelly, and rangers at Bryce, Grand Canyon, and Capitol Reef are learning to give nature talks in French and German. What is even more significant, the world that visits our national parks has copied them. There are now parks on the American model in 120 countries, and at a recent World Parks conference in Indonesia it was revealed that parkland throughout the world has grown by 82 percent in the past ten years.

By virtue of the General Authorities Act of 1970, all the varieties of reservation that make up the National Park System are *equally* parts of the system. That means that the rule of enjoyment without impairment, impossible or not, applies as surely to national recreation areas and seashores as to national parks, though with less stringency. That is important, because the "without impairment" clause has been the barricade upon which friends of the parks have many times rallied to fight off some threat. It has kept power dams out of Glacier and Dinosaur, it stopped the patriotic loggers from skinning Olympic of its spruce during World War II, it inhibits, though it cannot entirely prevent, wildflower picking, cactus stealing, pothunting, game poaching, and the dumping of cans and garbage in geysers. It is the basic principle by which the public has been gradually trained to understand the difference between a national park and a resort.

There are certain other laws, notably the Antiquities Act, the Wilderness Act, and the Land and Water Conservation Act, that are important in national park affairs. The first and third provide means for acquiring new parklands; the second allows even stricter protection than the National Park Act for what has already been set aside.

Passed ten years before the National Park Act, the Antiquities Act authorized the president, by proclamation, to set aside as national monuments natural or historic areas in the Public Domain that are under threat. Some of the great parks, including Grand Canyon, Lassen, Capitol Reef, Arches, and Glacier Bay, were first created by proclamation as monuments, and later upgraded to parks by Congress. It was the Antiquities Act that permitted President Carter to put big chunks of Alaska on hold while the Alaska National Interest Lands and Conservation Act struggled through Congress. It is still there as a last-ditch preservation instrument for any president with the nerve to invoke it in the face of powerful special interests.

The Wilderness Act of 1964 added nothing to the National Park System, but it gave added protection to wild and primitive areas within the system. In effect, it put the emphasis in those wild areas on protection of the resource, not service to the public. The machinery of designation has been slow and cumbersome, but as of 1982 there were 35 million acres in thirty-six national park areas that were part of the wilderness system, protected from roads, logging, structures, and any human use that leaves a track. Preexisting mineral claims are grandfathered (unfortunately), and wilderness areas require policing, but wilderness designation protects natural areas, takes a burden off the Park Service, and releases park rangers from being, as they often are elsewhere in the system, part-time garbagemen.

Finally, there is the Land and Water Conservation Act of 1965, a law of prime importance. In the beginning, national parks were carved out of the Public Domain, and therefore were all in the West. As the demand for parks in the East, Midwest, and South began to be felt, the problem of acquisition arose, for most land in those regions was in private ownership. Private donors, most notably the Rockefellers, made possible the Great Smokies, Acadia, Virgin Islands, and the Jackson Hole part of Grand Teton, and the Save-the-Redwoods League was vital in the creation of Redwood National Park. But demand far exceeded the supply of private money, and in 1965 Congress authorized a public fund for the purchase of federal parklands and for assisting states to create or enlarge state parks. The fund was to be derived from a tax on motorboat fuel. When that source proved inadequate, Congress in 1968 amended the act and enlarged the fund by tapping the royalties from offshore oil leases.

Two kinds of acquisition are promoted by the Land and Water Conservation Fund. One is the buying up of inholdings, those privately held parcels within existing park boundaries which are like a gun pointed at the head of the parks that enclose them. The other is the purchase of lands within new park areas authorized by Congress, such as the Santa Monica Mountains Recreation Area and many of the seashores, lakeshores, and urban parks. A salutary aspect of the fund is that it comes out of no taxpayers' pockets. It draws on what amounts to a severance tax on publicly owned Outer Continental Shelf resources, and devotes the proceeds to the acquisition of an alternative public resource, parkland.

A success story, the steady advance of a splendid idea through more than a century and throughout the world. Nevertheless, all is not well. Public pressures increase geometrically, appropriations arithmetically. And as its problems increase, the Park Service has been increasingly politicized.

Until 1980, most people, including former Interior Secretaries Stewart Udall and Cecil Andrus, have urged that the only way to take pressure off existing parks is to keep adding new ones. The 1960s and 1970s saw massive additions to the system. The Alaska Lands Act alone more than doubled the Park Service acreage, and the creation of such urban recreation areas as Gateway in New York, Golden Gate in San Francisco, and Santa Monica Mountains in Los Angeles democratized the park experience by bringing it within the reach of large population concentrations. But appropriations did not keep pace with expansion, especially after the Reagan budget cutting, and one effect has been to spread an already thin service even thinner. Since the public has traditionally been the primary obligation, protection has had to suffer.

A report entitled *State of the Parks, 1980* made clear the nature and extent of the threats to the health of the park system. It was initiated by Congress, not by the Park Service, but it was put together by superintendents and others in the field, and it was no whitewash.

Its conclusion: There is no park area, not even the most remote, that has not suffered demonstrable damage. One resounding lesson of *State of the Parks, 1980* is that no park is an island any more, or can be. Some of the threats from outside are as uncontrollable as acts of God. It would take the transformation of our industrial society, the transformation of the traveling public, and the creation of buffer zones 100 or 200 miles wide to defend against them.

Qualified Homage to Thoreau

Before I get around to saying why I think that Walden Woods absolutely must be preserved from subdivision and development, let me confess that, much as I admire Thoreau's hard-mouthed intellectual integrity and his knotty grappler's mind, I have some reservations about him. There are writings of his that I admire more than *Walden*—the essay "Walking," for example, which is superb from first line to last, and "Civil Disobedience," though this latter is as explosive as dynamite caps, and should not be left around where children might find it and play with it. Reading *Walden*, I am alternately exhilarated and exasperated, as some of the author's contemporaries were with the man himself. In one paragraph he may say something that has been waiting a thousand years to be said so well; in the next he is capable of something so outrageous that it sets my teeth on edge.

With the Thoreau who observed and participated in nature, the Thoreau who loved wildness, and the Thoreau who trusted physical labor so long as it was not a compulsion, and who mistrusted material ambition, I am completely in accord. It is Thoreau the moralizing enemy of the tradition to which he owes all his own authority who puts me off. Especially in the first chapter, "Economy," he reveals himself to be a Wordsworthian romantic, and a self-absorbed one at that, with an underdeveloped social sense, a limited patience with his fellow men, and an independence that frequently amounts to pig-headedness.

Like any zealot, he is intemperate. The individualism that in moderate doses would be bracing sometimes becomes shrill and toxic. At times he sounds perilously like his spiritual descendants of the 1960s, who trusted no one over thirty and believed that they existed outside of, and were exempt from, the society they were protesting. What I miss in him, as I missed it in the more extreme rebels of the 1960s, is the acknowledgment that their society shaped them, that without it every individual of them would be a sort of Sasquatch, a solitary animal without language, thought, tradition, obligation, or commitment. It is culture, tradition, that teaches us to be human, teaches us almost everything, including how to protest and what to protest about.

I never hear Thoreau admitting this—in fact, he often specifically denies it, and his denials raise my temperature. "How about a little well-deserved humility?" I feel like asking him. It is like arguing with a television screen, but it eases the mind.

The fact is, it is precisely Thoreau's repudiation of the dead hand of the past that makes him so excruciatingly American. He is a caricature of our ahistorical weakness. He pretends to believe that all experience is not merely fruitless, but damaging. "Men think they are wiser by experience, that is, by failure," he remarks in the "Economy" chapter. "I have always been regretting that I was not as wise as the day I was born." And further, "Age is no better, hardly as well, qualified for an instructor as youth, for it has not profited so much as it has lost." (Here come the spontaneous, blind-leading-the-blind Free Universities of the sixties.) And finally, in a foreshadowing of the "no one over thirty" proscription, "I have lived some thirty years on this planet, and I have yet to hear the first syllable of valuable or even earnest advice from my seniors."

No benefit from his experience at Harvard College, then? Who taught him to read Latin and Greek? Who directed him to the Bhagavad Gita? And what was clogging his ears during the seasons when he lived in Emerson's house as a member of the family?

Extreme statements have their value as shock; they stimulate response and debate. As an outline for action, which is more or less how they are proposed, they can be poisonous. Nobody, in fact, can fully mean such things, and Thoreau reveals that he doesn't, either. While denying authority to any elder, he reveres the elders of literature and philosophy, he quotes us Homer and Shakespeare and the Indian mystics. Denying that there are philosophers any more, but only professors of philosophy, he undermines himself and disparages the people who have been his tutors and friends. Denying the validity of experience, he constantly (and properly) cites his own to bolster his beliefs.

Civil disobedience came easier to Thoreau than to most people because he never cared much for the civil aspects of life in the first place. His antisocial stance is very American, like his independence, but it is less a philosophical position than a temperamental dislike of influence and control. He has a loner's aversion to society, a need for private space. Instead of working to improve the world, he said, one should try only to make oneself "one of the world's worthies." As a companion, he was rather chilly. Emerson said he would as lief take hold of an oak limb as Henry's arm.

Even his prose style and his literary tastes trouble me. His style is didactic and apothegmatic to a degree. ("The mass of men lead lives of quiet desperation." "In the long run, men hit only what they aim at." "Trade curses everything it handles; and though you trade in messages from heaven, the whole curse of trade attaches to the business.") Being a Transcendentalist, a product of his tradition and his times, he finds every natural object or act emblematic of some larger Truth. The sentences which report these truths are declarative and dogmatic, and when read aloud they tend to have the same tune. They suggest a mind impervious to interruption or diversion, the kind of mind that cannot discuss, but only assert. He adds insult to injury, and offends the storyteller in me, by expressing contempt for fictions of all kinds; and yet he frequently invents little fables and parables from which he plucks meanings like a man cracking and eating walnuts. It is the moral that interests him, not the story, and in that he differs temperamentally from me.

This sounds like a litany of offenses, a list of reasons why Walden Woods should *not* be preserved as a memorial to Thoreau. It has no such intention, but so long as we are running through it, let us make one addition. It is that Thoreau's experiment in spartan living fudged its declared restrictions, and that the lessons Thoreau drew from it are therefore less persuasive than they sound.

The land on which he built his cabin was not his; he squatted on it in a most American way. On this borrowed ground, for a few dollars' worth of old boards, bricks, mortar, and sand, and by the application of his own labor, he made himself a shelter that satisfied all his limited needs. His demonstration of how little it takes to live, and live healthily and well, stirs the mind. So does his demonstration of how far personal independence will take us. Over the past 140 years thousands of people, singly or in couples, have taken off to places where they can escape the rat-race, own their horizon, live close to nature, and subsist on fish and moose-burgers. Thoreau was the model for most of them, probably.

But notice the moral he draws from his Walden experience (experience being synonymous with failure, as he said): "I thus found that the student who wishes for a shelter can obtain one for a lifetime at an expense not greater than the rent he now pays annually." So? Maybe, if there is land out there free for the stealing or squatting on, and if we can find some complaisant freeholder who doesn't mind our cutting down his trees for lumber or firewood and thus, as Thoreau says, "improving the property." Maybe, if there are people, presumably some of those who live lives of quiet desperation, who will lend us the wheelbarrows, shovels, axes, hammers, and hoes we need; and if we know of friendly attics where chairs may be had for the labor of taking them away. And if our own independence allows us to sponge on those we scorn or pity.

Maybe it is the morality of property and ownership that makes this seem less than admirable to me. But I wish Thoreau had felt these squattings and borrowings as acts that entailed some sort of obligation. I am reminded of the hippie girl from the Haight-Ashbury district of San Francisco who some time in the sixties was stopped by a policeman from picking flowers from a bed in Golden Gate Park. She was angry. "They're not your flowers," she told the cop. "They're God's flowers." She might have been quoting one of the more extreme passages of *Walden*.

Thoreau does not strike me as a completely dependable guide to conduct. He refuses to pay the social dues that everybody owes. One reason for his continuing popularity is that he seems to offer an excuse for not doing what many overburdened people don't want to do. But for me, at least, his formula for plain living and high thinking has a flaw in it from the beginning. His economy is uncomfortably close to that of the desocialized hoboes of "The Bum Song":

> *For we are three bums, three jolly old bums*
> *We live like royal Turks.*
> *We have good luck in bumming our chuck,*
> *God bless the man that works.*

Nevertheless, having said all this, and assuming that it is all true, I have not diminished Thoreau's stature by a millimeter, or reduced the significance of Walden Woods by a milligram. Walden must be preserved and made into a shrine, not just because it is a pretty wood surrounding a little pond in suburban Massachusetts, or because any pretty little wood or pond saved is a step gained on a bearable future, but because this little pond is a glowing spot in the American memory, and because Thoreau made it so by living a couple of years on its shore.

Transcendentalist that he was, he made Walden Pond into a symbol of American possibility, and his own living routines into a paradigm of the American experience. If, as Robert Frost has said, the land was ours before we were the land's, Thoreau was one of those who showed us how to make ourselves the land's. His deeper and deeper penetration into Walden's secrets, his closer and closer participation in the pond's life and the pond's seasons, are a miniaturized and syncopated parallel to our invasion, use, and gradual understanding of the continent. His personal independence was the shadow of American cultural autonomy, his rebellion from Concord echoed America's rebellion from Europe.

He could be wrong, as I have surlily tried to demonstrate; but when he was right he was often spectacularly right, and he was, right or wrong, American to the marrow. His withdrawal from obligation and domination, his loner streak, were paralleled in thousands of lives across the whole history of America's frontiers. He did not invent the antisocial stance he sometimes took, but he gave it and all the cultural tendencies that surrounded it their most telling expression. The rebels of the 1960s found him unerringly, and overstated their case as he had overstated his.

But it was in his love of wildness, his perception that "in wildness is the preservation of the world," that he spoke his nation's mind at its best and highest reach. There is little of that in *Walden*—he was learning it there, but did not formulate it until later—but Walden is the proper place to commemorate it, for how do you make a significant human monument in the midst of the Maine woods?

No, Walden is the place for Thoreau's monument as surely as Washington is the place for the temples we have erected to Jefferson and Lincoln. This little lake within sight of the tracks and sound of the train whistle should be part of the American iconography. But we need no marble columns. The pond itself, and the creatures that find life in it and in the woods that surround it, are the most fitting monument for the man who took so much from them, and gave it back in unforgettable terms to his countrymen.

When it is dedicated, I will go there and walk the shore arguing with Thoreau's ghost. But I will go there.

Living on Our Principal

When this forming civilization assembles its Bible, its record of the physical and spiritual pilgrimage of the American people, the account of its stewardship in the Land of Canaan, Aldo Leopold's *A Sand County Almanac* will belong in it, one of the prophetic books, the utterance of an American Isaiah.

"To understand the fashion of any life," Mary Austin said in *The Land of Little Rain*, "one must know the land it is lived in and the procession of the year." Leopold's essays follow with love the procession of the year in a Wisconsin county raped and abandoned by the loggers, and slowly recovering. They cry woe for what we have done to the earth's fairest continent and to the plant and animal species we found in it. They also analyze the errors of understanding and attitude and aim that have led us to failure just short of calamitous; and they suggest a change of heart and mind, a personal conversion, a reversal of individual and communal carelessness, which might lead to changes in public policy and let us still salvage and partially reclaim our earth and ourselves. What Leopold hoped for was the gradual spread of a "land ethic," built upon a scientific understanding of the earth and earth processes, but infused with a personal, almost religious respect for life and for the earth that generates and supports it.

On the face of it, a land ethic does not seem much of a defense against the greed that has consistently moved us, nor against the conception of land as a commodity to be bought, sold, and exploited without regard for its living continuities, nor against the twentieth-century technology that gives us such power to destroy. Nevertheless, the land ethic goes to the heart of the matter. Leopold was not one of those throbbing nature lovers who, as he said, write bad verse on birchbark. He was a scientist, one of the first to profess the new science of ecology. As a forester and game manager he had seen for himself, in many places, the slow death of the land, and he knew that our unchecked effort to make everything safe and comfortable for our own species at the expense of all others could eventually destroy us along with the earth we depend on.

He told us many things that have by now become truisms of the environmental movement. "The old prairie (or any biome) lived by the diversity of its plants and animals," he wrote, "all of which were useful because the sum total of their cooperations and competitions achieved continuity." He had the faith in the natural order that some economists have in the free market. Human interference and management break down the food chains and tear the web of intricate interdependence. Unless done with care, discretion, and restraint, they are sure to result in land-sickness, and can result in total land death, as in the man-made deserts of the world.

Not only the burn-plant-and-move-on agriculture of some primitive peoples, but our own scientific agriculture is capable of great long-range harm. Monoculture, in which all the roots are at the same soil level and all the plants are subject to the same pests; over-grazing; manipulations of surface and sub-surface water; the cutting of timber on the watersheds; even deep plowing—these can bring on, severally or together, soil exhaustion, erosion, salinization, depletion of the water table, the death of species, and the spread of liberated or imported weeds.

We kill the thing we love, Leopold said, "and so we the pioneers have killed our wilderness. . . . The congressmen who voted money to clear the ranges of bears were the sons of pioneers. They acclaimed the superior virtues of the frontiersman, but they strove with might and main to make an end of the frontier."

None of that sounds new in 1985. Except in its scientific justifications it was not new even in 1949. The lament for our wastefulness and greed runs like a leitmotif through our literature from very early times. James Fenimore Cooper, our first significant novelist, voiced it before our frontier had moved beyond the Great Lakes. Read the scene in *The Pioneers* (1823) in which the townspeople of an upstate New York settlement, in their frenzy to reap God's plenty, fire into flocks of passenger pigeons with artillery. Read the passage in *The Prairie* (1827) in which Cooper asks passionately what the axemen will do when they have cut their way from sea to sea. (We know what some of them do. They sit in Eureka bars and foam at the mouth about Redwood National Park, or they slip into the Avenue of the Giants after dark and with their chainsaws, out of sheer spite, girdle thousand-year-old trees.)

Nature, and the love of it, is a major theme in others of that generation. It is there in Thoreau, Emerson, Muir, Burroughs, Whitman, and it continues into the present as an unbroken double song of love and lamentation. Lamentation is the conscience speaking. Below the energy, enthusiasm, and optimism of our early years—below the Whitman strain—there is always the dark bass of warning, nostalgia, loss, and somewhat bewildered guilt.

So it was not for its novelty that people responded to Leopold's call for a land ethic. It was for his assurance, an assurance forecast much earlier in the work of George Perkins Marsh and John Wesley Powell, that science corroborates our concern, not our optimism: that preserving the natural world we love has totally practical and unsentimental justifications. Many Americans will discount poets and mistrust barefoot nature lovers, and schoolmarms who cry "Woodman, spare that tree!" and Indians who revere the earth as their mother; but they find it harder to shrug off what they think of as the "practical" evidence of scientists.

It was Leopold's distinction that he combined and reconciled two strains of thought. He had no romantic revulsion against plowing, or cutting trees, or hunting birds and animals, or any of the things we do to make our living from the earth. He was only against the furious excess of our exploitation, our passion to live on our principal. It struck him as sad that unexploited land, land left alone, seemed actively to offend our continent-busters. (We hear them still. They are the people who resent what they call the "locking-up" of resources.)

151

"Progress," Leopold wrote, "cannot abide that farmland and marshland, wild and tame, exist in mutual toleration and harmony," and so we have assiduously drained most of the marshes where ducks, geese, and cranes used to add their seasonal magic to our life. Plowmen and stockmen were never able to resist putting every square rod of grassland to use and over-use, with the result that many once-luxuriant prairie plants are now extinct, and others survive only along fencelines where the plow could not reach, or within railroad rights-of-way fenced against both plows and grazing animals. The prairie biome is weakened in ways we can only guess.

Unlike many early conservationists, including John Muir, Leopold was as suspicious of recreation as he was of logging and agriculture. He noted that the impulse to refresh ourselves out of doors has damaged many of our remaining wild places—and he wrote before off-road vehicles had carried damage close to ruin. The lure of tourist money, he said, is a gun pointed at the heart of the wild, and he was right.

One example: for the last thirty years we have had to watch the congressional delegation of Utah, one of the most marvelously endowed of the fifty states, do its best to cheapen and imperil the magnificence of southern Utah by promoting freeways on which tourists could view it at seventy miles an hour. The only really creative part of recreational engineering, Leopold insisted, is to promote *perception*. "Recreational development is a job not of building roads into lovely country, but of building receptivity into the still unlovely human mind."

With Thoreau, he believed that "in wildness is the preservation of the world," and he believed in wildness not because it is sublime but because it is all our hope, the reservoir of all future possibility. "Wilderness was never a homogeneous raw material. It was very diverse, and the resulting artifacts are very diverse. These differences in the end product are known as cultures. The rich diversity of the world's cultures reflects a corresponding diversity in the wilds that gave them birth."

He was one who made us begin to understand that wilderness is indispensable for science and survival. We need to keep the wild gene pool diverse and healthy, if only because our domesticated species are subject to devastating pests, and may need some genetic assistance.

We need to understand, better than we do, why some species have disappeared forever and some have proliferated as weeds. Without rejecting Emerson's definition of a weed as a species for which man has not yet found a use, Leopold might have pointed to weeds as species that, imported into environments where they have no competitors, or liberated from their natural competitors by our intervention, have gone out of control. To counter weeds, as well as to deal with the other ills we bring on, we resort to what he called "land doctoring." The art of land doctoring, he wrote, "is being practiced with vigor, but the science of land health is still to be born."

New or old, those ideas were heretical in 1949, and in some quarters still are. They smack of socialism and the public good. They impose limits and restraints. They are anti-Progress. They dampen American initiative. They fly in the face of the faith that land is a commodity, the very foundation-stone of American opportunity, and that it must be put to the use that the assessor's office would certify as the highest use—meaning economic use. Oil drillers, miners, lumbermen, stockmen (all deeply involved in the rape of the public domain), recreation entrepreneurs (just as deeply involved), and farmers concerned to get maximum short-term productivity out of their family or corporate farms, water-users busily pumping down the water table of desert valleys, and developers hungry to squeeze the ultimate building site out of a parcel—none of these have adopted Leopold's views with enthusiasm.

Nevertheless, he thought there might be an outside chance of correcting our course—if we could expand our ethics to take in land as well as people. Those twelve slave girls whom Odysseus hanged for their indiscretions roused no sympathy or guilt in either Odysseus or Homer. We have developed a tenderer conscience about such matters in three thousand years, we inherit the world-wide revulsion against slavery that took place in the nineteenth century, we have been taught to respect human rights no matter whose. If we can do as much about understanding the rights of the natural environment we have a chance.

That was the way Aldo Leopold saw it at mid-century. His book has taught tens of thousands of Americans to see it in the same way, and the thirty-six years since the publication of *A Sand County Almanac* have surely been years of increasingly acute environmental awareness. But as the century explodes toward its end we may well ask if the strain of thought that Leopold developed and stimulated has had much effect on the vague, changeful, and uninformed entity we call the public mind.

Are we any closer than we were in 1949 to a land ethic as widely acknowledged (however widely evaded) as our commitment to civil rights? Or have we, indulging habits learned on our careless frontiers and given continuing force by the Reagan administration, pushed closer to the showdown that, if not so dramatic and totally annihilating as the atomic showdown we simultaneously risk, will surely bring a sharp decline in the quality of American life?

Certain inescapable facts are relevant. At mid-century the population of the United States was 150 million. Since then we have added more people than the whole country contained in 1900, and now number above 230 million. That 53 percent growth above the 1950 base has meant what we in our lives are witnessing: more mouths to feed, a greater and greater demand for energy to run our industries and our homes, more digging for minerals and coal, more cutting of timber, more drilling for oil on- and off-shore, more automobiles to carry us around and foul the air, more paving-over of land for freeways, roads, driveways, parking areas, and tennis courts, more orchards and fields gone into subdivisions or industrial plants or shopping centers, more bombing and missile ranges in the deserts, more ski resorts in the mountains, more smokestacks and acid rain, more Love Canals and toxic waste sites and more dirty politics to cover them up, less green, less space, less freedom, less health, more intensive working of the soils still left in agriculture, a longer and longer stretching of a rubber band not indefinitely stretchable, a temporarily more comfortable, ultimately less plentiful, increasingly less spiritually rewarding life.

Precisely because we could not ignore the symptoms, we managed some corrections, especially during the 1960s and 1970s, before the Reagan administration undertook to dismantle the gains. Most of the corrections we measure by federal laws; and though Leopold himself warned us against expecting the government to exercise our conscience for us, we would be in infinitely worse shape without the Clean Air Act, the Clean Water Act, the Strip Mining Act, the Wilderness Act, the Federal Land Policy and Management Act (FLPMA), the Land and Water

Conservation Fund Act, the Alaska National Interest Lands Conservation Act (ANILCA), and many other laws that have been enacted since Leopold wrote. Without such laws to evade or circumvent or confront, James Watt and Anne Gorsuch Burford would have done even greater harm than they succeeded in doing before being forced out of office.

Also, in the very fact that they were forced out of office, that they outraged the environmental conscience of enough people to do themselves in, there is evidence that Leopold's hope for a growing individual and public awareness was not totally naive. Their fall at least enforced caution on the administration, which discovered that it couldn't ride roughshod over the body of environmental law. One hardly expects a change in policy, but one expects greater circumspection.

Other indications: when Leopold wrote, there were only a few principal environmental organizations, each devoted to a single issue and none (not even the Audubon Society, which had begun that way) politically militant. In addition to the Audubon, which had been organized to protect birds from plume hunters, there was the Sierra Club, for mountaineers; the Izaak Walton League, for fishermen; the Wilderness Society, devoted to wilderness and wildlife; and the Save the Redwoods League, devoted to just what its title indicated.

Now there are dozens: the Nature Conservancy, the Trust for Public Land, the Open Space Trust, the Environmental Defense Fund, the Natural Resources Defense Council, the League of Conservation Voters, the Sempervirens Fund, Trout Unlimited, Ducks Unlimited, the National Wildlife Federation—a long list, plus a thousand regional and local defense committees organized to protect a valued local resource from destructive exploitation.

The spirit of all those groups is aroused and aggressive. James Watt himself noted that one of the first effects of his application of Reagan principles was to double or triple the membership of the conservation organizations—the "environmental extremists"—and to galvanize their political activism. Watt and Gorsuch walked into a buzzsaw that they had apparently thought was a wreath of wildflowers.

Thus, since Leopold's day we have seen not only a worsening of all the environmental sicknesses, but the development of an environmental constituency that grows steadily larger and more militant. Our national parks have always had a loyal party of backers, in and out of Congress, and until 1981 (with brief lapses during the Truman and Eisenhower administrations) they were steadily added to in order to provide for a growing public need. Essentially the same constituency pushed through ANILCA, which though signed by Mr. Reagan was really the last conservation act of Mr. Carter. The same constituency had brought about, in 1964, the wilderness system that Leopold had first proposed for the Gila country of New Mexico, back in the 1920s.

That old party of loyalists has been immensely augmented in the past twenty years as people began to protest dirty air, poisoned water, and creeping uglification. But how much evidence is there that a real conversion has taken place in a substantial part of the public? Earth Year fired up the college campuses briefly and subsided to something less than a conflagration. Is there anything to the environmental movement now besides the activity of those irreconcilable "environmental extremists" who so exasperated and frustrated Mr. Watt? Is environmentalism any more than the effort of a comfortable middle class to preserve its amenities? Do workers share in it? Blacks? Chicanos? College students? The young? The old? Is there perhaps even a backlash against environmentalism?

I can ask those questions, but not answer them. I am not a statistical man, and have no numbers, and probably would not trust them if I had them. But I have to believe that we have done better in pushing for and enacting environmental legislation than we have in creating and spreading a real environmental conscience. We have reached the immediately educable. The ineducable, who I am afraid include Mr. Reagan, continue to live by the myths of old-fashioned American enterprise, and are either indifferent or actively hostile.

The environmental lobby, potent during the 1960s and '70s, and still formidable, perhaps does represent the views of a special-interest minority rather than a broad and united public opinion. That it has been a disinterested special-interest group, bent upon securing a truly public good and resisting special privilege, gives it a suspiciously pinkish tinge to those who cannot conceive of disinterested action. It is hard to resist publicly because it asks nothing for itself, but it is easy to disparage as an impractical and probably socialist frill.

In our time we have seen the environmentalism that used to be a bipartisan movement fall by default to the Democrats. No Republican administration in recent memory has been better than tepid on conservation issues, and most have been reluctant or opposed. None has picked up the mantle of Theodore Roosevelt—and even Roosevelt came under fire from many in his own party who resented what "that damned cowboy" was doing to the country.

Herbert Hoover and his Secretary of the Interior Ray Lyman Wilbur did their best to give away the public domain to the states. Warren G. Harding and *his* Secretary of the Interior Albert B. Fall gave us the Teapot Dome scandal. Dwight D. Eisenhower and *his* Secretary of the Interior Douglas McKay threw the public lands to the corporate wolves. Ronald Reagan and *his* Secretary of the Interior James Watt sponsored the blind, greedy, and reactionary outburst from western stockmen that was known as the Sagebrush Rebellion, and did their best to open up the public lands on- and off-shore to coal and oil leasing at bargain basement prices. And even in Democratic administrations, but especially in Republican ones, the U.S. Forest Service for which Aldo Leopold worked many years of his life has persisted in its policy of board feet, at whatever cost to the environmental values that Leopold helped to define.

But if modern Republicans have not, as a party, espoused conservation, many individuals who would like to be Republicans have done so, and the Democratic party has happily adopted the environment as its own to save. The trouble is—and this is a commentary on how thinly distributed the environmental conscience is—it has not been a winning political issue. In the ordinary voter's hierarchy of problems it pretty clearly ranks below the economy, the arms race, the nuclear threat, the women's movement, social security, civil rights, and other matters.

Because environmental degradation is, as Stewart Udall said, a quiet crisis, a creeping calamity, it makes news only when it crests in some dramatic episode such as the Love Canal or Rita Lavelle's handling of toxic waste sites. It makes news because of people's fear or someone's misfeasance, not because of people's consciences.

And fear is much more likely to be aroused by poisoned air or polluted water than by diminishing soil fertility or increased erosion. The single environmental issue significant in the 1984 political campaigns was acid rain, and most Americans outside the affected Northeast probably didn't have much feeling even for that. Clean up the worst of the waste sites and improve the unbreathable air and the polluted groundwater, and the public environmental conscience might all but evaporate. Back in Ohio and Indiana, where the sulphur dioxide comes from and where cleaning up the stack emissions might cost every ratepayer some money, it has already all but evaporated.

What is more, the air, and to a lesser extent the water, exist in our minds as free public necessities. Land is something else: property. A land ethic calls not only for corporate scrupulousness but for a modification of our acquisitive impulses, something we have not yet learned with regard to real estate dealings. What is your saved open space and rescued air is my spoiled opportunity, and this is the land of opportunity, isn't it? And opportunity is measured in dollars, isn't it?

For every devoted individual who donates money to save a redwood grove, there are fifty who would, perhaps unhappily but moved by a higher necessity, cut it down for profit. Set up a new national park, with its opportunities for health, quiet, beauty, and the recreation of the spirit, against an opportunity for everyone to make a sum of hard dollars, and you know which opportunity most Americans would choose. Most people anywhere. Americans are no worse than other people. They have just had more practice in making money and wasting land, and more encouragement to go on doing so.

One area where a substantial number of people *have* had their minds changed is the preservation of wildlife and wildlife habitat. Not only the National Wildlife Federation, the largest of the environmental organizations, but hunters and gun clubs have realized the necessity of conservation if shooters are to have anything to shoot. And over the past thirty years there has been a flood of wildlife films that, being among the few things on television suitable for children's viewing, have beyond question educated many young people to feel kindly toward wildlife, including the predators with whose evil nature parents used to scare children a generation ago.

These films appeal to the Bambi impulse, featuring cute pairs of bear cubs, river otter pups, or cheetah kittens which go out into their wilderness environment and through comic misadventures learn about life. But better sentimentality than ruthlessness, better an impulse to pat and cuddle than to scream and shoot. By making a niche for itself in television programming, wildlife may have done more to save itself than all the devoted organizations together.

But cute otter pups, or a spotted fawn curled up in the concealing grass, threaten no one. A national park or a wilderness reservation that blocks development may seem to. The closer we are to economic insecurity, the more willing we are, by and large, to sacrifice grasslands for the jobs and short-term profits of a strip mine. The harder our noses are to the grindstone, the more willing we are to suffer the ugliness and poisons that emanate from the smokestack plant on which we depend for a paycheck. The lunch bucket argument has always been the most effective argument, even when it is misapplied, against environmental restraints.

Thus some citizens of Moab, Utah, and Hanford, Washington, vie for a nuclear waste dump in their community. Thus workers in Ohio and Indiana resent being told that their jobs are producing acid rain. The attitudes of bosses need not be considered, for they do not have to live with what they create. But an environmental conscience in people who live close to the margin may often seem more self-sacrificial than anyone has a right to ask.

Not only the struggling and desperate are hard to reach and persuade. Those who use the deserts, mountains, and beaches for wheeled recreation are at least as destructive and less forgivable. When I wonder whether the barbarians who tear up fragile desert eco-systems with their frenzied trail bike rallies ever stop to think what they are doing, I remember the remark of a nineteenth-century politician in another context. "Does a dog stop for a marriage license?"

We are a long way yet from where Leopold hoped we might one day arrive. Corporate greed may be controlled by legislation—though not likely during the present administration. Special lands may be set aside, as in the past, as national parks, wildlife refuges, seashores, lakeshores. But we are running out of the raw material for such reservations, and there is no more where it came from. Moreover, the tighter the pinch, the more persuasive the lunch bucket argument against "unproductive" stewardship. The only real success, the creation and spread of an environmental conscience which will be as angered by the abuse of land as most

159

consciences would now be angered by the abuse of a child—that may have to wait a few hundred or a few thousand years, and we may not have that much time.

The land ethic is not a widespread public conviction. If it were, the Reagan administration would not have been given a second term. The lunch bucket argument, and the deification of greed as the American Way, reelected by a landslide one of the most antienvironmental presidents in our history. Aldo Leopold would not be encouraged.

There will always be those who believe that the public domain is owned and maintained by the rest of us for our exclusive exploitation and use. There will always be those who never breathed deeply of the wind off clean grassland, or enjoyed the shade of a hillside oak on a July day, or watched with pleasure as some wild thing slid out of sight, and who will never see the reasons for living with the earth instead of against it.

The number of functional illiterates that our free public education produces does not make us sanguine about educating a majority of the public to respect the earth, a harder form of literacy. Leopold's land ethic is not a fact but a task. Like old age, it is nothing to be overly optimistic about. But consider the alternative.

Bernard DeVoto

When Bernard DeVoto died on November 13, 1955, he was one of the most visible and most controversial figures in America, and had been for thirty years. Though he had begun as a novelist, it was in other roles that most of his public knew him: as historian, essayist, editor, hack-writer, pamphleteer, custodian of the Bill of Rights and the public conscience and the public lands. "A literary department store," he called himself, and he was vehement in every department. Readers responded to him with equal vehemence. Many respected and revered him and depended on him for their thinking and their courage in public issues. Some hated him with a passion. All had ample opportunity to know his opinions, for he was not only a frequent contributor to all sorts of magazines, but he was for a short time (November 1936 to March 1938) editor of the *Saturday Review of Literature*, and for twenty years, from 1935 until his death, he wrote the Easy Chair in *Harper's Magazine*, the oldest and perhaps the most influential column in American journalism.

The staff at *Harper's* loved him as a curmudgeon with a heart of mush; they said he collected underdogs the way a blue serge suit collects lint. John Fischer, the editor of *Harper's* during DeVoto's last years, thought of him as "a combat journalist, who charged headlong into any public controversy that got his dander up," and who "enjoyed a fight more than any man I ever knew." Malcolm Cowley, who had felt the DeVoto lash early, did not meet the ogre until much later, and to his surprise found him personally a pleasant man. But when he got in front of a typewriter, Cowley said ruefully, "how he did like to swing the shellalagh!"

From the time in the mid-Twenties when he published his first essays in H. L. Mencken's *American Mercury*, his career had been controversy. He had broken spears against the progressive schools and the football colleges, against Van Wyck Brooks and the young intellectuals, against the literary censors of Watch and Ward, against the communists and Popular Fronters, against J. Edgar Hoover and the FBI, against Senator McCarthy, the Reece Committee, and other official enemies of civil liberties, against academic historians and southern revisionists, against the "beautiful thinking" of the literary who hunted in pack, against western stockmen and their political backers. To some he seemed merely contrary: when the public weathervane veered Left, he veered Right; when it veered Right, he veered Left. In the 1930s the *Daily Worker* called him a fascist. By the 1950s, the *Worker* was quoting his Easy Chairs with approval, old antagonists such as F. O. Matthiessen and the editors of *New Republic* were his somewhat astonished allies, and Senator McCarthy was denouncing "one Richard DeVoto" as a communist.

Early in 1937, pondering DeVoto's aggressive editorship of the *Saturday Review of Literature*, Edmund Wilson found him difficult to label, and rather plaintively called on him to stand and declare himself in the ideological struggles of his time. Who was he? What did he believe in? What did he want? Why was he so angry?

Some of the questions were rhetorical, some unanswerable. DeVoto could never have explained why he was so angry, any more than a fish could have explained why it breathed through gills. And Wilson had to know who DeVoto was—he had been around for considerably more than a decade, in postures of constant challenge. But there was every reason why Wilson could not understand DeVoto. There were enough differences of background and belief to make them incomprehensible to one another, though Wilson was probably more comprehensible to DeVoto than DeVoto was to Wilson. For DeVoto was a westerner, something easterners have seldom understood, and a belligerent westerner at that. Moreover, he was a shirtsleeve democrat, almost a populist—a

Declaration-of-Independence, Bill-of-Rights, Manifest-Destiny American democrat, inhabiting intellectual territory that the then-reigning arbiters of opinion thought uninhabitable.

Born in Ogden, Utah, on January 11, 1897, son of a Mormon mother and a Catholic father, DeVoto had studied first with the Sisters of the Sacred Heart and later in the Ogden public schools, had attended the University of Utah for one year, had transferred to Harvard, had been uprooted from there before graduation by World War I, had gone to OTC and been commissioned a second lieutenant of infantry, had served as a musketry instructor at Camp Perry, Ohio, and after being demobilized had returned to Harvard to graduate, *cum laude* and Phi Beta Kappa, with the class of 1920. After an interlude in Ogden made disastrous by a nervous breakdown, his mother's death, a collapsed love affair, and his hatred of his native town, he had escaped to a job as instructor of English at Northwestern University, in Evanston, Illinois, where he shortly married the prettiest girl in his freshman class, Helen Avis MacVicar, and set out to write his way to fame.

By the time Edmund Wilson was asking his questions in *New Republic*, DeVoto had already left Northwestern for Harvard, and Harvard for New York, and had written four novels: *The Crooked Mile* (1924), an unfriendly portrait of a western town very like Ogden; *Chariot of Fire* (1926), about a frontier prophet not unlike the Mormon prophet Joseph Smith; *The House of Sun-Goes-Down* (1928), a sequel to *The Crooked Mile*; and *We Accept with Pleasure* (1934), set in Boston and Cambridge during the Sacco and Vanzetti trial. Before he was done, DeVoto would publish a fifth novel, *Mountain Time* (1947), under his own name, and under the pseudonym of John August four others: *Troubled Star* (1939), *Rain before Seven* (1940), *Advance Agent* (1942), and *The Woman in the Picture* (1944). Before or after 1937, and under any name, his novels never brought him the recognition and reputation he hoped for, but the pseudonymous books, all serials written for *Collier's*, subsidized his more important writing. In the preface to *The Year of Decision: 1846* (1943), the first of his great trilogy of western histories, DeVoto ironically acknowledged the "periodic assistance from Mr. John August" that had made the book possible.

The major accomplishments were still in the future when Wilson called on DeVoto to stand and deliver, but the accomplishments of the past were not to be overlooked. Besides teaching at Northwestern and at Harvard—and his teaching had the same challenging provocativeness as his essays—DeVoto had had two years of experience in upsetting apple-carts as editor of the previously stuffy *Harvard Graduates' Magazine* (1930–1932). He had been general editor of a short-lived but admirable series of reprints of lost American classics, the Americana Deserta series. In 1936 he had collected in a book, *Forays and Rebuttals*, twenty-three of his essays which stood the test of time and a hard re-reading. (This was the first of four such collections; the others are *Minority Report*, 1940; *The Hour*, 1951; and *The Easy Chair*, 1955.) And he had published in 1932 the book that made him an instant reputation not only as a fierce controversialist but as a student of American society, especially frontier society. *Mark Twain's America*, which he captioned "an essay in the correction of ideas," examined Van Wyck Brooks's theory, expressed in *The Ordeal of Mark Twain*, that Mark Twain was stultified by a puritanical culture and a puritanical mother, and reduced by these malign influences from a potential artist to a mere humorist. It demolished Brooks's theory with a thoroughness and violence that appalled and infuriated Brooks's friends; but it also demonstrated Bernard DeVoto as a social historian of insight, range, and formidable learning, and forecast the historian of the West who was still to be developed in him.

In his foreword, DeVoto had rejected the temptation to explain Mark Twain simply or according to any formula, as he accused Brooks of doing. "I do not believe in simplicities about art, artists, or the subjects of criticism," he wrote. "I have no theory about Mark Twain. It is harder to conform one's book to ascertainable fact than to theorize, and harder to ascertain facts than to ignore them. In literature, beautiful simplicities usually result from the easier method, and, in literature, the armchair assertion that something must be true is the begetter of unity."

There, if Wilson had looked, was the explanation of DeVoto. Throughout his career, while opponents accused him of flipping back and forth, he held to the tests of fact and experience. Viewed in retrospect, his principles reveal themselves as completely consistent. He was a rock in the surf of changing minds, fickle fashions, liberal hesitations, doubts, recantations, and gods that failed. Though his interests moved steadily away from literature and toward history and politics and conservation, he distrusted *a priori* thinking wherever he found it, and his nickname among his colleagues at the Breadloaf Writers' Conference, where he taught for a good many summers during the 1930s and 1940s, was Ad Hoc.

Over a period of three decades, his writings say it in a hundred contexts. In a double editorial in the *Saturday Review* for February 13, 1937, he said it for Edmund Wilson, who had complained about his lack of "articulated ideas."

"This," he said, "is a demand for a gospel, and I have been acquainted with it since my earliest days. I was brought up in a religion which taught me that man was imperfect but might expect God's mercy—but I was surrounded by a revealed religion founded by a prophet of God, composed of people on their way to perfection, and possessed of an everlasting gospel. I early acquired a notion that all gospels were false and all my experience since then has confirmed it . . . I distrust absolutes. Rather, I long ago passed from distrust of them to opposition. And with them let me include prophecy, simplification, generalization, abstract logic, and especially the habit of mind which consults theory first and experience only afterward."

In a time which spent much of its intellectual and emotional energy debating whether America would go communist or fascist, and when most of the literary leaned left, that pragmatic, skeptical, equilibristic stance was glaringly unorthodox. Distrusting New York as the nest where all the current orthodoxies were laid and hatched, DeVoto consistently earned New York's dislike and disapproval. He refused all the fashionable hooks, however attractively baited. In 1943 he said, "Politically, I am a New Dealer on Election Day and a critic of the New Deal at other times." In 1950 he said, "I am a half-Mugwump, 60 percent New Dealer, 90 percent Populist dirt-roads historian." In 1944, in a last charge against accepted literary opinion, he put together some lectures delivered at the University of Indiana under the title *The Literary Fallacy*, in which he again defended American society from the commonplace assumption that it was a "great gaslighted barbarity" that destroyed its artists. He said instead that its artists had betrayed and misrepresented their society, and called down on his head the wrath of all the literary, especially Sinclair Lewis, whose attack in *The Saturday Review* of April 15, 1944, will probably persist in our literary history simply by virtue of its *ad hominem* virulence.

Through the literary unrest of the Twenties, the leftist temptations of the Thirties, the crisis patriotism of the war years, and the demoralizing witch-hunts of the late Forties and early Fifties, DeVoto reiterated, in woodwinds, strings, and brass, the declaration of belief to which he had been forced by Wilson; and as the political air darkened, so did the DeVoto analysis. Ideas as systematic constructs, ideas unresponsive to the facts of a nation's history and the habits and needs of people, were not merely intellectually offensive but politically dangerous, no matter whether well-meant or ill-meant. (DeVoto's one-time intimate and surrogate father, Robert Frost, put it succinctly in a comment on Henry Wallace. "Henry," he said, "is bound to reform you whether you want to be reformed or not.")

To a mind as truculently independent as DeVoto's, all dogma, whether in religion, literature, history, teaching, or any other endeavor, suppressed thought. In politics, it was a constant threat to freedom. Passionate political dogmas led to machine-gun government; and "idealism, whether moral or metaphysical or literary, may be defined as a cross-lots path to the psychopathic ward, Berchtesgaden, and St. Bartholomew's Eve. Absolutes mean absolutism."

In the pre-war and war years when left-leaning intellectuals had more or less cornered American publications (with the marked exceptions of *Harper's* and *The Saturday Review*) DeVoto was as completely anathema to the political intellectuals as he had earlier been to the literary. He got his revenge, and could not resist airing it, when the faithful began to recant and fall off the Moscow Express, as Malcolm Cowley put it, after the Moscow Trials and especially the Hitler-Stalin pact. In a 1951 Easy Chair entitled "The Ex-Communists," DeVoto commented on these born-again democrats: "The road to an understanding of democracy crosses the communist east forty. Before you can add a column of figures correctly you must first add them wrong. He who would use his mind must first lose it. Various ex-communist intellectuals are offering themselves on just that basis as authorities about what has happened and guides to what must be done. Understand, I am right now *because* I was wrong then. *Only* the ex-communist can understand communism. Trust me to lead you aright now *because* I tried earlier to lead you astray. My intelligence has been vindicated *in that* it made an all-out commitment to error."

In DeVoto's view, the ex-communist had arrived, proud of his mistakes, at precisely the place where any non-communist American had stood all along. "Where, for God's sake, was he when they were distributing minds?" One thing he could be sure of—he himself had been more stoutly at the barricades than the twice-born ones. During the war he had repeatedly tried to free the hands of his friend Elmer Davis, then head of the Office of War Information, to disseminate information instead of soothing syrup and propaganda. "The way to have an informed public opinion is to inform the public." And in the October, 1949, Easy Chair he had capped his long career in defense of civil liberties with "Due Notice to the FBI," an essay that made him stronger and more lasting friends than all his controversies together had made him enemies. He would no longer, he said, discuss anyone in private with any FBI operative. If it was his duty to do so, he would discuss anyone, but only in court, and in the presence of his attorney, not for the dubious uses of a system of informers and secret police.

"I like a country where it's nobody's damned business what magazines anyone reads, what he thinks, whom he has cocktails with. I like a country where we do not have to stuff the chimney against listening ears and where what we say does not go into the FBI files along with a note from S-17 that I may have another wife in California. I like a country where no college-trained flatfeet collect memoranda about us and ask judicial protection for them, a country where when someone makes statements about us to officials he can be held to account. We had that kind of country only a little while ago and I'm for getting it back."

That was who Bernard DeVoto was, and had been, and would continue to be—as dedicated a cultural patriot as the country has had since Emerson, light years away from the literary and political coteries with their Anglophile, Francophile, or Russophile addictions, and 90° divergent from H. L. Mencken, under whose enthusiastic Booboisie-thumping tutelage he had begun. In spite of its frequent failure to live up to itself and its willingness to listen to siren voices, America was what he believed in. He believed in its political principles and its democratic strength, in its always-tumultuous present and its probably-distracted future, and he was stimulated and invigorated by its past.

His enemies called him a philistine. He did not mind—he even embraced the role. And before he was done he would make three major contributions to the American tradition. (1) His essays on civil liberties and public affairs (see especially those in *The Easy Chair*) stand re-reading better than the work of any commentator of his time except E. B. White, who for some years shared the pages of *Harper's* with him and helped make it the most influential magazine of the period. A few of those essays, such as "Due Notice to the FBI" and "Guilt by Distinction," belong among the very best statements of the American gospels. (2) His essays on the West, especially those written during the late 1940s and early 1950s in an almost-singlehanded and spectacularly successful attempt to forestall a grab of public lands by western resource interests, explained the West and the public lands to the rest of the nation as no one else had succeeded in doing, and gave him unquestioned leadership in the modern conservation movement. And (3), his histories, among which one should probably classify *Mark Twain's America*, finally won him the praise and recognition that his novels had failed to win him, including the Pulitzer and Bancroft prizes and the National Book Award.

Before he left a floundering *Saturday Review* in the spring of 1938 and returned to Cambridge, he had undertaken the curatorship of the Mark Twain papers. Out of an eight-year struggle with those and with the Mark Twain Estate would come a book of critical essays, *Mark Twain at Work* (1942), as well as two collections of previously unpublished Mark Twain writings: *Mark Twain in Eruption* (1940) and *Letters from the Earth,* the latter held up by the scruples of Mark Twain's daughter and not published until after DeVoto's death. He continued writing the Easy Chair, to which he always gave a high priority. To support himself he called several times on John August. But to satisfy his own deepest needs, to focus his mind, to bring together what he knew and what he believed about America and especially the West, he began work on the history of a critical year, the year 1846, in which, he felt, the continental surge of Manifest Destiny was consummated, and by the end of which the forces that would bring about the Civil War had all clicked into place like cartridges into the magazine of a rifle. Forced out of teaching and editing, he was ready to become a historian.

Those who had read him on the subject of Ogden, Utah, might have been surprised. Those who had heard him scorn the literary might be astonished. For the historian in DeVoto, when he finally emerged, was a historian of the West, and he was both literary and romantic. The impulse that had driven him to write novels lingered in him like an embarrassing adolescent acne: he approached the history of the West as an enthusiast. Also, the training he had given himself in the handling of character, action, and scene asserted itself strongly when he began to deal with the historical characters and actions of the westward movement. He wrote history like a romantic novelist.

His view of American history was as sweeping as Parkman's. He saw it as a vast panorama, the greatest story in the record of civilized man, shot with lurid colors, strenuous adventures, appalling risks, spectacular follies, broken dreams, outrageous crimes, the loftiest heroisms, and the profoundest tragedies—a panorama rolled forward by mysterious and irresistible forces, social and political, of which the most potent came to be called Manifest Destiny. And if readers asked how someone who thought of the West as a place first plundered by eastern capital and then vulgarized by its own efforts could be so exhilarated by the story of how it was explored and opened, DeVoto could have answered that in this, at least, he was orthodox. Nearly every western writer of quality since Ed Howe wrote *The Story of a Country Town* in 1883 has demonstrated the same ambivalence. Willa Cather did, Mari Sandoz did. Bernard DeVoto did it at the top of his voice. The western present, this feeling goes, is vulgarized and spoiled. The western past was adventure, high purpose, grand country, unspoiled magnificence, an unparalleled spectacle of civilization at its most daring making contact with the virgin continent at its most splendid.

"Sure you're romantic about American history," DeVoto wrote Catherine Drinker Bowen, ". . . it is the most romantic of all histories. . . . If the mad, impossible voyage of Columbus or Cartier or La Salle or Coronado or John Ledyard is not romantic, if the stars did not dance in the sky when the Constitutional Convention met, if Atlantis has any landscape stranger or the other side of the moon any lights or colors or shapes more unearthly than the customary homespun of Lincoln or the morning coat of Jackson, well, I don't know what romance is. Ours is a story mad with the impossible, it is by chaos out of dream . . . and of our dreams there are two things above all others to be said, that only madmen could have dreamed them or would have dared to—and that we have shown a considerable faculty for making them come true."

The Civil War, DeVoto often said, was the single greatest subject available to an American historian. For one reason or another—probably that he himself derived from neither the North nor the South—he felt unqualified to write about the great testing of the Republic. But the second greatest subject, the westward movement, he did feel qualified for, by birth, experience, training, and understanding. He saw the West whole, and he saw it, moreover, in context, as part of the nation's development. A boyhood in the canyons of the Wasatch, coupled with a long exile in the East, had sharpened his senses to the western landscape and western air and light. Some significant part of his beginning as historian may be traced to nostalgia. That should not minimize the knowledge, the masterful overview, that gave his histories scope. It only allowed him to do what he said *The Year of Decision: 1846* aimed to do—"to realize the pre–Civil War, Far Western frontier as personal experience."

Not a small task for one who described himself as a journalist, a man trained not as a historian but as a novelist, and a man who, without an academic job to support him and without a single foundation grant in his entire life, had to support his family and numerous dependents by his unceasing industry as a pamphleteer and hack. He stole the time for it as he could, between Easy Chairs, magazine articles, serials, public controversies, book reviews, and all the demands of a furious twelve- to fifteen-hour day, and in the end these were the books that represented and justified him.

But no one could call Bernard DeVoto an orthodox historian. For one thing, the romantic novelist in him takes advantage of every opportunity for drama and color. As he told his friend Garrett Mattingly, most historians stop on second because there is some theory in the profession that historians do not hit home runs. DeVoto himself never stopped on second if there was a chance of going to third. Though he would not invent dramatic scenes, he would take advantage of everything his sources offered him—as, for instance, he took advantage of the spectacle of the fur rendezvous on the upper Green River in *Across the Wide Missouri*, and the pitiful flight of the Mormons from Nauvoo, the march of the Mormon Battalion, the ghastly camp of the Donner party, and much else, in *The Year of Decision: 1846*.

He was able to recreate these scenes with extraordinary vividness, partly because he relied by preference on first-hand accounts, partly because he himself knew the West, partly because he thought like a novelist and his subject was people in action. But also, by trial and error during the writing of *The Year of Decision: 1846*, he had devised a narrative method that he called "simultaneity." Faced with the problem of carrying forward all the complex actions of his climactic year, he learned to drive them like a twenty-mule team, with his hands full of lines. The Mormon exodus from Nauvoo; the adventures of young Francis Parkman in and around Fort Laramie; the glory-hunting of John Charles Frémont and Commodore Stockton, and the quiet diplomacy of Consul Larkin, in California; the progress of the Mexican War from bluster to declaration to comic opera to deadly combat that trained most of the officers of the greater war that would follow in fifteen years; General Kearney's march to Santa Fe and on to the Pacific, with its sub-plot of the Mormon Battalion; the slow doom of the Donner-Reed party rocking toward its climax in the Sierra—these and other strands move, pause, start again, meet, interweave, illuminate one another. It is a virtuoso performance both in the dexterity of its handling and the vividness with which these actions, the men who made them, and the country they were made in are realized.

The method devised for *The Year of Decision: 1846* worked even better for *Across the Wide Missouri*, which, starting as a set of captions and the story of the western excursions of the Scottish sportsman William Drummond Stewart, evolved into a brilliant history of the mountain fur trade during its peak years. The great men of the fur trade—Bridger, Fitzpatrick, Joe Meek, Black Harris, the enigmatic Captain Bonneville—are all there. So are the missionaries who passed through on their way to Oregon: Marcus Whitman and his opulent wife Narcissa, Henry Spalding who had wooed Narcissa and lost, and had married frail and faded Eliza on the bounce. The two couples shared a tent, not always amicably, all the way across the plains and mountains. And the Indians are there— Sioux, Shoshones, Nez Percés, Blackfeet, in their turmoil of incessant war. Tying all this together and giving it depth and color are the Scottish laird and his party, including the painter Alfred Jacob Miller, sketching and making watercolors of all they saw. If *Across the Wide Missouri* seems now a greater achievement, a more brilliant evocation, than *The Year of Decision: 1846*, put it down to the greater simplicity of the action, the smaller cast of characters, the more manageable scope; but also to the fact that it was the fur trade, above all other aspects of western history, that had fascinated DeVoto ever since boyhood, and to the further fact that the fur trade had mainly taken place, as it were, in his boyhood backyard. His very first essay in history, back in 1926, had been called "The Mountain Men," and it was purely celebratory. His second, the next year, had been a piece on the Platte Valley route of migration called "The Great Medicine Road." In more ways than one, *Across the Wide Missouri* was a culmination, the one book that Bernard DeVoto had been born to write.

But it did not quite complete him. His two histories, between them, covered only the years from 1832 to 1846, and though he had looked ahead from 1846 to the consequences of that year's fateful decisions, and so did not have to deal with them, he had done little back-looking to the actions that had brought Europeans to North America and finally across the wide Missouri. That story he told in *The Course of Empire*.

It began with the feeling that Lewis and Clark were somehow central to all western history, but as he wrote Garrett Mattingly in December, 1948, "There's no reason to write a book about how a well-conducted party got to the mouth of the Columbia and back. . . . The only thing worth my writing or anyone's writing is a book that says, hey, this seems to have been left out of the picture." What seemed to have been left out of the picture occupied his mind and disturbed his sleep for several years, and the deeper he got into it the more it maddened him. He could not dramatize it as he had dramatized the plains crossing of Narcissa Whitman or the march of the Mormon Battalion. There were few distinctive portraits in it, and no room for the blunt judgments of character that had offended some orthodox historians in the earlier books. His whole method had to be adjusted or abandoned. In October, 1950, he again wrote to Mattingly:

"I have, in nomine Patris et Filii, this day got the French out of North America. One year to the day, and three million words, after I began a book that had no intention of getting the French into North America. . . . So where are we? With thirteen million words written, or by our Lady some two score million, we have now accounted for 229 years that do not enter at all into my book, and have only forty more years to go, or say an even million words . . . before we reach the beginning of my book and, with a sigh of infinite satisfaction and a suffusing glow of happy realization that only ten million words lie ahead, take up a blank, virgin sheet of paper and write at the top of it Page One."

He had, Mattingly advised, a mild case of *regressus historicus*. And he was writing another kind of history from what he had essayed before. He couldn't expect to skip across the centuries at the same pace, and with the same attention to the roadside, as when he had been walking wide-eyed through a single year. But there was another reason why DeVoto had difficulty with his third volume. He found no way to treat it in terms of characteristic figures and characteristic actions, no way to select from it parts that would stand for the whole. As a historian, he was incurably what he and Robert Frost called a "synecdochist." He operated by sampling, and gave his samples vividness. In *The Course of Empire* he had to deal much less particularly with the whole thing. Or almost did. He was saved by the Lewis and Clark expedition, to which he gave the final 120 pages of a book that had begun with a letter from Columbus to Isabella of Spain. That culminating adventure completed a circuit, found a sort of Northwest Passage, and confirmed in the Americans the growing perception that they were fated to spread their country from sea to sea.

Different though it is, *The Course of Empire* is essential to the continental theme, and the adventure which concludes it is put into the context of centuries. When he had put a final footnote to the task by editing the Lewis and Clark *Journals*, DeVoto had finished his job as historian and—though he had to go on writing the journalism that supported him and his family—as writer. He died of a heart attack in New York City, where he would not have wanted to be found dead, on November 13, 1955.

Conservation Equals Survival

In the spring of 1969 thousands of Californians, warned by soothsayers that earthquakes impended, shut themselves up in their houses or fled to what they thought safe places, where they waited for disaster through a day and a night like nineteenth-century Millerites gathered for the Second Coming. The earth did not tremble and gape—the San Andreas fault is fairly unresponsive to soothsaying—but the gullible demonstrated one important human truth: we can be more frightened by fictions and phantasms than by the things that should really scare us to death. These frightened people huddled in houses that were sunk in air murky with poisonous smog; they should have sniffed panic with every breath they drew. Those who fled rushed past endless overcrowded subdivisions down freeways that roared with cars bumper to bumper, four lanes each way, at seventy or eighty miles an hour; they should have heard apocalypse rumbling before and beside and behind. Above the murk and the traffic the firmament split with sonic booms. The passing roadside showed them the devastated redwood groves of Eureka and Arcata. They drove past Santa Barbara, where crude oil bubbled from below the off-shore drilling platforms and moved in great black rafts of tar toward the beaches; or through the Santa Clara Valley, where bulldozers pushed down prune orchards to clear the way for cheesebox housing; or up into

Yosemite, where the gibbering of pre-apocalypse dementia greeted them from the thousand transistors on every campground; or down into the desert, where rallies of Hondas and Yamahas roared past in a mass frenzy called outdoor recreation.

People had every reason to turn pale, hide, flee, in the spring of 1969. But they hid or fled from the shadow of a fear, not from the true substance of their danger. From the thing that should have terrified them there is no hiding. How do we flee from ourselves, from our incontinent fertility, our wastes and poisons, the industrial society in which we are guilty, suffering participants?

Some years ago Stewart L. Udall, then Secretary of the Interior, published a book summarizing the history of land use and abuse in the United States and suggesting a "land ethic" by which we might be guided. He called his book *The Quiet Crisis*; most readers probably read "quiet" as also meaning "slow," "delayed." Many probably assumed that he was talking primarily about open space and scenic beauty. To the average city dweller of the early 1960s—and more and more we all tend to be city dwellers—such concerns probably seemed minor by comparison with the cold war, the bomb, racial strife, inflation, the disintegrating cities, and much else. To people living in the ghetto these matters may have seemed, and may still seem, frivolous.

They were not frivolous—that was Mr. Udall's point. Neither were they limited to open space and scenic beauty. Neither have they remained quiet. While we watched the horizon for mushroom clouds, a funnel-shaped one came up behind us with terrifying swiftness. It is perfectly clear now that we can destroy ourselves quite as completely, if not quite so spectacularly, through continuing abuse of our environment as we can through some mad or vengeful or preventive finger on the atomic trigger. Conservation still properly concerns itself with national parks and wildernesses, but it has not for some years been confined to them. As Mr. Udall says in another context, true conservation begins wherever people are and with whatever trouble they are in.

People are everywhere, and in trouble wherever they are. It is not only amenity, not only quality of living, not only a supply of raw materials or open space for our grandchildren, that we must fight for. Paul B. Sears and William Vogt and others told us what was at stake sixty-odd years ago in the Dust Bowl years: survival. It is even more at stake now—survival of this civilization, perhaps even survival of the living world. And it is later than we think.

Even in America, some wise men have always known how to live with the earth instead of against it. If we had had more husbandmen like Thomas Jefferson and John Bartram, the American farm might have remained as stable as those of northern Europe, where the soil has been farmed for two thousand years without becoming less fertile. If our lumbermen had been foresters as sane as Gifford Pinchot, we would not have mined the forests of New England, the Great Lakes region, and the Northwest and left so many of them scrub country unproductive for generations. If our dry-land settlers and their congressmen had made use of the foresight of John Wesley Powell, there would have been no dust bowls in the shortgrass plains. If more attention had been paid to a book called *Man and Nature*, published over one hundred years ago, we would not now have to learn, little and late, the principles of ecology.

It seems to us a relatively new science, but George Perkins Marsh comprehended its basic laws as early as 1864. As a Vermont farm boy he had observed how woods, streams, lakes, ponds, swamps, plants, animals, fish, insects, earthworms, and weather form a flexible and dynamic system in which every part—even the earthworm—has a function. As Lincoln's ambassador to Italy, he had seen in Mediterranean countries the man-made deserts that taught him how civilizations are brought to an end. He was one of the first to point out that man is an agent of erosion and, in his book, to warn against "the dangers of imprudence and the necessity of caution in all operations which, on a large scale, interfere with the spontaneous arrangements of the organic and inorganic world."

We could have found our land ethic long ago in Marsh, or Bartram, or Jefferson, or Powell. We could have found it in Aldo Leopold's *Sand County Almanac* (1949), one of the great love letters to the natural world.

If we read their books at all, we read them as metaphor, or something applicable to other parts of the world or to a time centuries away. Our faith in science told us that when minerals and fossil fuels ran out, science would find substitutes; when earth's fertility declined, science would feed us on fish meal and plankton that the taste buds could not distinguish from prime ribs. We forgot Paul Sears's warning that nature is not an "inert stockroom" but "an active system, a pattern and a process." We forgot that every human act against the earth has consequences, sometimes big consequences.

One Santa Barbara with its fouled beaches and its slimed and dying sea birds and seals is enough to make a conservationist of a confirmed exploiter and force us to ask ourselves how much an oil field is worth. The poisoning of the Rhine reminds us that American rivers—including the Mississippi—have been similarly poisoned,* that Lake Erie is so clogged with sewage and industrial sludge that fish cannot live in its oxygenless waters, that whole catches of the painstakingly cultivated coho salmon of Lake Michigan have been declared inedible because of the amount of DDT in their bodies, that our eagles and peregrine falcons and perhaps our pelicans as well are dying out from eating DDT-contaminated prey. The plight of the angry Dutch at the Rhine's mouth is not so different from the plight of any of us. It is dangerous to live downwind or downstream from an industrial community, and in this global world every place is ultimately downstream or downwind. Penguins at the South Pole have DDT in their livers; the Greenland ice cap has a dark modern layer, courtesy of the smog blanket of Los Angeles, Tokyo, and London.

Smog has been one of our best teachers. A recent poll indicates that more than half the people of the United States think air pollution one of our most pressing problems. Most of us, on reflection, would rate water pollution as being just as serious. Hardly a river in New England runs Class A—drinkable—water. Many run Class E—sewage. And all of them have poisons washed into them from sprayed and dusted fields or forests or swamps.

We show signs of putting certain villains down: DDT, dieldrin, and the other chlorinated hydrocarbons. These so-called "hard" pesticides are man-made compounds that do not exist in nature; they were never born and they are all but eternal. Instead of dispersing and becoming harmless, they concentrate in living forms, moving from food to feeder, prey to predator, accumulating as they go.

---

*While the discussion in these few paragraphs refers to issues current in 1969, the points being made are still depressingly relevant.

Suppose we do ban the worst of these poisons, as we seem likely to do. What then do we do with the vast quantities already in existence? What do I do with the junk in my garden shed? Bury it in the ground? Dump it in the ocean? Incinerate it so that it can be blown around the world? Sweep it under the rug? Whatever I do with it, it is in danger of joining those amounts that already contaminate the natural world and are sneaking up on me through the food chain. It is a problem that promises to be as difficult of solution as the disposal of radioactive wastes, which have a half-life infinitely longer than that of any container in which they can be locked. Those lead canisters we sink in the sea will be cracking open one day to leak their contents into the water from which, the scientists assure us, much of our food will ultimately come.

Sooner or later our wastes and poisons become part of the garbage problem. In this high-consumption country every one of us generates 5.3 pounds of refuse a day exclusive of sewage, which is a separate problem. It is no longer possible, because of air pollution, to burn even those parts of it that are combustible. We spend more on garbage collection and disposal than on any public service except schools and roads, and still we fall behind.

Not one of our environmental problems—ecological disruption, depletion, pollution, the shrinking of healthy open space—gets anything but worse, despite all our ingenuity. For as we mine from nature more than we have a right to take, we make it possible to go on multiplying in exponential ways the real root of our difficulties: ourselves. There are too many of us now. Like bacteria, we multiply to the edge of our agar dish. When we arrive there, as many nations already have, we will either starve or strangle in our own wastes.

Unless.

Unless, being men and not bacteria, and living not in an agar dish but on a renewable earth, we apply to ourselves and our habitat the intelligence that has endangered both. That means drastically and voluntarily reducing our numbers, decontaminating our earth, and thereafter husbanding, building, and nourishing, instead of squandering and poisoning.

Some say the world will end in fire, Robert Frost wrote, some say in ice. His alternatives do not exhaust the possibilities. For destruction, overpopulation is very adequate; pollution and depletion are also great,

178

and will suffice. If Professor Lamont Cole of Cornell is right, our large-scale burning of fossil fuels endangers the atmosphere in other ways than pollution. The percentage of oxygen in the air we breathe goes imperceptibly down as pollutants and carbon dioxide go up. We will feel it first at night, when photosynthesis stops, and in winter, when it is slowed. But ultimately we will feel it. Two conclusions emerge: fossil energy is the worst discovery man ever made, and his disruption of the carbon-oxygen cycle is the greatest of his triumphs over nature. Through thinner and thinner air we labor toward our last end, conquerors finally of even the earth chemistry that created us.

These are hard doctrines, and an America lulled by four and a half centuries of careless plenty accepts them unwillingly if at all. I myself find them difficult to accept, sitting in my woodsy shack on a bright Vermont morning, with a junco working in the balsam fir outside and a spider knitting up a captured fly in the corner of the window—weather and plants and creatures and I all going about our comfortable business. American optimism asserts itself against the doomsday demographers. I comfort myself that one demographer, Donald Bogue of the University of Chicago, predicts not a geometric progression of our numbers but a levelling off of the American population at about 220 million in the next decade, and relative stability thereafter. Japan has succeeded in controlling its population, though Tokyo in 1969 is a horror, a paradigm of the merely bearable world that we will all go through on our way to doomsday if we do not make peace with the earth and learn what conservationists have long known: that living with the earth is healthier, saner, and more rewarding than living against it.

The conservation movement that began as a small group of nature lovers working for the preservation of natural beauty has expanded in numbers and influence and broadened its areas of concern. The Sierra Club, born in the early part of this century of John Muir's fight to save Hetch Hetchy Valley from a storage dam, has grown from ten thousand members to eighty thousand since World War II. The Wilderness Society, formed by Aldo Leopold and other ecologists to help save for science small remnants of the untouched American biota, has similarly grown. So has the Audubon Society, created to save from extinction the egrets of the Everglades. United with other groups—Izaak Walton League, National

Parks Association, Federation of Western Outdoor Clubs—they have had their surge of militancy as our environmental problems thickened and the outdoors came under greater threat. They have had their victories—they blocked the proposed Echo Park Dam in Dinosaur National Monument and the Marble and Bridge Canyon dams in the Grand Canyon; they appear to have won in Red River Gorge in Kentucky; they have played watchdog on the government agencies charged with the care of the national parks and forests; they are locked in battle with Consolidated Edison over the Hudson and with Walt Disney Productions over the Mineral King. They helped make Stewart Udall's eight years as Secretary of the Interior productive of sixty-four new additions to the national park system, including four new national parks, six national seashores and two national lakeshores, seven national monuments, and dozens of historical parks and sites and recreation areas. If they have sometimes sounded alarmist, their alarm has not been unjustified.

Conservationists, being the first to comprehend ecology, are the people best equipped to spread their knowledge of how inextricably related our environmental problems are. They comprise the indispensable counterforce to industrial exploitation. They have a political base; they can swing elections; their zeal often takes precedence over party and must be wooed by both sides. If there is a hope for the American habitat and for the quality of American life, it is the hope that they represent through their capacity to educate and to get environmental sanity incorporated into law.

Froelich Rainey, Loren Eiseley, and some of their associates at the University Museum, University of Pennsylvania, are currently working on an exhibit that will demonstrate both man's disastrous effect on his environment and the single hope they see of recovering from his abuses. Their exhibit will be in three parts: the first showing the world in its natural balance, nature in full charge, man no more than one more primate; the second showing man in charge, progressing through higher and higher technologies with greater and greater damage to the earth and all its interdependent forms of life; the third, a hypothetical stage barely suggested by our present small efforts at correction and adjustment, showing man learning how to rejoin and develop in harmony with the nature he has previously slashed, burned, gutted, mined, poisoned, and overused.

What that projected exhibit is trying to come at in its third section is precisely what Leopold, Udall, and all the forces of ecology and conservation have been working toward: the development of a land ethic, a respect for the earth and its healthy relationships, a wise stewardship instead of wasteful greed, a rationing of our resources and ourselves for the purpose of promoting a sane, healthy, and renewable living place.

It is very late. But if we are not at the brink of a Spenglerian decline, with the conquest of the moon the last mad achievement of a mad society, we could be on the brink of the greatest period of human history. And it could begin with the little individuals, the kind of people many would call cranks, who insist on organically grown vegetables and unsprayed fruits, who do not pick the wildflowers, who fight against needless dams and roads. For that is the sort of small personal action that a land ethic suggests. Widespread enough, it can keep men from moving mountains.

Now, If I Ruled the World . . .

I am sorry to tell you that I cannot accept your invitation to be environmental dictator of the world. I fear any dictator, even an environmental one, and even when the dictator is myself. The health of the planet's land, air, and water depends on the development of an environmental conscience in a majority of people, and I doubt that a conscience is ever created by decree.

But if the job of Environmental President of the United States is open, and I see no evidence that it is not, then I would accept appointment to that post. It could be temporary: The essential requirements of the job could be demonstrated within weeks or months by a few policy decisions, reversals of direction, and strategic appointments.

The policy decisions would have to be real ones, not the public-relations capers we have grown used to. When a Clean Air Act is in the works, we won't attempt to stall it with more "studies." When international groups meet to deal with global warming, or pollution of the oceans, or a long-term policy for Antarctica, we will be out in front, setting an example, not dragging our heels and coming aboard, if at all, as the last reluctant, unconvinced member. When some scheme to exploit some resource in the public domain comes up, we will say, "If it comes at the expense of the health, the sustainable health, of the environment, we don't want it."

Sooner or later, with or without an Environmental President, the United States will have to phase out chlorofluorocarbons and reduce automobile emissions and close down polluting smokestack industries. I will, as president, encourage every move in that direction, and not let a public-speaking or photo opportunity go by without a specific lesson. But I will not break my neck trying to get it all done overnight.

Other things I will be more prompt about: I will urge Congress to declare the Arctic National Wildlife Refuge a wilderness area, and if Congress won't, I will declare it a national monument under the Antiquities Act, so that our greatest remaining wildlife wilderness will not be destroyed for a week or two of oil. I will lean on Congress to repeal the outdated 1872 Mining Law.

I will appoint a Secretary of the Interior who believes that the earth is, in Aldo Leopold's words, a community to which we belong, not a commodity it is our privilege to exploit. That will mean subordinate appointments in the National Park Service, Fish and Wildlife Service, and Bureau of Land Management that will ensure enforcement of existing protective laws and the imposition of adequate fees for grazing (the present $1.35 per animal-unit-month is about a fifth of what graziers must pay for privately held land). And if cattlemen in the West can't make a living without all the federal subsidies that they have enjoyed for decades, that may be the market economy telling us that cattle are not a viable industry in that erodible and fragile and depleted region.

I will appoint a Secretary of Agriculture who understands the need to reduce our dependence on poisons and who knows that a forest is not just a bunch of trees, who can think in terms larger than board-feet and getting out the cut. I would stop, by any means I could find, all cutting in the ancient forests of the Northwest—what remains of them. I would give every aid to timber-dependent communities, even those that hate environmentalists as the supposed cause of their loss of jobs. I would stop all shipments of round logs and even of rough-sawn lumber out of the country, and give liberal aid to the establishment of mills and wood-products factories within the former logging regions. I would encourage timber companies to develop and maintain sustainable cutting programs where harvest and growth are in balance.

There will be logging and ranching, but on a smaller and more careful scale. Logging and ranching communities face a difficult transition, and deserve every assistance while they make it. But we do not need to sacrifice our few remnant ancient forests, or further erode our grasslands, to save jobs in industries that have had their day.

All this will, I am sure, make me enemies, and concentrate political opposition to my reelection. But I don't care about my reelection, and I am persuaded that my actions will bring me more friends than enemies. For Americans are already more than halfway toward an environmental conscience—and about time, too. The majority understand, and so will the timber-dependent and grass-dependent communities eventually, that some jobs once valid and accepted can come to the point where they are socially undesirable.

Part Three

INHERITANCE

Editor's Note

Dan Flores, the A. B. Hammond Professor of History at the University of Montana, once wrote that what distinguished Wallace Stegner's vision of the American West from most other environmentalist manifestos was "a far deeper knowledge of history" and "harder, more penetrating thinking. History and intelligent thought were the main weapons in Stegner's arsenal. . . ."

Nowhere is that vision more reflectively or elegantly synthesized than in the essays that comprise the concluding section of this book—particularly "The Twilight of Self-Reliance: Frontier Values and Contemporary America," and "Living Dry." "The Twilight of Self-Reliance," which by no means confines itself to sociopolitical issues of the American West, is a broad expansion on the Crèvecoeurian question "Who then is the American, this new man?" And "Living Dry" explores as intelligently and gracefully as any essay ever has the deceptively simple fact about the American West—aridity—and the ways in which aridity defines not only the history of the region but all its possibilities.

"The Twilight of Self-Reliance" was one of the Tanner Lectures on Human Values delivered at the University of Utah in February of 1980; "Living Dry" was the first of three William W. Cook Lectures, delivered at the University of Michigan in October 1986, later published by the university press in a small paperback called *The American West as Living Space*. All three essays were reprinted in *Where the Bluebird Sings to the Lemonade Springs* in 1992. "Land: America's History Teacher" appeared in *Living Wilderness* in 1981. "The Rocky Mountain West" was a chapter from *The Romance of North America*, edited by Hardwick Moseley and published by Houghton Mifflin in 1958.

The Twilight of Self-Reliance

Frontier Values and Contemporary America

1

Henry David Thoreau was a philosopher not unwilling to criticize his country and his countrymen, but when he wrote the essay entitled "Walking" in 1862, at a time when his country was engaged in a desperate civil war, he wrote with what Mark Twain would have called the calm confidence of a Christian with four aces. He spoke America's stoutest self-confidence and most optimistic expectations. Eastward, he said, he walked only by force, but westward he walked free: he must walk toward Oregon and not toward Europe, and his trust in the future was total.

> If the moon looks larger here than in Europe, probably the sun looks larger also. If the heavens of America appear infinitely higher, and the stars brighter, I trust that these facts are symbolical of the height to which the philosophy and poetry and religion of her inhabitants may one day soar. . . . I trust that we shall be more imaginative, that our thoughts will be clearer, fresher, and more ethereal, as our sky—our understanding more comprehensive and broader, like our plains—our intellect generally on a grander scale,

like our thunder and lightning, our rivers and mountains and forests—and our hearts shall even correspond in breadth and depth and grandeur to our inland seas. Perchance there will appear to the traveler something, he knows not what, of *laeta* and *glabra*, of joyous and serene, in our very faces. Else to what end does the world go on, and why was America discovered?

The question was rhetorical; he knew the answer. To an American of his generation it was unthinkable that the greatest story in the history of civilized man—the finding and peopling of the New World—and the greatest opportunity since the Creation—the chance to remake men and their society into something cleansed of past mistakes, and closer to the heart's desire—should end as one more betrayal of human credulity and hope.

Some moderns find that idea perfectly thinkable. Leslie Fiedler finds in the Montana Face, which whatever else it is is an authentically American one, not something joyous and serene, but the large vacuity of self-deluding myth. Popular books which attempt to come to grips with American values in these times walk neither toward Oregon nor toward Europe, but toward dead ends and jumping-off places. They bear such titles as *The Lonely Crowd*, *The Organization Man*, *Future Shock*, *The Culture of Narcissism*. This last, subtitled "American Life in an Age of Diminishing Expectations," reports "a way of life that is dying—the culture of competitive individualism, which in its decadence has carried the logic of individualism to the extreme of a war of all against all, the pursuit of happiness to the dead end of a narcissistic preoccupation with the self." It describes "a political system in which public lying has become endemic and routine," and a typical citizen who is haunted by anxiety and spends his time trying to find a meaning in his life. "His sexual attitudes are permissive rather than puritanical, even though his emancipation from ancient taboos brings him no sexual peace. . . . Acquisitive in the sense that his cravings have no limits, he does not accumulate goods and provisions against the future, in the manner of the acquisitive individualist of the nineteenth century political economy, but demands immediate gratification and lives in a state of restless, perpetually unsatisfied desire."

Assuming that Thoreau spoke for his time, as he surely did, and that

Christopher Lasch speaks for at least elements and aspects of his, how did we get from there to here in little more than a century? Have the sturdiness of the American character and the faith in America's destiny that Thoreau took for granted been eroded entirely away? What happened to confidence, what happened to initiative and strenuousness and sobriety and responsibility, what happened to high purpose, what happened to hope? Are they gone, along with the Puritans' fear of pleasure? Was the American future, so clear in Thoreau's day, no more than a reflection of apparently unlimited resources, and does democracy dwindle along with the resources that begot it? Were we never really free, but only rich? In any event, if America was discovered only so that its citizens could pursue pleasure or grope for a meaning in their lives, then Thoreau and Lasch would be in agreement: Columbus should have stood at home.

Even if I knew answers, I could not detail them in an hour's lecture, or in a book. But since I believe that one of our most damaging American traits is our contempt for all history, including our own, I might spend an hour looking backward at what we were and how America changed us. A certain kind of modern American in the throes of an identity crisis is likely to ask, or bleat, "Who am I?" It might help him to find out who he started out to be, and having found that out, to ask himself if what he started out to be is still valid. And if most of what I touch on in this summary is sixth-grade American history, I do not apologize for that. History is not the proper midden for digging up novelties. Perhaps that is one reason why a nation bent on novelty ignores it. The obvious, especially the ignored obvious, is worth more than a Fourth of July or Bicentennial look.

2

Under many names—Atlantis, the Hesperides, Groenland, Brazillia, the Fortunate Isles—America was Europe's oldest dream. Found by Norsemen about the year 1000, it was lost again for half a millennium, and only emerged into reality at the beginning of the modern era, which we customarily date from the year 1500. There is even a theory, propounded by the historian Walter Webb in *The Great Frontier*, that the new world created the modern era—stimulated its birth, funded it, fueled it, fed it, gave it its impetus and direction and state of mind, formed its expectations and institutions, and provided it with a prosperity unexampled in history, a boom that lasted fully 400 years. If Professor Webb pushes his thesis a little hard, and if it has in it traces of the logical fallacy known as *post hoc, ergo propter hoc*, it still seems to me provocative and in some ways inescapable, and Webb seems entirely justified in beginning his discussion of America in medieval Europe. I shall do the same.

Pre-Columbian Europe, then. For 150 years it has been living close to the limit of its resources. It is always short of money, which means gold and silver, fiat money being still in the future. Its land is frozen in the structures of feudalism, owned by the crown, the church, and an aristocracy whose domains are shielded by laws of primogeniture and entail from sale or subdivision—from everything except the royal whim which gave, and can take away. Its food supply comes from sources that cannot be expanded, and its population, periodically reduced by the Black Death, is static or in decline. Peasants are bound to the soil, and both they and their masters are tied by feudal loyalties and obligations. Except among the powerful, individual freedom is not even a dream. Merchants, the guilds, and the middle class generally, struggle against the arrogance of the crown and an aristocracy dedicated to the anachronistic code of chivalry, which is often indistinguishable from brigandage. Faith is invested in a politicized, corrupt, but universal church just breaking up in the Reformation that will drown Europe in blood. Politics are a nest of snakes: ambitious nobles against ambitious kings, kings against pretenders and against each other, all of them trying to fill, by means of wars and strategic marriages, the periodic power vacuums created by the cracking of the Holy Roman Empire. The late Middle Ages still look on earthly life as a testing and preparation for the Hereafter. Fed on this opium, the little individual comes to expect his reward in heaven, or in the neck. Learning is just beginning to open out from scholastic rationalism into the empiricism of the Renaissance. Science, with all it will mean to men's lives and ways of thinking, has barely pipped its shell.

Out of this closed world Columbus sails in 1492 looking for a new route to Asia, whose jewels and silks are coveted by Europe's elite, and whose spices are indispensable to nations with no means of preserving food except smoking and salting, and whose meat is often eaten high. The voyage of the three tiny ships is full of anxiety and hardship, but the end is miracle, one of those luminous moments in history: an after-midnight cry from the lookout on the *Pinta*, Columbus and his sailors crowding to the decks, and in the soft tropical night, by the light of a moon just past full, staring at a dark ambiguous shore and sniffing the perfumed breeze off an utterly new world.

Not Asia. Vasco da Gama will find one way to that, Magellan another. What Columbus has found is puzzling, of unknown size and unknown relation to anything. The imagination has difficulty taking it in. Though within ten years of Columbus' first voyage Vespucci will demonstrate that the Americas are clearly not Asia, Europe is a long time accepting the newness of the new world. Pedro de Castañeda, crossing the plains of New Mexico, Oklahoma, and Kansas with Coronado in 1541, is confident that they make one continuous land mass with China and Peru; and when Champlain sends Jean Nicolet to explore among the Nipissings on the way to Georgian Bay and the great interior lakes in 1635—133 years after Vespucci—Nicolet will take along in his bark canoe an embroidered mandarin robe, just in case, out on those wild rivers among those wild forests, he should come to the palace of the Great Khan and need ceremonial dress.

Understanding is a slow dawning, each exploration bringing a little more light. But when the dawn arrives, it is a blazing one. It finds its way through every door and illuminates every cellar and dungeon in Europe. Though the discovery of America is itself part of Europe's awakening, and results from purely European advances—foreshadowings of Copernican astronomy, a method for determining latitude, the development of the caravel and the lateen sail—the new world responds by accelerating every stir of curiosity, science, adventure, individualism, and hope in the old.

Because Europe has always dreamed westward, America, once realized, touches men's minds like fulfilled prophecy. It has lain out there in the gray wastes of the Atlantic, not only a continent waiting to be discovered, but a fable waiting to be agreed upon. It is not unrelated to the Hereafter. Beyond question, before it is half known, it will breed utopias and noble savages, fantasies of Perfection, New Jerusalems.

Professor Webb believes that to closed and limited Europe America came as a pure windfall, a once-in-the-history-of-the-world opportunity. Consider only one instance: the gold that Sir Francis Drake looted from Spanish galleons was the merest fragment of a tithe of what the Spaniards had looted from Mexico and Peru; and yet Queen Elizabeth out of her one-fifth royal share of the *Golden Hind*'s plunder was able to pay off the entire national debt of England and have enough left to help found the East India Company.

Perhaps, as Milton Friedman would insist, increasing the money supply only raised prices. Certainly American gold didn't help Europe's poor. It made the rich richer and kings more powerful and wars more implacable. Nevertheless, trickling outward from Spain as gift or expenditure, or taken from its ships by piracy, that gold affected all of Europe, stimulating trade and discovery, science, invention, everything that we associate with the unfolding of the Renaissance. It surely helped take European eyes off the Hereafter, and it did a good deal toward legitimizing the profit motive. And as the French and English, and to a lesser extent the Dutch and Swedes, began raiding America, other and more substantial riches than gold flooded back: new food plants, especially Indian corn and the potato, which revolutionized eating habits and brought on a steep rise in population that lasted more than a century; furs; fish from the swarming Newfoundland banks, especially important to countries still largely Catholic; tobacco for the indulgence of a fashionable new habit; timber for ships and masts; sugar and rum from the West Indies.

Those spoils alone might have rejuvenated Europe. But there was something else, at first not valued or exploited, that eventually would lure Europeans across the Atlantic and transform them. The most revolutionary gift of the new world was land itself, and the independence and aggressiveness that land ownership meant. Land, unoccupied and unused except by savages who in European eyes did not count, land available to anyone with the initiative to take it, made America, Opportunity, and Freedom synonymous terms.

But only later. The early comers were raiders, not settlers. The first Spanish towns were beachheads from which to scour the country for treasure, the first French settlements on the St. Lawrence were beachheads of the fur trade. Even the English on Roanoke Island, and later at Jamestown, though authentic settlers, were hardly pioneers seeking the promised land. Many were bond servants and the scourings of debtors' prisons. They did not come, they were sent. Their hope of working off their bondage and starting new in a new country was not always rewarded, either. Bruce and William Catton estimate that eight out of ten indentured servants freed to make new lives in America failed—returned to pauperism, or became the founders of a poor-white class, or died of fevers trying to compete with black slaves on tobacco or sugar plantations, or turned outlaw.

Nevertheless, for the English who at Jamestown and Plymouth and the Massachusetts Bay Colony began to take ownership of American land in the early seventeenth century, land was the transfiguring gift. The historian who remarked that the entire history of the United States could be read in terms of real estate was not simply making words.

Here was an entire continent which, by the quaint assumptions of the raiders, was owned by certain absentee crowned heads whose subjects had made the first symbolic gesture of claiming it. They had rowed a boat into a rivermouth, sighted and named a cape, raised a cross on a beach, buried a brass plate, or harangued a crowd of bewildered Indians. Therefore Ferdinand and Isabella, or Elizabeth, or Louis owned from that point to the farthest boundary in every direction. But land without people was valueless. The Spaniards imported the *encomienda* system—that is, transplanted feudalism—and used the Indians as peons. The French built only forts at which to collect the wilderness wealth of furs. But the English were another kind, and they were the ones who created the American pattern.

"Are you ignorant of the difference between the king of England and the king of France?" Duquesne asked the Iroquois in the 1750s. "Go see the forts that our king has established and you will see that you can still hunt under their very walls. . . . The English, on the contrary, are no sooner in possession of a place than the game is driven away. The forest falls before them as they advance, and the soil is laid bare so that you can scarce find the wherewithal to erect a shelter for the night."

To be made valuable, land must be sold cheap or given away to people who would work it, and out of that necessity was born a persistent American expectation. The very word "claim" that we came to use for a parcel of land reflected our feeling that free or cheap land was a right, and that the land itself was a commodity. The Virginia Company and Lord Calvert both tried to encourage landed estates on the English pattern, and both failed because in America men would not work land unless they owned it, and would not be tied to a proprietor's acres when they could go off into the woods and have any land they wanted, simply for the taking. Their claim might not be strictly legal, but it often held: hence the development of what came to be known as squatters' rights. As Jefferson would later write in *Notes on Virginia*, Europe had an abundance of labor and a dearth of land, America an abundance of land and a dearth of labor. That made all the difference. The opportunity to own land not only freed men, it made labor honorable and opened up the future to hope and the possibility of independence, perhaps of a fortune.

The consequences inform every notion we have of ourselves. Admittedly there were all kinds of people in early America, as there are all kinds in our time—saints and criminals, dreamers and drudges, pushers and con men. But the new world did something similar to all of them. Of the most energetic ones it made ground-floor capitalists; out of nearly everyone it leached the last traces of servility. Cut off from control, ungoverned and virtually untaxed, people learned to resent the imposition of authority, even that which they had created for themselves. Dependent on their own strength and ingenuity in a strange land, they learned to dismiss tradition and old habit, or rather, simply forgot them. Up in Massachusetts the idea of the equality of souls before God probably helped promote the idea of earthly equality; the notion of a personal covenant with God made the way easier for social and political agreements such as the Plymouth Compact and eventually the Constitution of the United States. In the observed freedom of the Indian from formal government there may have been a dangerous example for people who had lived under governments notably unjust and oppressive. Freedom itself forced the creation not only of a capitalist economy based on land, but of new forms of social contract. When thirteen loosely allied colonies made common cause against the mother country, the League of the Iroquois may well have provided one model of confederation.

"The rich stay in Europe," wrote Hector St. John de Crèvecoeur before the Revolution. "It is only the middling and poor that emigrate." Middle-class values emigrated with them, and middle-class ambitions. Resentment of aristocrats and class distinctions accompanied the elevation of the work ethic. Hardship, equal opportunity to rise, the need for common defense against the Indians, and the necessity for all to postpone the rewards of labor brought the English colonists to nearly the same level and imbued all but the retarded and the most ne'er-do-well with the impulse of upward mobility. And if the practical need to hew a foothold out of the continent left many of them unlettered and ignorant, that deficiency, combined with pride, often led to the disparagement of cultivation and the cultivated as effete and European. Like work, barbarism and boorishness tended to acquire status, and in some parts of America still retain it.

Land was the base, freedom the consequence. Not even the little parochial tyranny of the Puritans in Massachusetts could be made to stick indefinitely. In fact, the Puritans' chief objection to Roger Williams, when they expelled him, was not his unorthodoxy but his declaration that the Colonists had no right to their lands, the king not having had the right to grant them in the first place. Williams also expressed an early pessimistic view of the American experiment that clashed with prevailing assumptions and forecast future disillusion. "The common trinity of the world—Profit, Preferment, and Pleasure—will be here the tria omnia, as in all the world besides . . . and God Land will be as great a God with us English as God Gold was with the Spaniard." A sour prophet indeed—altogether too American in his dissenting opinions and his challenging of authority. And right besides. No wonder they chased him off to Rhode Island.

Students of the Revolution have wondered whether it was really British tyranny that lit rebellion, or simply American outrage at the imposition of even the mildest imperial control after decades of benign neglect. Certainly one of George III's worst blunders was his 1763 decree forbidding settlement beyond the crest of the Alleghenies. That was worse than the Stamp Act or the Navigation Acts, for land speculators were already sniffing the western wind. When Daniel Boone took settlers over the Cumberland Gap in 1775 he was working for speculators. George Washington and Benjamin Franklin, who had a good deal to do with the Revolution, both had interests in western land. Only a very revisionist historian would call our revolution a real estate rebellion, a revolt of the subdividers, but it did have that aspect.

And very surely, as surely as the endless American forests put a curve in the helves of the axes that chopped them down, the continent worked on those who settled it. From the first frontiers in Virginia and Massachusetts through all the successive frontiers that, as Jefferson said, required Americans to start fresh every generation, America was in the process of creating a democratic, energetic, practical, profit-motivated society that resembled Europe less and less as it worked westward. At the same time, it was creating the complicated creature we spent our first century as a nation learning to recognize and trying to define: the American.

3

"Who then is the American, this new man?" asked Crèvecoeur, and answered his own question in a book published in 1782 as *Letters from an American Farmer*. We were, he said, a nation of cultivators; and it was the small farmer, the independent, frugal, hard-working, self-respecting freeholder, that he idealized—the same yeoman farmer that only a little later Jefferson would call the foundation of the republic. But out on the fringes of settlement Crèvecoeur recognized another type. Restless, migratory, they lived as much by hunting as by farming, for protecting their crops and stock against wild animals put the gun in their hands, and "once hunters, farewell to the plough. The chase renders them ferocious, gloomy, and unsocial"; they exhibit "a strange sort of lawless profligacy"; and their children, having no models except their parents, "grow up a mongrel breed, half civilized, half savage."

Crèvecoeur, familiar only with the eastern seaboard, thought the frontiersman already superseded almost everywhere by the more sober and industrious farmer. He could not know that on farther frontiers beyond the Appalachians, beyond the Mississippi, beyond the Missouri and the Rocky Mountains, the breed would renew itself for another hundred years, repeating over and over the experience that had created it in the first place. The Revolutionary War was only the climax of the American Revolution, which was the most radical revolution in history because it started from scratch, from wilderness, and repeated that beginning over and over.

The pioneer farmer has a respectable place in our tradition and an equally respectable place in our literature, from Cooper's *The Pioneers* to Rölvaag's *Giants in the Earth*. But it was the border hunter who captured our imaginations and became a myth. He was never a soft or necessarily attractive figure. Ferocious he always was, gloomy often, antisocial by definition. As D. H. Lawrence and a whole school of critics have pointed out, he was a loner, often symbolically an orphan, strangely sexless (though more in literature than in fact), and a killer. We know him not only from the Boones, Crocketts, Carsons, and Bridgers of history, but from Cooper's Leatherstocking and all his literary descendants. His most memorable recent portrait is Boone Caudill in A. B. Guthrie's *Big Sky*, who most appropriately heads for the mountains and a life of savage freedom after a murderous fight with his father. Most appropriately, for according to Lawrence's *Studies in Classic American Literature*, one essential symbolic act of the American is the murder of Father Europe, and another is re-baptism in the wilderness.

We may observe those symbolic acts throughout our tradition, in a hundred variations from the crude and barbarous to the highly sophisticated. Emerson was performing them in such essays as "Self-Reliance" ("Trust thyself: every heart vibrates to that iron string") and "The American Scholar" ("We have listened too long to the courtly muses of Europe"). Whitman sent them as a barbaric yawp over the rooftops of the world. Thoreau spoke them in the quotation with which I began this lecture, and put them into practice in his year on Walden Pond.

The virtues of the frontiersman, real or literary, are Indian virtues, warrior qualities of bravery, endurance, stoical indifference to pain and hardship, recklessness, contempt for law, a hawk-like need of freedom. Often in practice an outlaw, the frontiersman in literature is likely to display a certain noble savagery, a degree of natural goodness that has a more sophisticated parallel in the common American delusion, shared even by Jefferson, who should have known better, that untutored genius is more to be admired than genius schooled. In the variants of the frontiersman that Henry Nash Smith traces in *Virgin Land*—in flatboatman, logger, cowboy, miner, in literary and mythic figures from the

Virginian to the Lone Ranger and Superman—the Indian qualities persist, no matter how overlaid with comedy or occupational detail. Malcolm Cowley has shown how they emerge in a quite different sort of literature in the stiff-upper-lip code hero of Ernest Hemingway.

We need not admire them wholeheartedly in order to recognize them in their modern forms. They put the Winchesters on the gunracks of pickups and the fury into the arguments of the gun lobby. They dictate the leather of Hell's Angels and the whanged buckskin of drugstore Carsons. Our most ruthless industrial, financial, and military buccaneers have displayed them. The Sagebrush Rebellion and those who would open Alaska to a final stage of American continent-busting adopt them as a platform. Without them there would have been no John Wayne movies. At least as much as the sobriety and self-reliant industry of the pioneer farmer, it is the restlessness and intractability of the frontiersman that drives our modern atavists away from civilization into the woods and deserts, there to build their yurts and geodesic domes and live self-reliant lives with no help except from trust funds, unemployment insurance, and food stamps.

This mythic figure lasts. He is a model of conduct of many kinds. He directs our fantasies. Curiously, in almost all his historic forms he is both landless and destructive, his kiss is the kiss of death. The hunter roams the wilderness but owns none of it. As Daniel Boone, he served the interests of speculators and capitalists; even as Henry David Thoreau he ended his life as a surveyor of town lots. As mountain man he was virtually a bond servant to the company, and his indefatigable labors all but eliminated the beaver and undid all the conservation work of beaver engineering. The logger achieved his roughhouse liberty within the constraints of a brutally punishing job whose result was the enrichment of great capitalist families such as the Weyerhausers and the destruction of most of the magnificent American forests. The cowboy, so mythically free in books and movies, was a hired man on horseback, a slave to cows and the deadliest enemy of the range he used to ride.

Do these figures represent our wistful dream of freedom from the shackles of family and property? Probably they do. It may be important to note that it is the mountain man, logger, and cowboy whom we have made into myths, not the Astors and General Ashleys, the Weyerhausers, or the cattle kings. The lowlier figures, besides being more democratic and so matching the folk image better, may incorporate a dream not only of freedom but of irresponsibility. In any case, any variety of the frontiersman is more attractive to modern Americans than is the responsible, pedestrian, hard-working pioneer farmer breaking his back in a furrow to achieve ownership of his claim and give his children a start in the world. The freedom of the frontiersman is a form of mortal risk and contains the seed of its own destruction. The shibboleth of this breed is prowess.

The pioneer farmer is another matter. He had his own forms of self-reliance; he was a mighty coper, but his freedom of movement was restricted by family and property, and his shibboleth was not prowess but growth. He put off the present in favor of the future. Travelers on the Midwestern frontier during the 1820s, '30s, and '40s were universally moved to amazement at how farms, villages, even cities, had risen magically where only a few years before bears had been measuring their reach on the trunks of trees. British travelers such as Mrs. Trollope found the pioneer farms primitive, the towns crude, and the brag of the townsmen offensive, but Americans such as Timothy Flint, Thomas Nuttall, and John James Audubon regarded the settlement of the Midwest with a pride that was close to awe. Mormons looking back on their communal miracles in Nauvoo and Salt Lake City feel that same pride. Progress we have always measured quantitatively, in terms of acres plowed, turnpikes graded, miles of railroad built, bridges and canals constructed. I heard former Governor Pat Brown of California chortle with delight when the word came that California had passed New York in the population race. All through our history we have had the faith that growth is good, and bigger is better.

And here we may observe a division, a fault-line, in American feeling. Cooper had it right in *The Pioneers* nearly 160 years ago. Leatherstocking owns Cooper's imagination, but the town builders own the future, and Leatherstocking has to give way. *The Pioneers* is at once an exuberant picture of the breaking of the wilderness and a lament for its passing; and it is as much the last of the frontiersmen as the last of the Mohicans that the Leatherstocking series mourns. Many of Cooper's successors have felt the

same way—hence the elegiac tone of so many of our novels of the settlement and the land. We hear it in Willa Cather's *A Lost Lady*, where the
railroad builder Captain Forrester is so much larger than anyone in the
shrunken present. We hear it in Larry McMurtry's *Horseman, Pass By*,
which before it was made into the movie *Hud* was a requiem for the old-
time cattleman. A country virtually without history and with no regard
for history—history is bunk, said Henry Ford—exhibits an odd mourn-
fulness over the passing of its brief golden age.

The romantic figure of the frontiersman was doomed to pass with
the wilderness that made him. He was essentially over by the 1840s,
though in parts of the West he lingered on as an anachronism. His
epitaph was read, as Frederick Jackson Turner noted in a famous historical essay, by the census of 1890, which found no continuous line of
frontier existing anywhere in the United States. He was not the only one
who died of that census report. The pioneer farmer died too, for without
a frontier there was no more free land. But whether the qualities that the
frontier had built into both frontiersman and farmer died when the line of
settlement withered at the edge of the shortgrass plains—that is not so
clear.

4

Not only was free land gone by 1890, or at least any free land capable of
settlement, but by the second decade of the twentieth century the population of the United States, despite all the empty spaces in the arid West,
had reached the density which historians estimate congested Europe had
had in 1500. The growth that Jefferson had warned against had gone on
with astounding speed. The urban poor of Europe whose immigration he
would have discouraged had swamped the original nation of mainly
Protestant, mainly North European origins, and together with the industrial revolution, accelerated by the Civil War, had created precisely
the sort of manufacturing nation, complete with urban slums and urban
discontents, that he had feared. We were just at the brink of changing over from the nation of cultivators that Crèvecoeur had described
and Jefferson advocated into an industrial nation dominated by corpora-

tions and capitalistic buccaneers still unchecked by any social or political controls.

The typical American was not a self-reliant and independent landowner, but a wage earner; and the victory of the Union in the Civil War had released into the society millions of former slaves whose struggle to achieve full citizenship was sure to trouble the waters of national complacency for a century and perhaps much longer. The conditions that had given us freedom and opportunity and optimism were over, or seemed to be. We were entering the era of the muckrakers, and we gave them plenty of muck to rake. And even by 1890 the note of disenchantment, the gloomy Dostoyevskyan note that William Dean Howells said did not belong in American literature, which should deal with the more smiling aspects of life, had begun to make its way into our novels.

After 1890 we could ask ourselves in increasing anxiety the question that Thoreau had asked rhetorically in 1862. To what end *did* the world go on, and why *was* America discovered? Had the four hundred years of American experience created anything new, apart from some myths as remote as Romulus and Remus, or were we back in the unbreakable circle from which Columbus had sprung us?

From 1890 to the present there have been plenty of commentators, with plenty of evidence on their side, to say that indeed we have slipped back into that vicious circle; and when we examine the products of the Melting Pot we find lugubrious reminders that it has not melted everybody down into any sort of standard American. What we see instead is a warring melee of minority groups—racial, ethnic, economic, sexual, linguistic—all claiming their right to the American standard without surrendering the cultural identities that make them still unstandard. We seem to be less a nation than a collection of what current cant calls "communities": the Black Community, the Puerto Rican Community, the Chicano Community, the Chinese Community, the Gay Community, the Financial Community, the Academic Community, and a hundred others. We seem to approach not the standard product of the Melting Pot but the mosaic that Canadians look forward to, and that they think will save them from becoming the stereotypes they think we are.

With all respect to Canada, we are not a set of clones. We are the wildest mixture of colors, creeds, opinions, regional differences, occupations, and types. Nor is Canada the permanent mosaic it says it wants to be. Both nations, I am convinced, move with glacial slowness toward that unity in diversity, that *e pluribus unum* of a North American synthesis, that is inevitable, or nearly so, no matter which end it is approached from. When we arrive there, a century or two or three hence, darker of skin and more united in mind, the earlier kind of American who was shaped by the frontier will still be part of us—of each of us, even if our ancestors came to this continent after the frontier as a fact was gone.

For as Turner pointed out, the repeated experience of the frontier through more than 250 years coalesced gradually into a package of beliefs, habits, faiths, assumptions, and values, and these values in turn gave birth to laws and institutions that have had a continuous shaping effect on every newer American who enters the society either by birth or immigration. These are the things that bind us together no matter how many other forces may be pushing us apart. Language is one thing. I believe it has to be English, for language is at the core of every culture and inseparable from its other manifestations. If we permit bilingualism or multilingualism more than temporarily as an aid to assimilation, we will be balkanized and undone, as Canada is in danger of being by the apparently irremediable division between the Anglophones and the Francophones. The Bill of Rights is another unifier. We rely on it daily— even our enemies rely on it. And the images of ourselves, including the variant myths, that we developed when we were a younger, simpler, and more hopeful nation are still another. The national character, diffuse or not, recognizable if not definable, admirable and otherwise, bends newcomers to its image and outlasts time, change, crowding, shrinking resources, and fashionable pessimism. It has bent those apparently untouched by the Melting Pot, bent them more than they may know. Thus James Baldwin, visiting Africa, discovered to his surprise that though black, he was no African: he was an American, and thought and felt like one.

Time makes slow changes in our images of ourselves, but at their best, the qualities our writers and mythmakers have perpetuated are worth our imitation. The untutored decency and mongrel smartness of Huckleberry Finn, as well as the dignity that the slave Jim salvaged out of an oppressed life, could only have been imagined in America. The innocent philistinism of Howells' Silas Lapham could have been imagined by a European observer, but the ethical worth that nearly ennobles Lapham in his financial crisis is—realistic or not—pure American. Henry James' American, significantly named Christopher Newman, has a magnanimity that matches his naïveté. And the literary archetypes of the pre–1890 period are not the only ones. We have had political leaders who have represented us in more than political ways, and two at least who have taught us at the highest level who we are and who we might be.

Washington I could never get next to; he is a noble impersonal obelisk on the Mall. But Jefferson and Lincoln are something else. Jefferson did more than any other man to shape this democracy: formulated its principles in the Declaration of Independence and insisted on the incorporation of the Bill of Rights into the Constitution; had a hand in preventing the establishment of a state church; created the monetary system; framed the rules for the government of the western territories; invented the pattern for the survey of the public domain; bought Louisiana; sent Lewis and Clark to the western ocean and back, thus fathering one of our most heroic legends and inventing Manifest Destiny. If he had a clouded love affair with the slave half-sister of his dead wife, that only winds him more tightly into the ambiguous history of his country. As for Lincoln, he gave eloquence and nobility to the homespun values of frontier democracy. He was native mind and native virtue at their highest reach, and he too, like Jefferson but more sternly, was mortally entangled in the slave question that threatened to break America apart before it came of age.

Historians in these anti-heroic times have sometimes scolded the folk mind for apotheosizing Jefferson and Lincoln; and certainly, from their temples on the Potomac, they do brood over our national life like demigods. But as Bernard DeVoto said in one of his stoutly American "Easy Chairs," the folk mind is often wiser than the intellectuals. It knows its heroes and clings to them stubbornly even when heroes are out of fashion. Unfortunately, it is about as unreliable in its choice of heroes as in its creation of myths. It has a dream of jackpots as well as a dream of moral nobility and political freedom; it can make a model for imitation out of Jim Fisk or a myth out of a psychopathic killer like Billy the Kid almost as readily as it makes them out of the Great Emancipator.

5

These days, young people do not stride into their future with the confidence their grandparents knew. Over and over, in recent years, I have heard the cold undertone of doubt and uncertainty when I talk with college students. The American Dream has suffered distortion and attrition; for many, it is a dream glumly awakened from.

Per Hansa, in *Giants in the Earth*, could homestead Dakota farmland, gamble his strength against nature, lose his life in the struggle, but win in the end by handing down a productive farm to his son, and insuring him a solid, self-respecting place in the world. Per Hansa's grandsons have no such chances. Only one of them can inherit the family farm, for it would not be an economic unit if divided (it barely is while still undivided), and so something like primogeniture must be invoked to protect it. The other sons cannot hope to buy farms of their own. Land is too high, money is too expensive, machinery is too costly. The products of a farm acquired on those terms could not even pay the interest on the debt. So the other sons have a choice between leaving the farm, which they know and like, and going into the job market; or hiring out as tenant farmers or hired hands to some factory in the field. All over the United States, for several decades, farms have become fewer, larger, and more mechanized, and family ownership has grown less. Though I have no statistics in the matter, I would not be surprised to hear before the end of the 1980s that investors from the Middle East, Hong Kong, and Japan own as much American farmland as independent American farmers do.

For the vast majority of American youth who are not farmers, the options of independence have likewise shrunk. What they have to consider, more likely than not, is a job—a good job, in a company with a good pay scale, preferably, and with guaranteed promotions and a sound retirement plan. The future is not a thing we want to risk; when possible, we insure against it. And for the economically disadvantaged, the core-city youth, the minorities ethnic or otherwise, the people with inferior capacities or bad training or no luck, it is as risky as it ever was in frontier times, but without the promise it used to hold, and with no safety valve such as free land used to provide.

So we return to the vision of Christopher Lasch in *The Culture of Narcissism*. With some of it, especially its glib Freudian analyses of straw men, I am not in sympathy. By some parts, even when I think accurate observations are being marshaled to a dubious conclusion, I have to be impressed. The vision is apocalyptic. Lasch sees our cities as bankrupt or ungovernable or both, our political life corrupt, our bureaucracies greedy and expanding, our great corporations pervaded by the dog-eat-dog individualism of managerial ambition, maximized profits, and "business ethics"—which bear the same relation to ethics that military intelligence bears to intelligence. He sees Americans degraded by selfishness, cynicism, and venality, religion giving way to therapy and lunatic cults, education diluted by the no-fail concept, high school graduates unable to sign their names, family life shattered and supervision of children increasingly passed on to courts, clinics, or the state. He sees sexuality rampant, love extinct, work avoided, instant pleasure pursued as the whole aim of life. He sees excellence disparaged because our expectations so far exceed our deserving that any real excellence is a threat. He sees the Horatio Alger hero replaced in the American Pantheon by the Happy Hooker, the upright sportsmanship of Frank Merriwell replaced by the sports manners of John McEnroe, and all the contradictory strains of American life beginning to focus in the struggle between a Far Right asserting frontier ruthlessness and unhampered free enterprise, and a welfare liberalism to which even the requirement of reading English in order to vote may seem like a violation of civil rights.

The culture hero of Lasch's America is no Jefferson or Lincoln, no Leatherstocking or Carson, no Huck Finn or Silas Lapham. He is no hero at all, but the limp, whining anti-hero of Joseph Heller's *Something Happened*—self-indulgent, sneaky, scared of his superiors, treacherous to his inferiors, held together only by clandestine sex and by a sticky sentiment for the children to whom he has given nothing, the wife whom he ignores and betrays, and the mother whom he filed away in a nursing home and forgot.

Not quite what Thoreau predicted. The question is—and it is a question forced by Lasch's implication that his generalizations, and Heller's character, speak for the whole culture—does the Lasch-Heller characteristic American match the Americans you know in Salt Lake City and I know in California and other people know in Omaha and Des Moines and Wichita and Dallas and Hartford and Bangor?

I doubt that we know many such limp dishrags as Heller's Bob Slocum, but we recognize elements of the world he lives in. We have watched the progress of the sexual revolution and the one-hoss-shay collapse of the family. We have observed how, in the mass media and hence in the popular imagination, celebrity has crowded out distinction. We have seen the gap widen between rich and poor, have seen crime push itself into high places and make itself all but impregnable, have watched the drug culture work outward from the ghettos into every level of American life. We are not unaware of how the Pleasure Principle, promoted about equally by prosperity, advertisers, and a certain kind of therapist, has eaten the pilings out from under dedication and accomplishment; how we have given up saving for the future and started spending for the present, because the Pleasure Principle preaches gratification, because the tax laws and inflation discourage saving and encourage borrowing. We have stood by uneasily while the Pleasure Principle invaded the schools, and teachers tried desperately to save something out of the wreck by pretending to be entertainers. Johnny can't read, but he expects his English class to be as entertaining as an X-rated movie. Increasingly he seems to be a vessel which dries out and deteriorates if it is not kept filled, and so for his leisure hours he must have a four-hundred-dollar stereo and/or a color TV, and when he walks around he carries a transistor radio, tuned loud. If he doesn't get a ski weekend during the winter term, he calls a school strike. He has never worn a tie, but he can vote, being eighteen.

We have lived through times when it has seemed that everything ran downhill, when great corporations were constantly being caught in bribery, price fixing, or the dumping of chemical wastes in the public's backyard—when corporate liberty, in other words, was indulged at the public expense. We have seen the proliferation of government bureaus, some of them designed to curb corporate abuses and some apparently designed only to inhibit the freedom of citizens. We have watched some of our greatest cities erupt in mindless violence. We have built ourselves a vast industrial trap in which, far from being the self-reliant individuals we once were, and still are in fantasy, we are absolutely helpless when the power fails.

Can any of the values left over from the frontier speak persuasively to the nation we have become? Some of the most antisocial of them still do, especially the ruthless go-getterism of an earlier phase of capitalism. Single-minded dedication, self-reliance, a willingness to work long and hard persist most visibly not in the average democratic individual but in the managers of exploitative industry and in spokesmen for the Far Right. Expressed in a modern context, they inspire not admiration but repulsion, they make us remember that some of the worst things we have done to our continent, our society, and our character have been done under their auspices. We remain a nation of real estate operators, trading increasingly small portions of the increasingly overburdened continent back and forth at increasingly inflated prices.

But I have a faith that, however obscured and overlooked, other tendencies remain from our frontier time. In spite of multiplying crises, galloping inflation, energy shortages, a declining dollar, shaken confidence, crumbling certainties, we cannot know many Americans without perceiving stubborn residues of toughness, ingenuity, and cheerfulness. The American is far less antisocial than he used to be; he has had to learn social values as he created them. Outside of business, where he still has a great deal to learn, he is very often such a human being as the future would be safe with.

I recognize Heller's Bob Slocum as one kind of contemporary American, but I do not commonly meet him in my own life. The kind I do meet may be luckier than most, but he seems to me far more representative than Bob Slocum, and I have met him all over the country and among most of the shifting grades of American life. He is likely to work reasonably hard, but not kill himself working; he doesn't have to, whether he is an electronics plant manager or a professor or a bricklayer. If he is still an individualist in many ways, he is also a belonger. If he belongs to a minority he is probably a civil rights activist, or at least sympathizer. If he belongs to that group of "middle Americans" about whom Robert Coles wrote a perceptive book, he may be confused and shaken by some equal-opportunity developments, but as often as not he understands the historical context and the necessity for increasing the access to opportunity, and if not supportive, is at least acquiescent.

He has not given up the future, as Lasch believes. He is often very generous. He gives to good causes, or causes he thinks good, and in a uniquely American way he associates himself with others in ad hoc organizations to fight for better schools, more parks, political reforms, social justice. That is the remote but unmistakable echo of the Plymouth Compact—government improvised for the occasion; government of, by, and for the people.

This American may be pinched, but he is not poor by any definition. He is lower middle, middle middle, upper middle. Whether he works for a corporation, a university, a hospital, a government bureau, whether he is a skilled laborer or a professional, he has a considerable stake in this society. He is always respectful of money, but he cannot be called money-crazy: money-craziness occurs much more commonly among the poor who have far too little or the rich who have far too much. Unless he is financially involved in growth, in which case he may be everything I have just said he is not, he is wary of uncontrolled growth and even opposed to it. Free enterprise in the matter of real estate speculation strikes him as more often fruitful of social ill than social good, just as industrialization strikes him not as the cure for our ills but the cause of many of them. He takes his pleasures and relaxations, and expects far more of them than his frontier grandparents did, but he can hardly be called a pleasure freak bent on instant gratification. He is capable, as many of us observed during a recent California drought, of abstinence and economy and personal sacrifice in the public interest, and would be capable of much more of those if he had leaders who encouraged them.

This sort of American is either disregarded or disparaged in the alarming books that assay our culture. Lasch, though he would like him better than the kind he describes, seems to think him gone past retrieval. But Lasch, like some other commentators, is making a point and selects his evidence. To some extent also, he makes the New Yorker mistake of mistaking New York for the United States. To an even greater extent he reads a certain class as if it were a cross section of the entire population. He would honestly like to get us back onto the tracks he thinks we have left, or onto new tracks that lead somewhere, and he deplores what he sees as much as anyone would.

But in fact we may be more on the tracks than he believes we are. His book is rather like the books of captious British travelers in the first half of the nineteenth century. Not having experienced the potency of the dream of starting from scratch, he sees imperfections as failures, not as stages of a long slow effort. But there is something very American about *The Culture of Narcissism*, too. We have always had a habit, when we were not bragging, of accepting Father Europe's view that we are short on cultural finesse and that our fabled moral superiority is a delusion. It may *be* a delusion; that does not make an American a creature unworthy of study, or American society a dismal failure. We have never given up the habit we acquired while resisting George III: we knock government and authority, including our own; we bad-mouth ourselves; like Robert Frost's liberal, we won't take our own side in an argument.

It is time we did. In 1992, twelve years from now, it will be half a millennium since Columbus and his sailors poured out on deck to see the new world. In half a millennium we should have gone at least partway toward what we started out to be. In spite of becoming the dominant world power, the dominant industrial as well as agricultural nation, the dominant force for freedom in the world, in spite of the fact that historically our most significant article of export has been the principle of liberty, in spite of the fact that the persecuted and poor of the earth still look to the United States as their haven and their hope—ask a Mexican wetback family, ask a family of Vietnamese boat people—many of us have never quite got it straight what it was we started out to be, and some of us have forgotten.

Habits change with time, but the principles have not changed. We remain a free and self-reliant people and a land of opportunity, and if our expectations are not quite what they once were, they are still greater expectations than any people in the world can indulge. A little less prosperity might be good for some of us, and I think we can confidently expect God to provide what we need. We could also do with a little less pleasure, learn to limit it in quantity and upgrade it in quality. Like money, pleasure is an admirable by-product and a contemptible goal. That lesson will still take some learning.

Give us time. Half a millennium is not enough. Give us time to wear out the worst of the selfishness and greed and turn our energy to humane and socially useful purposes. Give us a perennial few (a few is all any society can expect, and all any society really needs) who do not forget the high purpose that marked our beginnings, and Thoreau may yet be proved right in his prophecy.

Above all, let us not forget or mislay our optimism about the possible. In all our history we have never been more than a few years without a crisis, and some of those crises, the Civil War for one, and the whole problem of slavery, have been graver and more alarming than our present one. We have never stopped criticizing the performance of our elected leaders, and we have indeed had some bad ones and have survived them. The system was developed by accident and opportunity, but it is a system of extraordinary resilience. The United States has a ramshackle government, Robert Frost told Khrushchev in a notable conversation. The more you ram us, the harder we shackle. In the midst of our anxiety we should remember that this is the oldest and stablest republic in the world. Whatever its weaknesses and failures, we show no inclination to defect. The currents of defection flow the other way.

Let us not forget who we started out to be, or be surprised that we have not yet arrived. Robert Frost can again, as so often, be our spokesman. "The land was ours before we were the land's," he wrote. "Something we were withholding made us weak, until we found that it was ourselves we were withholding from our land of living." He was a complex, difficult, often malicious man, with grave faults. He was also one of our great poets, as much in the American grain as Lincoln or Thoreau. He contained within himself many of our most contradictory qualities, he never learned to subdue his selfish personal demon—and he was never a favorite of the New York critics, who thought him a country bumpkin.

But like the folk mind, he was wiser than the intellectuals. No American was ever wiser. Listening to him, we can refresh ourselves with our own best image, and renew our vision of America: not as Perfection, not as Heaven on Earth, not as New Jerusalem, but as flawed glory and exhilarating task.

Living Dry

The West is a region of extraordinary variety within its abiding unity, and of an iron immutability beneath its surface of change. The most splendid part of the American habitat, it is also the most fragile. It has been misinterpreted and mistreated because, coming to it from earlier frontiers where conditions were not unlike those of northern Europe, we found it different, daunting, exhilarating, dangerous, and unpredictable, and we entered it carrying habits that were often inappropriate, and expectations that were surely excessive. The dreams we brought to it were recognizable American dreams—a new chance, a little gray home in the West, adventure, danger, bonanza, total freedom from constraint and law and obligation, the Big Rock Candy Mountain, the New Jerusalem. Those dreams had often paid off in earlier parts of America, and they paid off for some in the West. For the majority, no. The West has had a way of warping well-carpentered habits, and raising the grain on exposed dreams.

The fact is, it has been as notable for mirages as for the realization of dreams. Illusion and mirage have been built into it since Coronado came seeking the Seven Cities of Cíbola in 1540. Coronado's failure was an early, spectacular trial run for other and humbler failures. Witness the young men from all over the world who fill graveyards in California's

Mother Lode country. There is one I remember: *Nato a Parma 1830, morto a Morfi 1850*, an inscription as significant for its revelation of the youth of many argonauts as for its misspelling of Murphy's, the camp where this boy died. Witness too the homesteaders who retreated eastward from the dry plains with signs on their covered wagons: "In God we trusted, in Kansas we busted." Yet we have not even yet fully lost our faith in Cíbola, or the nugget as big as a turnip, or even Kansas.

Anyone pretending to be a guide through wild and fabulous territory should know the territory. I wish I knew it better than I do. I am not Jed Smith. But Jed Smith was not available for this assignment, and I was. I accepted it eagerly, at least as much for what I myself might learn as for what I might be able to tell others. I can't come to even tentative conclusions about the West without coming to some conclusions about myself.

I have lived in the West, many parts of it, for the best part of seventy-seven years. I have found stories and novels in it, have studied its history and written some of it, have tried to know its landscapes and understand its people, have loved and lamented it, and sometimes rejected its most "western" opinions and prejudices, and pretty consistently despised its most powerful politicians and the general trend of their politics. I have been a lover but not much of a booster. Nevertheless, for better or worse, the West is in my computer, the biggest part of my software.

If there is such a thing as being conditioned by climate and geography, and I think there is, it is the West that has conditioned me. It has the forms and lights and colors that I respond to in nature and in art. If there is a western speech, I speak it; if there is a western character or personality, I am some variant of it; if there is a western culture in the small-*c*, anthropological sense, I have not escaped it. It has to have shaped me. I may even have contributed to it in minor ways, for culture is a pyramid to which each of us brings a stone.

Therefore I ask your indulgence if I sometimes speak in terms of my personal experience, feelings, and values, and put the anecdotal and normative ahead of the statistical, and emphasize personal judgments and trial syntheses rather than the analysis that necessarily preceded them. In doing so, I shall be trying to define myself as well as my native region.

Perhaps we will all know better what I think when we see what I say.

There are other ways of defining the West, but since Major John Wesley Powell's 1878 *Report on the Lands of the Arid Region* it has usually been said that it starts at about the 98th meridian of west longitude and ends at the Pacific Ocean. Neither boundary has the Euclidean perfection of a fixed imaginary line, for on the west the Pacific plate is restless, constantly shoving Los Angeles northward where it is not wanted, and on the east the boundary between Middle West and West fluctuates a degree or two east or west depending on wet and dry cycles.

Actually it is not the arbitrary 98th meridian that marks the West's beginning, but a perceptible line of real import that roughly coincides with it, reaching southward about a third of the way across the Dakotas, Nebraska, and Kansas, and then swerving more southwestward across Oklahoma and Texas. This is the isohyetal line of twenty inches, beyond which the mean annual rainfall is less than the twenty inches normally necessary for unirrigated crops.

A very little deficiency, even a slight distortion of the season in which the rain falls, makes all the difference. My family homesteaded on the Montana-Saskatchewan border in 1915, and burned out by 1920, after laying the foundation for a little dust bowl by plowing up a lot of buffalo grass. If the rains had been kind, my father would have proved up on that land and become a naturalized Canadian. I estimate that I missed becoming Canadian by no more than an inch or two of rain; but that same deficiency confirmed me as a citizen of the West.

The West is defined, that is, by inadequate rainfall, which means a general deficiency of water. We have water only between the time of its falling as rain or snow and the time when it flows or percolates back into the sea or the deep subsurface reservoirs of the earth. We can't create water, or increase the supply. We can only hold back and redistribute what there is. If rainfall is inadequate, then streams will be inadequate, lakes will be few and sometimes saline, underground water will be slow to renew itself when it has been pumped down, the air will be very dry, and surface evaporation from lakes and reservoirs will be extreme. In desert parts of the West it is as much as ten feet a year.

The only exception to western aridity, apart from the mountains that provide the absolutely indispensable snowsheds, is the northwest corner, on the Pacific side of the Cascades. It is a narrow exception: everything east of the mountains, which means two-thirds to three-quarters of Washington and Oregon, is in the rain shadow.

California, which might seem to be an exception, is not. Though from San Francisco northward the coast gets plenty of rain, that rain, like the lesser rains elsewhere in the state, falls not in the growing season but in winter. From April to November it just about can't rain. In spite of the mild coastal climate and an economy greater than that of all but a handful of nations, California fits Walter Webb's definition of the West as "a semi-desert with a desert heart." It took only the two-year drought of 1976–77, when my part of California got eight inches of rain each year instead of the normal eighteen, to bring the whole state to a panting pause. A five-year drought of the same severity would half depopulate the state.

So—the West that we are talking about comprises a dry core of eight public lands states—Arizona, Colorado, Idaho, Montana, Nevada, New Mexico, Utah, and Wyoming—plus two marginal areas. The first of these is the western part of the Dakotas, Nebraska, Kansas, Oklahoma, and Texas, authentically dry but with only minimal public lands. The second is the West Coast—Washington, Oregon, and California—with extensive arid lands but with well-watered coastal strips and with many rivers. Those marginal areas I do not intend to exclude, but they do complicate statistics. If I cite figures, they will often be for the states of the dry core.

Aridity, and aridity alone, makes the various Wests one. The distinctive western plants and animals, the hard clarity (before power plants and metropolitan traffic altered it) of the western air, the look and location of western towns, the empty spaces that separate them, the way farms and ranches are either densely concentrated where water is plentiful or widely scattered where it is scarce, the pervasive presence of the federal government as landowner and land manager, the even more noticeable federal presence as dam builder and water broker, the snarling states'-rights and antifederal feelings whose burden Bernard DeVoto once characterized in a sentence—"Get out and give us more money"—those are all consequences, and by no means all the consequences, of aridity.

Aridity first brought settlement to a halt at the edge of the dry country and then forced changes in the patterns of settlement. The best guide to those changes is Walter Webb's seminal study, *The Great Plains* (1931). As Webb pointed out, it took a lot of industrial invention to conquer the plains: the Colt revolver, a horseman's weapon, to subdue the horse Indians; barbed wire to control cattle; windmills to fill stock tanks and irrigate little gardens and hayfields; railroads to open otherwise unlivable spaces and bring first buffalo hides and buffalo bones and then cattle and wheat to market; gang machinery to plow, plant, and harvest big fields.

As it altered farming methods, weapons, and tools, so the dry country bent water law and the structure of land ownership. Eastern water law, adopted with little change from English common law, was essentially riparian. The owner of a stream bank, say a miller, could divert water from the stream to run his mill, but must flow it back when it had done his work for him. But in the arid lands only a little of the water diverted from a stream for any purpose—gold mining, irrigation, municipal or domestic consumption—ever finds its way back. Much is evaporated and lost. Following the practice of Gold Rush miners who diverted streams for their rockers and monitors, all of the dry core states subscribe to the so-called Colorado Doctrine of prior appropriation. First come, first served. The three coastal states go by some version of the California Doctrine, which is modified riparian.

Because water is precious, and because either prior appropriation or riparian rights, ruthlessly exercised, could give monopolistic power to an upstream or riparian landowner, both doctrines, over time, have been hedged with safeguards. Not even yet have we fully adapted our water law to western conditions, as was demonstrated when the California Supreme Court in 1983 invoked the "Public Trust" principle to prevent a single user, in this case the Los Angeles Water and Power Authority, from ever again draining a total water supply, in this case the streams that once watered the Owens Valley and fed Mono Lake. The court did not question the validity of Los Angeles' water rights. It only said that those rights could not be exercised at the expense of the public's legitimate interest.

The conditions that modified water use and water law also changed the character of western agriculture. The open range cattle outfits working north from Texas after the Civil War had only a brief time of uninhibited freedom before they ran into nesters and barbed wire. But the homesteaders who began disputing the plains with cattlemen quickly found that 160 acres of dry land were a hand without even openers. Many threw in. Those who stuck either found land on streams or installed windmills; and they moved toward larger acreages and the stock farm, just as the cattlemen eventually moved toward the same adjustment from the other end.

Powell had advocated just such an adjustment in 1878. In country where it took 20, 30, even 50 acres to feed one steer, quarter-section homesteads were of no use to a stock raiser. But 160 acres of intensively worked irrigated land were more than one family needed or could handle. Furthermore, the rectangular cadastral surveys that had been in use ever since the Northwest Ordinance of 1787 paid no attention to water. Out on the plains, a single quarter or half section might contain all the water within miles, and all the adjacent range was dominated by whoever owned that water.

Powell therefore recommended a new kind of survey defining irrigable homesteads of 80 acres and grazing homesteads of 2,560, four full sections. Every plot should have access to water, and every water right should be tied to land title. Obviously, that program would leave a lot of dry land unsettled.

Unfortunately for homesteaders and the West, Powell's report was buried under dead leaves by Congress. Ten years later, his attempt to close the Public Domain until he could get it surveyed and its irrigable lands identified was defeated by Senator "Big Bill" Stewart of Nevada, the first of a long line of incomparably bad Nevada senators. In 1889 and 1890 the constitutional conventions of Montana, Idaho, and Wyoming territories would not listen when Powell urged them to lay out their political boundaries along drainage divides, so that watershed and timber lands, foothill grazing lands, and valley irrigated lands could be managed intelligently without conflict. The only place where a drainage divide does mark a political boundary is a stretch of the Continental Divide between Idaho and Montana. And to cap this history of old habits stubbornly clung to and hopes out of proportion to possibilities, when Powell addressed the boosters of the Irrigation Congress in Los Angeles in 1893 and warned them that they were laying up a heritage of litigation and failure because there was only enough water to irrigate a fifth of the western lands, the boosters didn't listen either. They booed him.

Powell understood the consequences of aridity, as the boosters did not, and still do not. Westerners who would like to return to the old days of free grab, people of the kind described as having made America great by their initiative and energy in committing mass trespass on the minerals, grass, timber, and water of the Public Domain, complain that no western state is master in its own house. Half its land is not its own—85 percent of Nevada is not Nevada, but the United States; two-thirds of Utah and Idaho likewise; nearly half of California, Arizona, and Wyoming—48 percent of the eleven public lands states.

There are periodic movements, the latest of which was the so-called Sagebrush Rebellion of the 1970s, to get these lands "returned" to the states, which could then dispose of them at bargain-basement rates to favored stockmen, corporations, and entrepreneurs.

The fact is, the states never owned those lands, and gave up all claim to them when they became states. They were always federal lands, acquired by purchase, negotiation, or conquest before any western state existed. The original thirteen colonies created the first Public Domain when they relinquished to the federal government their several claims to what was then the West. The states between the Alleghenies and the Mississippi River were made out of it. All but one of the rest of the contiguous forty-eight were made out of the Louisiana and Florida purchases, the land acquired by the Oregon settlement with Great Britain, and the territory taken from Mexico in the Mexican War or obtained by purchase afterward. All of the western states except Texas, which entered the Union as an independent republic and never had any Public Domain, were created out of federal territory by formal acts of Congress, which then did everything it could to dispose of the public lands within them.

As far as a little beyond the Missouri, the system of disposal worked. Beyond the 98th meridian it did not, except in the spotty way that led Webb to call the West an "oasis civilization." Over time, large areas of forest land and the most spectacular scenery were reserved in the public interest, but much land was not considered worth reserving, and could not be settled or given away. The land laws—the Preemption Act, Homestead

Act, Desert Land Act, Carey Act, Timber and Stone Act—produced more failure and fraud than family farms. Not even the Newlands Act of 1902, though it has transformed the West, has put into private hands more than a modest amount of the Public Domain.

Despite all efforts, the West remained substantially federal. In 1930 Herbert Hoover and his Secretary of the Interior Ray Lyman Wilbur tried to give a lot of abused dry land to the states, and the states just laughed. Then in 1934, in the worst Dust Bowl year, the Taylor Grazing Act acknowledged the federal government's reluctant decision to retain—and rescue and manage—the overgrazed, eroded Public Domain. In the 1940s the stockmen's associations tried to steal it, as well as the Forest Service's grazing lands, in a dry rehearsal of the later Sagebrush Rebellion. Bernard DeVoto, in the Easy Chair pages of *Harper's Magazine*, almost single-handedly frustrated that grab.

But by the 1940s more than stockmen were interested, and more than grass was at stake. During and after World War II the West had revealed treasures of oil, coal, uranium, molybdenum, phosphates, and much else. States whose extractive industries were prevented from unhampered exploitation of these resources again cried foul, demanding "back" the lands they had never owned, cared for, or really wanted, and complaining that the acreages of the Bureau of Land Management, national forests, national parks and monuments, wildlife refuges, military reservations, and dam sites, as well as the arid poor farms where we had filed away our Indian responsibilities, were off the state tax rolls and outside of state control and "locked up" from developers who, given a free hand, would make the West rich and prosperous.

Never mind that grazing fees and coal and oil lease fees and timber sale prices are so low that they amount to a fat subsidy to those who enjoy them. (The flat fee of $1.35 per animal-unit-month set by the Reagan Administration as a grazing fee is about 20 percent of what leasers of private land must pay in most districts. Many timber sales are below cost.) Never mind that half of the money that does come in from fees and leases is given to the states in lieu of taxes. Never mind that the feds spend the other half, and more, rescuing and rehabilitating the lands whose proper management would bankrupt the states in which they lie. Never mind the federal aid highways, and the federally financed dams, and the write-offs against flood control, and the irrigation water delivered at a few dollars an acre foot. Take for granted federal assistance, but damn federal control. Your presence as absentee landlord offends us, Uncle. Get out, and give us more money.

There are other objections, too, some of them more legitimate than those of stockmen, lumbermen, and miners greedy for even more than they are getting. There are real difficulties of management when the landscape is checkerboarded with private, state, and federal ownership. And federal space is tempting whenever the nation needs a bombing range, an atomic test site, missile silo locations, or places to dump nuclear waste or store nerve gas. Generally, the West protests that because of its public lands it gets all the garbage; but sometimes, so odd we are as a species, one or another western state will fight for the garbage, and lobby to become the home of a nuclear dump.

More by oversight than intention, the federal government allowed the states to assert ownership of the water within their boundaries, and that is actually an ownership far more valuable but more complicated than that of land. The feds own the watersheds, the stream and lake beds, the dam sites. Federal bureaus, with the enthusiastic concurrence of western chambers of commerce, have since 1902 done most of the costly impoundment and distribution of water. And federal law, in a pinch, can and does occasionally veto what states and irrigation districts do with that water. It is a good guess that it will have to do so more and more—that unless the states arrive at some relatively uniform set of rules, order will have to be imposed on western water by the federal government.

It will not be easy, and the federal government has created a nasty dilemma for itself by giving its blessing both to the legal fiction of state water ownership and to certain Native American rights to water. As early as 1908, in the so-called Winters Doctrine decision, the Supreme Court confirmed the Indians' rights in water originating within or flowing through their reservations. Though those rights have never been quantified or put to use (a beginning has been made by the tribes on the Fort Peck Reservation), Indian tribes all across the West have legitimate but unspecified claims to water already granted by the states to white individuals and corporations. Even without the Indian claims, many western streams—for a prime example the Colorado—are already oversubscribed.

The Colorado River Compact allocated 17.5 million acre feet annually among the upper basin, lower basin, and Mexico. The actual annual flow since 1930 has averaged about 12 million acre feet.

Aridity arranged all that complicated natural and human mess, too. In the view of some, it also helped to create a large, spacious, independent, sunburned, self-reliant western character, and a large, open, democratic western society. Of that, despite a wistful desire to believe, I am less than confident.

Nineteenth-century America, overwhelmingly agricultural, assumed that settlement meant agricultural settlement. That assumption underlies—some say it undermines—Frederick Jackson Turner's famous hypothesis, expressed in his 1893 lecture "The Significance of the Frontier in American History," that both democratic institutions and the American character have been largely shaped by the experience of successive frontiers, with their repeated dream of betterment, their repeated acceptance of primitive hardships, their repeated hope and strenuousness and buoyancy, and their repeated fulfillment as smiling and productive commonwealths of agrarian democrats.

Turner was so intent upon the mass movement toward free land that he paid too little attention to a growing movement toward the industrial cities, and his version of the American character is therefore open to some qualifications. He also paid too little attention to the drastic changes enforced by aridity beyond the 98th meridian, the changes that Powell before him and Webb after him concentrated upon.

The fact is, agriculture at first made little headway in the West, and when it was finally imposed upon the susceptible—and some unsusceptible—spots, it was established pretty much by brute force, and not entirely by agrarian democrats.

Until the Civil War and after, most of the West was not a goal but a barrier. Webb properly remarks that if it had turned out to be country adapted to the slave economy, the South would have fought for it, and its history would have been greatly different. He also points out that if the country beyond the Missouri had been wooded and well watered, there would have been no Oregon Trail.

• • •

Emigrants bound up the Platte Valley on their way to Oregon, California, or Utah, the first targets of the westward migration, almost universally noted in their journals that a little beyond Grand Island their nostrils dried out and their lips cracked, their wagon wheels began to shrink and wobble, and their estimates of distance began to be ludicrously off the mark. They observed that green had ceased to be the prevailing color of the earth, and had given way to tans, grays, rusty reds, and toned white; that salt often crusted the bottoms of dry lakes (they used some of it, the sodium or potassium bicarbonate that they called saleratus, to leaven their bread); that the grass no longer made a turf, but grew in isolated clumps with bare earth between them; that there was now no timber except on the islands in the Platte; that unfamiliar animals had appeared: horned toads and prairie dogs that seemed to require no water at all, and buffalo, antelope, jackrabbits, and coyotes that could travel long distances for it.

They were at the border of strangeness. Only a few miles into the West, they felt the difference; and as Webb says, the degree of strangeness can be measured by the fact that almost all the new animals they saw they misnamed. The prairie dog is not a dog, the horned toad it not a toad, the jackrabbit is not a rabbit, the buffalo is not a buffalo, and the pronghorn antelope is more goat than antelope. But they could not mistake the aridity. They just didn't know how much their habits would have to change if they wanted to live beyond the 98th meridian. None of them in that generation would have denied aridity to its face, as William Gilpin, the first territorial governor of Colorado, would do a generation later, asserting that it was a simple matter on the plains to *dig* for wood and water, that irrigation was as easy as fencing, which it supplanted, and that the dry plains and the Rockies could handily support a population of two hundred million. That kind of fantasy, like Cyrus Thomas's theory that cultivation increases rainfall, that "rain follows the plow," would have to wait for the boosters.

Two lessons all western travelers had to learn: mobility and sparseness. Mobility was the condition of life beyond the Missouri. Once they acquired the horse, the Plains Indians were as migrant as the buffalo they lived by. The mountain men working the beaver streams were no more fixed than the clouds. And when the change in hat fashions killed the fur trade, and mountain men turned to guiding wagon trains, the whole intention of those trains was to get an early start, as soon as the grass greened up, and then get *through* the West as fast as possible. The Mormons were an exception, a special breed headed for sanctuary in the heart of the desert, a people with a uniquely cohesive social order and a theocratic discipline that made them better able to survive.

But even the Mormons were villages on the march, as mobile as the rest until, like Moses from Pisgah's top, they looked upon Zion. Once there, they quickly made themselves into the West's stablest society. But notice: Now, 140 years after their hegira, they have managed to put only about 3 percent of Utah's land under cultivation; and because they took seriously the Lord's command to be fruitful and multiply, Zion has been overpopulated, and exporting manpower, for at least half a century. One of the bitterest conflicts in modern Utah is that between the environmentalists who want to see much of that superlative wilderness preserved roadless and wild, and the stubborn Mormon determination to make it support more Saints than it possibly can.

Lieutenant Zebulon Pike, sent out in 1806 to explore the country between the Missouri and Santa Fe, had called the high plains the Great American Desert. In 1819 the expedition of Major Stephen Long corroborated that finding, and for two generations nobody seriously questioned it. The plains were unfit for settlement by a civilized, meaning an agricultural, people, and the farther west you went, the worse things got. So for the emigrants who in 1840 began to take wheels westward up the Platte Valley, the interior West was not a place but a way, a trail to the Promised Land, an adventurous, dangerous rite of passage. In the beginning there were only two *places* on its two-thousand-mile length: Fort Laramie on the North Platte and Fort Hall on the Snake. And those were less settlements than way stations, refreshment and recruitment stops different only in style from motel-and-gas-and-lunchroom turnouts on a modern interstate.

Insofar as the West was a civilization at all between the time of Lewis and Clark's explorations and about 1870, it was largely a civilization in motion, driven by dreams. The people who composed and represented it were part of a true Folk-Wandering, credulous, hopeful, hardy, largely uninformed. The dreams are not dead even today, and the habit of mobility has only been reinforced by time. If, as Wendell Berry says, most Americans are not placed but displaced persons, then western Americans are the most displaced persons of all.

Ever since Daniel Boone took his first excursion over Cumberland Gap, Americans have been wanderers. When Charles Dickens, in the Mississippi Valley, met a full-sized dwelling house coming down the road at a round trot, he was looking at the American people head-on. With a continent to take over and Manifest Destiny to goad us, we could not have avoided being footloose. The initial act of emigration from Europe, an act of extreme, deliberate disaffiliation, was the beginning of a national habit.

It should not be denied, either, that being footloose has always exhilarated us. It is associated in our minds with escape from history and oppression and law and irksome obligations, with absolute freedom, and the road has always led west. Our folk heroes and our archetypal literary figures accurately reflect that side of us. Leatherstocking, Huckleberry Finn, the narrator of *Moby Dick*, all are orphans and wanderers: any of them could say, "Call me Ishmael." The Lone Ranger has no dwelling place except the saddle. And when teenagers run away these days, in the belief that they are running toward freedom, they more often than not run west. Listen to the Haight-Ashbury dialogues in Joan Didion's *Slouching toward Bethlehem*. Examine the American character as it is self-described in *Habits of the Heart*, by Robert Bellah and others.

But the rootlessness that expresses energy and a thirst for the new and an aspiration toward freedom and personal fulfillment has just as often been a curse. Migrants deprive themselves of the physical and spiritual bonds that develop within a place and a society. Our migratoriness has hindered us from becoming a people of communities and traditions, especially in the West. It has robbed us of the gods who make places holy. It has cut off individuals and families and communities from memory and the continuum of time. It has left at least some of us with a kind of spiritual pellagra, a deficiency disease, a hungering for the ties of a rich and stable social order. Not only is the American home a launching pad, as Margaret Mead said; the American community, especially in the West, is an overnight camp. American individualism, much celebrated and cherished, has developed without its essential corrective, which is belonging. Freedom, when found, can turn out to be airless and unsustaining. Especially in the West, what we have instead of place is space. Place is more than half memory, shared memory. Rarely do Westerners stay long enough at one stop to share much of anything.

The principal invention of western American culture is the motel, the principal exhibit of that culture the automotive roadside. The principal western industry is tourism, which is not only mobile but seasonal. Whatever it might want to be, the West is still primarily a series of brief visitations or a trail to somewhere else; and western literature, from *Roughing It* to *On the Road*, from *The Log of a Cowboy* to *Lonesome Dove*, from *The Big Rock Candy Mountain* to *The Big Sky*, has been largely a literature not of place but of motion.

Trying to capture America in a sentence, Gertrude Stein said, "Conceive a space that is filled with moving." If she had been reared in Boston she might not have seen it so plainly; but she was reared in Oakland. She knew that few Westerners die where they were born, that most live out their lives as a series of uprootings.

Adaptation is the covenant that all successful organisms sign with the dry country. Mary Austin, writing of the Owens Valley in the rain shadow of the Sierra, remarked that "the manner of the country makes the usage of life there, and the land will not be lived in except in its own fashion. The Shoshones live like their trees, with great spaces between. . . ."

She might have added, though I don't remember that she did, how often Shoshonean place names contain the syllable *-pah:* Tonopah, Ivanpah, Pahrump, Paria. In the Shoshonean language, *-pah* means water, or water hole. The Pah-Utes are the Water Utes, taking their name from their rarest and most precious resource. They live mainly in Utah and Nevada, the two driest states in the Union, and in those regions water is safety, home, life, *place*. All around those precious watered places, forbidding and unlivable, is only space, what one must travel through between places of safety.

Thoroughly adapted, the Pah-Utes (Paiutes) were migratory between fixed points marked by seasonal food supplies and by water. White Americans, once they began to edge into the dry country from east, west, and south, likewise established their settlements on dependable water, and those towns have a special shared quality, a family resemblance.

For the moment, forget the Pacific Coast, furiously bent on becoming Conurbia from Portland to San Diego. Forget the metropolitan sprawl of Denver, Phoenix, Tucson, Albuquerque, Dallas–Fort Worth, and Salt Lake City, growing to the limits of their water and beyond, like bacterial cultures overflowing the edges of their agar dishes and beginning to sicken on their own wastes. If we want characteristic western towns we must look for them, paradoxically, beyond the West's prevailing urbanism, out in the boondocks where the interstates do not reach, mainline planes do not fly, and branch plants do not locate. The towns that are most western have had to strike a balance between mobility and stability, and the law of sparseness has kept them from growing too big. They are the places where the stickers stuck, and perhaps were stuck; the places where adaptation has gone furthest.

Whether they are winter wheat towns on the subhumid edge, whose elevators and bulbous silver water towers announce them miles away, or county towns in ranch country, or intensely green towns in irrigated desert valleys, they have a sort of forlorn, proud rightness. They look at once lost and self-sufficient, scruffy and indispensable. A road leads in out of wide emptiness, threads a fringe of service stations, taverns, and a motel or two, widens to a couple of blocks of commercial buildings, some still false-fronted, with glimpses of side streets and green lawns, narrows to another strip of automotive roadside, and disappears into more wide emptiness.

The loneliness and vulnerability of those towns always moves me, for I have lived in them. I know how the world of a child in one of them is bounded by weedy prairie, or the spine of the nearest dry range, or by flats where plugged tin cans lie rusting and the wind has pasted paper and plastic against the sagebrush. I know how precious is the safety of a few known streets and vacant lots and familiar houses. I know how the road in both directions both threatens and beckons. I know that most of the children in such a town will sooner or later take that road, and that only a few will take it back.

In mining country, vulnerability has already gone most or all of the way to death. In those ghosts or near ghosts where the placers have been gutted or the lodes played out, the shafts and drifts and tailings piles, the saloons and stores and hotels and houses, have been left to the lizards and a few survivors who have rejected the command of mobility. The deader the town, the more oppressive the emptiness that surrounds and will soon reclaim it. Unless, of course, the federal government has installed an atomic testing site, or new migrant entrepreneurs have come in to exploit the winter skiing or bring summer-festival culture. Then the ghost will have turned, at least temporarily, into a Searchlight, an Aspen, a Telluride, a Park City—a new way station for new kinds of migrants.

We return to mobility and the space that enforces it. Consider the observations of William Least Heat Moon, touring the blue highways of America. "The true West," he says (and notice that he too finds the true West somewhere outside the cities where 75 percent of Westerners live),

> differs from the East in one great, pervasive, influential, and awesome way: space. The vast openness changes the roads, towns, houses, farms, crops, machinery, politics, economics, and, naturally, ways of thinking. . . . Space west of the line is perceptible and often palpable, especially when it appears empty, and it's that apparent emptiness which makes matter look alone, exiled, and unconnected. . . . But as the space diminishes man and his constructions in a material fashion it also—paradoxically—makes them more noticeable. *Things show up out here.* The terrible distances eat up speed. Even dawn takes nearly an hour just to cross Texas. (*Blue Highways*, p. 136)

Distance, space, affects people as surely as it has bred keen eyesight into pronghorn antelope. And what makes that western space and distance? The same condition that enforces mobility on all adapted creatures, and tolerates only small or temporary concentrations of human or other life.

Aridity.

And what do you do about aridity, if you are a nation inured to plenty and impatient of restrictions and led westward by pillars of fire and cloud? You may deny it for a while. Then you must either adapt to it or try to engineer it out of existence.

The Rocky Mountain West

When I was a boy on the steppe-like Saskatchewan plains I used to watch, full of fantasies and longings, the crests of the Bearpaws that floated on the heat-waves along the southern horizon far down in Montana; and I can remember well when, at the age of eleven, I finally got to the mountains for the first time. The Bearpaws and the Little Belts, outlying ranges, would in themselves have been wonder enough after the withered plains. The forests, lakes, glaciers, and geysers of Yellowstone left me bug-eyed and awed. But what I most remember is a camp we made by Upper Mesa Falls, on Henry's Fork of the Snake.

I knew neither geography nor history. I didn't know that this marvelous torrent rose on the west side of Targhee Pass and flowed barely a hundred miles, through two Idaho counties, before joining the Snake near Rexburg; or that in 1810, only four years after Lewis and Clark came back across Lolo Pass with the first authentic information about the Northwest, Andrew Henry built on Henry's Fork near modern St. Anthony the first American post west of the continental divide. The divide itself meant nothing to me. My imagination was not stretched by the wonder of the parted waters—the Yellowstone and Gallatin and other rivers rising only a few miles eastward to flow out toward the Missouri, the Mississippi, and the Gulf, while this bright pounding stream was starting through its thousand miles of canyons to the Columbia and the Pacific.

All I knew was that it was pure delight to be where the land lifted in peaks and plunged in canyons, to sniff air that was thin, spray-cooled, full of the smells of pine and fir, to be so close-seeming to the improbable indigo sky. I gave my heart to the mountains the minute I stood beside this river with its spray in my face and watched it thunder into foam, smooth to green glass over sunken rocks, shatter to foam again. I was fascinated by how it sped by and yet was always there. Its roar shook both the earth and me.

When the sun dropped over the rim, the shadows chilled sharply; evening lingered until foam on water was ghostly and luminous in the near-dark. Alders caught in the current sawed like things alive, and the noise was louder. It was rare and comforting to waken late and hear the undiminished shouting of the water in the night. At sunup it was still there, powerful and incessant, with the sun tangled in its spray and the grass blue with wetness and the air, scented with campfire smoke, as heady as ether.

By such a river it is impossible to believe that one will ever be tired or old. Every sense applauds it. Taste it, feel its chill on the teeth: It is purity absolute. Watch its racing current, its steady renewal of force: It is transient and eternal. Listen again to its sounds, get far enough away so that the noise of falling tons of water does not stun the ears, and hear how much is going on underneath: a whole symphony of smaller sounds, hiss and splash and gurgle, the small talk of side channels, the whisper of blown and scattered spray gathering itself and beginning to flow again, secret and irresistible, among the wet rocks.

In the day or two we spent on Henry's Fork I think I got from the mountains one of their most precious gifts, wonder; and I learned something about their most precious resource, water. Both are indispensable to any discussion of the Rocky Mountains. Wonder, delight, freedom, adventure, excitement, are as much a part of the mountains as peaks and forests. Realism is for tamer landscapes; the mountains are inescapably romantic. And water, while an exhilarating element of the mountain scene, is in the West of more than aesthetic interest. By Upper Mesa Falls I had the wit to be awed by what was most vital. The water of the Rockies is the very source and fountain of the West's life. Without it the dry plains that front the mountains and the deserts that back them would be all but uninhabitable.

Let us limit the area under discussion. What we speak of is the Rocky Mountain states, but not the entire Rocky Mountains, whose multiple ranges extend all the way from Alaska down through Mexico, and which may, with no great distortion of topographical fact, be made continuous with the ranges of Central and South America. We do not even include all of the American Rockies, for our region stops in the middle of the Sangre de Cristo range in southern Colorado, at the foot of San Luis Valley. Below that is the Southwest, which ethnography and history, if not topography, have made another country.

Six states—Montana, Wyoming, Colorado, Utah, Idaho, and Nevada—comprise the Rocky Mountain West as distinguished from the Southwest, California, and the Pacific Northwest. Even these six are by no means all mountains. The whole eastern side of Montana, Wyoming, and Colorado is high plains, the gently sloping "long hill" which the swinging rivers have built and down which they run. Montana, named for its mountains, is three-fifths high plains; in Wyoming and Colorado the mountain chain is wider and the plains correspondingly narrower. But plains or mountains, these states are all within the "West," they lie beyond the invisible boundary which marks the true West's beginning. The boundary is the isohyetal line of twenty inches. Beyond it unassisted agriculture is dubious or foolhardy, and beyond it one knows the characteristic western feel—a dryness in the nostrils, a cracking of the lips, a transparent crystalline quality of the light, a new palette of gray and sage-green and sulfur-yellow and buff and toned white and rust-red, a new flora and a new fauna, a new ecology. The boundary is as unmistakable as if a wall had been built between East and West, roughly along the 98th meridian. If political boundary lines were logical, that is where our western states would begin, about a third of the way across Kansas, Nebraska, and the Dakotas.

But the Rocky Mountain West, if topography dictated boundaries, would begin at the mountains. Walling the high plains along the West, tilting the earth violently upward, they reach down out of the northwest corner of Montana, from where Chief Mountain is overthrust onto the short-grass prairie before Glacier National Park. Widening as they go, they run south-southwest, a chain of linked and interlocking ranges with several isolated outliers—the Sweetgrass Hills, the Highwoods, the Bearpaws, the Little Rockies, the Little Belts, the Big Snowies, and farther south the Big Horns and the Black Hills—until they reach a kind of corner at the Laramie Range, west of Cheyenne, Wyoming. There the whole system, which has now reached its widest spread, turns due south. The ranges that leap up in waves back of Boulder, Denver, and Colorado Springs are the highest in the whole American Rockies, with fifty-four peaks over 14,000 feet. Front Range, Park Range, Sawatch, Sangre de Cristo, San Miguel, La Plata—they fill western Colorado nearly to the Utah border, where the plateaus begin; and southward they reach into New Mexico to link the Rockies with the Southwest.

The eastern tier of Rocky Mountain states is thus made of plains on the east, mountains on the west. The western tier, not quite so symmetrically, is made of mountains and plateaus on the east and deserts on the west. Nevada, in fact, almost a region in itself, is nearly all desert, and its mountains, though they sometimes lift out of the Great Basin to lofty altitudes, are transitional between the Rockies and the Sierra Nevada rather than an integral part of the Rockies chain. Throughout the region, altitude has both good and bad effects: The mountains not only catch rain, but they throw a rain shadow. As the Montana, Wyoming, and Colorado plains lie in the rain shadow of the Rockies, the deserts of southwestern Idaho, western Utah, and Nevada lie in the rain shadow of the Cascade-Sierra-Coast Range uplifts. And these deserts, says the historian Walter Webb, are the truest West, its dead and arid heart. The rest of the West is a semihabitable fringe subject to cyclic disasters and dust bowls, and to a chronic and incurable shortage of water.

Professor Webb's thesis, whose central points were first phrased by Major John Wesley Powell in his extraordinary *Report on the Lands of the Arid Region* in 1878, needs periodic and stentorian restating in a region where optimism consistently outruns resources. But I should like it stated in a slightly different way. Instead of a country with a dead heart and semiarid fringes, I conceive the Rocky Mountain West to be composed of two long belts, one of dry steppe-like plains and one of true desert, with the multiple fountain of the Rockies between them. The fountain, even if every reclamation damsite should be developed, cannot water a fraction of the land that lies under it, but it is a fountain nevertheless. A simple comparison of annual rainfall figures, such as that between the 35-inch precipitation of the Yellowstone plateau and the 6-inch precipitation of the Big Hole Basin, tells only part of the story. The difference is actually much more than the apparent six to one, for the snowpack in the higher, cooler altitudes melts more slowly, the forest cover retards the runoff, the evaporation rate is much lower. Both the surface streams and the underground water table for hundreds of miles out on the plains may benefit from the fact that water is not only made in the mountains, but stored there. Without the highlands, the lowlands would be at the worst utter desert, which parts of them are anyway, and at best a thinly populated grazing country always on the dusty edge of trouble. And despite the help of the mountains, great sections of the plains periodically suffer terrible droughts and dust storms, loss of topsoil, ruin of farms and ranches. The 1950s repeated the 1930s, which in turn repeated the late 1880s and early 1890s.

Apart from its abiding unity of aridity, the Rocky Mountain West is a region of bewildering variety. Its life zones go all the way from arctic to subtropical, from reindeer moss to cactus, from mountain goat to horned toad. Its range of temperatures is as wide as its range of precipitation; it runs through twelve degrees of latitude and two miles or more of altitude. It is bald alkali flats, creosote-bush deserts, short-grass plains, irrigated alluvial valleys, subarctic fir forests, bare stone. It is, by common consent and the advertising of local booster clubs, the biggest, the best, the widest, the highest, the most invigorating, the friendliest. And of this gigantic sandwich with its two dry slabs and its moist center it is possible to cite the statistics of the Promised Land.

Within its area of roughly 400,000,000 acres—about one-fifth of the United States—lived in 1950 only 3,644,224 people. They were densest in Colorado, at 12.8 per square mile, thinnest in Nevada at 1.5 (the population density over the whole nation that year was 50.7). More than that, this skimpy population was concentrated in certain areas of plentiful water, and rather surprisingly, showed in the statistics as more urban

than rural. Over half of Colorado's people were packed into the ten counties along the east face of the Rockies, the rest scattered thinly through
fifty-three counties; more than two-thirds of Utah's population made a
narrow dense band of settlement in the six counties along the foot of the
Wasatch, the other third occupied oasis spots through Utah's remaining
twenty-three counties. And what was true in a marked way for Utah and
Colorado was true to a somewhat lesser extent for the whole region. As
Professor Webb has remarked, the West is an oasis civilization.

Room, then—great open spaces, as advertised. Also, those great
open spaces contained the mineral heart of the country, the source of
much of our gold, silver, lead, zinc, copper, molybdenum, antimony,
coal, iron, petroleum, uranium. The single mine of the Utah Copper at
Bingham produces, year in, year out, roughly 30 percent of the country's
copper, 10 percent of the world's. Now that the Mesabi Range in
Minnesota approaches exhaustion, Iron County in Utah becomes one of
our major sources of iron ore; the steel industry based upon Utah ore and
limestone and on Utah, Wyoming, and Colorado coal is the indispensable
first step in the West's industrial maturity. It has been estimated that
the upper Colorado River basin contains a sixth of the world's known
coal reserves. Since the railroads dieselized, and towns converted to
natural gas, all but the coking coals lie nearly untouched, and coal mining
is in a deadly slump; but at least the coal is there, in case anyone wants it.
When the accessible petroleum, including that in the extensive fields in
Montana, Wyoming, Colorado, and Utah, is used up the oil shales of
eastern Utah and western Colorado, already in experimental production
in Parachute Canyon, may be literally the world's major resource of oil.
And though there are no public figures, it is a foolproof guess that
most of the uranium mined in the United States comes from the San
Juan country where Utah, Colorado, New Mexico, and Arizona meet.
Recently, on a road across the top of the Navajo Reservation near the
Four Corners, where a few years ago you were lucky to meet so much as
a lizard, I was stalled by an oil exploration rig that broke an axle fording
Chinle Wash after a cloudburst. Behind me, in the hour I waited, stacked
up fifteen or twenty cars and parts of three other exploration outfits. And
who pulled the broken-down one out and let us get on? A truck loaded

with twenty tons of uranium ore. At Farmington, Ship Rock, Grand Junction, Moab, the wondering traveler will see repeated, with the addition of a mechanization then undreamed-of, a frenzy of boom not matched in this country since the gold rush.

The statistics say that the Rocky Mountain region is extravagantly endowed with sources of energy, including solar energy. And more: Down its entire length from Alberta to New Mexico, nearly a thousand miles by airline and much more as the ridgepole bends, the mountains form the nation's roof, and on them are generated the three great western river systems, the Missouri, the Columbia, and the Colorado, not to mention the Southwest's great river, the Rio Grande. Along all those rivers, and along all their tributaries, most of the most feasible power, reclamation, and flood-control damsites are already developed; for the others, two great government agencies and an assortment of private power companies now contend. But never mind, for the moment, who develops and harnesses the rivers, whether Corps of Engineers or Bureau of Reclamation, Idaho Power, Montana Power, or Utah Power and Light. Whoever puts them to work, they are formidable fountains of energy. Just one installation, Grand Coulee, made an industrial revolution in the Pacific Northwest; and Hollywood's Sunset Strip glares with the light of water falling through the penstocks of Hoover Dam on the Colorado. The Upper Colorado River Basin Project, already authorized and elements of it begun at Flaming Gorge and Glen Canyon, will provide the power for the exploitation of rich mineral and oil deposits, especially in the Uinta Basin of Utah and Colorado, and may well turn into an industrial complex "beyond the Urals" a region that until now has been submarginal farm land, desert grazing land, or total wasteland.

Power. Also, at least hopefully, the power of attraction, though historically the mountain region has never had this except sporadically. Even yet most people go, not to it, but through it. Much as it means to the six mountain states, the tourist business of all six is still minor—their total take of $715,000,000 in 1955 was less than that of California alone, and far less than that of New York or Florida. They are too far from the great centers of population—one is inclined to add Thank God—to be overrun with visitors. But within the region lie some of the continent's most impressive natural spectacles, including Glacier, Yellowstone, Rocky

Mountain, Grand Teton, Mesa Verde, Zion, and Bryce Canyon National Parks and twenty national monuments, besides hundreds of square miles of mountain, forest, plateau, and canyon that anywhere else would be called superlative. Within them also are many of the country's finest ski resorts—Sun Valley, Jackson Hole, Alta, Brighton, Aspen, Steamboat Springs. Some indication of the discrepancy between resources and use may be gained from the fact that so famous a ski area as Alta, held by many to have the finest snow and the best slopes on the continent, has accommodation for no more than 250 people as of 1957, and its sister resort, Brighton, a few miles of lovely high-altitude ski-touring over the divide, has only one real ski lodge, the Alpine Rose. Though even at the present rate of visitation, so unsatisfactory to local improvement committees, the annual visitors to the mountain states outnumber the native population by at least five to one, the fact remains that in the tourist business, as in the field of industrial energy, what so far exists is an enormous potential.

When you have run through the extravagant statistics and assayed the promise of the future, add this: That all the West's resources, even water power, even scenery, are more vulnerable than the resources of other regions, and that the social and economic structure of much of the West is tentative, uncertain, and shifting. The reasons are partly short-haul freight rates and partly distance from sizable industrial markets; but a more compelling reason is that the basic resources of water and soil, which can be mismanaged in other regions without drastic consequences, cannot be mismanaged in the West without consequences both immediate and catastrophic—consequences, moreover, that may spread far beyond the boundaries of the mountain states proper. The overgrazing or clear-cutting of a watershed on the Milk or the Yampa can carry consequences clear to St. Louis or Yuma. And the history of the Rocky Mountain West, when we hold at arm's length the excitement, the adventure, the romance, and the legendry, is a history of resources often mismanaged and of conditions often misunderstood or disregarded. Here, as elsewhere, settlement went principally by trial and error—only here the trials were sometimes terrible for those who suffered them, and the errors were sometimes disastrous to the land.

Specifically, the history of the Rocky Mountain West until very

237

recently has been a history of the importation of inherited humid-land habits (and carelessnesses) into a dry land that will not tolerate them; and of the indulgence of an unprecedented personal freedom, an atomic individualism, in a country which experience says can only be successfully tamed and lived in by a high degree of co-operation. The inherited wet-land habits have given us an endangered and partly damaged domain; the exacerbated personal freedom of the frontier has left us with a myth, a folklore, a set of beliefs and automatic acceptances, that are often comically at odds with the facts of life. Because that myth and that folk-lore have been embedded in a literary—or sub-literary—tradition, and through the movies and television and radio have the widest and most incessant distribution, this West is a place where life may very often be seen to copy art. Nobody so devours Westerns as the bona fide cowhand; nobody so religiously attends horse opera; nobody is so helplessly mod-eled by a fictitious image of himself. And what directly affects the working cowhand affects, in its subtler and less stereotyped forms, a lot of people in professional or service or industrial occupations, in cities like Denver and Great Falls and Salt Lake City and Boise. The West, and the Westerner, are partly what in fact and history they are and have been; and they are partly what the romantic imagination has made them.

Bernard DeVoto once described the West as a plundered province. Certainly, until the industrial boom that began with World War II, its products generally went to provide dividends for corporations chartered in Missouri or Maine or New Jersey, and to enrich investors living in Boston and Upper Montclair. And certainly, for at least seventy-five years from the opening of this frontier, it was not so much settled as raided. Until the 1880s it saw few true settlers except the Mormons, and some of the few it did see should have been talked out of coming, for their heroic efforts to make homesteads in the arid belt succeeded mainly in making dust bowls. Mainly what the West saw was explorers, through travelers bound for Oregon or California, and a series of hit-and-run plunderers, picturesque, robust, romantic, and destructive.

Newest of our regions, raw, brash, still nascent, still discovering its endowment, and still learning how to live within its natural conditions, the Rocky Mountain West cannot fairly be charged with its cultural limi-tations, as one literary Easterner did in describing the vacant, stunned, deprived or undeveloped "Montana Face." I suspect that the Montana Face is an illusion as romantic, in its way, as the archetypal figure of the Westerner that the Westerner himself is likely to accept. And it would be remarkable indeed if the cultural stirrings that agitate the campuses and the clubs of the West were not often naive, almost always derivative, and frequently fumbling. It is as permissible for a region to be young as for an individual to pass through the stages of childhood. The Rocky Mountain region has a total recorded history of hardly more than a century and a half, and a settled—or exploited—history of not much more than a century—some parts of it much less than that.

Before the beginning of the nineteenth century white men had seen the Rocky Mountains twice. In 1743 Pierre and Chevalier de la Vérendrye, exploring far down into the plains from the Saskatchewan country, described "high" and "well-wooded" mountains that might have been the Big Horns, the Black Hills, or even the Laramie Range. In 1776 Fathers Escalante and Dominguez crossed from Taos to the Utah Valley, turned southwest along the eastern wall of the Great Basin, recrossed the Colorado at the Crossing of the Fathers near the present Glen Canyon damsite, and found their way back across the Painted Desert to New Mexico. They left both Escalante's journal and Miera's map, and both added immeasurably to knowledge. But the history of the Rocky Mountain states for Anglo-Americans begins with the official explorers from the United States, with Lewis and Clark in 1804–06, with Zebulon Pike in 1810, with Major Stephen Long in 1820. Especially with Lewis and Clark, the first, the most intelligent and resolute, incomparably the most successful. Pike, whose impetuosity got him into difficulties first with the country and then with the Spaniards, has left his name on the great landmark peak above Colorado Springs. Long, as over-cautious as Pike was headstrong, retreated without major discoveries but also left his name on a peak, this one above Estes Park. Lewis and Clark left their names on no such peaks, but they opened the West.

From St. Louis up the Missouri through the plains that would some day be Nebraska, the Dakotas, Montana; past the Great Falls and through the "Gates of the Rocky Mountains," up the dwindling forks, they went by water until the water would no longer float them. Then they stalked Sacajawea's suspicious Snake relatives until they caught some and made friends, and with a few horses and information about a difficult way over the mountains, they struggled up over Lolo Pass and stood, the first Americans to do so, on the western slope of the continental divide. Next spring, having passed a dreary winter in the rain at the mouth of the Columbia, they came back over the Bitterroots, split forces so that Clark could explore the Yellowstone while Lewis went up the Marias, and were reunited below the mouth of the Yellowstone, from where—Lewis with an accidental gunshot wound in his thigh—they floated the long river homeward to St. Louis and triumph.

Their word on the unknown reaches of Louisiana and "the Oregon" was added to by Pike and Long, as well as by Frémont, who surveyed the Oregon Trail in 1842 and other parts of the West in 1844–46. It was given detail by the Pacific Railroad Surveys of the 1850s, and topographical knowledge was brought close to its final form by Major Powell's brilliant exploration down the Green and Colorado Rivers in 1869. The last act of all in the record of official exploration belonged to Powell's brother-in-law, Almon Thompson, who in 1871 added to the map of southern Utah the last-discovered river—the Escalante, whose mouth Powell had missed. But long before the 1870s, when explorers had become surveyors and the King, Hayden, Powell, and Wheeler Surveys were triangulating the West, another breed had lived its short hot life and disappeared: the first of the raiders, the first of the picturesque and destructive ones, the first shapes of myth—the mountain men.

Returning out of the wilderness on Clark's heels in 1806, Lewis had met, below the mouth of the Yellowstone, two trappers named Dickson and Hancock, the first to follow upriver the path the explorers had opened. One of the expedition's men, John Colter, turned out to be still unsated with wilderness after two years of hardship, starvation, wounds, scurvy, and venereal Chinook squaws. He asked leave to turn back with the trappers, and having been a faithful man, was granted it. He helped build in 1807, at the mouth of the Big Horn, the fort that was the first building in Montana and probably the first in the Rocky Mountain states. That same year he returned from a trip up the Yellowstone with tales of boiling springs, fountains of steam, quaking and smoking earth, mountains of glass. Sixty-five years later a body of enthusiasts assisted by members of the Hayden Survey and armed with photographs by William

Henry Jackson and water colors by Thomas Moran would succeed in having Congress set aside Colter's Hell as Yellowstone National Park. Both the discovery and the reservation are significant; they bracket a substantial part of the West's history, from uninhibited exploitation of the public domain to federal ownership, conservation, and management of the more crucial parts of it in the interest of all the people and of the future. A hundred and fifty years after Colter made the first white moccasin tracks in the Yellowstone country, an annual invasion of a million and a quarter tourists would be threatening to trample it to death, and would have done so long since except for the protection of a federal bureau, the National Park Service.

After 1808 the Northwest Company had posts in western Montana, in 1810 Andrew Henry built his post on Henry's Fork, in 1829 the American Fur Company erected Fort Union at the mouth of the Yellowstone, and this was for a time the ultimate outpost of the raiders in a hostile country. But the trade was already shifting westward, away from the river that was so unreliable and dangerous a highway, with so many belligerent tribes in a constant boil along its banks. Soon the raiders would operate without bases; and in their wanderings they would locate a road. Wilson Henry Hunt led his fifty Astorians down the Snake and the Columbia in 1811, following roughly the route of Lewis and Clark. Next year, Robert Stuart brought a small party back, swerving southward in search of an easier way; crossing the mountains far to the south and east, he may have made the first crossing of South Pass. The effective discovery of that route, the one with consequences, was made by a party of General Ashley's trappers under Thomas Fitzpatrick and Jedediah Smith in 1824. Intent upon new beaver country, they prepared the way for a new phase of the frontier.

Over the same featureless plateau, Jason Lee and the Spaldings and Marcus and Narcissa Whitman would go missionarying to Oregon. Whitman would drag a wagon over it all the way to Fort Hall in 1836; in 1840, mountain men and other missionaries would print the mark of wheels all the way to Whitman's mission at Waiilatpu. While fixed posts such as Fort Laramie and Fort Hall began to take over from the annual rendezvous of the fur brigades, and while Nathaniel Wyeth disputed the Snake River country with Peter Skene Ogden and John Work of the

Hudson's Bay Company, the fur trade guttered out. Marcus Whitman would enforce the new order on the imagination of the nation, first making his epic journey from the West Coast to preach the gospel of Oregon into eastern ears, and on his return in 1842 taking a wagon train all the way through, to show that it could be done. These things would take time, almost two decades after the effective discovery of an easy wagon pass, but the discovery made them inevitable. There lay the open track to—or through—the West; the route of the Donner-Reed party doomed to their grisly ordeal in the snow-blocked Sierra in 1846, the way of the Mormon pioneer company, moving out of the infested bottoms at Winter Quarters, on the Missouri, in 1847; the road of the Gold Rush; the road that the Handcart Companies would walk to their snowdrift graves along the Sweetwater in 1856.

Stand on South Pass now, and you will find it as still and peaceful as if no clamor of empire had ever surged through it. Antelope will drift close to see what you are up to; no smokes stain the dark blue sky; the riotous rendezvous of the fur brigades, held in this vicinity for a dozen years after 1825, have left neither mark nor echo, not even a tepee ring. The wheels that between 1836 and 1869 rocked and creaked and squealed up the Sweetwater and down past the westward-falling trickle of Pacific Creek have left ruts that are still visible in places among the sage and bunchgrass if you look hard, but modern travel does not go this way. Both Highway 30 and the railroad cross the divide at Creston. All that crosses South Pass now is Wyoming 28, a secondary road.

And here is a lesson, not only in history, but in the fallibility of prophecy based on false premises. In 1860 William Gilpin, first territorial governor of Colorado and a loud voice for Manifest Destiny, foresaw that South Pass would become a gateway more thronging than Gibraltar, and that the population of the Rocky Mountain region would be numbered in hundreds of millions.

Ask the antelope, coming back after a long period of near-extinction, where those hundreds of millions are. Ask the people from the Bureau of Land Management, the Soil Conservation Service, the Bureau of Reclamation, and the Forest Service, who have the job of restoring the overgrazed ranges and impounding the little available water and protecting the watersheds, how they would like to entertain that many guests. Look

242

back eastward a little, back where the Sweetwater flows down into the North Platte, and see in the Seminole, Kortes, and Pathfinder Dams, one of the salient reasons why this part of what Gilpin called the great Cordilleran Region is habitable at all. The dams represent sanity, acceptance, planning—the act of acquired wisdom, the acknowledgement of inexorable aridity. Gilpin made one principal error: He forgot that people live on water as much as on land.

Nobody stopped here to accommodate Gilpin's prophecies. Except for the Mormons who after 1847 were building an agricultural society in the irrigable valleys of Utah and southern Idaho and the western edge of Nevada, nobody stopped anywhere in the Rocky Mountain country— especially after John Marshall stooped to examine the glitter in the bottom of Sutter's millrace at Coloma, California, in January 1848. For a round decade everybody went straight on through, cussing every dusty mile that lay between him and the Pacific coast. From John Colter on, men with the itch of the wild in them had found the Rockies a place of savage freedom; but they apparently offered nothing to the homemaker, and their minerals were not yet discovered. Oregon wagons and Forty-niners were part of the history but not the life of the Rocky Mountains. The Mormons were another matter. They were not headed anywhere else; their destination was a desert valley between the Wasatch and Great Salt Lake. On the very first afternoon they made their peace with at least one of the West's inflexible conditions. They diverted water from City Creek to soften the ground for a potato field, and began Anglo-American irrigation on this continent—began, that is, the adjustment that north-European peoples were compelled to make before they could learn to live in the West.

The ferocious partisans of the fur companies had cleaned out the beaver by 1840, and turned to guiding wagon trains, scouting for the United States Cavalry, or hunting buffalo for the hides. Nearly twenty years before they had the buffalo wiped out and the cavalry had suppressed the last desperate Indian uprisings, a new wave of raiders swept in upon the Rockies from both east and west. In 1858 there were gold strikes on Clear Creek, near modern Denver, and on Cripple Creek back of Pike's Peak, and on Gold Creek in Montana. The next year the fabulous Comstock Lode sucked half the miners in California over the mountains into Nevada, and intercepted most of the emigrants from the east. Idaho joined the excitement with the strike on Orofino Creek in 1861, and in 1862 with strikes in the Boise Basin and at Bannack in the Beaverhead country. In 1863 the discovery of the richest of all placers brought into existence a Montana Virginia City to match the Nevada city of the same name on the Comstock. By that time General Connor's soldiers, posted in Salt Lake City to keep an eye on the Mormons, had been turned loose to find gold in Bingham Canyon and in the Wasatch, and a Gentile society of raiders, which gradually transformed itself into a more permanent cluster of camps to exploit lode mines, was developing in competition with the Mormon society of irrigation farmers.

Insofar as the non-Mormon West was settled at all by 1869, when Union Pacific and Central Pacific bumped cowcatchers at Promontory and opened a new age of accessibility for the mountains, it was settled by miners, and miners are notoriously prone to vanish from their mushroom towns as quickly as they gather. Quartz mines can last a long time, and new discoveries and new mining and smelting methods have kept alive such towns as Bingham, Butte, Anaconda, Park City, Ely. For that matter Salt Lake City, the heart of Mormon agrarianism, is the largest nonferrous smelting center in the world. But if the West depended entirely on minerals to support a civilization, it could look forward to an extinction as complete as that of the Land of Midian, where King Solomon's mines have heard only the dry whisper of blowing sand for millennia. Mineral resources are not renewable, and placers especially are resources of a year or two or ten, hardly more; the early placer camps went out like blown matches. In such of them as now show any standing buildings, the doors swing in the wind and snow blows in the broken windows of saloons and stores, the nails are tufted with the hair of animals, the gutted gulches spill their gravel into the valleys on the spring freshets or in summer cloudbursts, and the mountainsides whose pines went to prop shafts or flumes show now the deep scorings of erosion gulleys. Some lode camps, like Virginia City, Nevada, and Leadville, Colorado, survive as fractions or remnants; some, like Virginia City, Montana, Aspen, Colorado, and Alta, Utah, have been rejuvenated as resort or ski towns. But many of these too are ghosts. Tourists and antiquarians often profess to find them charming, and it is true that some of them, buried among the mountains, occupy spectacular sites. But charming they hardly are with the single exception of Aspen. They are the leavings of the second careless rush of hit-and-run exploiters, a breed generally as thoughtless of the future or of consequences as the mountain men slaughtering their way through a wilderness of fur and meat that seemed inexhaustible and then was suddenly gone. The towns which *did* expect a future, looking upon their mineral wealth as inexhaustible, and which erected opera houses and ice palaces and hotels and cultivated the high-toned arts (the two Virginia Cities, Leadville, Central City), have a rather wistful lease on life as quaint tourist attractions or as sites of summer opera festivals. They survive, that is, on transfusions.

Montana, Colorado, most of Idaho, and Nevada all drew their first inhabitants to the mineralized mountains, not to their agricultural land. Utah and its southern Idaho outposts maintained their pastoral and cooperative societies based on irrigation even through the mining rushes, and made money selling services, farm produce, mules, and Valley Tan whiskey to the infidel. Wyoming, with vast ranges of grasslands, became above all a cattle country. The raid here, as on the plains of Colorado and Montana, was on the grass. Many of the cattle corporations, like the fur companies and the mining companies, were absentee-owned, some in England and Scotland. The men who set out to get rich from the western grasslands shared the psychology—and the ignorance of consequences— of the men who had cleaned out the beaver streams and were busy cleaning out the precious metals. Who among the mountain men would have paused to consider, or would have cared, that beaver were a water resource, and that beaver engineering was of great importance in the maintenance of stream flow and the prevention of floods? Who among the miners worried about what happened to the watersheds where they logged their timbers or the stream beds where their monitors or dredges tore up the gravel? Who among the cattlemen knew, or cared, that in a dry land grass, like minerals, might be non-renewable; that some of the best grasses were annuals that reproduced only from seed, and that overgrazing both prevented reseeding and encouraged erosion? The cattleman like his predecessors lived a large, free life; he is even more deeply embedded in our folklore than mountain man or miner; in terms of the enduring capacity of the West to sustain a civilization, he did more harm than either.

Late as they came to it, settlers were in the West before much of it was surveyed, before there were laws adequate to its conditions. The public domain lay wide open to anyone with the energy to take it. Also there were, for those who chose to use them, short cuts to an empire. By having your cowhands homestead a quarter-section apiece and commute it to you for a small consideration, you could assemble the core of a noble range. By homesteading, buying, or merely appropriating the land along the watercourses or around sources of water, you could dominate many square miles of dry grazing land. By using the public domain as if it were really your own, you could perhaps convince yourself that you had exclusive rights to it, and by intimidation or the method known as dry-gulching you might discourage rivals or sheepmen or nesters, saying in justification that they were trespassers or rustlers. The history of the West is full of murderous quarrels over property that neither of the contestants owned, and over rights that no law had approved. Transformed, these quarrels are often the stuff of horse opera. Read, for instance, the history of the Johnson County War in Wyoming, when cattlemen rode north-ward from Cheyenne with a list of "rustlers" and "trespassers" they intended to rub out. They rubbed out two before the law belatedly began to assert that the rustlers and trespassers had as much right where they were as the cattlemen who tried to gun them off. That is an ugly story. But put in the terms Owen Wister gave it in *The Virginian*, it takes on all the beguiling qualities of myth. The culture hero, torn between friendship and duty to "law," does not seem like a lyncher and a vigilante. By such transformations it is even possible to make a sort of hero of Tom Horn, the cattlemen's hired assassin, or of Billy the Kid, a psychopathic killer.

The mythic West is the West that everyone knows. Every American child grows up in it. The dream of total emancipation from inhibition, law, convention, and restraint is a potent dream. The West, wide open, fostered it as few environments have. And if the emancipated and unin-hibited were also lawless, if they were scoundrels as so many western characters turn out to be on close examination, let us make them rebels against the system, friends of the poor, according to a formula well known to the creators of Robin Hood and Jesse James. If law officers turn out, on close look, to be bandits with badges on, and if the posses who made themselves judge, jury, legislature, and executioner look sometimes like dupes, sometimes like a bloody-minded rabble, put into their mouths such excuses as the Virginian uses, and further palliate their vigilantism by making them courteous to women and tender to little children and to old men; give them a stern faith in honesty, property, the sanctity of contract. Commit them fully to the mores of the middle-class community and give them all the lineaments of the Lone Ranger, let them be lawless in defense of law, unconventional in the service of convention, and the peculiarity of their ethics, like the dubiousness of their exploitation of natural resources, blurs and disappears in a blaze of picturesqueness.

The mythic western hero, the apostle of a most rugged individualism, is a curious hangover, and may sometimes be caught sanctifying some odd practices and policies. He has codified and perpetuated an honor as high-colored as the feudal code of the old South—which, by way of the Virginian and a lot of ex-Confederates among the Texas cattle drivers, was probably its source. He suggests that the resolution of every quarrel is ultimately violence: The walkdown is a fixture of all highbrow horse opera, as the stagecoach chase is of the lowbrow variety. He represents a Cockaigne, a Poictesme, a Never-Never West, but he is propped with the most scrupulous and niggling realism. Try to write a Western with your gun lore crooked, or with holes in your lingo! He is sometimes—and this is the principal danger in what would otherwise only be wistful or amusing—invoked to justify new outbreaks of rugged individualism, irresponsibility, intemperance, and the economics of the raid. The real people of the West are generally not cowboys and never myths; they live in places like Denver and Salt Lake, Dillon and Boise, American Fork and American Falls, and they confront the real problems of real life in a real region and have gone a long way toward understanding the conditions of western life and accepting the agencies that have been slowly evoked to meet them. But those who live by the myth, or pretend to, have never yet admitted that they live in a land of little rain and big consequences. Whether they are resisting the gift of Grand Teton National Monument from the Rockefellers to the people of the United States, or maneuvering for the transfer of grazing, timber, oil, or mineral lands from national parks and forests to state and ultimately to private ownership for the quick profit of a few, they represent the survival of a gospel that left to its own devices would ultimately reduce the West to a desert as barren as Lebanon. One would be more inclined to indulge the fiction of western largeness and western freedom if it did not consistently obfuscate the facts that Westerners who can learn have been painfully learning for a century.

Say of the mountain West that it is extravagantly endowed, but that it has one critical deficiency, water, and that therefore its soil, its watersheds, its timber, and its grass are all vulnerable. There have been man-made deserts before in the world's history; some, like the valley of Oaxaca, in Mexico, are being made while we watch. The West could be one of those, and it is not comforting to know that its range is at least 50 percent deteriorated under our handling, and that its rivers run muddy where they used to run clear. The very jokes that strike us as most western are likely to have an edge of grimness: "Throw a gopher in the air, and if he starts to burrow, it ain't a clear day"; "The best place to locate a farm in western Colorado is in eastern Kansas."

Say of the West too that it has been plundered and has plundered itself, or collaborated with its plunderers, but that little by little whole communities and districts have learned how to manage their environment and have made superb living-places out of their oases. Say that the West is everyone's romantic home, for we have all spent a part of our childhood there. And say that in its territory, as in its legendry, much of the West is public domain.

Next to aridity, this is the most important fact about the Rocky Mountain states. Of their 400,000,000 acres, more than half is federal land. Of the state of Nevada, you and I own 87 percent. Drive from Glacier Park to the Spanish Peaks, and from the Sierra Nevada to the high plains, and you are never out of sight of lands reserved and managed by public agencies in the public interest. Why? Not because Westerners are more socialist than other Americans; they are, on the contrary, inclined to conservatism politically. And not because a conspiracy within the government is using the West as a pawn in a game to overthrow the American way of life. Some of these lands have been reserved to keep them from ruinous private exploitation, some to protect the regions in which they lie, some simply because despite all its efforts the government was never able to get anyone to homestead or buy them.

Some of the management is a good deal less effective than it ought to be. The Bureau of Land Management's 116 million acres of range and wasteland are overgrazed, partly because of heavy pressure from permit holders against reduction, partly because the bureau has never been given a budget big enough to do anything: In 1956 the Forest Service was handling 6 million acres of rescue work as "land utilization projects" because the Bureau of Land Management had no staff to put on them. And if history means anything, any future bureau which did get an adequate budget and start seriously to work to bring the range back would find itself bucking the embattled graziers and leaseholders and stockmen's associations.

Who else runs the public West? Well, in our six states the Bureau of Reclamation has 5.5 million acres reserved for dam and canal sites, there are 4.5 million strictly set aside for "use without impairment" as national parks and monuments, there are 3.5 million acres in game and bird refuges and feeding stations run by the Fish and Wildlife Service. The Bureau of Indian Affairs, apart from the Indian Reservations proper, which are not federal but tribal land, has 188,000 acres. The withdrawals for the use of the armed services are large—islands in Great Salt Lake and patches of the salt desert for bombing ranges, A- and H-bomb testing areas near Las Vegas, desert proving grounds, airfields, training centers, the Air Force Academy near Colorado Springs. But it is the 75 million acres of national forests in these six states which are the most critical acres in the whole West. They are important for their resources—their reserves of timber, their annual crop of water, their summer grazing, their priceless and mushrooming value as places of outdoor recreation for millions of people—but even more for what they prevent. The Forest Service lands lie almost entirely in the high country and on the watersheds where the West's life is made and stored, where floods can begin, where erosion can be most disastrous. Any forester these days is likely to admit that watershed control, and after that recreation, are both more important in the national forests than the growing, selective marketing, or conservation of trees for timber. The Forest Service is a key bureau because, operating on a policy of multiple use and sustained yield, it harvests some of its resources, especially lumber, water, and grass, each year, and is always under pressure to let go of more. If watershed control, or recreation, or the maintenance of wildlife habitat, or any of the other interests involved, are in conflict with the interest of holders of grazing permits or the bidders for timber-cutting contracts, the service has the unpleasing job of deciding among the conflicting claims. It takes a steady pounding, year in and year out; and year in and year out it is the principal force which keeps the short-term profit-takers, the raiders who see no farther than mountain man or miner, from doing the region in.

The fact is, neither the Forest Service nor most of the other federal agencies are likely to go out of business in the West, because too many Westerners have found out how important is the work they do. It is not merely a question of federal payrolls in local communities, though those are an item. Who, for example, can measure the dollar value of the A-bomb testing area to Las Vegas, or the dollar value of Rocky Mountain National Park to Colorado? The annual payroll for Denver's more-than-two-hundred federal bureau offices was over $20,000,000 as far back as ten years ago. Not many Westerners are inclined to question federal participation in the local life when it means a power or reclamation or flood-control dam in the area: Listen to the logs rolling among western senators on that issue! Few Westerners will deplore the spending of public funds to rescue the trumpeter swan from the edge of extinction, or to cure ducks sick with botulism in the Bear River marshes, or to winter-feed the elk in Jackson Hole. The collaboration between state fish and game departments, which hatch and plant and manage the fish and game birds, and the Forest Service, which manages the habitat, is close and cordial, and the degree to which Westerners actually make use of the national forests for "harvesting" the fish and game is clear from one figure from Utah. On the opening day of the 1957 deer season, one Utahn out of every six was out with a rifle, and along with them were tens of thousands of out-of-state hunters, mainly from California.

No Westerner in his right mind would dream for a moment of trying to get along without the constant aid and support of the federal agencies. It is easy to see why. Stand, as I did once, on the high grade of the Union Pacific between Salt Lake and Ogden, and watch a cloudburst roll a fifteen-foot wall of mud and rocks and water down the canyons onto the farm land, and come back later to see houses full to the second story with mud and gravel, and gravel and boulders ten feet deep over the fields. Reflect that floods like that arise from one cause alone—the stripping of the mountain slopes of timber in the 1880s. And then visit the regional forest office in Ogden and learn what they are doing in watershed research and (in small, local pilot projects) in watershed restoration, and you will know why this and other agencies have friends when the sniping begins. Watch the parachutes of smoke-jumpers balloon out against a sky ominous with the smoke of forest fires, and the lesson acquires excitement, even heroics. For research that preserves a national forest helps state forests or private forests, saved watershed reflects good all around it, a fire halted in your woods and mine is money in the pocket of everyone anywhere near there. To give the public lands to the states, as the raiders periodically propose—they say "restore," but the word is a smoke screen, for the public lands have never belonged to the states— could have only one of two effects. The states would go bankrupt trying to keep them up, or they would let them deteriorate. Most people in the West know when they are well off.

It is a pity, in a way, that so many Americans know the West only from the roadside. The original Oregon-Mormon-California trail through it has proliferated into many through routes—U.S. 2, 12, 14, 20, 30, 40, 50, with their north-south links U.S. 85, 87, 91 and scores of good secondary roads. But present and past are alike in this, that the majority of travelers see the West on the fly, customarily on their way somewhere else, and that in consequence roadside accommodations and services are a primary function of western towns. They are considerably less open to criticism than the stage stops on the Overland against which Mark Twain complained so bitterly in *Roughing It* ("At the Green River Station we had breakfast— hot biscuits, fresh antelope steaks, and coffee—the only decent meal we tasted between the United States and Great Salt Lake City . . ."). You do not rough it now, and you may choose among many caravanserais, so many that a lot of western towns appear to exist only as adjuncts of the road. A town on a through highway, such a town as Ely or Elko, Nevada, or Rock Springs, Wyoming, crouches like a spider on the trip-thread of asphalt, and everything in it vibrates to the passing thunder of wheels. Being oases, western towns are inevitably way stations as well.

The West invented the motel, and the motel here has come a long way from the homemade cabin with "running water" and "flush toilet" that used to be advertised along western roads. It has graduated from the back-yard home-labor class and become big business. Nowadays it is likely to be the equal of a first-rate, often a luxury, hotel; it may be one of a chain; the best ones are likely to belong to an association bent upon improving the tourist's comfort, and if you follow one of the guides (the AAA publishes a good one) you can sleep every night in a tastefully decorated room, on a Posturepedic mattress, insulated from traffic noise, and in the morning after your shower you can open the curtains quite often on a superb view through your picture window. If you do not follow a guide, you can get stung, but not nearly so badly as in some other regions, because here competition does what competition is classically reputed to do. When a motel fails, it is much more likely to fail in taste rather than in comfort, and it is for their breaches of taste, rather than for any failure of essential service, that one has to deplore the roadside institutions that have learned to cluster around the motels on incoming and outgoing roads: the hamburger stands, diners, drive-ins, restaurants, bars, taverns, service stations; the drug stores featuring postcards of cows stepping on their dragging udders, over the caption, "You think *you* got troubles!"; the curio shops featuring strange wooden and leather items and Ute beadwork made in Hong Kong. No matter how well designed and carefully planned these roadside businesses may be individually, they are collectively an eyesore. With their advertising, they make the outskirts of nearly every western town feverishly ugly. Here again, the West is not so different from the rest of the country; the trouble is only that in a dry country, without masking grass, shrubs, trees, the ugliness shows more.

Sooner or later the West will learn that scenery, the natural beauty which is the region's noblest endowment, can be ruined as surely by billboards, neon, and the ferocious glare of competing colors, as range can be ruined by overgrazing or a watershed by indiscriminate timber cutting. Somebody should read to the western roadside the story of the man who killed the goose that laid the golden eggs. Anyone can sample the goose, before and after killing: Drive through a typical motel strip, say that of Colorado Springs, and on through the desecrated entrance to Ute Pass, and then on into the unbillboarded wilderness—unbillboarded because certain federal bureaus, here the Forest Service, have had the will and the power to prohibit the posting of outdoor advertising and the smearing of paint on cliffs, even the paint that says "Jesus Saves."

Maybe He does save; maybe He will some day save the West from its habit of exploiting and destroying by human heedlessness resources that are not automatically renewable. Add outdoor advertisers, big and little, to the list that contains mountain men, miners, and cattlemen. Add scenery to the things that haste and folly can destroy.

It is too bad, one insists, that America knows the West from the roadside, for the roadside is the hoked-up West, the dude West, the tourist West, the West with its eye on the traveling dollar. Remembering earlier and more innocent years when I knew this country all the way from the Canadian border to Monument Valley, I have taken to traveling whenever possible by the back roads, and giving up the comforts along with the billboards. That is one way of getting behind the West's roadside face. Another is to live in some part of it a while, sample it as a human dwelling place, as the formative stage of a unique civilization, as a place to go *to*, not through.

Try, since this is an oasis civilization, some of the oasis cities. Try Denver, Salt Lake City, Reno, which, spaced like the stars in the belt of Orion, span the Rocky Mountain West at its broadest part. Highway 40 will lead you through all of them, across 1,100 miles of mountain, plateau, and desert, and will lead you also through all three of the West's zones. Denver is a plains city, Salt Lake a mountain city, Reno a desert city. Each is the metropolis of its subregion, each one of the earliest settlements in its cultural area. They all depend for their life upon the water of the mountains that overhang them—Denver upon the Rockies, Salt Lake upon the Wasatch which forms the eastern rim of the Great Basin, Reno upon the Sierra which forms its western rim. They are all recognizably western, they know the same high, dry air, the same purity of light, the same quality of youth and cleanliness. But they are very different, nevertheless.

Denver, being a plains town, is spread wide; in spite of the mountains behind it, and in spite of its altitude of one mile, it impresses a visitor (and for all I know a native) as the Midwest at its farthest west remove. It has more in common with Wichita than with Salt Lake City or the Pacific coast. It is a family town, a home-owning town, a business town, a regional-office town, a town proud of its schools, its parks, its civic center, its community spirit. In the *Denver Post* and the *Rocky Mountain News* it has two newspapers each unique in its way and with more-than-metropolitan influence. It is a good place to grow up, though it has its own local segregations and snobberies, and East High may hold itself above South or Manual Training High, and Indians, Mexicans, and more recently Negroes have had to resist survivals of frontier prejudice. But a good town, and one its children are proud of, and one that illustrates something about the whole West and about the whole habit of man as a homemaker and a builder of civilizations. Lacking adequate rainfall, Denver has made its water supply from the mountains, even tapping the watersheds of the western slope by tunnel. Lacking natural greenery, it has produced it by pooled effort, and the qualities of Denver as a park city are in direct proportion to the community co-operation it has taken to create them. The great agricultural civilizations, we are reminded, were born in deserts: Egypt, Mesopotamia, the Indus Valley. And the most settled and civilized Indians in the territory of the continental United States were desert agriculturists—the Pueblo, Hopi, and Zuñi of the Southwest. There is much to be said for a civilization that has to be planned for and continuously worked for. No one need be afraid of Denver's future; she will remain the "Queen City of the Plains and Peaks"—though my private reservation is that her influence is shed east, north, and south much more than it is shed west. Before you get very deep in the mountains, you begin to feel the influence of the next metropolis.

Salt Lake City is less than half Denver's size, but it is even more surely a provincial capital. A mountain town, it does not spread like Denver: It is cupped, cradled, in the broad valley between the Wasatch and the Oquirrh Range. As Denver lies at the beginning of the Rockies, Salt Lake lies at their end; it is exactly at the breaking line between mountains and desert. It too is a business town, a milling and smelting center, a center of deferred shopping (watch the stores and shops during the spring and fall conferences of the Mormon Church, when out-of-towners combine the godly with the necessary). Like Denver, it lies a little to one side of the main transportation routes—the Union Pacific hits Cheyenne and Ogden rather than Denver and Salt Lake, and the airlines characteristically fly right over nonstop to Chicago or New York. Nevertheless, the Utah (and Mormon) symbol of the beehive is very apt. This is an industrious and thriving city, intensely domestic, intensely self-sufficient. Hidden behind its mountains, it feels the winds of politics and international hysteria less than most places; it has, uniquely, the qualities one might ask of a "home" town. Since it was my own home town for fifteen years or more, I speak from prejudice, but I know of no evidence to confute the local boast that this is "the most beautifully situated city in America," and I know few cities which display more community spirit in keeping themselves attractive. At least as much as Denver, this is a city of parks, of broad grassed parkways, of clean streets, of monuments. The monuments are a little hard to account for, in spite of Mormon devotion to the Church's history and an almost Shintoist reverence for ancestors. I suspect that partly they derive from the heavy proportion of Danes among the early converts, and from the Danes' inherited tradition of sculpture. In any case the city has the beginnings of a monumental quality: Its pioneer Mormon company of 1847 is commemorated in Mahonri Young's "This Is the Place" monument at the mouth of Emigration Canyon. The Mormon Battalion of the Mexican War has its memorial in the Capitol grounds, Brigham Young's solid frock-coated figure dominates the intersection at the corner of the Temple Block, the Temple Block itself has its grateful sculptural acknowledgement to the sea gulls who descended to end a locust plague in 1848.

Somehow the monuments are symptomatic: These were people who intended from the beginning to stay, and they brought their gods with them. As the holy city of the Church of Jesus Christ of Latter-Day Saints, Salt Lake City has its religious shrines and its religious tourist attractions, but even for a "Gentile," or non-Mormon, it is a good town to grow up in. And Mormon or Gentile, these, much more than the mythical men in high heels and big hats, are the people of the West. They do little dry-gulching or racing after runaway stage coaches, but they do a lot of sprinkling of their fragrant lawns in the evenings when the canyon breeze begins to feel its way down from the mountains toward the more slowly cooling lake; they dig night crawlers with flashlights after dark; they do a lot of fishing and hunting; they haunt the canyons which open in their very back yards—the Wasatch National Forest in 1956 entertained, of all kinds of visitors from casual travelers to campers and hunters, nearly 13,000,000 people (if we count repeaters), most of them locals. These are mountain people and they use their mountains.

From Salt Lake City it is nearly 600 miles by road to Reno—600 miles of desert, salt flats, arid ranges half buried in their own alluvium. There are some minor oases on the way, such as Elko under the Ruby Mountains, but Reno is the true oasis because it has the Sierra behind it. It lies on the Truckee Meadows, the Truckee River flows through its heart and provides a suitable wishing well for divorcées to throw their wedding rings into. It has long been known as a divorce capital and a gambling mecca, and it is both. But it is also, like Denver and Salt Lake City, a university town—the University of Nevada is situated there. And back of or behind or interwoven with the divorce mills and the resorts and the clubs is a surprisingly stable and sober community. I lived in it once for a good part of a year (for non-divorce purposes), and found it astonishingly like Salt Lake. It even smelled the same, and on some of its streets in June the whole sky snowed down cottonwood fluff from big rattly leaved trees in just the same way, and the climate was variable and stimulating and the nights had the same softness, the moon the same silvery paleness, the horizon the same abrupt thrusting into the sky. Even if you don't want to gamble or shed a wife, Reno is a good town.

I cannot, personally, say the same for Las Vegas, once a sleepy way station on Highway 89 and now the focus for A- and H-bomb testing, for a lot of shenanigans by refugees from Hollywood, and for an extravagant night-club life. It is all very hectic and glossy, but I have not liked it since I went a few years ago into a bar I had used to frequent—a real oasis in prohibition times—and found it a place of chrome and blue glass, with a bartender who was above conversation and a clientele that was beneath notice. While I was there a prospector with a dog came in, put a nickel in the juke box, and started the dog to dancing. The bartender ran him out. We went out too. They can have Las Vegas.

They cannot have a lot of other western towns. They can't have Great Falls, where I used to wade in the Missouri and catch carp with my hands, where I used to sell ice-cream cones in Black Eagle Park and take Boy Scout hikes up the river to Third and Fourth Island. They can't have Boise, where I know the best Basque restaurant that ever made a delirium out of lamb. They can't have the green, irrigated Mormon potato towns along the Snake River. They can't have Jackson, Wyoming, in spite of the fact that the gamblers and the Hollywood refugees have come in there, too. They can't have Missoula or Provo or any of the small, provincial college towns, for whenever I visit them I am brought to the conclusion that the word "provincial" is a very dangerous word: It means, generally, "different—different from what I am used to," or it means "inadequate by the standards that I have chosen to set." I do not care whether or not Missoula may be provincial by the standards of New York or Cambridge. By standards appropriate to this fledgling civilization, it is something new and potentially fine and exciting. It has health and hope and ambition and a future.

The Rocky Mountain West is good at any season, and it has all four, sharply defined. Try Denver or Salt Lake in May, when the chestnut trees are tossing up cones of blossom, and the scent of lilacs and snowballs perfumes the whole air and mockingbirds go wild on moonlit nights. Try the Aspen or Alta or Brighton or Jackson Hole snow, any time from Thanksgiving to April. Try the summers, with their sharp distinction between sun and shade, their hot days and shirt-sleeve nights. Or try autumn, after all the tourists have gone home for the summer, and the winter ones have not yet arrived, when for a brief while the mountain people have their mountains to themselves. The color of autumn in the mountains is gold, and it is gold the "Aspencades" go out to see. But gold is a limited word. On a single aspen, if you stop to examine it carefully—examine it, say, from the chair lift at Aspen, as you cruise up over the glowing mountainside toward the Sundeck—you can see thirty shades of gold, all the way from the purest palest jonquil to a red-gold that is nearly vermilion. Every leaf of every white-boled tree is in motion; the very air is gold; the mountainsides opposite, and the mountains beyond those, lift into view wider and wider tilted planes of color. You could bottle the air and sell it for vintage prices. At Aspen, where taste has restrained garish advertising and where the natural setting was superb to begin with and where the old mining camp had a certain Victorian charm that later buildings have not departed from too markedly, there is more the feeling of a Swiss village, more a feeling of community within the mountains, than in most Rocky Mountain towns. Another of the same, not known to skiers because skiing has not been developed there yet, but known to Salt Lake City families who for four generations have used it as a local, quiet resort, is the Heber Valley, sixty miles southeast of Salt Lake in the Wasatch. Lie there in your bed in the Homestead Inn at Midway, under the magnificent terraced east face of Mt. Timpanogos, and in the high pure morning before sunup listen to the tuned Swiss bells of Mormon cows going down the village street.

There are a hundred things to do and know in the West that the roadside-tourist does not do or know. If you want to fish and camp and climb, and swim in lakes so cold they electrocute you at the touch, try the Permanent Wilderness of the Grand-daddy Lakes Basin, in the Uinta Mountains of eastern Utah. Try the rivers, though this is not notably a country of rivers. Try boat trips on the Yampa or the Green, or down Glen Canyon of the Colorado as far as it is still possible to float. Or try any mountain creek in an inner tube—that is the way kids from Provo or Ashton or Jackson would do it. Try getting out in back country and breaking down; stick yourself in sand or mud and learn the unfailing hearty helpfulness of the people who will rescue you. Heedless of their resources they may be, but never of a fellow creature in a jam. I have been stuck by cloudbursts in the Arizona Strip, below Zion National Park; and in both sand and cloudbursts in the Navajo Reservation; and by car trouble in the Capitol Reef and in Clear Creek Canyon in central Utah; and by washouts on Togwotee Pass in Wyoming; and by other cloudbursts out in the barren sagebrush stretches of the Wyoming Plateau; and I have slept in root cellars with mud dripping through on me, and in a shack where the bach homesteader had a water bucket full of rattlesnake tails—his hobby and consolation—and under cottonwood trees and beside irrigation ditches (in Idaho pronounced "airigation" ditches)—and I never failed to end by loving the catastrophes that marooned me among so much human kindness.

There is no Montana Face—there is no western face. The people of the West come from everywhere, practically, and it takes more generations than they have yet had in this home to stabilize a breed, as the Yankee was stabilized. It takes more generations than they have yet had for the making of a native culture. The West is still nascent, still forming, and that is where much of its excitement comes from. It has a shine on it, it isn't tired: Even the sometimes-dubious activities of the boosters reflect an energy that doesn't know what it means to be licked or to give up. The face of the West changes; a decade is much. Generally speaking, the country lives up to its water supply. As long as there is only so much water, for so much farm land, so many towns, so much industry, Mormon boys from the Salt Lake and Utah Valleys, boys from Montana cow towns and mining camps, boys from Sheridan and Ucross and Twin Falls, will be heading toward the West Coast or toward the Midwest or the East: The Rocky Mountain states export manpower as a general rule, though all of them grow in population—Nevada most because it has no state income tax, Utah and Colorado next because they have richer mineral and industrial possibilities. They will continue to grow until they again crowd the limits of their water; if they want to grow indefinitely they will have to make the sort of effort for water that Los Angeles makes, and bring it in, perhaps, by an 800-mile pipeline from condensing plants on the Pacific Ocean. The fountain itself, the Rocky Mountains in their many folds and ranges, can produce even with maximum efficiency a crop of only so many acre-feet per year.

There will always, that is, be some open spaces. Not all the irrigation works of the next two hundred years are likely to affect the climate enough to take that dry clarity out of the air or change the gray and tawny country to a green one. There will still be the smell of sagebrush after a shower, the bitter tang of aspen in the mountains; the smoke of juniper or piñon fires: western smells. Thanks to the collaboration between private and public, local and federal, that western conditions have begotten, there will always be some roadless wilderness, quite a lot of accessible national forests, the indispensable scenic core of the national parks and monuments, a managed harvest of fish and game, a touch of the old wonder at mountain water, mountain peaks, mountain sky. Angry as one sometimes gets at what heedless men do to a noble human habitat, one cannot be pessimistic about the West. This is where optimism was born. And when the West learns more surely that co-operation, not rugged individualism, is the quality that most characterizes and most preserves it, I will seize the harp and join the boosters, for this will be one of the world's great lands.

Land: America's History Teacher

When Europeans found it, North America was very sparsely peopled, and by their standards unowned. Therefore subject to seizure. To men from a continent where land was a resource and not a commodity, where it was entailed and primogenitured and encumbered and parceled out by aristocrats to peasants under feudal rules of tenure, free or unoccupied land was explosive with possibility. As Walter Webb pointed out in *The Great Frontier*, only in America has the word "claim" come to mean a parcel of land. That single word expresses a revolution in attitudes. The historian who remarked that America's whole history could be read as one continuous real estate transaction was not too far off.

Land has been the creator of our wealth and the shaper of our expectations. From the sixteenth century onward we considered the virgin continent ours for the taking. Some among us feel exactly the same way about the unappropriated remnants that we call the public domain. The value of that public domain has increased exponentially during the very years when public policy was changing from disposal to retention and management by the federal government. Earlier raids upon it have been inconsequential and abortive. But the raid that began to gather force at the end of the 1970s, and that early acquired the name of Sagebrush Rebellion, is not inconsequential. It could be so important to the future of the nation, and especially the West, that it might even drive us back to history to learn what the public domain means and where it came from.

Quieting native unrest with beads, bullets, and treaties not meant to be kept, Europeans claimed whole empires on the grounds that one of their kind had first sighted a headland, or put into a river mouth, or planted a cross. Francis Parkman describes what happened when LaSalle beached his canoes at the mouth of the Arkansas in 1692 and harangued a crowd of Indians in a language they didn't understand. "On that day," Parkman says in a famous passage, "the realm of France received on parchment a stupendous accession. The fertile plains of Texas; the vast basin of the Mississippi, from its frozen northern springs to the sultry borders of the Gulf; from the woody ridges of the Alleghenies to the peaks of the Rocky Mountains—a region of savannas and forests, sun-cracked deserts, and grassy prairies, watered by a thousand rivers, ranged by a thousand warlike tribes, passed beneath the sceptre of the Sultan of Versailles; and all by virtue of a feeble human voice, inaudible at half a mile."

Great expectations, unlimited opportunity. The fabulous treasures that the Spaniards found in Mexico and Peru led all the competing empires to hope for similar jackpots. All of Europe found a treasure of fish on the Newfoundland Banks, and the French found a strenuous treasure of furs in Canada. But most of the New World proved to be worthless unless settled, and so the monarchs who had acquired it by proclamation began giving it away to court favorites or colonizing companies, who in turn either disposed of it as headrights to settlers, or turned it into plantations worked by Indians, black slaves, or indentured servants, many of whom soon fled the coop and went off into the woods and settled on some land of their own by squatters' rights. In a country that, as Jefferson said, was rich in land and poor in labor, land to settle on and work came to be part of the human expectation.

The protracted real estate transactions went on. France lost Canada to the British on the Plains of Abraham in 1759. Twenty years later the American colonies forced England to acknowledge their independence. In 1803 Napoleon sold to the infant United States all that Louisiana Territory that LaSalle had claimed and named. Once started, the Americans spread like impetigo. In 1819 they forced Spain to sell Florida. In 1845 they absorbed the Republic of Texas and thus took over a big chunk of the old Spanish empire in America. In 1846, by the Oregon Treaty, they made good their claim to the Northwest. In 1848, defeated Mexico ceded the Southwest and California and five years later, in the Gadsden Purchase, sold the rest of what is now Arizona and New Mexico. Seventy years after the Revolution the mongrel Republic had spread from sea to sea, and from the 49th Parallel to the Rio Grande. The Alaska Purchase of 1867, and some island loot from Caribbean and Pacific wars, expanded the boundaries but had little effect on the formation of the national set of mind.

Seven of the original thirteen colonies held crown grants to western lands between the Alleghenies and the Mississippi. Six had no such lands. When the time came to sign the Articles of Confederation in 1777 Maryland, one of the six, refused to sign unless New York, Massachusetts, Connecticut, Virginia, Georgia, and the two Carolinas would cede their western lands to the federal government so that all could start equal. Beginning with New York in 1781 and ending with Georgia in 1802, the landed colonies made the cession. Congress in 1780 had defined the policy with regard to the proposed public domain: "Resolved, that the unappropriated lands that may be ceded or relinquished to the United States, by any particular states, pursuant to the recommendation of Congress . . . shall be disposed of for the common benefit of the United States, and be settled and formed into distinct republican states, which shall become members of the Federal Union, and shall have the same rights of sovereignty, freedom, and independence, as the other states."

Three laws were significant in the administration and disposal of that first public domain. The Ordinance of 1785 established the rectangular surveys into mile-square sections, and gave one section in every thirty-six to the new states for support of education. The Northwest Ordinance of 1787, among other things, required that all new states formed out of the public domain formally renounce any claim to public domain lands, and agree to respect the right of the federal government to dispose of them. That early, there were insurrectionary states'-rights feelings that had to be squelched. And finally, in 1789, the Constitution, in Article IV, Section 3, gave Congress power to regulate and dispose of public lands. That authority has never been shaken in any court test.

Nevertheless, there was no intention, then or for a long time later, to retain any permanent public domain or extend federal ownership beyond the small amounts of land needed for military reservations, post offices, and other federal enterprises. Eventually, virtually all of that original public domain was disposed of to state, private, or corporate ownership and in accordance with the 1780 resolution was formed into new sovereign states.

The public domain that was added west of the Mississippi by purchase and conquest after 1803 was of a different sort. It had never belonged to any of the states, and was never ceded by them to the federal government. It was federal from the beginning. The demand today of some that the public domain be "returned" to the states is either ignorant or disingenuous. It could be *given* to them, conceivably; it could never be returned. Except for Texas, which was annexed as an independent republic and hence never has had any public domain, no state west of the Mississippi has ever had title to any of its territory except that granted it by Congress.

From the Articles of Confederation until 1872, every substantive land law dealt with ways by which the public lands should be sold or given away. The year 1872, which saw the reservation of Yellowstone National Park as a "pleasuring ground for all the people," marked the beginning of a change from disposal to retention. But the general policy of disposal was not substantially ended until the Taylor Grazing Act of 1934 and not formally repudiated until 1976, with the passage of the Federal Land Policy and Management Act.

The early land sales were mainly to speculators, and in wholesale lots. Individual settlers hunting land had either to buy it from speculators or go out ahead of the surveys and squat on a piece of the unappropriated continent. In 1841, through the Preemption Law, the government acknowledged the reality of their settlements and let them obtain legal title to 160 acres on payment of $1.25 an acre. A homestead law, many times proposed, was for a long time blocked by the South, which feared the creation of new free states in the West. But in 1862, after the outbreak of war, Congress passed, and Abraham Lincoln signed, the Homestead Act that would give any settler 160 acres in exchange for stipulated improvements and residence. Two years later the Morrill Act made large grants of lands to the states for the support of agricultural colleges, and after the Civil

War the Desert Land Act, the Timber and Stone Act, and the Carey Act all continued the effort of the federal government to get rid of its domain. Enormous grants went to railroads, others to the states in support of canals, turnpikes, and other public improvements beneficial to the nation as a whole. Eventually, by one law or another, almost all the land east of the 100th meridian was disposed of.

But west of the 100th meridian, it began to be apparent, the patterns of settlement and the laws of disposal that worked well in fertile country with dependable rainfall did *not* work well. Settlers found it possible to hold on only on land with access to the water of springs, creeks, or rivers, and in altitudes that permitted farming or ranching. In the mining regions, beginning with the California Gold Rush and spreading later into Nevada, Colorado, Montana, Idaho, and Utah, the gold hunters were all out ahead of the surveys. Every gold or silver strike precipitated mass trespass on government land that was not only not policed, but literally had no laws. Miners made their own laws, including water laws, and eventually saw them validated. But homesteaders trying to operate beyond the 100th meridian under the Homestead, Preemption, and Desert Land laws had to bet their lives against 160 acres that they could make agriculture pay in the dry country, and most of them lost. Vast areas were either never settled at all, or came back into the government's hands as the homesteaders dried up and blew away. Water was the difference between making it and not making it. The West grew up as an oasis civilization, and that is what is still is. The residual public domain is the unappropriated and long-unwanted land that holds the oases apart.

The individual who saw most clearly what was happening in the West, and who had the clearest vision of how settlement must be adapted to western conditions, was Major John Wesley Powell. He began as a public hero for his exploration of the Colorado River, rose swiftly to become the most powerful scientist and most effective bureaucrat in Washington (he headed both the United States Geological Survey and the Bureau of Ethnology), and ended up a defeated old man, put down by the West he had tried to educate, guide, and save.

His *Report on the Lands of the Arid Region*, in 1878, said more truth about the West in its first three chapters than had been said altogether up to then. Manifest Destiny and the boosterism that it encouraged were envisioning a West more densely peopled than the Roman Empire under Trajan and the Antonines, believed that rain followed the plow and that settlement made the climate wetter, saw South Pass as a gateway more thronging than Gibraltar, held to the faith of William Gilpin that on the dry plains settlers could *dig* both for wood and for water. Powell's *Report* said otherwise.

It asserted what the boosters and promoters were denying, that beyond the 100th meridian agriculture was possible only with the aid of irrigation, which was generally too much for the individual farmer to handle; that much of the well-watered land was too high, and most of the arable land too dry, for the raising of crops; that the rectangular surveys that worked well in humid country left thousands of square miles of potential homesteads in the West without access to water; and that the 160 acres allowed under the Homestead Act, though more than an intensive irrigation farmer could work, were totally inadequate for a stock farmer, who needed at least four sections, 2,560 acres. He thought the system should be changed to allow the formation of cooperative irrigation districts in which the surveys should conform to the terrain, so that every parcel, whether farm or ranch, should have a water right and a portion of irrigable land. Farm size should vary from 80 to 2,560 acres. Reservoirs and canals, impossible for individuals, should be built cooperatively. The federal government, except for providing a system within which homesteaders could succeed, should stay out of it.

The alternatives, Powell said, were already apparent: they were widespread homesteader failure and the monopolization of land through monopoly of water. Using their cowboys as fraudulent filers of homestead claims, cattle outfits were picking up the quarter and half sections containing springs, or land along the banks of rivers, and thus controlling whole dukedoms of the public grass. Those homesteaders, "nesters," who had managed to find land where they had a chance, were coming into conflict with the stockmen, who cut their fences, shot their animals, threatened their families, and sometimes fired their haystacks or their houses.

Powell was a sort of early Populist. He was on the side of the Jeffersonian yeoman and the family farm and against the highhanded practices of some cattle outfits, many of which in that day were foreign-owned. His heresy, in the eyes of the Westerners who ultimately defeated him, was that he thought in terms of the democratic health of the society and the health of the resources upon which it must be built: land and water.

His *Report* brought about controversy, but little change. In that same year, 1878, Congress did put a 160-acre limitation into the Timber and Stone Act, but like the similar limitation in the Homestead Act, it was essentially an invitation to fraud. The Forest Service estimates that nearly one-third of the privately owned timber land in the Pacific Northwest was obtained through fraudulent entries—such practices as taking a whole shipload of sailors to the land office, having them file individual claims, and then giving them ten dollars, or a few drinks, for commutation of their claims to the company. In similar ways, such enormous land accumulations as those of Miller and Lux, on the San Joaquin River in California's Central Valley, were steering the West toward monopoly and factories in the field. On the plains, the trouble between the nesters and the cattlemen came to a head in Johnson County, Wyoming, in 1892, when a posse of cattlemen rode north from Cheyenne to rub out some "rustlers." Some of them may indeed have been rustlers, but some of them were simply homesteaders trying to exercise their rights under American law, and all of them were harder to handle than the cattlemen anticipated. The posse in that "Johnson County War" was made up of ancestors of the Sagebrush Rebels. And Owen Wister, a friend of the leader of that ignoble outfit, cast their principles in bronze. He made the good-guy Virginian, that knight errant on a cowhorse, one of the vigilantes, and wrung readers' hearts with the Virginian's anguish at having to help string up Shorty—a friend, but a cattle thief, and hence subject to summary justice.

By 1888 the West was enduring a severe drought, and western members of Congress known to history as the "Irrigation Clique," under the leadership of Senator William Stewart of Nevada, pushed through legislation calling for a survey of reservoir sites. Powell, as the man who knew most about western land and water, and as head of the Geological Survey, was put in charge of the new survey, and he leaped at the opportunity to put some of his reforms into effect. He proposed to survey and inventory all the public lands in the West, locate reservoir and canal sites, designate lands as irrigable or non-irrigable, and thus give settlers an opportunity to locate on lands where they had a chance to survive. Senator Stewart's intentions were probably less altruistic, for when he found that by a freakish amendment to his legislation the public domain had been utterly closed to entry, he blew up. His friends in Reno and Carson City, having inside information, could not now file on reservoir sites as they were designated and make a good thing of them. What was worse, there was no quick way of re-opening the public domain to entry. Only when Powell had finished his survey and designated western lands as irrigable or non-irrigable would he be required to certify certain areas to the President, who in turn would re-open them. And Powell was apparently going to take years about a task that Stewart had conceived as a quick reconnaissance.

Within a year Senator Stewart perceived that he had embraced a serpent. He became the bitter enemy of his own legislation and of Powell. By 1892 he and his colleagues of the Irrigation Clique had killed the appropriation for the irrigation surveys and cut Powell's Geological Survey budget; by 1894 they had forced Powell's resignation. They had also killed the first farsighted effort to give the West a system under which it could develop without either bitter individual failures or land and water monopoly by large interests. If Powell's plans had been given a chance to develop, the West would have reached a settlement equilibrium a great deal sooner, and the federal presence would probably be less. And it was the West itself, or its oligarchies, that broke Powell.

During 1889, when he and Senator Stewart were touring the West in something like harmony, Powell addressed the constitutional conventions of North Dakota, Montana, and Wyoming. He urged all of them, in planning their states, to lay out their counties not by arbitrary political lines but by drainage divides, so that watershed and timber, grazing-land foothills, and irrigable bottomland would all be inter-dependent parts of the same unit. He urged what later came to be called the Wyoming Doctrine, which tied water rights to land. And he made very little headway against habit, optimism, boosterism, and self-interest. In 1893, addressing the Irrigation Congress in Los Angeles, he told those blue-sky boosters that they were laying up trouble, because there was only enough water in the West to take care of about 20 percent of the land. They booed him, as boosters might boo him now if he should return to tell them that they can't expect to fill the West with new towns, new cities, new resorts, strip-mines, power plants, synfuel plants, slurry pipelines, and such goodies, and still have water for the traditional uses which have made the enduring life patterns of the West: ranching, irrigation farming, trout fishing, outdoor recreation, and Coors beer.

The West is full of ghost towns, and may be hatching a new crop. It is also full of vast ranges of what was once good grassland and is now mainly sagebrush, rabbitbrush, shadscale, and dust. (The basin of the Escalante River in Utah once carried 4,000 cattle and 12,000 sheep. Now it carries none.) One of the reasons for ghost towns and deteriorated ranges is that the West has always been subjected to the economics of liquidation. Another is that it is a collection of fragile ecosystems that too few of the people who lived in it understood, or do yet. Still another is that for decades everybody's land was nobody's land, and was used without management, restriction, or responsibility.

A policy of disposal has to change if you find out that you can't dispose of something. With regard to the public domain the disposal policy began to change, as we have seen, when Yellowstone National Park was set aside in 1872. It took a big step toward retention in 1891, when an amendment to the General Land Law Revision Act authorized the President to create forest reserves from public lands, and thus save at least a portion of the American forests from what had happened in Michigan and Wisconsin. Grover Cleveland and Theodore Roosevelt took full advantage of that authorization, and because only in the West was untouched forest land available their reservations were made west of the 100th meridian.

There were complaints from hungry timber interests, but the forest reserves were by no means imposed upon protesting western states by an authoritarian federal government. Many western cities wanted forest reserves around them to protect their vital watersheds. The Oregon legislature in 1889 *petitioned* the government in Washington, asking that the Cascade forests be set aside. (The request came to nothing because of the resistance of stock and timber interests.) After 1897, western landowners could take advantage of the "lieu lands" clause, and trade poor land

268

within a proposed forest reserve for better land outside. That generated a good deal of local enthusiasm for forest reserves. And it should be noted that the Utah national forests that Senator Hatch wants "returned" to the state were carved out of land that had never been anything but federal, with the enthusiastic backing of both Utah officials and the Mormon Church.

Not that the disposal policy or its states' rights corollary submitted meekly to this gradual conversion. In the 1890s, Irrigation Congresses regularly asked that the unappropriated public lands be ceded to the states in support of irrigation projects—a plan that would have made some sense if the states had been financially capable of swinging such projects. The Carey Act of 1894, in fact, granted up to a million acres to any state willing to irrigate them. Willing or not, the states did not have the ability; historically only California has managed to develop and support a water plan of its own, and most of California's system is based on federally built projects. The Irrigation Congress was not long in understanding the facts of life, and the demand for cession was replaced by a demand for federal appropriations to assist irrigation and protect watersheds. The result was the Newlands (or Reclamation) Act of 1902, which in the next eighty years poured more money into western water projects than the lands they would water were worth.

In the beginning, the national forests had been under Interior, a department with a long history of corruption and land fraud. In 1905, on the urging of Gifford Pinchot, they were moved to Agriculture and put under Pinchot's aggressive direction. The multiple-use policy had not yet developed, and timber cutting on the reserves was minimal; the principal *use* of the forests was for grazing. Pinchot promptly proposed what had never been required before, a grazing fee. It struck stockmen, accustomed to free use of the public domain, as un-American. They refused to pay, sued the Forest Service, and stirred up their Congressmen.

By 1907 they had succeeded in attaching to the Agricultural Appropriations Bill a rider banning creation of any further forest reserves in Washington, Oregon, Idaho, Montana, Wyoming, and Colorado without the consent of Congress, which in effect meant the consent of the western-dominated land committees. When the bill came to Roosevelt's desk for signature he knew that a veto could not be sustained. So he held the bill through the last days of his administration, worked furiously laying out new reserves, and only when he had created sixteen million acres of new federal forests, signed the bill that would have prevented him from doing so. Except for about 20,000 acres in Washington that promptly disappeared into the hands of the lumbermen, the reservations stuck, primarily because western public opinion was more for than against them.

Once initiated, permanent withdrawals from the public domain increased in number and multiplied in kind. Getting the Indian tribes onto reservations meant carving out large areas, many of them out of the poorest and apparently least usable land. Though national forests remained more or less fixed, national parks continued to be set aside, some of them out of the unappropriated public domain, some out of former national forests. The Antiquities Act of 1906 authorized the President to create national monuments in areas of great natural, historical, or archaeological value. Wildlife sanctuaries, national seashores and lakeshores, wild and scenic rivers, wilderness areas created under the Wilderness Act of 1964, all represent a strengthening of the decision to hold on to and manage large sections of the public domain rather than try to dispose of them or let them deteriorate. Apart from the Indian reservations, these withdrawals represent pretty much the cream of the remaining public lands. What about the leftovers, the sage plains, the deserts, the barren mountains where the potential was thought to be almost exclusively minerals and grazing?

Mineral lands especially were of continuing interest to Westerners, and the traditional practices of free exploration and entry were well established. When Theodore Roosevelt and William Howard Taft, between 1907 and 1910, withdrew from entry many non-metallic mineral deposits and potential water-power sites, they encountered immediate stiff resistance. Western legislatures in 1913, 1914, and again in 1919 demanded (the old cry where apparently valuable resources were involved) that all remaining public lands be ceded to the states. They did not get the lands, perhaps did not expect to, but as is often the case in these federal-state disputes they got something just as good or better: the Mineral Leasing Act and the Water Power Act of 1920, which opened the Roosevelt-Taft reserves to exploitation under lease, and gave the states 90 percent of the mineral lease revenues and 87.5 percent from the licensing of power sites.

After that resounding success, states' rights agitation subsided for more than a decade. Why buy a cow when the milk is so cheap? Why take the risk of owning and managing lands that the federal government will manage in your behalf, giving you 90 percent of the proceeds? So in 1930, when Herbert Hoover and his Secretary of the Interior, Ray Lyman Wilbur, proposed to give to the states all the unappropriated public domain, minus its minerals, the states laughed. They already, said Governor George Dern of Utah, had more than plenty of that kind of land. "Why should the states want more of this precious heritage of desert?"

That was in 1930, the beginning of the Depression, the beginning of the Dust Bowl, when plowing, overgrazing, and cyclic drought had turned much of the Plains country into a disaster area. By 1934 the dust had blown clear to Washington, D.C., and converted an old fed-hater, Congressman Edward Taylor of Colorado, into a believer in federal rescue and management. He fathered the Taylor Grazing Act, which organized most of the remaining public lands into grazing districts and closed them to entry under any existing land law. The federal government, represented by the new Taylor Grazing Service, would manage them with the advice and consent of local district boards.

Predictably, some die-hard cattlemen resisted, denying that overgrazing had anything to do with erosion. Congressman Ayers of Montana introduced yet another bill that would have turned over the public domain to the states. But some people learned faster than Congressman Ayers. The appalling evidence of range deterioration through the western states was reinforced by the success of the Mizpah–Pumpkin Creek experiment in Montana, where careful range management increased the carrying capacity from 2,000 animals to 5,000 in six years. The Taylor Grazing Act, with its built-in range rehabilitation financed by the federal government, had broad support. But Senator Pat McCarran of Nevada (they're generally from Nevada, at once the driest and least reasonable of the western states) worked out his method of letting the feds pay for the restoration of the range while frustrating their efforts to regulate grazing:

fill out the district advisory boards with local stockmen and keep the Grazing Service budget down to starvation levels. McCarran, one of the best friends special interests ever had, kept the Grazing Service poor and impotent through its short life. After the Grazing Service was fused with the General Land Office to form the Bureau of Land Management, the effectiveness of McCarran's formula did not decrease.

The Taylor Grazing Act virtually closed the public domain and ended the long-lived policy of disposal. But it did not *say* it did, and so did not overtly repudiate a bankrupt policy. From the cattleman's point of view, it put the grazing lands in the hands of a bureau that could be milked for benefits while being controlled by its permittees. But the BLM Organic Act, FLPMA, passed by Congress in 1976, indicated an alarming change. It said outright that the public domain would hereafter be retained in perpetuity and managed in the national interest. It gave BLM, for the first time, not only an adequate budget but also greatly expanded powers and an expanded staff. It gave it specific management directives and an obligation to serve not only grazing interests but also other, and sometimes competing, interests such as wildlife management, wilderness protection, and public recreation. It asserted federal sovereignty over local tradition, the integrity of land and water resources over local and sometimes (not always) self-interested freedom of action. Unquestionably, the new hard line of the BLM Organic Act was dictated by a new perception of the national interest as against the regional western interest, and by a new perception of the importance of the resources buried under the scruffy grass and inaccessible mountains of the West.

To the BLM Organic Act stockmen reacted predictably: FLPMA has been generally conceded to be the precipitating cause of the Sagebrush Rebellion. A good thing was threatened; federal managers were empowered to manage; AUMs (animal units per month) might be cut; fees might be increased; deliberate trespass might not be condoned. And this at a time when cattle ranching was marginal or threatened with failure, when there were no beef price supports to match tobacco supports or milk supports (and hard-nosed cattlemen wouldn't have accepted beef price supports anyway; they would rather cut off their noses to spite their faces). Some BLM lands were closed to mineral exploration while being studied as permanent wilderness. It could even be that in the euphoria of sudden power, some BLM officials threw their weight around; at least they failed to observe the traditional subservience to local graziers and their politicians. And wildlife, whatever that meant, was held to be a legitimate use of the public domain. When Uncle Sam's elk or deer, wild burros or wild horses used the range or broke into a rancher's haystacks, he was supposed not to get out his rifle but appeal to the local BLM office, which would probably cite him the multiple-use regulations.

Those were irritations to a traditional, well-organized, and barely economic industry. There was something else, within a year of the passage of FLPMA, that really scared the West and brought a good many allies to the original Sagebrush Rebels. In 1977 Jimmy Carter announced his "hit list" of proposed water projects that he intended to block. Of nineteen projects, seven were in the West, four in the Colorado River drainage basin. His announcement seemed to mean that after seventy-five years of pouring money into western reclamation, the eastern states which have paid most of the bills were getting tired of doing so. At the same time, President Carter indicated that he hoped to develop a national water policy. The double threat of reduced federal aid and increased federal participation in water decisions trod on every toe in the West, and the 100th meridian began to seem like a north-south Mason Dixon line. Western congressmen of both parties rose up and aborted most of President Carter's plans and cut his hit list drastically.

However justified it may have seemed as national policy, Carter's move was a political blunder and certainly had something to do with Reagan's 1980 sweep of the western states. On water matters, the otherwise diverse and disunited West is traditionally unanimous, or at the very least states are willing to trade support for the projects of others in exchange for support of their own.

The feds, despite serious mistakes and despite a recent tendency of the Forest Service to defect to the enemy, have always been the West's best chance for survival. They have made some parts of it what they are, and brought some parts of it halfway back from ruin. In its relations with Washington the West has been subsidized, not victimized; the land managing bureaus have more often been patsies than tyrants.

The grazing fee on Taylor lands from 1936 to 1946 was a nickel per animal unit month. By 1966 it had gone up to thirty-three cents, by 1974 to a dollar. In the 1980s, at something over two dollars in the Jackson Hole area, it is less than half of what comparable private grazing land leases for; and if there are hindrances and restrictions on federal land that are not imposed on private land, that fact should be matched against the controlling fact that there isn't nearly enough private land to serve ranchers' needs. Though less a bargain than they were, the BLM and forest grazing leases are the resource that keeps many ranchers afloat, and there is every prospect that with improved management they will get better, not worse. Moreover, half the grazing fees collected go to the state, and half of the federal half is plowed back into range improvement. Furthermore, the states get big federal payrolls; extra highway aid through public lands; free development of national parks, which in some states are the biggest source of tourist revenue; free management of forests and watersheds, which to cities such as Salt Lake are virtually local parks and playgrounds. They still get half the mineral-lease bonuses, royalties, and rentals, amounting in most western states to several millions each year, and in Wyoming to $39.4 million in 1979. From the Outer Continental Shelf lands in Oregon, once granted to a railroad and on collapse of the railroad reclaimed by the federal government, the timber payments totaled $86.7 million in that same year. Of that, according to the prevailing formula, 50 percent went to the state, 50 percent to the federal government, which in turn invested half of its half in timber improvement programs. Also, all public lands states get many millions in lieu of taxes.

And not only money. That open space that fills your vision and lifts your heart when you drive across the West is federal open space, most of it. Federally owned, protected, managed, federally kept open to almost any sort of reasonable public use. If it brings some irritations from hordes of tourists, it also fills the local treasury, and it gives a large part of the spaciousness and satisfaction to western living. As for wilderness areas, if we had had to depend on the states for their protection, there would pretty clearly be none.

The Sagebrush Rebels, bemused by their own mythology, are fond of asserting that rugged individualism built the West, pioneer grit and self-reliance. It is true that the West's history is punctuated with the lives of rugged individualists—Henry Villard, Marcus Dailey, Henry Miller, Jim Hill—but they built such things as railroad empires, land empires, and the Anaconda Copper Company. Who built the West as a living-place, a frugal, hard, gloriously satisfying civilization scrabbling for its existence against the forces of weather and a land as fragile as it is demanding, was not rugged individuals but cooperators, neighbors who knew how to help out in crises, who could get together to build a school and figure out a way to get the kids there, pool their efforts to search for lost cattle or lost people, and join in infrequent blowouts, dances, and fairs. It was rugged individualists who *raped* the West, some successfully, some not. One remembers Bernard DeVoto's remark that the only true rugged individualists in the West generally wound up at the end of a rope whose other end was in the hands of the cooperating citizenry.

Unfortunately, the West has already gone a long way on the booster road, and federally developed water has made possible a lot of what is called Progress but might well be called something else. A river such as the Colorado is dammed and managed from its headwaters to what used to be its mouth—there isn't a mouth now, the river dies in the sand miles from the Gulf. One keeps remembering that reservoir sites have a predictable life, on the Colorado, of not much more than a hundred years, and Boulder Dam was built nearly fifty years ago. One can't help being aware that the closer it gets to its end, the more saline the Colorado's many-times-used water becomes, and that only an expensive desalinization plant allows the United States to fulfill its obligation of 1,500,000 acre-feet of usable water to Mexico.

No western states except those on the Pacific Coast can permanently support large populations. Nor can they support, without drastic consequences, continued application of the economics of liquidation. The extermination of the beaver and the bison, the gold and silver rushes, could be recovered from; the rivers still run, though without the flood protection of beaver engineering; the abandoned drifts crumble in the dry hills; the grass, with great effort, can be brought back after decades of overgrazing.

But the contemporary raids on coal, oil, gas, and uranium, the high-powered explorations for every sort of extractable wealth, threaten to destroy the one appropriate, enduring, and renewable future for much of the West, especially of the northern plains and Rockies, which is grass. Industry threatens the integrity of every western town exposed to it, and the thousands of megawatts of electricity from coal that are already being produced or on the drawing boards threaten both the air and the clean space. Immigrants hungry for just the goodness of life that much of the West still provides endanger what they come seeking. Much of the West, sparse as its population is by comparison with that of the Midwest or Northeast or even California, is over-populated right now. The rivers are over-subscribed, the ground water is pumped down—and that is the ultimate bank account. When that is gone a place is in trouble, like a Vermont farmer who has been forced to log his sugarbush in a last desperate effort to stay solvent.

If the West is going to be saved in anything like its present state, it will not be by the states or the oligarchs who dominate most western capitals. It will be accomplished, if at all, by the greatest cooperation possible between state and federal, private and federal, private and state, business and agriculture. The Sagebrush Rebellion is a delusion, an anachronism, in some part a selfish attempt at a grab whose consequences the grabbers either do not see or do not care about.

A little less boosterism, a little less mobility (it is graveyards that give stability to towns, and most western graveyards hold only one generation of a family), a little more consideration of the earth which is all we have to live on and the water which is all we have to live by, would become us. The West is not only beautiful and spacious and exhilarating, it is also very fragile. Westerners would do well to examine their own relation to it, and learn to live in harmony with it, instead of joining those who, as Aldo Leopold said, are trying to remodel the Alhambra with a bulldozer, and proud of their yardage.

If Westerners are uneasy about the future, they have reason. But it seems to this observer that federal control of the public domain and the continuing strength of the federal land-managing bureaus are indispensable parts of the future. Without them, in fact, there may not *be* much of a future.

Part Four

GENESIS

Editor's Note

"Genesis" was one of several stories intended for inclusion in *Wolf Willow*, a combined history, memoir, and fictional account of the Cypress Hills country of Saskatchewan that Stegner wrote during a fellowship year at the Center for Advanced Studies in the Behavioral Sciences in 1955, and completed and published in 1962. "I had some kind of half-assed notion that I wanted to do a study in village democracy," he remarked in a conversation with Richard Etulain. "One was Saskatchewan, where I had spent my boyhood. Another was Vermont, which had a village democracy for two hundred years at least. . . . What it finally came down to was concentrated on the Saskatchewan . . . because that was obviously the one that interested me most."

Only two of the stories made it into the book, "Carrion Spring" and "Genesis," and many readers feel the latter is one of the best pieces of fiction Stegner ever wrote. In 1970 I had an occasion to record a conversation of my own with him on the genesis of "Genesis," a small portion of which follows:

"The form and length of the story were as vague as the theme, and of course I did not have the title until the theme had been discovered and worked out in actions which suggested not only the beginning of manhood but the beginnings of a new country.

"What I began with was a notion of writing a story about the winter of 1906, which put the open range cattle outfits out of business and opened the way for homesteaders. I was telling the story of a disaster. Tradition may have steered the story into becoming, as well, the story of a testing. Perhaps the plain logic of my material forced me in that direction. Perhaps memory played a part in it, since I was remembering places and events close to my own childhood, and the childhood of a somewhat frail child on a rough frontier is full of testings.

"But the testing theme did not insist upon itself at once. When I began writing I had no tenderfoot hero—I had the exact reverse, for I started telling it from the point of view of Ray Henry, the foreman, who had already won his manhood and didn't need to prove anything. All I began with were the specific events of the belated roundup, in which all the cattle outfits in that country fought to save their stock, and lost. I began with the story of a physical defeat; the theme of a spiritual gain as a consequence of the struggle came in later.

"An ordeal must be long enough to be nearly unbearable, not long enough to become either dispersed or tiresome. The typical ordeal story is a very long short story or a pretty short novel—in short, a *nouvelle*. Styron's *The Long March* is such a story. Conrad wrote some of the great ones—*Youth, Typhoon, The Nigger of the Narcissus*. And if I were to confess the full truth I would have to admit that all the time I was writing 'Genesis' I felt a good deal like Conrad on a cowhorse."

Genesis

The summer of 1906 was very wet. It seemed to rain for weeks and the coulees ran knee deep and the Frenchman River was as high as a spring flood. The dirt roofs of the log houses of that day became so sodden that water dripped from them whether it rained or not. It stayed so wet that we had difficulty getting the hay in. The winter started early with a light snow on the 5th of November, followed by a terrific three-day blizzard that started on the 11th. From then till Christmas was a succession of bad storms. The range cattle were dying in December.

Corky Jones as an old man

It seemed to the young Englishman that if anyone had been watching from the bench he would have seen them like a print of Life on the Western Plains, or like a medieval procession. The sun was just rising, its dazzle not yet quite clear of the horizon, and flooding down the river valley whitened with the dust of snow, it gilded the yellow leaves that still clung to the willows, stretched the shadow of every bush and post, glazed the eastern faces of the log ranch buildings whose other side was braced with long blue shadows. And moving now, starting to roll, the outfit was strung out along the Mounted Police patrol trail. He was enclosed in it, moving with it, but in his excitement he saw it as it would look from outside and above, and it made him want to stand up in his stirrups and yell.

Leading the lithograph procession went the five hounds—the four Russian wolfhounds and the thing its owner called a staghound, a dog as big as a calf and with a head like a lioness. Across the bottoms in the morning cold they cut loose and ran for the love of running; within seconds they were out of sight among the willows by the ford. Behind them rode Schulz, the wolfer, as new to the outfit as the Englishman himself; and after him his fifteen-year-old son driving a packhorse; and after them old Jesse in the wagon pulled by a team of hairy-footed Clydesdale stallions. Then the horse herd, seventy or eighty saddle horses in a flow of dark tossing motion across the flat, and then the riders, two and two.

They carried no lances or pennons, the sun found no armor from which to strike light, but in the incandescence of being nineteen, and full of health, and assaulted in all his senses by the realization of everything splendid he had ever imagined, the English boy knew that no more romantic procession had ever set forth. The Crusades could not have thrilled him more. Though they went, and he with them, like an illumination in an old manuscript, they had their own authentic color. Among the bays and blacks and browns and buckskins and roans of the horse herd was one bright piebald; in substitution for slashed doublets and shining silks they offered two pairs of woolly goatskin chaps and Ed Spurlock's red mackinaw.

Only a week in that country, the Englishman with practically no urging would have started running with the dogs. It rattled the brains in his head like seeds in a pod to think where he was—here, in Saskatchewan, not merely on the way to the great lone land, or on its edge, but in it, and going deeper. He had lived a dream in which everything went right. Within an hour of the time he stepped off the train in Maple Creek, hesitant and a little scared, he had learned that all the big cattle outfits using the open range east of the Cypress Hills were short-handed. Within two hours, he had found a ride with Joe Renaud, the mail driver. Within twelve, he was sleeping in the T-Down bunkhouse, an authentic cowboy. Within a week here he went, part of a company bound for adventure, on the late fall roundup to gather and bring in to feeding stations the calves that could not be expected to winter on the range.

He was face to shining face with everything new. Names he had heard here knocked and clanged in his mind—places where anything could happen, and from the sound of them, *had* happened—Jumbo's Butte, Fifty-Mile, Pinto Horse Butte, Horse Camp Coulee, the War Holes. He blew his exultant breath out between his pony's ears, and when he breathed in again he felt the cold at the root of every bared tooth. He noticed that the horses felt as he did: though they had been on the roundup and then on the long drive to Montana and then on the long drive back, and had been worked steadily since May, they were full of run; they joined him in snorting smoke.

The column turned down toward the river, and looking back the Englishman saw Molly Henry, the foreman's wife, hugging her elbows by the ranch-house door. He waved; her hand lifted. He and Ed Spurlock were the last in the line, and he saw how they would look to her, his new sheepskin and Spurlock's red mackinaw just disappearing into the willows. He thought it a lonesome piece of luck for a girl married only three weeks to be left now, with no help except a crippled handy man and no company except the Mountie on his weekly patrol from Eastend, and no woman nearer than twenty-five miles. To Spurlock, jogging beside him with his mittened hands stacked on the horn, he said with feeling, "I'm certainly glad it's not *me* being left behind!"

Spurlock glanced sideward with restless brown eyes; he said nothing; his expression did not change.

The Englishman grew aware, under Spurlock's glance, that he was posting to his pony's jogtrot. As if stretching muscles he pushed down hard into the unfamiliarly long stirrups, shoved back against the cantle, leaned a little, and stacked his hands casually on the horn in imitation of Spurlock's. As soon as he had them there he felt that he seemed to be hanging on to ease the jolt of sitting the trot, and he took his hands away again. With a complex sense of being green, young, red-headed, and British—all potentially shameful—but at the same time strong, bold, high-spirited, and ready for anything, he appraised Spurlock's taciturnity and adjusted his seat in the big strange saddle and threw at random into the air a look that was cocky, self-conscious, and ingratiating all at once.

The wagon had crushed through the thin ice at the ford, and the horses waded into the broken wake and stood knee deep, bobbing away ice-pans with their noses, plunging their muzzles to suck strongly. Here and there one pulled its nose out and stood with a thoughtful, puckered, tasting expression at the corners of its dripping lips; they looked as if the water had made their teeth ache.

Then Slippers and Little Horn and Ray Henry rode in and hazed them across, and Buck and Panguingue and Spurlock and the Englishman picked up the stragglers. The cold sound of splashing became a drumming and thudding on the bank. Above and ahead, the wagon was just tilting out of sight over the dugway edge. They took the herd up after it in a rush, and burst out onto the great glittering plain.

It was tremendous, it was like a plunge over a cliff. The sun looked them straight in the eyes, the earth dazzled them. Over and under and around, above, below, behind, before, the Englishman felt the unfamiliar element, a cleanness like the blade of a knife, a distance without limits, a horizon that did not bound the world but only suggested endless space beyond. Shading his eyes with his hand while his pony rocked into a lope, he saw all ahead of him the disk of the white and yellow world, the bowl of the colorless sky unbearable with light. Squatting on the horizon right under the searchlight sun were a pair of low mounds, one far off, one nearer. The closer one must be Jumbo's Butte, the far one Stonepile. They were the only breaks he saw in the plains except when, twisting backward, he found the Cypress Hills arched across the west, showing in coulees and ravines the faded white and gold of aspen, the black of jack-pines. By the time they had ridden five minutes the river valley out of which they had risen was almost invisible, sunk below the level of sight.

The wolfer and his son were already far ahead, the dogs only running specks out on the shining plain. Jesse and the pilot wagon were leading the rest of them on a beeline toward Jumbo's Butte, and as the Englishman settled down and breathed out his excitement and relaxed to the shuffle of his pony he watched the broad wheels drop and jolt into holes and burnouts and old Jesse lurch and sway on the high seat, and he let his back ache with sympathy. Then he saw Jesse's teeth flash in his face as he turned to shout something at Ray Henry riding beside the wagon, and he decided that sympathy was wasted. Jesse had been a bullwhacker with supply trains between Fort Benton and the Montana mining camps in the early days, he had known these plains when the buffalo were still shaking them, he had been jolting his kidneys loose across country like this for thirty years. If he had wanted another kind of job he could have had it. The Englishman admired him as a man who did well what he was hired to do. He believed old Jesse to be skilled, resourceful, humorous, close-mouthed, a character. Briefly he contemplated growing a mustache and trying to train it like Jesse's into a silky oxbow.

The saddle horses followed along smartly after the pilot wagon, and there was hardly any need to herd them, but the boys were fanned out in a wide semicircle, riding, as if by preference, each by himself. And among them—this was the wonder, this was what made him want to raise his face and ki-yi in pure happiness—rode Lionel Cullen, by now known as Rusty, the least of eight (as he admitted without real humility) but willing, and never more pleased with himself. That morning in early November, 1906, he would not have traded places with Sir Wilfrid Laurier.

He wanted to see everything, miss nothing, forget nothing. To make sure that he would not forget what happened to him and what he saw, he had begun a journal on the train coming west from Montreal, and every evening since then he had written in it seriously with posterity looking over his shoulder. He watched every minute of every day for the vivid and the wonderful, and he kept an alert eye on himself for the changes that were certain to occur. He had the feeling that there would be a test of some sort, that he would enter manhood—or cowboyhood, manhood in Saskatchewan terms—as one would enter a house. For the moment he was a tenderfoot, a greenhorn, on probation, under scrutiny. But at some moment there would be a door to open, or to force, and inside would be the self-assurance that he respected and envied in Jesse, Slippers, or Little Horn, the calm confidence of a top hand.

As they moved like the scattered shadow of a cloud across the face of the plain he knew practically nothing except how to sit a horse, and even that he knew in a fashion to get him laughed at. But he was prepared to serve an apprenticeship, he would prove himself as and when he must. And in the pocket of his flannel shirt he had a notebook and two pencils, ready for anything.

• • •

At noon, a little to the east of Jumbo's Butte, they stopped to boil coffee and heat a kettle of beans. The thin snow did not cover the grass; the crust that had blazed in their eyes all morning was thawing in drops that clung to the curly prairie wool. On a tarpaulin spread by the wagon they sprawled and ate the beans that Jesse might just as well not have heated, for the cold tin plates congealed them again within seconds. But the coffee burned their mouths, and the tin cups were so hot to hold that they drank with their mittens on. The steam of their coffee-heated breath was a satisfaction; Rusty tried to blow rings with it.

When he finished he lay on the tarp next to Panguingue. There was always, it seemed, room next to Panguingue: it was said of him that he took a bath every spring whether he needed it or not. In the cold, and so long as Panguingue wore a sheepskin and overshoes, Rusty did not mind. And anyway, since arriving he had seen no one take a bath, not even Buck, who was fastidious; certainly he had taken none himself. So he relaxed by Panguingue and felt the ground satisfyingly hard under the tarp, and let Panguingue thump him monotonously between the shoulder blades and dust cigarette ashes through his hair. Through half-closed eyes he heard the horses working on the curly grass all around, he saw a snowbird come boldly to pick at a scrap of salt pork by the edge of the tarp; his ears heard the sounds of ease, the scratchings, the crackle of a match; his nose smelled sour pipe, smelled Bull Durham, smelled Ray Henry's sybaritic cigar. He loved every minute, every sensation, and when, just as they were rising to tighten cinches and move on, they heard the hysterical yapping of hounds, and saw Schulz's pack, two miles away, pursue and run down a coyote, he climbed on the wagon and watched as eager as a spectator at a horse race. He thought of Schulz as belonging somehow with Jesse, the two of them survivors of an earlier stage of plains life; he rather envied Schulz's boy, brought up to lonely cabins, skimpy cowchip campfires on the prairies, familiarity with wild animals, the knack and habit of casual killing. From high on the wagon seat, bracing himself on Jesse's shoulder, he watched Schulz ride in and scatter the hounds and dismount, while the boy gathered up the loose packhorse. He expected that the wolfers would come in and get something to eat, but he saw Schulz mount again and the three horses and the five dogs move out eastward. Even more than the cowboys, these were the wild ones; they had gone as far as it was possible to go back toward savagery. He regretted not seeing them ride in with the scalp of the coyote, the hounds bloody-muzzled from the kill. He hoped to get a chance to course a coyote or a wolf across such a marvelous plain as this on such a glorious day, when you could see for twenty miles. It was tremendous, every bit of it.

During the afternoon the country roughened, broke into coulees that opened down toward the river. They rode, it seemed, endlessly, without a break and with little talk. Rusty stiffened in the saddle, he rode lounging, stood in the stirrups, hung his feet free while under him the shaggy little horse shuffled on. The sun went down the sky toward the Cypress Hills, now no more than a faint clean lifting of the horizon. They felt the thin warmth on their necks if their collars were down; their faces felt the cold.

When they arrived at Stonepile the sun was already down. The sky back over the hills was red, the snow ahead of them lay rosy across the flats. Until they reached the coulee's rim they would not have known it was there; as for the river, it was sunk among indistinguishable rough coulees to the north, but no more than a mile away. As they dipped downward toward the Stonepile buildings, once a Mounted Police patrol post, the valley was already full of violet shadow. Rusty creaked and eased himself, letting the horse pick his way. He was stiff and chilled, his face felt like sheet metal, his eyes watered and smarted from the day's glare.

They were not talkative as they unsaddled and turned the horses loose, or during the time while they lugged bedrolls and food into the old barracks. Two or three men would be stationed here later to feed to the calves the three hundred and fifty tons of wild hay stacked in the coulee; they had brought flour, rice, oatmeal, sugar, matches and prunes, tinned corn and syrup and jam and peas, dried apples and peaches, to stock the place. There was a good deal of tracking in and out from the cold blue dusk. Jesse had stuck two tallow dips in china holders that said *Peerless Hotel*. They were all in each other's way in the narrow bunkhouse, and all in the way of Jesse, trying to get supper going. They bumped shoulders, growled. Rusty, who had thrown his bedroll forehandedly into one of the upper bunks, came in with a load later and found that Ed Spurlock had thrown it out and put his own in its place. There were only six bunks for the ten of them. In the end, Rusty spread his bed beside Panguingue's on the floor, and the wolfers, coming in a half hour after them, looked in the door briefly and decided to sleep in the stable with the Clydes, the night horses, and the dogs.

"Be careful them studs," Jesse told Schulz. "It wouldn't do if them and your lion got to mixing it."

The wolfer was a man, Rusty thought, to be noticed, perhaps to be watchful of. He still wore, in the warming barracks, a muskrat cap with earlaps. Under it his eyes were gray as agates, as sudden as an elbow in the solar plexus. His face was red, his mustache sandy. Between his eyes, even when he smiled, which was not often, he wore a deep vertical wrinkle. He had what Rusty thought of as a passionate taciturnity. He looked watchful and besieged, he would be quick to strike back, he was not a man you could make a joke with. In a low growling voice he said that he valued his hound too highly to let any forty-dollar horse kick him in the head.

Jesse looked at him, holding a stove lid half off the smoking fire, and his silky mustaches moved as if a small animal had crawled under the thatch. He said, "If one of the Clydes hit him, that wouldn't be no forty-dollar kick. That would be a genuine gold-plated eight-hundred-dollar kick guaranteed to last."

Schulz grunted and went out: Rusty told himself that he had been right in guessing him as a man with whom you did not joke. The boy, sullen-looking, with a drooping lip and eyes that looked always out their corners, went silently after him. They came back in for supper, cleaned their plates, and went out again for good.

"What's the matter with him?" Spurlock asked. "Don't he like our company?"

"Likes his dogs better," Buck said. He reared his red turkey neck up and glared out into the jammed corridor between the bunks. From the end, where he sat braced against the wall fooling with the harmonica, Rusty saw the disgust on his skinned-looking face. "What about some-body that would sleep with a God damn dog?" Buck said.

From the lower, talking around the dead cigar that poked upward from his face, Little Horn said gently, "We ain't got any right to criticize. We all been sleepin' with Panguingue for a year."

"B.S.," Panguingue said. "My feet don't smell no worse'n yours."

"Well for the love of God," Jesse said, hanging the dishpan on the wall, "let's not have any contests. There ain't a man here would survive it."

Rusty took the slick metal of the harmonica from his mouth and ventured: his feelers, tentative always to estimate his own position as one of them, told him that now, while they were criticizing the unsociable wolfer, his own position was more solid; and yet he admired the wildness and the obvious competence of the wolfer, too. The very fact that he rode in moccasins and thick German socks gave him a distinction over the rest of them in their overshoes. Rusty said, "Do you suppose it's only that he's used to living out alone, don't you know . . . that he's almost like a wild animal himself? He seems that way to me . . . or is that only fancy?"

They hooted at him, and he felt his ears grow red. "Aow, it's only fawncy, p'raps," they told each other for the next minute or two. "Deah!" they said. "Rilly?" Rusty blew into the mouth organ. He heard Little Horn saying, "It's natural enough. Yell at a dog, he minds. Yell at one of you sonsofbitches, what does he do? I don't blame the guy. There's no satisfaction in a cowpuncher's company like there is in a dog's."

Spurlock said, "Can his kid talk? I never heard him say a word yet."

"Probably all he knows is 'bow-wow,' " Buck said.

Jesse pawed his yellow-white silky mustache and said with the look of foolery in his faded blue eyes, "Schulz don't look to me like he's got a steady conscience. I'd say mebbe he was a windigo."

Rusty waited, hoping someone else would take the bait, but resigning himself when no one spoke. And anyway, he was interested. "What's a windigo?"

"What the Crees used to call an Injun that had made use of manmeat," Jesse said. "Most generally seemed to sort of drive a man wild, he wasn't right afterwards. I recall hearing Bert Willoughby tell about one the Mounties had to go get up on the Swift Current, back in the early days. His tribe got suspicious, he come out of a starvin' winter lookin' so fat and slick. Also his fambly was missin'. So they collared this buck and he took 'em up to his winter camp on Bigstick Lake, and here was all these bones and skulls around, and he'd kick 'em and laugh, and say,

'This one my wife, hee hee hee,' and 'That one my mother-in-law, ho ho,' and 'This one here my father, ha ha.' He'd et the whole damn bunch, one after the other."

"Well," Little Horn said. "I wonder if somebody is settin' oncomfortable on old Schulzie's stomach?"

"Maybe we could get him to eat Panguingue before he gets too God damn high," Spurlock said.

Little Horn said regretfully, "I doubt if even a windigo would take a chance on Panguingue."

"B.S.," Panguingue said.

From the white cloud of cigar smoke that filled the enclosed space above his bunk, Ray Henry whispered, "You can all take it easy. Schulz and his boy will be stayin' here or at Bates Camp all winter, while you boys is up to your ass in dried apple pies back at the ranch."

"Good," Buck said.

"Sure, Ray," said Jesse, "I know that was the arrangement. But is it safe?"

"Safe, how?"

Jesse kicked the stove leg. "This-here my boy," he said. "Hee hee hee."

They left Schulz and his silent boy behind them at the Stonepile camp and made a hard drive eastward to the Fifty-Mile Crossing of the Whitemud, on the eastern boundary of the range that, by mutual consent among all the outfits, was called the T-Down's. Already, within a day, Rusty felt how circumstances had hardened, how what had been an adventure revealed itself as a job. He rose from his bed on the floor so stiff he hobbled like a rheumatic dog, and when he stumbled out of the foul barracks and took a breath of the morning air it was as if he had had an icicle rammed clear to his wishbone. Another cold day—colder than the one before by a good deal—and an even harder ride ahead. And leaving the Schulzes affected him unpleasantly: these two were being separated off to carry on a specific and essential duty, but no one was sorry to see them go. The outfit that he had thought of as ten was really only eight. If the others chose to find him as disagreeable as they found Schultz, it was only seven. He hung at their fringes, hoping to earn a place among them. He was painfully alert, trying to anticipate what was expected of him. What was expected was that he should climb in the saddle, on a new pony this morning—one with a trot like a springless wagon over cobblestones—and ride, and ride, and ride, straight into the blinding glare of the sun.

The night before, he had entered in his journal information on how the open range from Wood Mountain on the east to Medicine Lodge Coulee on the west was run. From the Whitemud north to the Canadian Pacific tracks the Circle Diamond and the 76, both very large outfits, divided it. South of the river there were several. Between Wood Mountain and Fifty-Mile was the Turkey Track, running about 25,000 head. Then their own outfit, the T-Down Bar, running 10,000. Between the T-Down ranch house and the Cypress Hills the Z-X ran about 2,000 purebred shorthorns and whitefaces, and through the Cypress Hills to Medicine Lodge Coulee an association of small ranchers called the Whitemud pool ran their herds together. It seemed reasonable; it even seemed neat; but it seemed terribly large when you had to ride across it at the wagon's pace.

By noon the sky had hazed over. They blessed it because of their eyes and cursed it because the wind developed a sting. Then away out on the flats in the middle of a bleak afternoon they met the wagon and four riders from the Turkey Track, bound for a camp they had on the big coulee called the War Holes. They were on the same errand as the T-Down boys: combing parts of the range missed in the spring roundup, and separating out the calves and bulls to be wintered on hay in the sheltered bottoms. Their greeting was taciturn and numb. The T-Down boys looked to them exactly as they looked to the T-Down, probably: frostbitten, with swollen watery eyes, their backs humped to the cold wind, their ponies' tails blowing between their legs as they waited out the fifteen minutes of meeting.

It had not been made clear to Rusty Cullen, until then, that they were on a belated and half-desperate job. A green hand did not inquire too closely for fear of asking foolish questions; an experienced hand volunteered nothing. And so he was surprised by the gloominess of the Turkey Track boys and their predictions of heavy losses on the range. They quoted signs and omens. They ran mittened hands against the grain of their ponies' winter hair, to show how much heavier it was than normal. They had seen muskrat houses built six feet high in the sloughs—and when the rats built high you could depend on a hard winter. Mounted Police freighters reported a steady drift of antelope from the north across the CPR tracks.

The chinook winds, he gathered, should keep the range clear enough for the stronger animals to get feed, but calves didn't winter well. Fortunately all the stock was fat: the summer range had been good. If they could get the calves in where there was feed, maybe there wouldn't be too much loss. Having exchanged omens, predictions, reassurances, and invitations to Christmas blowouts, they raised their mitts to each other and ducked each his own way into or away from the wind, and the tracks that had briefly met crawled apart again across the snow.

Somehow the brief, chilled, laconic encounter in the emptiness and cold of the flats left Rusty depressed. By the time they dragged in to camp in the willows of the river bottom at Fifty-Mile his eyes were swollen almost shut, and burned and smarted as if every little capillary and nerve in them had been twisted and tied in knots; he knew how streaked and bloodshot they were by looking at the eyes of the others. He was tired, stiff, cold; there was no immediate comfort in camp, but only more cold hard work, and the snow that was only a thin scum on the prairie was three inches deep down here. They shoveled off a space and got the tent set up in the blue dusk, and he looked it over and felt that their situation was gloomily naked and exposed. When he chopped through the river's inch of ice and watched the water well up and overflow the hole it seemed like some dark force from the ancient heart of the earth that could at any time rise around them silently and obliterate their little human noises and tracks and restore the plain to its emptiness again.

The wind dropped after sundown, the night came on clear and cold. Before turning in Rusty stepped outside and looked around. The other boys were all in their bedrolls, and the light in the tent had been blown out so that even that pale human efflorescence was gone; the tent was a misty pyramid, the wagon a shadow. Tied to the wheels, the blanketed night horses and the Clydes moved their feet uncomfortably and rustled for a last grain of oats in the seams of their nosebags.

The earth showed him nothing; it lay pallid, the willows bare sticks, the snow touched with bluish luminescence. A horn of moon was declining toward the western horizon. But in the north the lights were beginning, casting out a pale band that trembled and stretched and fell back and stretched out again until it went from horizon to horizon. Out of it streaks and flares and streamers began to reach up toward the zenith and pale the stars there as if smoke were being blown across them.

He had never felt so small, so lost, so inconsequential; his impulse was to sneak away. If anyone had asked his name and his business, inquiring what he was doing in the middle of that empty plain, he would have mumbled some foolish and embarrassed answer. In his mind's eye he saw the Turkey Track camp ten or fifteen or twenty miles out in the emptiness, the only other thing like themselves, a little lonesome spark that would soon go out and leave only the smudge of the wagon, the blur of the tent, under the cold flare of the Northern Lights. It was easy to doubt their very existence; it was easy to doubt his own.

A night horse moved again, a halter ring clinked, a sound tiny and lost. He shuddered his shoulders, worked his stiffened face, stirred up his numbed brains, and shook the swimming from his eyes. When the tent flap dropped behind him and he stooped to fumble the ties shut the shiver that went through him was exultant, as if he had just been brushed by a great danger and had escaped. The warmth and the rank human odors of the tent were mystically rich with life. He made such a loud, happy, unnecessary row about the smell of Panguingue's feet when he crawled into his bedroll in their cramped head-to-foot sleeping space that three or four sleepy voices cursed him viciously and Panguingue kicked him a few good hard ones through his blankets and kicked the vapors out of him.

Sometime during that roundup they may have had a day of decent weather, but it seemed to Rusty it was a procession of trials: icy nights, days when a bitter wind lashed and stung the face with a dry sand of snow, mornings when the crust flashed up a glare so blinding that they rode with eyes closed to slits and looked at the world through their eyelashes. There was one afternoon when the whole world was overwhelmed under a white freezing fog, when horses, cattle, clothes, wagon, grew a fur of hoar frost and the herd they had gathered had to be held together in spooky white darkness mainly by ear.

On bright days they were all nearly blind, in spite of painting their cheekbones with charcoal and riding with hats pulled clear down; if they could see to work at all, they worked with tears leaking through swollen and smarting lids. Their faces grew black with sun and glare, their skin and lips cracked as crisp as the skin of a fried fish, and yet they froze. Every night the thermometer dropped near zero, and there was an almost continuous snake-tongue of wind licking out of the north or west.

The river bottom and the big rough coulees entering from the south held many cattle, and they soon collected a large herd. They were hard to move; if he had had a gun Rusty would have been tempted more than once to make immediate beef of them. The Canadian cattle, whiteface or whiteface-and-shorthorn cross, were impenetrably stupid and slow; their whole unswerving intention was to break past a rider and get back into the bottoms. The longhorns, most of which carried the Turkey Track or Circle Diamond brand and which had to be cut away from their own, were exactly the opposite: fast, agile, wicked, and smart. They could lead a man a wild chase, always in a direction he didn't want to go; they hid among other cattle and couldn't be cut out; they milled and stampeded the T-Down herd at every chance; all the boys had spills, chasing long-horns through rough country and across the icy flats; and they wore the horses, already weak and thin, to the bone.

On the third day out from Fifty-Mile, Slip, Panguingue, and Rusty were cutting out a bunch of ten or fifteen Circle Diamond longhorns from a dozen T-Down whitefaces. They wanted the whitefaces up on the bench where they could turn them into the herd; the longhorns were welcome to the coulee. Of course the whitefaces hung on to the coulee and the longhorns stampeded up onto the flats. It was astonishing how fast those cattle could move and how much noise they made. Their horns cracked; their hoofs cracked; their joints cracked; it seemed as if even their tails snapped like bullwhips. In a wild clamor they went up the coulee bank, agile as goats, with Rusty after them.

He came out onto the rim in a sting of snow and wind. The longhorns were well ahead of him, racing with their bag-of-bones clatter toward the wagon and the herd that Jesse and Spurlock were holding there. Rusty ducked his head and squinted back at Slip; he was waving and shouting: Rusty understood that he was to head the longhorns before they got too close to the herd.

The cattle, very fast for a short distance, began to slack off. His dogged little horse came up on a roan haunch, then on a brindle, then past a set of wild horns, and finally up on the leader, so close the boy could have kicked his laboring shoulder or reached out and grabbed his thirty-inch horn. He lashed him with the rope across the face; still going hard, the steer ducked and began to turn.

The next he knew, Rusty was over the pony's head like a rock shot from a slingshot. It happened so fast he knew nothing about it until he was flying through the air frantically clawing at nothing, and lit sliding, and rolled. His wind and wits went out of him together; he sat up groggily, spitting blood and snow.

And oh, how beautiful a thing it is to work with men who know their job! He sat up into a drama of danger and rescue. The steer had turned and was coming for him; Slip was riding in hard from the side to head him off. But he was too far back; Rusty saw it with the hardest sort of clarity, and he was up on hands and knees, into a crouch, his eyes estimating distances, watching the wide horns and the red eyes of the steer, noting even how the stiff ice-encased hairs sprayed back from his nostrils. While he crouched there laboring to get wind back into his lungs, Rusty saw Slip's bay in the air with all four legs stiff, coming down to a braced landing. The wide loop came snaking in the air, Slip's left hand was making a lightning dally around the horn. The timing was so close that the rope did not even sag before the steer's rush took up the slack. It simply whistled out straight and was snapped tight and humming as the pony came down stiff-legged in the snow. The steer was yanked off his feet, the horse slipped, went nearly down, recovered, the air was full of hoofs and horns, and the longhorn crashed as if he had fallen from the sky. Liquid dung rolled from under his tail; Rusty thought he had broken his neck.

Shakily he went toward the steer to unhook Slip's rope for him, but Slip warned him sharply away. His horse stepped nervously, keeping the rope tight when the steer tried to rise. A little way off, Panguingue was reaching from his saddle to catch the trailing reins of Rusty's pony. "Bust anythin'?" Slip said.

"No," Rusty said. He had sense enough to swallow his gratitude. With his cracked and blackened face, Slip looked like a dwarfish Negro jockey on that big strong horse. He was watching the herd, and Rusty turned to look too, just as Panguingue rode up and handed him his reins. All three stood a moment looking toward the wagon and listening to the uproar of shouts and curses that came from Spurlock and Jesse.

"God damn!" Panguingue said.

The longhorns, bursting into the compact herd of whitefaces, were stirring them like a great spoon. Even as they watched, the milling movement spread, the edges scattered, the whole herd was on the run back toward the coulee. Slip shook off his rope and he and Panguingue started off at a lope without a glance at Rusty. The steer rose and stood spraddling, watching him with red eyes. Limping, cursing the treacherous icy hole-pocked prairie, sorry for himself in his unregarded pain, Rusty reached his numb left arm up and took hold of the horn and mounted. Gritting his teeth, he spurred the pony into a trot, but that so agonized his arm and shoulder that in a moment he slowed to a walk. Then he swore and kicked him into a canter. He would show them. He would ride it out the whole mortal day, and they would never know until that night, after he had done without a complaint all the duty demanded of him, that he was really a stretcher case with a broken shoulder or collarbone or something. He knew he was going to be laid up, but he would stay in the saddle till he dropped. A grim campaigner, a man with the right stuff in him, he crippled along after Slip and Panguingue and the accursed cows.

He managed to get through the rest of the day, but when he was unsaddling that night at the wagon, his face skinned, his left hand helpless, and his right fumbling and clumsy, no one came around with help or sympathy. One or two of them gave him bleary glances and went on past as he picked at the latigo with one freezing unmittened hand. Perhaps he dropped a tear or two of rage and weakness and pain into the snow. When he finally got the saddle off and turned the pony loose, he stumbled into the tent and lay down and turned his back to them. He heard Jesse's cooking noises, he smelled the smoke of frying meat, he felt the heat of the stove filling the canvas space. The boys talked a little, growling and monosyllabic. The wind puffed on the tent wall near his face; he cradled his aching arm the best he could and concentrated on stoicism.

Panguingue came in, crawled into his bed to warm up, and kicked

Rusty companionably to get his attention. The jar shook such pain through the boy that he rose up with gritted teeth. Panguingue's astonished grin glimmered through his beard, and he said to the tent at large, "You should of seen old Rusty get piled today. How'd that feel, Rusty? You was up in the air long enough to grow feathers."

"It felt like hell, if you want to know. I think I broke my shoulder."

"Oh well," Panguingue said. "Long as it wasn't your neck."

His callousness absolutely enraged Rusty, but Spurlock enraged him more when he remarked from the other corner of the tent, "You sure chose a hell of a time to get piled, I'll say that. You fall off and we lose the whole God damn herd."

"Fall off?" Rusty said shrilly. "*Fall* off? What do *you* do when your pony steps in a hole?"

"Not what you did," Spurlock said. In the light of the two candles Jesse had stuck onto his grub box, his bloodshot eyes moved restlessly, here, there, first on Rusty, then on one of the others, never still. There was a drooping, provocative smile on his face. Rusty pulled his anger in and stayed silent.

Slippers said into the air from where he lay on his back next to Panguingue, "Rusty was doin' all right. He was headin' 'em."

"When he see his horse was too slow, he took off and flew," Panguingue said.

In imbecile good nature his rough hand jarred out, half blow and half push, and Rusty fell awkwardly on the bad shoulder. "Look out, you silly bastard!" he screamed, so much like a hysterical schoolboy that he turned again, ashamed, and gave his back to them. He knew they were watching, speculatively and with expressions of calculated neutrality. Judgment was going on in their minds, and he hated what they were thinking.

In a few minutes Ray Henry came in, the last but one into camp.

"Somebody'll have to spell Buck in an hour," he said. "After that we can take it in two-hour shifts. Little Horn, you take it first, then Panguingue, then Slip." His inflamed eyes came around to Rusty, blinked at him across the stove and candles. "Rusty, you healthy? Was that you took a spill today?"

"That was me."

"Hurt yourself?"

"I don't know. I can't move my left arm."

The foreman picked his way between the bedrolls and squatted. "Roll over and let's see." Obediently, justified and finally vindicated, Rusty helped unbutton sheepskin and both flannel shirts he wore, and the thick hands probed and squeezed and punched around his shoulder and collar-bone and down the arm. Rusty flattered himself that he did not wince.

For a second or two Ray stayed squatting there, dark-faced, burly as a boulder, expressionless. "I don't think she's bust," he said. "It don't wiggle anywhere. I'll take your shift tonight, and you better lay up with the wagon tomorrow and see how it goes."

"No," Rusty said. "I can work."

"Excelsior," said Spurlock from his corner.

"What?" Ray said.

Nobody said anything.

That was always a bad time, that few minutes before supper, when they came in and lay around the tent waiting for food with their bones melting away with tiredness. But it didn't last. They were cheerful enough afterward, lying in bed, smoking, and Spurlock even went to the length of rolling Rusty a cigarette and passing it across in silence. "Oh, I say," Rusty said. "Thanks very much!" Spurlock threw his muzzle in the air and gave himself up to silent laughter, or to communion with his ironic gods, and shook his head in amused despair, but the edge was out of him, out of all of them.

Buck came in, cold and morose, and fussily hunted up a pan and heated water in it and washed himself before he ate the supper Jesse had kept warm. Little Horn, groaning, hunched into his sheepskin and went out. They could hear him asking the sympathy of the horse as he saddled up.

One by one the other boys made their way outside and in a few seconds came chattering in again. When it came Rusty's turn he ducked out with his arm hugged against his chest. The cold froze his teeth clear to the roots at the first breath; he shuddered and shook. It is awkward enough for a man to button and unbutton his pants with his right hand at any time, but in that freezing circumstance he might as well have tried to do it with tongs. The big pale earth was around him, the big mottled sky arched over with a slice of very white moon shining on icy-looking clouds. It was so quiet he heard his own heart thudding. For a moment he stood taking it in, and then he opened his mouth and let out a very loud yell, simply to announce himself and to crack the silence. When he went back in, hissing and shaking, he found them all staring at him.

"What in hell was that?" Buck said.

"That was me," Rusty said. "It was too quiet to suit me."

Jesse was paring a sliver of tobacco off a plug, working at it slowly and carefully as he might have peeled an apple. His faded eyes glinted up, his oxbow mustaches parted briefly. "You hadn't ought to do a thing like that, son," he said. "I reckon you don't know, though."

"Know what?"

"When it's this cold," Jesse said, "man has to be careful how loud he talks."

"What?" Rusty said. "Get too cold air into your lungs, you mean? Freeze your windpipe?"

"Tell you," Jesse said. "I used to know this feller name Dan Shields."

Rusty crept into his blankets, not willing to give any of them, even Jesse, a handle. "Anybody feel like a game of stud?" Spurlock said.

"Too damn cold," Panguinge said. "You'd freeze your hands."

"Down by where I used to work," Jesse said, in his soft insisting voice, "down there by Sheridan, there's this guy Dan Shields. He's tellin' me one time about some cold weather *he* seen. Said him and another guy was up on the mountain workin' a gold mine one winter, and it chilled off considerable. Man walk along outside, he'd steam like a laundry. Wood froze so hard it'd last all night in the stove—they never had a bit of fuel trouble. Go to spit, you'd have to break yourself free before you could walk away. They figured seventy-five, eighty below. Couldn't tell, the thermometer froze solid at sixty-five."

"I hope they had a stream-heated backhouse," Panguingue said. "I had to break myself free out there just now."

"Better look close, Pan," said Spurlock. "Man could make a serious mistake breakin' too careless."

"B.S.," Panguingue said. "Even broke off short I'll match you."

"Said they had them a nice warm cabin and they made out fine," Jesse said, "except the grub began to run low. One mornin' they're talkin' about what they should do, and they step outside to sort of look at the weather. They're standin' there talkin', and it seems to Dan this other guy's voice is sort of failin' him. He gets squeakier and squeakier, and finally he pinches out. The fella looks surprised and clears his throat, and spits, and breaks himself loose, and tries again. Not a whisper.

" 'Is your tonsils froze, or what?' Dan says to him—and you know, *he* don't break the silence any, either. He tries his lips, and they're workin', and he wags his tongue, and *it* ain't bogged down, and he takes a big breath and tries to rip off a cussword, and nothin' happens at all.

"His partner is lookin' at him very queer. He says somethin' that Dan don't get. 'By God,' says Dan at the top of his voice, 'there's somethin' almighty damn funny here!' and all he hears is nothin', just nothin'. They turn their heads and listen, and there ain't a sound.

"Dan cusses some more, thinkin' he may jar somethin' loose the way you'd kick a jammed endgate. He can't make a peep. Said he was beginnin' to get scared. Said he looks across at his partner and the sweat was up on the guy's forehead size of buckshot. The drops froze as fast as they popped out, and they roll off his face and hit the snow. You'd think they'd patter—sort of human hailstones. Not a speck, Dan says. They roll off his partner's brow and hit the ground and he can see them bounce and they don't make no more noise than feathers.

"The partner begins to get excited. His mouth is goin' like a stamp-mill, and yet it's just as quiet as three o'clock in the mornin'. His eyes bug out, and he makes these yellin' motions, and all of a sudden he bursts inside the cabin and throws his stuff together and takes off down the mountain."

"And never was seen again," Spurlock said. "The end."

"Well, that relieves the grub situation, and after Dan has gone inside and warmed up he tries out his voice again and it works, so he stays on. The weather never lets up, though, not till way 'long in the spring. Then one mornin' the sun comes up bright and first thing Dan notices the thermometer has thawed out and begun to slide up, and she's only sixty below, and then a little later she's fifty. She's gettin' so mild he sits down on the doorstep after breakfast and smokes a pipe. While he's sitting there he hears his partner, somewhere a good ways away, but comin' closer, sayin' somethin' like, 'Figger we could get down and back in three-four days if on'y it wasn't so God damn cold.'

300

"Said it cheered him like anythin' to hear a human voice again, and he raises up on the doorstep and looks down the trail, but ain't a sign of anybody. He's lookin' all around when his partner says, quite close, 'I don't mind bein' out of sugar, but I sure as hell don't aim to stay long where they ain't any Climax Plug.'

" 'I see what you mean,' Dan says conversationally. 'I expect you get the bulk of your nourishment thataway,' and then he looks very fast behind him and all around that front yard, because it ain't him that's said it, he ain't moved his mouth or had any intention of sayin' anything. It ain't him but it's his voice.

" 'My notion is we ought to go on down,' the partner says, very clear and close, and then there is a good deal of hackin' and spittin' and clearin' of the throat and the partner says, 'What in the God damn hell is happenin' to me?' and Dan hears his own voice say, 'Is your tonsils froze, or what?' and then there is a very considerable duet of cussin' and yellin', and more throat clearin' and more yellin' and a sound like a hailstorm patterin' all around, and out of this big uproar the partner says, 'By God, I'm gettin' out of here!' Well that's just what Dan does. He ducks inside that cabin and leans against the door till all the fuss dies down outside, and when she's quiet he gathers together his plunder and he hightails her off the mountain too.

"He had it figured out by then, easy enough. It was so cold out there while they was talkin' that their words froze right there in the air, froze up plumb solid and silent. Then when that quick thaw comes on they broke up all at once and come down on old Dan's head like icicles off a roof. But Dan said he didn't want to stay up there even after he figured it out. Said it made him uncomfortable to think that any time somebody might yell right in his ear three months ago. Said he never did learn to care for cold-storage conversation as well as the fresh article."

"Now ain't it funny?" Buck said. "That ain't my taste at all. I'd just as soon have everything you just said all froze up nice and solid so the coyotes could listen to it next spring and I could just lay here now with no noise going on and get some sleep."

"That's the biggest pile of cold-storage bullshit I ever heard," Spurlock said. "Jesse, you could chop that up and use it for cowchips for a month."

"I guess," Jesse said mildly. "But I tell you, kid, don't you go yellin' so loud outside there no more. This is one of those winters when you might deefen somebody in 1907."

With his arm hanging in a sling made of a flour sack and a horse-blanket pin, and the loose sleeve of his sheepskin flapping, Rusty managed to go on riding. The weather was clear and bitter, full of signs that the boys said meant change—sundogs by day, Northern Lights by night. Even the noontime thermometer never climbed much above twenty. Flushing the stubborn cattle out of coulees and draws, they left behind them a good many cold-storage curses to startle the badgers and coyotes in the first thaw.

Day by day they worked their herd a few miles closer to Horse Camp Coulee; night by night they took turns riding around and around them, beating their arms to keep warm, and after interminable star-struck icy hours stumbled into the sighs and snores and faint warmth of the tent and shook the shoulder of the victim and benefactor who would relieve them. Some days one or another couldn't see to work, and when that happened they all suffered, for Jesse rode with the hands, instead of making camp, and in the icy evening they all had to fall to and shovel off a patch of prairie and set up the tent and fit the sooty lengths of stovepipe through the roof thimble, and anchor themselves to the earth with iron picket pins, the only thing they could drive into the frozen ground.

After an hour or two the stove would soften up the ground close around it, but near the edges and under their beds it never thawed more than just enough to moisten the tarps and freeze the beds fast, so that they pulled them up in the morning with great ripping sounds. The tent walls that they banked with snow to keep out the wind had to be chopped free every morning, and wore their clots and sheets of ice from one day to the next.

That cloth house stamped itself into Rusty's mind and memory. It spoke so plainly of the frailty and impermanence of their intrusion. And yet that frailty, and the implication of danger behind it, was what most nettled and dared and challenged him. Difficult as this job was, it was still only a job, and one done in collaboration with seven others. It called only for endurance; it had very little of the quality of the heroic that he had imagined Saskatchewan enforced upon the men who took its dare. Sometime, somehow, after he had gone through this apprenticeship in the skills of survival, he would challenge the country alone—some journey, some feat, some action that would demand of him every ounce of what he knew he had to give. There would be a real testing, and a real proof, and the certainty ever afterward of what one was. The expectation had no shape in his mind, but he thought of it in the same way he might have thought of sailing a small boat singlehanded across the Atlantic, or making a one-man expedition to climb Everest. It would be something big and it would crack every muscle and nerve and he would have to stand up to it alone, as Henry Kelsey had, wandering two years alone among unheard-of tribes in country not even rumored, or as young Alexander Mackenzie did when he took off from Fort Chippewyan to open the mysterious Northwest and track down the river that carried his name. There were even times when he thought of the wolfer Schulz with near envy. Like him or not, he didn't run in pack, he was of an older and tougher breed, he knew precisely what he was made of and what he could do, and he was the sort from whom one might learn something.

Meantime he was the greenhorn, the outcast tenderfoot of the outfit, and he would remain so until he personally turned a stampeding herd, or rode seventy-five miles and back in twenty-four hours to bring a doctor for someone critically hurt, or plucked somebody from under the horns of a crazy longhorn steer. He nursed his sore shoulder, evidence of his so-far failure to perform heroically, like a grudge that must sometime be settled, or a humiliation that must be wiped out.

The first night, when he had come out and confronted a sinking moon and a rising banner of Northern Lights, and the other one, after his fall, when he had been tempted into a yell of defiance, had several counterparts. Sometimes, riding around the dark mass of the herd, numbly aware of the click of hoofs, the sigh of a cow heaving to her feet, the flurry of movement from a scared or lost calf, the muted tramplings and mooings and lowings, it seemed he guarded all life inside his round, and heard its confusion and discomfort and dismay, and witnessed its unsleeping vigilance against the dangers that might come at it from outside the ritual circle his pony trod. The fact of living, more even than the fact of a job or a duty or the personal need to prove himself fit to call himself man in this country's own terms, bound him to the cattle. The steam that hung above them was relative to the breath that plumed before his own face. It seemed to him a fact of tremendous significance that a cow never closed its eyes in sleep in all its life. These calves were on watch against the world from the time their mothers licked away the membrane from their wet faces until the axe fell between their eyes in Kansas City or Chicago. He felt that nothing living could afford *not* to be on guard, and that the warm blood of men and cattle was in league against the forces of cold and death. Like theirs, his mortality mooed and bellowed, keeping up its courage with its voice or complaining of its discomfort. He sang to the herd, or to himself, and sometimes played them tunes on the harmonica.

They had to be content with a limited repertoire—the mouth organ had been his study for no more than ten days, on the boat coming over—so that he found himself running through a few songs many times. Sometimes, for variety, he rendered, talking aloud to himself, the pony, and the cattle, like a fool or a hermit, certain poems, especially one he had memorized in his first enthusiasm for Canada—a ballad of *coureurs de bois* and of a stranger that walked beside them and left no footprints in the snow. When he had succeeded in scaring himself with ghosts and shadows he might fall back upon a jigging Canuck tune,

> *Rouli roulant, ma boule roulant,*
> *Rouli roulant ma boule.*

But everything he said or played or sang during his hours on the night herd was meant seriously, even soberly, even ritually, for he felt in every deceptive snow-shadow and every pulse of the Northern Lights and every movement of the night wind the presence of something ancient and terrible, to which the brief stir and warmth of life were totally alien, and which must be met head on.

On those miraculously beautiful and murderously cold nights glittering with the green and blue darts from a sky like polished dark metal, when the moon had gone down, leaving the hollow heavens to the stars and the overflowing cold light of the Aurora, he thought he had moments of the clearest vision and saw himself plain in a universe simple, callous, and magnificent. In every direction from their pallid soapbubble of shelter the snow spread; here and there the implacable plain glinted back a spark—the beam of a cold star reflected in a crystal of ice.

He was young and susceptible, but he was probably not far wrong in his feeling that there never was a lonelier land, and one in which men lived more uneasily on sufferance. And he thought he knew the answer to the challenge Saskatchewan tossed him: to be invincibly strong, indefinitely enduring, uncompromisingly self-reliant, to depend on no one, to contain within himself every strength and every skill. There were evenings when he sorted through the outfit, examining models, trying on for fit Ray Henry's iron, Slip's whalebone, Little Horn's leather. Though he had ambitions beyond any of them, he admitted that there was not a man in the outfit who could not teach him something, unless it was Spurlock. And Spurlock, he perceived, was the one on whom he might have to prove himself. The others would tease him, Little Horn and Jesse would pull his leg, Panguingue would thump him in brainless good humor, but Spurlock would push his nasty little nagging persecution until he might have to be smashed. It even occurred to Rusty once or twice that that was exactly what Spurlock wanted: a test of strength. Well, so be it. Riding narrow-eyed, he compared their physical equipment. Spurlock probably had some weight on him, and Rusty had a picture in his mind of big hands, thick wrists. On the other hand, Spurlock must be at least thirty-five, and it was said that for five years he had dealt in a Butte gambling joint, an occupation to soften and weaken a man. Let him come; he might not be half as tough as he sounded or acted; and in any case, let him come.

And then, with singing stopped, and talking stopped, and harmonica stopped, riding slowly, thinking of challenges and anticipating crises and bracing himself against whatever might come, he might have word from his night companions of the prairie, and hear the *yap-yap-yap* and the shivering howl of coyotes, or the faint dark monotone of the wolves. Far more than the cattle or their protectors, they were the proper possessors of the wilderness, and their yelling was a sound more appropriate there than human curses or growls or songs, or the wheezy chords of the mouth organ, and certainly than the half-scared screech of defiance he had let off that one night. The wolves' hunting noises were always far off, back north in the river bottoms. In the eerie clarity of the white nights they seemed to cry from inexpressible distances, faint and musical and clear, and he might have been tempted to think of them as something not earthly at all, as creatures immune to cold and hunger and pain, hunting only for the wolfish joy of running and perhaps not even visible to human eyes, if he had not one afternoon ridden through a coulee where they had bloodied half an acre with a calf.

By day the labor and the cold and the stiffness of many hours in the saddle, the bawling of calves, the crackle and crunch of hoofs and wheels, the reluctant herded movement of two or three hundred cows and calves and six dozen horses, all of whom stopped at every patch of grass blown bare and had to be whacked into moving again. By night the patient circling ride around the herd, the exposure to stars and space and the eloquent speech of the wolves, and finally the crowded sleep.

Nothing between them and the stars, nothing between them and the North Pole, nothing between them and the wolves, except a twelve-by-sixteen house of cloth so thin that every wind moved it and light showed through it and the shadows of men hulked angling along its slope, its roof so peppered with spark holes that lying in their beds they caught squinting glimpses of the stars. The silence gulped their little disturbances, their little tinklings and snorings and sighs and the muffled noises of discomfort and weariness. The earth and the sky gaped for them like opened jaws; they lay there like lozenges on a tongue, ready to be swallowed.

In spite of his dream of a test hoped-for, met, and passed, the tenderfoot pitied himself, rather. The pain of his arm as he lay on the frozen ground kept him turning sleeplessly. Some nights his fingers throbbed as if he had smashed them with a maul, and his feet ached all night with chilblains. To be compelled to bear these discomforts and these crippling but unvaliant pains he considered privately an outrage.

They told each other that it couldn't last—and yet they half prayed it would, because cold as it was, it was working weather: they could collect and move their herd in it. Nevertheless the boys spoke of change, and said that this early in November, weather like this shouldn't last more than a few days, and that the sundogs meant something for sure. Not at all fond of what they had, they feared what might replace it.

At the end of the eighth day, with a herd of nearly four hundred cows and calves and two dozen bulls, they camped within ten miles of Horse Camp Coulee. The streaked sky of sunset hazed out in dusk. Before Jesse had supper hot the wind was whistling in the tent ropes and leaning on the roof in strange erratic patches, as if animals were jumping on the canvas. In an hour more they were outside trying to keep the tent from blowing away, half a dozen of them hauling the wagon by hand around on the windward side and anchoring the tent to it. The darkness was full of snow pebbles hard and stinging as shot, whether falling or only drifting they couldn't tell, that beat their eyes shut and melted in their beards and froze again. While they were fighting with the tent, Slip came in from the cattle herd and talked with Ray. He did not go back; it would have been risking a man's life to try to keep him riding. They did not discuss what was likely to happen to the cattle, though even Rusty could guess; they crawled into their beds to keep warm, let the fire go out to save fuel, gave at least modified thanks for the fact that they would not have to ride night herd, and because they could do nothing else, they slept.

They slept most of the time for the next two days. When the wind eased off and they dug their way out, the wagon and the tent were surrounded by a horned dune of snow. Snow lay out across the plains in the gray, overcast afternoon, long rippled drifts like an ocean petrified in mid-swell, a dull, expressionless, unlit and unshadowed sea. There was not a sign of the herd; the only horses in sight were the four they had kept miserably tied to the wagon—Jesse's Clydes and two night saddle ponies.

Slip and Little Horn hunted up the horses, far downwind, before dark. They reported bunches of cattle scattered through all the coulees in that direction for a dozen miles. They also found that range steers had drifted in among them during the storm, which meant that all of that separation of whiteface and longhorn and steer and cow and calf had to be gone through again.

The prospect appalled Rusty Cullen; he waited for them to say it couldn't be done, that they would give it up and head for the ranch. It apparently never even occurred to Ray that they might quit. They simply chased and swore and floundered through the drifts, and wore out horses and changed to others, and worked till they couldn't see, and fell into their beds after dark with about a hundred head reassembled. Next day they swung around in a big half circle to the south and east and brought together about a hundred and fifty more.

Sweeping up a few strays as they went, they moved on the third day toward the corrals at Horse Camp Coulee and made half of the ten miles they had to cover. The hard part was about over. They spoke at supper of Molly Henry's dried apple pies, disparaging Jesse's beefsteak and beans. That night, sometime between midnight and dawn, the wind reached down out of the iron north and brought them a new blizzard.

Into a night unfamiliarly black, whirling with snow, a chaos of dark and cold and the howl of a wind that sometimes all but lifted them from their feet, they struggled out stiff and clumsy with sleep, voiceless with outrage, and again anchored themselves to that unspeakable plain. While they fought and groped with ropes in their hands, ducking from the lash of wind and snow, apparitions appeared right among them, stumbled over a guy rope and almost tore the tent down, snorted and bolted blindly into the smother: range horses drifting before the storm. The cowboys cursed them and repaired their damage and got themselves as secure as they could and crawled back into their blankets, knowing sullenly what the drifting horses meant. When they dug out of this one they would have lost their herd again.

Jesse had started the fire as soon as it seemed clear that the tent would not go down. When Rusty had got back into his bed next to Buck, with Panguingue's feet jammed for a headboard against his skull, he could see the glow through the draft door and feel his stung face loosening in the warmth. The canvas roof bucked and strained, slacked off, stiffened in a blast. The wind came through in needles of cold. It was close to morning; he could make out the faint shapes inside the tent. He waited for Ray to say something—something to console them, perhaps, for their failure and their bad luck—but no one spoke at all. They lay appraising the turmoil half seen and half heard on the straining roof. Finally, after several minutes, Jesse said, "Anybody feel like a cup of coffee?"

Only then did Ray speak. His hoarse, ironic whisper croaked across the tent, "Looks like you boys could have the day off. Sleep in, if you want."

"Sleep!" Ed Spurlock said. "How could anybody sleep when he thinks where them God damn cows are going?"

"Just the same you better sleep," Ray whispered. "You'll need your rest, boy."

"You going to try rounding them up again?"

Ray said, "We're in this business to raise calves, not fertilize some prairie with their carcasses."

"*Jesus!*" Spurlock said. He rocked his head back and forth on his rolled mackinaw, glaring at the tent roof with eyes that shone oilily in the glimmer from the firebox. The wind took hold of the tent and shook it, testing every rope; they waited till the blast let go again. "You can't drive cows in this kind of weather, Ray," Spurlock said.

"I know it," Ray whispered. "That's why you get the day off."

"I bet you we end up by leaving the whole herd to scatter."

"We do, we'll lose ever' damn calf," Ray said. His face turned and craned toward Spurlock, above and across from him. His indomitable croak said, "I don't aim to lose any, if work'll save 'em."

"No, I can see," Spurlock said. "You might lose a few of us though."

Ray laughed through his nose. "Why, Ed," he said, "you sound like you thought you was more valuable than a calf."

"I'd kind of like some coffee, myself," old Jesse said. "Don't anybody else feel thataway?"

"Shut up!" said Buck's voice from under the blankets. He had a capacity for always sounding furious, even when he was talking through four layers of wool. "Shut up and let a guy get some sleep."

Panguingue produced a few exaggerated snores.

There was a brief silence. The wind gripped the tent, fell away, pounced once more; they could hear it whining and ricocheting off the guy ropes. "Good God," Ed Spurlock said restlessly, "listen to the God damn wind blow."

"I think I'll just put the pot on anyhow, long as we got that fire," Jesse's soft voice said. Rusty heard the stiff creak of his bedroll tarp and the fumbling sounds as he got on his boots. There was a grunt, and Spurlock said savagely, "God damn it to hell, Jesse, watch out where you put your feet!"

"Don't leave your face hanging out, then," Jesse said. "How can I see your face in this dark? I been huntin' for ten minutes with both hands, and I just now found my ass."

"Step on me once more and you'll find it in a sling," Spurlock said. "Why can't you stay in bed? There's nothing to get up for."

"Yes there is," Jesse said. "Coffee."

His shape reared up against the graying canvas; when he opened the lid the glow from the stove illuminated his intent face with the white bristles on cheeks and chin, and the mustache drooping in a smooth oxbow. This, Rusty thought, was all familiar to Jesse. He must have done this same thing, camped in the same brutal kind of weather, a hundred times, with Indians, with *métis hivernants*, with hide hunters, with wagon trains hauling supplies into the Montana camps, with cattle outfits like this one. His relation to the country was almost as simple as that of the wolves; no matter how fast the province changed, it remained to Jesse merely a few known forms of hardship, a known violence of weather, one or two simple but irreplaceable skills. He had the air, standing ruminatively above his stove, of a man who could conceive of no evil that a cup of hot coffee or a beefsteak fried in flour would not cure.

Daylight came as dusk and stayed that way. They dozed, and when the fire was up high for cooking they took advantage of the warmth to play poker or blackjack. When anyone had to go outside he took a look at the horses, which they had picketed to give them a little more chance to move around and keep warm, but which crowded close up against the wagon for the little shelter it gave them. Morning and evening someone hung on their noses a nosebag of their limited oat supply.

Their wood was running low too; they had been depending on getting fuel from the willows in Horse Camp Coulee. After meals they had to let the fire die, and then if they played cards they passed around a lighted candle to warm their hands by. When even that got too cold they dug down under their blankets to sleep or think. Talk flared up like matches and went out again; they cocked their ears to the howl of the wind, remoter as the tent snowed in. Once or twice one of them went out and carefully cleared the worst of the snow off the roof while the rest, inside, watched with concern the sausage-tight canvas which a careless shovel might easily slit, leaving them exposed to the storm like an out-turned nest of mice. Every hour or so Ray Henry, taciturn and expressionless, took a look outside.

When he had got his hands well warmed under the blankets, Rusty played the harmonica. There were more requests than he could gratify, with a heavy favoritism for old Red River tunes which they tried to teach him by whistling or humming. If he quit, with his hands too numb to feel the fingers and his chapped lips sore from the sliding of the little honeycomb back and forth across them, they urged him for a while, and then cursed him languidly and gave up. The afternoon waned; they yawned; they lay resting.

Once the notebook in his shirt pocket crunched as Rusty turned over, and he took it out and amused himself for a while reading the journal entries he had made. There was nothing since his catalog of information about the Stonepile Camp, but before that there was a very windy and prize-essay series of notations. He had put them down in the first place as colorful items to be incorporated into letters home: they expected him not to write very often, and he would oblige them; but they expected him, when he did write, to fill pages with cowboys and Indians and wild game and the adventures and observations of a well-educated young gentleman in the North American wilderness. In this too he had set out to oblige them. He read what he had had to say about the ranch, and the thumbnail sketches he had made of some of the cowboys, and the lyrical flights he had gone into during the days of perfect Indian Summer haymaking weather that preceded the first storm—only the night before they had set out on this belated roundup. He could imagine the family all around his mother as she read, and he cocked an inner ear to the sound of his own prose describing the apelike Panguingue with his good nature and his total disregard for cleanliness, and wry little birdy Slippers with his sore feet, as if he had walked all the way from Texas; even on roundup he wore no boots like the rest of them but elastic-sided slippers under his overshoes. Rusty told them Slip was the best bronc rider in Saskatchewan, which may have been going it a bit strong, and about how Buck kept a row of tobacco tins on the two-by-four above his bunk, with all his smaller private effects filed away in them in neat and labeled order. He described, with the proper tone of sober appraisal and respect, Ray Henry and his new wife, whom he had brought from Malta, Montana, in a buckboard, a hundred and twenty miles across country, for a wedding trip. Rusty had loaded that part of the journal with data on the country, much of it, as he saw now, in error. It was the sort of stuff which, written as a letter, would surely set his younger brother to itching, and produce another emigration from the family, but it seemed false and shrilly enthusiastic and very, very young when he read it over in the tent, while a frozen guy rope outside, within three feet of his ear, hummed like a great struck cable.

"What you got there, Rusty?" Little Horn said. "Something to read?"

"No," he said. "Oh no, just an old notebook."

"Notebook?" Spurlock said.

"Just . . . notes, don't you know," Rusty said. He was frantic with the notion that they would sit on him and take it away from him and read in it what he had said about them. If they tried it he would die fighting. He put it in his shirt pocket and buttoned it down. "Things I wanted to remember to put in letters home," he said.

"All about the cow country and the cattle business, uh?" Little Horn said.

"More or less."

"She's a real good business," Little Horn said. "You ought to think about her, Rusty." Staring at the roof, his red nose one of a half dozen projecting toward the lashed and laboring canvas, he plucked a thread from the frayed edge of his blanket and drew it dreamily between his front teeth. "Young fella from the old country could do a lot worse," he said. "There's this Englishman over on Medicine Lodge Coulee, kind of a remittance-man colony they got over there, he was tellin' me about cattle ranchin' one time. He said there was millions in it. All you do, you just get some cows and a few bulls, and you turn 'em out on the range. Say you start with a hundred cows. You get a hundred calves the first year, and fifty of them are cows and fifty you make into steers. Next year you got a hundred and fifty cows and they give you a hundred and fifty calves, and you make seventy-five steers and keep the seventy-five cows, and that builds your breeding herd to two hundred and twenty-five. That year you get two hundred and twenty-five calves, and by now you're sellin' your two-year-old and three-year-old steers, and your herd keeps growin' and you keep sellin' the bull calves, and that's all they is to her. He had it all mapped out. You ought to talk to him, Rusty."

"I'll look into it the first chance I get," Rusty said. "I've been inquiring around for a good opportunity."

"You do that," Little Horn said. "If I didn't have me this job here with Ray, I'd do somethin' about it myself. There ain't a thing to her. Once you get your herd and start them cows to calfin', all you do is set back and count the dollars rollin' in.

"They'll tell you: mange. Hell, they ain't nothin' to mange. All you got to do about that, you dip 'em twice a year. You get yourself one of them steam boilers and a tank, and you lay in some sulphur and so on. And you dig yourself a big hole in the ground, maybe a hundred feet long, say, and thirty wide, and at one end you build a couple corrals, one big one to hold maybe a couple hundred head and the other a little one to take a dozen or so. From this little one you build a chute that leads down into the hole. At the other end of the hole you make a slatted slope out of planks for the cows to climb out on, and a couple drippin' pens where the ones that has been dipped can stand, and under those pens you dig a ditch so the dip that runs off them can run back into the vat. It ain't anything, hardly. If you got ten or fifteen hands around it'll only take you a couple-three weeks' hard work altogether to build this rig.

"Then you bring your stock into the big corral, see, and feed 'em out a few at a time into the little corral and on into the chute, and on both sides of the vat you put guys with long poles with a yoke onto them, and they get the yoke over these cattle as they come down the chute and duck 'em clear under. Then you prod 'em on through the vat and up the slope and into the drippin' pens and you're done with that bunch.

"They'll tell you it's lots of work. Shucks. You got, say, ten thousand head to dip, like we would on the T-Down, and you got maybe twelve men in the outfit. You can do a dozen ever' twenty minutes, thirty-six an hour, three hundred and sixty in a ten-hour day, thirty-six hundred in ten days. You can get the whole herd through in three or four weeks, if you can get the inspector there when you want him. They'll tell you it's hell to catch the inspector, and hard to keep the herd together that long, and hard to keep the sulphur mixture strong enough and the right temperature, and a lot like that, but it ain't nothing to bother a man. Some people would talk down anything.

"Or they'll tell you it's dangerous. Shoot! Suppose one of them steers does get on the peck when he's pushed under and gets his eyes full of sulphur, what can he do? He can thrash around in the vat, maybe, and drowned himself or some other steer, or maybe he climbs out and chases you up onto the barn, or he scrambles back into the corral and gets them to millin' there till they break something down, but that ain't only a little delay. Even if some old ringy longhorn catches you before you can climb out of the corral, what can he do to you? His horns is so wide he just rams you against the fence with his forehead and holds you there till somebody twists his tail or spits Bull Durham in his eye and pulls him off, and there you are good as ever, maybe bruised up some is all.

"No, sir," Little Horn said, pulling his thread back and forth, "it's a mistake to listen to these calamity howlers about what a tough business the cow business is. Mange, that's only a sample of how they exaggerate. They'll tell you: wolves. Wolves! They won't pick off more'n one calf in ten or twenty all winter long. Sure three or four of them will pull down a cow sometimes, get her by the hind leg and a flank and pull her over and pile on, but mostly it's just calves. Say you start with two thousand head in the fall, you still got eighteen hundred in the spring. And if you want to, you can hire somebody like this Schulz to wolf your range."

"Schulz!" Buck said from down under. "I wonder if he's et his boy yet?"

"Only cost you ten dollars a scalp," Little Horn said. "If he puts out poison baits, course you might lose a few dogs. Sure a wolf is hard to poison and he's too smart to step in a trap or come within gunshot very often, but that don't have to bother you. There's other ways of handlin' wolves. You just lay around and keep an eye open and when you catch one out on the flats you can run him down on a horse. I did it once myself. I had me a little old pony that could run, and I come right up on that old white wolf and run over him. I missed him that first time, somehow, and had to come over him again, and I missed him again, but I kep' tryin'. This wolf can't get away—he's down there under the pony's feet somewhere duckin' and snarlin'. I'd of had him sure if the pony hadn't of stepped in a hole. The wolf run off then and I couldn't chase him. I was out quite a few miles, and after I shot the horse I had me quite a walk carryin' the saddle, but that experience taught me quite a bit about runnin' down wolves, and I know how it's done. I'll show you sometime, if you want."

"Oh, I say, thanks," Rusty said.

"Old Rusty, I bet he figures just like your other Englishman," Spurlock said. "Ain't it the fact, Rusty? You come out here thinking you'd get yourself a few thousand acres and a herd of cows and be a lord of the manor like Dan Tenaille, uh?"

"That's right," Rusty said. "Just now, I'm out here learning the business firsthand from the experts."

"Or did you *have* to come out?" Spurlock said. "You're a remittance man too, ain't you? Tell us the story of how you happened to leave England. I bet it'd be interesting. Help pass the time, don't you know."

"I'm afraid you'd find it a bit dull."

"A bit dull?" Spurlock said heartily. "Not at all, lad, not at all. Come on, give us your reasons for trailing out to the cow country."

They were not a talking bunch, and so far as he knew they had not discussed him. He was too common a phenomenon. Unless he took pains to prove himself otherwise, any young Englishman in that country was assumed to be the second son, third son, scapegrace son, of a baronet, a KCB, a shooting partner of Edward VII. Or he was a cashiered guardsman or disgraced country vicar. Rusty was none of those, but it seemed unnecessary to insist. He said only, "I'm afraid my reasons wouldn't be as colorful as yours."

He put into his voice just the quantity of sneer that would make Spurlock rise up without realizing precisely where he was stung. Or perhaps the sneer did not do it at all, perhaps Spurlock was only bored, uncomfortable, irritable, ready to pluck any little thread that would ravel, quarrelsome out of no motive except tedium. If that was it, fine; let him come. And there he came, rearing up on one elbow and throwing across the tent a literary badman look as if he thought he was wearing black gloves and black guns like a villain in *The Virginian.* "What do you mean by that, exactly?"

From the side, Ray Henry's whisper said, "The kid's not crowding you any, Ed."

"I can tell when I'm crowded," Spurlock said.

"Pull in your elbows," Ray whispered, amused. "Then you'll have more room."

Spurlock lay down again. "Little English punks," he said. "Coming out pretending to be cowhands."

Rusty looked at Ray, but Ray only smiled. The boy said, fairly hotly, "The cows can't tell the difference."

"No," Spurlock said, "no, but a man sure can."

"I haven't heard any *men* discussing it."

Once more he reared up on his elbow. "Is its little arm sore?" he said. "Got piled, did it?"

"How are its little sore eyes?" Rusty said. Out of nothing, out of nowhere, as random and unprepared for as an August whirlwind kicking up a dust, Spurlock had produced the quarrel he evidently wanted. Rusty was angry enough to take him on, arm or no arm. He pretended to himself that he was annoyed with Ray when the foreman whispered equably, "In about a second I'm kickin' both you quarrelsome bastards out in the snow."

Rusty lay ready, smoldering, waiting for Spurlock to say something else that could not be borne, or to rise and stalk outside where it would be necessary to go out and fight him. But Spurlock did not move or speak; he only breathed through his nose in so eloquent and contemptuous a way that Rusty had to hold himself back from springing over and smashing him. The wind slammed against their canvas roof in a furious gust. Against some rope or edge or corner it howled like a wolf, and then trailed off to the steady whisper and rush again.

"They'll tell you," Little Horn said dreamily, "they'll say to you it's terrible hard work. Why, God damn, now, you just can't pay attention to that. How long we been on this-here roundup? Since first of May, more or less? And it's only November now. And they'll tell you it gets cold, but where would you find a nicer, more comfortable little tent than this one, if we only had some wood?"

Jesse crawled out and stood stretching in the narrow space among the mussed beds. Rusty noticed that he was careful to stay clear of Ed Spurlock's blankets. "Well," he said, "time for a little grub?"

Ray went past Jesse and pulled the flap aside and looked out. Beyond him the horizontal blast streaked with snow dipped and swirled; flakes settled and whirled away again; there was a curved drift building up at the tent corner. Ray's back looked bulky and solid; he was a powerful man, single-minded and devoted. A little hollow in the solar plexus from the nearness of a fight, Rusty had a wry feeling that if Spurlock and he had started something, and the foreman wanted to interfere, he could have thrashed them both. But what his hunched back and his bent head reminded Rusty of really was the burden he bore. He was foreman, he wore responsibility for both men and cattle, and he had left his bride of less than a month at the ranch house with only a crippled handy man for company. Rusty did not envy Ray, but he respected him a great deal. He wanted to do well for him; he was ashamed of having had to be reprimanded along with Spurlock. The foreman dropped the flap and came back and sat down.

"They'll tell you," Little Horn said, endless and ironic and contemplative, "they'll say, all that ridin' and brandin' and weanin' and nuttin' and chasin' cows up and down the hills and dales. How else would you want a cowpuncher to spend his time? He don't have any work to do, he just gets himself into trouble playin' cyards and fightin' and chasin' women. Lots better for him to be out in a nice tent like this, camped out comfortable in some blizzard."

Sometime before the gray afternoon howled itself out, Ray Henry shouldered into his sheepskin and went outside. The rest lay in their blankets, which they had inhabited too long for their blankets' good or their own, in their postures that were like the postures of men fallen in war. Panguingue sprawled with his drawn-up knees wide, his whiskered face glimmering a vacant grin straight upward. Little Horn and Buck were unexpected angles of arms and legs, Slip lay curled as if around a mortal body wound. Spurlock had locked his hands under the back of his head and crossed his knees under the covers. They listened to the undiminished wind. After what may have been ten minutes Jesse rose and said he guessed he'd take a look at the Clydes. He followed his jet of white breath outside, and they lay on.

Their cloth house shook, and gave way, and shuddered stiff and tight again. They heard the whistle and scream go flying through and away, and in a lull Buck said, "This one's the worst one yet." They lay considering this for quite a long time. At last Rusty heard the sound of feet, and with a relief that astonished him he cried, "Here they are!"

But no one entered. The wind pounded through and over and past. It had a curving sound; it dipped to the ear like telegraph wires to the eye. Everyone in the tent was listening for the steps Rusty had announced. At last Spurlock grumbled, "Just fawncy." Panguingue blurted a laugh.

"Christ A'mighty!" Slip said abruptly, and snapped nimble as a monkey out of his bed. He was stepping in his slippers across Ray Henry's tarp when the flap opened and Ray and Jesse stooped in on a flurry of snow. Slippers sat quietly down again on his blankets. His leathery, deeply lined, big-nosed face said nothing. Neither did any of the other smudged and whiskered faces around the tent. But they were all sitting up or half propped on their elbows; the concern that had moved Slip had been a fear in all of them. In silence they watched Ray throw down beside the cold stove three or four round cake-like chunks of ice. Rusty reached across and picked up a frozen cowchip.

"Are we burning ice now?"

With a wipe of a bare hand around on his wet, beef-red face, the foreman said, "We may be lucky to have that to burn, it's drifting pretty deep all over."

"Still from the northwest?" Buck asked.

"Oh dear," said Little Horn. "All those poor little calves and their mamas. They'll be clear the hell and gone down to Wood Mountain."

"Or else they'll be piled up in some draw," Ray said.

"You think it's pretty bad, then," Rusty said—a small, inconsequent, intrusive voice of ignorance and greenness that he himself heard with shame and dismay.

"Yes, kid," Ray said. "I think it's pretty bad."

They ebbed away into silence. With only a few sticks of wood left Jesse gave them no more for supper than warm gravy poured over frozen biscuits; not even coffee. Part of the stove, while the gravy was warming, held two of the cowchips that Ray had kicked up from under the snow, and the smell of wetted and baking manure flavored their supper. But at least the cakes dried out enough so that Jesse could use them for the breakfast fire.

The single candle gave a blotted light. When they were all still Rusty saw the humps of bedrolls fuming like a geyser basin with their eight breaths, until Little Horn said, "Well, nighty-night, kids," and blew out the candle. The wind seemed to come down on their sudden darkness with such violence that in the cold tent they lay tensely, afraid something would give. Both Slip and Little Horn had pulled their goatskin chaps over their beds for extra cover. Rusty's icy hands were folded into his armpits; he wore all his clothes except sheepskin and boots. He blew his breath into the air, moved his sore shoulder experimentally, smelled his own stale nest, thinking Holy Mother, if my people could see me now! There was a brief, vivid picture of rescuers in the spring reverently uncovering eight huddled figures, identifying each one, folding the tarp back over the frozen face. His head was full of vague heroisms related to Commodore Peary and the North Pole.

Once the thought popped whole and astonishing into his head: I might, except for one or two decisions made in excitement and stuck to through tears and argument, be sleeping in my old room right now, and if I opened my eyes I would see the model of the *Kraken* hanging from the ceiling like a ship of thanksgiving in a Danish church. Except for the excitement that his father thought wild whimsy and his mother thought heartlessness, he might be getting his exercise these days pushing a punt up and down the Cher, disturbing the swans (Swans! From here they sounded fabulous as gryphons), or drinking too much port with sporty undergraduates from his college, or sitting on some cricket pitch, or (assuming he *hadn't* chosen Oxford and the family's program) he might be guiding the tiller of the yawl with his backside while he shouted questions, jeers, comments, or other conversation at sailors leaning over the stern rails of old rustpots anchored in the stream off Spithead.

The fact that he was here in a tent on the freezing Saskatchewan plains, that one decision rashly made and stubbornly stuck to had taken him not only out of the university, out of home, out of England, but out of a whole life and culture that had been assumed for him, left him dazed. A good job he didn't have much chance to think, or he might funk it yet, and run straight home with his tail tucked. He was appalled at the effectiveness of his own will.

A numbness like freezing to death stole through him gradually, Panguingue restored him to wakefulness with a kick in the head, and he cursed Panguingue with a freedom he would not have adopted toward anyone else in the outfit. Sometime during or just after the flurry of profane protest he fell asleep.

Solitary flutes, songs from the Vienna woods, chirpings and twitterings so that he opened his eyes thinking *Birds?* and heard the awakening sounds of the outfit, and old Jesse whistling with loose lips while he stood over the stove. He lifted a can and tipped it in a quick gesture; the tent filled with the smell of kerosene. Jesse hobbled about in his boots like an old crone. His right knee crooked upward, there was a swoop and a snap, and a match popped into flame across his tight seat. The stove *whoofed* out a puff of smoke. The lids clanged on. Fire gleamed through the cracks in the ash door and Jesse shoved the coffee pot against the stovepipe. Looking, Rusty saw that Ray, Slip, and Buck were missing.

He sat up. "I say! The wind's died!"

"You say, hey?" Jesse said.

Rusty hustled to the door and looked out. Deep tracks went through the drift that curved all around them; the sky was palest blue, absolutely clear. Ray was trotting the Clydes up and down a fifty-foot trampled space, getting them warm. Their breasts and rumps and legs were completely coated in ice. Buck and Slip already had saddles on the night ponies. Whatever had been brown in the landscape had disappeared. There were no scraggly patches of bare grass in the snow waves, but packed, rippled white ran off into the southeast where the sun was just rising. He could almost see the plain move as if a current ran strongly toward where the sun squatted on the rim and sent its dazzle skipping across the million little wave crests into his eyes. Spurlock, looking over his shoulder, swore foully. "Here goes for some more God damn snowblindness." He stepped past Rusty and blew his nose with his fingers, first one nostril, then the other. Rusty shouted over to Ray, "Working weather!"

"Yeah." He laughed his dry laugh through his nose. "Come here and curry some of the ice out of these studs."

"Uh-huh!" Spurlock said behind Rusty, with I-told-you-so emphasis. The boy stared at him. "Working weather!" Spurlock said. "Jesus Christ! I guess."

His guess was right. Within minutes of the time Rusty woke he was working; they paused only long enough to bolt a steak and gulp scalding coffee and warm their hands over the fire; their last wood and all the cowchips had gone into it. Before they had more than spread their palms to the beautiful heat, Slip and Buck came in with the horse herd.

"Jesse," Ray said, "you better tear down here and get loaded and beat it on a beeline for Horse Camp. If we ain't there when you get there, which we won't be, you can improve your time and warm your blood gettin' in wood, and there ain't any such thing as too much. The rest of you is goin' to round up every cow within fifteen miles downwind, and we're going to put them all in the corrals at Horse Camp before we sleep any more. So pick you a pony with some bottom."

They looked at the shaggy, scrawny, long-maned and long-tailed herd picking at the wisps of a few forkfuls of hay that the boys had thrown out. There was not a pony among them whose ribs did not show plainly under the rough winter hair. Here and there one stood spraddled, head hanging, done in, ready to fall.

"Boneracks," Little Horn said. "Some of them ponies ain't goin' to make it, Boss."

"Then we got to leave them," Ray said. "They can maybe make out, poor as they are, but unless we get a chinook this is starvin' time for cattle."

They saddled and rode out, Ray, Slip, Panguingue, and Rusty to the southeast, straight into the sun, Spurlock and Buck and Little Horn to the northeast. They would pinch everything in to the middle and then swing and bring them back. The tent was already coming down as they rode off.

They rode a long way before they raised any cattle. When they did, down in a draw, they were humped in the deep snow, making no effort to get out. They stood and bellowed; they moved as if their blood had frozen thick, and they had among them range steers, including a few longhorns, which the boys did not want at all but had no time to cut out. They threw them all into a bunch, and attended by an intensely black and unlikely looking crow, rode on into the diamond glitter, gradually swinging eastward so that they could get some relief by ducking their heads and pulling their hats clear down on the sun side. Ray kept them pushing hard through the difficult going, knee high sometimes, hock high the next moment, crusted just enough to hold the horse's weight for a split second before he broke down through. It was hard enough in the saddle; it must have been a good deal worse under it.

"Got to hustle," Ray said. "For some reason I'm gettin' so I don't trust the damn weather." They fanned out, riding wide. Far north, across a spread of flats and one or two shallow coulees whose depressions could hardly be seen in the even glare, the black dots that were Spurlock and Little Horn and Buck were strung out across a mile or so of snow. They headed in toward the center of their loop every sad whiteface whose red hide showed. The cattle bellowed, blinking white eyelashes, and they moved reluctantly, but they moved. The crow flapped over, following companionably, flying off on some investigation of his own and returning after a few minutes to coast over and cock his wise eye down and caw with laughter to hear them talk.

About noon, far to the south and east of where they had camped, they came to the river, angling down from the northwest in its shallow valley. The willows along the banks looked thin as a Chinaman's whiskers, hardly more than weeds, but they held a surprising number of cattle, which the outfit flushed out by the dozens and scores and hazed, plunging and ducking and blindly swinging back until a horse blocked them or a rope cut across their noses, up onto the flats. They had everything in that herd: whiteface, shorthorn, longhorn, all sorts of crosses; steers, cows, bulls, calves; T-Down, Circle Diamond, Turkey Track. Ray pointed some out to Rusty when they rested their ponies for a minute on the flat and let Slip chase a half-dozen whiteface yearlings back into the bottoms. "The Seventy-Six," he said. "Their range is way up by Gull Lake, on the CPR. They've drifted twenty-five miles."

Whatever they were, whoever they belonged to, if they could not be easily cut out the riders swept them in and drove them westward, pushing them without a pause toward Horse Camp. The afternoon changed from blue-white to lavender. The crow had left them—disgusted, Rusty thought, that they never stopped to eat and threw away no scraps. The trampled waste of snow bloomed for a minute or two a pure untroubled rose, and the sun was gone as if it had stepped in a hole. Gray-blue dusk, grateful to their seared eyes, lay in every slightest hollow; the snowplain was broken with unexpected irregularities. The "drag" of cows and calves slowed, poked along, stopped and had to be cursed and flogged into starting. Their ponies, poor boneracks, plodded gamely, and if a cow tried to break away or swing back they had to gather themselves like a tired swimmer taking one last stroke. Their breath was frozen all over them, stirrups and overshoes were enameled in ice; Rusty could hear his pony wheezing in his pipes, and his skinny ewe neck was down. He stumbled in the trodden snow.

It grew dark, and they went on, following Jesse's track, or whatever track it was that Ray kept, or no track at all, but only his wild-animal's sense of direction. The faint eruption of color in the west was gone; and then as the sky darkened, the stars were there, big and frosty and glittering, bright as lamps, and Rusty found the Dipper and Cassiopeia and the Pole Star, his total astronomy. He moved in his saddle, lame and numb, his face stiff, his shoulder aching clear down across his collarbone into his chest. Ahead of him, a moving blur on the snow, the herd stumbled and clicked and mooed, the joints of their random longhorns cracked, the traveling steam went up. Off to his right he heard Buck trying to sing—a sound so strange, revelatory, and forlorn that he had to laugh, and startled himself with the voiceless croak he produced.

How much farther? Up above, the sky was pure; the Northern Lights were beginning to flare and stretch. He heard his old friend the wolf hunting down the river valleys and coulees of his ordained home and speaking his wolfish mind to the indifferent stars. Lord God, how much longer? They had been in the saddle since six, had eaten nothing since then. Neither horse nor rider could take much more of this. But nobody said, We can stop now. Nobody said, We'll camp here. They couldn't, obviously. Jesse had taken their bubble of shelter God knew how many more empty miles to Horse Camp. He thought to himself, with a qualm of panic, My God, this is *desperate*. What if we don't find him? What if a horse should give clear out?

He gave his pony clumsy mittened pats; he enlisted its loyalty with words; it plodded and stumbled on.

Eventually there was a soft orange bloom of light, and shouts cut through the luminous murk, and as he stopped, confused, Ray Henry came riding from his left and they crowded the cattle into a tighter mass.

Over their moving backs and the sounds of their distress and irritation he heard poles rattle; someone ki-yi-ed. Ray pushed his horse against the rear cattle and in his almost-gone whisper drove and urged them on. They moved, they broke aside, they were turned back; the mass crawled ahead, tedious, interminable, a toss and seethe of heads and horns, until suddenly it had shrunk and dwindled and was gone, and Panguingue was down in the snow, ramming gate poles home. The whole world smelled of cow.

They sat there all together, stupid with cold and fatigue; they dismounted like skeletons tied together with wire. Ray croaked, "Let's see if Jesse ain't got a spare oat or two for these ponies," and they walked toward the wagon and the bloom of the tent. The air, which had been bright at sunset and in the first hour of dark, was blurred as if a fog were rising from the snow; beyond the tent the faint shadow of the coulee fell away, but the other side was misted out. Rusty's eyes were so longingly on Jesse's shadow as he hopped around the stove, obviously cooking, that he fell over the pile of willows stacked by the wagon: Jesse had not wasted his time; there was cooking wood for a week.

"Dad," Ray called, "you got any oats? These ponies are about done." The white head appeared in the flap, a hand with a fork in it held the canvas back, the soft old voice said, "I got a couple-three bushel left, I guess. That has to hold the Clydes and the night horses till we get back to the ranch."

"They'll have to get along," Ray said. "I'm afraid we're going to lose some ponies anyway. They just don't have the flesh for this kind of a job."

Rusty stood with the reins in his hand, letting Jesse and Ray heave the oat bag out of the wagon. The tent with its bloom of light and its smell of frying was a paradise he yearned for as he had never yearned for anything, but he had to stand there and care for the horse first, and he hated the poor beast for its dependence. It was no tireder than he was. Nevertheless Ray's was an inescapable example. He unsaddled and threw the saddle into the wagon; he tramped a little hollow in the snow and poured out a quart or two of oats and pulled his pony's bridle and let him drop his head to them. One after the other the outfit did the same. After what seemed an hour Rusty found the tent flap and crept in. The little stove was red hot; the air was full of smoke. Jesse had unrolled their beds for them. Rusty stepped over Buck and fell full length and shut his eyes. What little strength he had left flowed out of him and was soaked up; his bones and veins and skin held nothing but tiredness and pain.

Jesse hopped around, juggling pans, going on cheerfully. He had thought by God they were never going to get in. Chopped wood till he like to bust his back. (Yeah, said somebody, *you* did a day's work!) Horse herd come all the way with him, right along behind the pilot. Those few scraps of hay the other day made tame ponies of the whole bunch. Looks like you guys got a pretty good herd of calves, considering. Anybody like a cup of coffee now?

"By God," he said after a short silence, "you fellers look *beat*."

And after another little silence in which nobody spoke, but somebody groaned or grunted, Jesse said, "Here, I don't reckon coffee has got enough nourishment for the occasion."

Beside Rusty, Buck rolled over. Rusty opened his eyes. Slip and Little Horn had rolled over too. Ray was sitting on his bed, holding a quart of whiskey, shaking his head. "Jesse," he said, "by God, remind me to raise your wages."

Their common emotion while Ray worked on the cork was reverence. They sat or lay around in a ring, as bleary a crew as ever ate with its fingers or blew its nose with the same all-purpose tool, and they watched each motion of his thick wrist and big dirty hand. None of them had shaved for more than two weeks; they had all, except possibly Buck, lost any right to browbeat Panguingue about his filthiness. They felt—or at least Rusty did—that they had endured much and labored incredibly. He wondered, as the greenest hand there, how well he had done, and hoped he had done at least passably, and knew with unaccustomed humility that he could not have done more. Considering everything, the three hundred–odd cattle they had finally brought to the Horse Camp corrals were an achievement. The work still to be done, the separating and weaning, and the driving of calves and bulls to the home ranch, could only be trifling after what they had been through.

The stove's heat beat on their bearded red faces, the candles gleamed in their bloodshot eyes. They watched Ray Henry's thick hands, and when the cork slipped out of the neck with a soft *pok* some of them smiled involuntarily, and Panguingue giggled, a high, falsetto sound that set off another round of smiles and made Jesse say, "Listen at old Pan, he sounds like a jack after a mare."

Ray held the bottle to the light and looked through it; he shook it and watched the bead rise. He was like a priest before an altar. He would not hurry this. "Well," he said at last, "here's looking at you, boys," and tipped the bottle to his blackened mouth. They watched the contents gurgle around the spark of candle that lived inside the amber bottle. He let the bottle down. "Whah!" he said. "Kee-rist!" and wiped the neck politely with the heel of his palm and passed it to Slip, whose bed lay beside his next to the wall. The smell of whiskey cut through the smoke of the tent; they sat like Indians in the medicine lodge and passed the cere-monial vessel around, and each, as he finished, wiped the neck carefully with his palm. Slip to Jesse, Jesse to Little Horn, Little Horn to Spurlock, Spurlock to Panguingue. Panguingue drank and shook his head and wiped the neck once and started to pass the bottle and then, as if not sat-isfied, wiped it again. Rusty loved him for it, he loved them all; he felt that he had never known so mannerly a group of men. Buck took the bottle from Panguingue, and from Buck it came to the greenhorn, its neck flavored with all their seven mouths and hands. He raised it to his mouth and let its fire wash down his throat and felt it sting in his cracked lips. His eyes watered. He lowered the bottle and choked down a cough, and as he passed the bottle back to Ray and talk broke out all at once, he took advantage of the noise and cleared his throat and so was not shamed.

"Well, Jesse," Ray said, "what do you think? Want to save that little-bitty dab?"

"Why, I can't see it'd be much good from now on," Jesse said.

They passed it around again, and their tongues were loosened. They told each other how cold it had been and how hard they had worked. Jesse had made up a raisin-and-rice pudding, practically a pailful. It was pure ambrosia; they ate it all and scraped the kettle, and for a few min-utes after supper Rusty even roused up enough strength to get out the harmonica. There was not the slightest remnant left of the irritability they had felt with one another in the snowed-in time; the boy could feel how they had been welded and riveted into a society of friends and brothers. Little Horn sang some filthy verses of "The Old Chisholm Trail." Spurlock supplied some even filthier ones from "Johnny McGraw." The whole bunch joined in a couple of songs.

Then all at once they were done in again. The talk dropped away, Rusty put the harmonica in his pocket. They went outside and walked a few steps from the tent and stood in a row and made water, lifting their faces into the night air that was mistier than ever, and warmer than any night since they had left the ranch.

"I don't know," Ray said, sniffing for wind. "I don't quite like the looks of the sky."

"Oh but hell," they said. "Feel how warm it is."

He gave in doubtfully to their optimism. The mild air might mean snow, but it also might mean a chinook coming in, and that was the best luck they could hope for. There was not enough grass bare, even out on the flats, to give the cattle a chance to feed. Rusty had never seen or felt a chinook, but he was so positive this was the birth of one that he offered to bet Little Horn and Panguingue a dollar each that it was a chinook coming. They refused, saying they did not want to hoodoo the weather. Ray remarked that such weather as they had had couldn't be hoodooed any worse. They kicked the snow around, smelling the night air soft in their faces; it smelled like a thaw, though the snow underfoot was still as dry and granular as salt. Every minute or so a hungry calf bawled over in the corral.

"Well," Ray said, "maybe this is our break."

Rusty hardly heard him. His eyes were knotted, the nerves and veins snarled together, the lids heavy with sleep. Back inside the tent there was a brief flurry of movement as they crawled in. Somebody cursed somebody else feebly for throwing his chaps across him. He heard the fire settle in the stove; after a minute or two he was not sure whether it was the stove or the first whiffling of some sleeper. Then he was asleep too, one of the first.

But not even his dead tiredness could lift from him the habits of the last ten days. In his dreams he struggled against winds, he felt the bite of cold, he heard the clamor of men and animals and he knew that he had a duty to perform, he had somehow to shout "Here!" as one did at a roll call, but he was far down under something, struggling in the dark to come up and to break his voice free. His own nightmared sounds told him he was dreaming, and moaning in his sleep, and still he could not break free into wakefulness and shove the dream aside. Things were falling on him from above; he sheltered his head with his arms, rolled, and with a wrench broke loose from tormented sleep and sat up.

Panguingue was kicking him in the head through his blankets. He was freezing cold, with all his blankets wound around his neck and shoulders like shawls. By the light of a candle stuck on the cold stove lid he saw the rest all in the same state of confused, unbelieving awakening. There was a wild sound of wind; while he sat leaning away from Panguingue's feet, stupidly groping for his wits, a screeching blast hit the tent so hard that old Jesse, standing by the flap, grabbed the pole and held it until the shuddering strain gave way a little and the screech died to a howl.

Rusty saw the look of disbelief and outrage on every face; Panguingue's grin was a wolfish baring of teeth, his ordinary dull-witted good nature shocked clear out of him. "What is it?" Rusty asked idiotically. "Is it a chinook?"

"Chinook!" Buck said furiously.

He yanked his stiff chaps on over his pants and groped chattering for his boots. They were all dressing as fast as their dazed minds and numbed fingers would let them. Jesse let go the tent pole to break some willow twigs in his hands and shove them into the stove. At that moment the wind swooped on them again and the tent came down.

Half dressed, minus mittens, boots, mackinaws, hats, they struggled under the obliterating canvas. Somebody was swearing in an uninterrupted stream. Rusty stumbled over the fallen stovepipe and his nostrils were filled with soot. Then the smothering canvas lifted a couple of feet and somebody struck a match to expose them like bugs under a kicked log, dismayed and scuttling, glaring around for whatever article they needed. He saw Jesse and Ray bracing the front pole, and as the match died he jumped to the rear one; it was like holding a fishing rod with a thousand-pound fish on: the whole sail-like mass of canvas flapped and caved and wanted to fly. One or two ropes on the windward side had broken loose and the wall plastered itself against his legs, and wind and snow poured like ice water across his stockinged feet. "Somebody get outside and tie us down," Ray's grating whisper said. Little Horn scrambled past, then Spurlock. Panguingue crawled toward the front flap on hands and knees, Slip and Buck followed him. Braced against the pole, old Jesse was laughing; he lit a match on his pants and got a candle going and stuck it in its own drip on the stove. The stovepipe lay in sooty sections across the beds.

Ropes outside jerked; the wall came away from Rusty's legs, the tent rose to nearly its proper position, the strain on the pole eased. Eventually it reached a wobbly equilibrium so that he could let go and locate his boots in the mess of his bed. The five outsiders came in gasping, beating their numbed hands. In the gray light of storm and morning, they all looked like old men; the blizzard had sown white age in their beards.

"*God* A'mighty!" Slip said, and wiped away an icicle from under his nose.

"Cold, uh?" Ray whispered.

"Must be thirty below."

"Will the tent hold?"

"I dunno," Slip said. "Corner ropes is onto the wheels, but one of the middle ones is pulled plumb out."

They stood a second or two, estimating the strain on the ropes, and as if to oblige their curiosity the wind lit on them and heeled them halfway over again. The whole middle of the windward wall bellied inward; the wind got under the side and for an instant they were a balloon; Rusty thought for certain they would go up in the air. He shut his eyes and hung on, and when he looked again three of the boys had grappled the uplifting skirt of the cloth and pinned it down.

"We got to get in off these flats," Jesse said.

"I guess," Ray said. "The question is how. It's three-four miles to the river."

"We could keep the wind on our left and drift a little with it. That'd bring us in somewhere below Bates Camp."

"Well," Ray said, and looked at the rest of them, holding the tent down, "we haven't got much choice. Slip, you reckon we could find any horses in this?"

"I reckon we could try."

"No," Ray said. "It'd be too risky. We couldn't drive them against this wind if we found them."

"What about the cattle?" Buck said.

"Yeah," said Little Horn. "What about them?"

"D'you suppose," Ray whispered, and a spasm like silent mirth moved his iron face, "after we get things ready to go, you boys could pull about three poles out of the corral gate?"

"You mean turn 'em loose?"

"I mean turn 'em loose."

Ed Spurlock said, "So after all this, we wind up without a single God damn calf?" and Ray said, "You rather have a corral full of dead ones?"

Rusty leaned against the swaying pole while the furious wind whined and howled down out of the Arctic, and he listened to them with a bitterness that was personal and aggrieved. It seemed to him atrocious, a wrong against every principle and every expectation, that the devoted and herculean labors of eight good men should be thwarted by a blind force of nature, a meteorological freak, a mere condition of wind and cold.

Now on with the boots over feet bruised and numb from walking stocking-footed on the frozen ground, and on with the overshoes, and stamp to get life going. Now button the sheepskin collar close and pull the fur cap down, earlaps and forehead piece, leaving exposed only the eyes, the chattering jaw, the agonized spuming of the breath, *huh-huh-huh, huh-huh-huh-huh*. Clumsy with clothing, beat mittened hands in armpits, stoop with the others to get the stovepipe together, the grub box packed, the beds rolled. "Keep out a blanket apiece," Ray Henry says.

The tent tugs and strains, wanting to be off. In the gray light, snow sifts dry as sand down through the open stovepipe thimble and onto the stove—a stove so useless that if anyone touched it with a bare hand he would freeze fast.

As in a nightmare where everything is full of shock and terror and nothing is ever explained, Rusty looks around their numb huddle and sees only a glare of living eyes, and among them Panguingue's eyes that roll whitely toward the tent roof to ask a question.

"We'll leave it up till we get set," Ray says. "It ain't a hell of a lot, but it's something."

They duck outside, and shielding faces behind shoulders and collars, drive into the wind. The paralyzing wind hammers drift against eyelids, nose, and lips, and their breath comes in gasps and sobs as they throw things into the wagon. Jesse and Ray are harnessing the Clydes over their yellow blankets, Slip pounds ice off the blanket of the night pony getting ready to throw the saddle on. From their feet plumes of drift streak away southward. Beyond the figures in the squirming dusk the whole visible world moves—no sky, no horizon, no earth, no air, only this gray-white streaming, with a sound like a rush of water, across and through it other sounds like howling and shouting far off, high for a moment and lost again in the whistle and rush.

The cheek Rusty has exposed feels scorched as if by flame. Back in the icy, half-cleared tent, the hollow of quiet amid the wind seems a most extravagant sanctuary, and he heaves a great breath as if he has been running. He does not need to be told that what moves them now is not caution, not good judgment, not anything over which they have any control, but desperation. The tent will not stand much more, and no tent means no fire. With no horses left but the Clydes and one night pony, they will have to walk, and to reach either of the possible shelters, either Stonepile or Bates Camp, they will have to go north and west, bucking the wind that just now, in the space of a dozen breaths, has seared his face like a blowtorch. He has a feeling outraged and self-pitying and yet remotely contemplating a deserved punishment, a predicted retribution, the sort of feeling that he used to have in childhood when something tempted him beyond all caution and all warnings and he brought himself to a caning in the iodine- and carbolic-smelling office where his father, the doctor, used to look him down into shame before laying the yardstick around his legs. They have got what they deserved for daring Authority; the country has warned them three separate times. Now the punishment.

Into the wagon, jumbled any old way, goes everything the tent holds—grub box, saddles, stove, stovepipe, kerosene can, and again they gather in the still, icy hollow, strangely empty without the stove. Ray Henry has two lariats in his hands, Buck an axe, and Jesse a lighted lantern. The foreman wipes his nose on the back of his mitt and squints at old Jesse. "Dad, you sure you want to drive? It'll be colder up there than walkin'."

The old-timer shakes the lantern, and his eyes gleam and his square teeth gleam. "Lantern between m'feet, buffler robe over the top," he says, "I don't care how cold I get upstairs if I'm warm from the tail down."

"Long as you don't set yourself afire," Ray says. "How about somebody ridin' up there with you?"

"Dee-lighted!" Jesse says, flashing his teeth like Teddy Roosevelt, and they laugh as if they were all short of wind. The foreman's gray thinking eyes go over them. When his look pauses on Rusty Cullen, the boy's breath is held for a moment in sneaking hope, for he has never been so miserable or so cold; the thought of going out there and fighting across six miles of snowflats in the terrible wind has paralyzed his nerve. Also, he tells himself, he is the injured one; his arm still hurts him. The possibility pictures itself seductively before him: to ride, bundled under the buffalo robe and with the lantern's warmth. Like a child pretending sleep when a night emergency arises and the rain beats in an open window or the wind has blown something loose, to sit snug beside old Jesse, relieved of responsibility, while the grownups take care of it. . . . He cannot read the foreman's gray eyes; he feels his own wavering down. A crawl of shame moves in his guts, and he thinks, If he picks me it will be because I'm the weakest as well as the greenest.

The thinking eye moves on. "Slip," Ray says, "you ain't got the feet for walkin'. You can spell Dad with the lines. It'll be bad on the hands."

To cover his relief Rusty is beating his hands rhythmically in his armpits and jiggling on nerveless feet. He watches Ray pass the lariats to Little Horn. "If you're tied together, we won't lose nobody."

"Where'll you be?"

"I'll be ridin' pilot."

They are all moving constantly, clumsily. Spurlock has wrapped a woolen muffler around his mouth so that only his restless eyes show. Buck and Panguingue already have hung blankets over their heads and shoulders. Little Horn pulls off a mitt to pat the chimney of Jesse's lantern with a bare hand. "Well," Ray says, "I guess it's time she came down."

They lurch outside. Rusty, unsure of what to do, astonished at their instant obedience, finds himself standing stupidly while Buck with the butt of the axe knocks out one picket pin, then another, and chops off the ropes that tie the tent to the wheels. Jesse and Panguingue, at the ends, reach inside the flaps and lift and yank at the poles, and down it comes in a puddle of frozen canvas that they fall upon and grapple together and heave into the wagon. They curse and fight the wind, pushing and folding the tent down, throwing the poles and two saddles on it to hold it, hauling and lashing the wagon cover tight. Rusty looks back at where their shelter has been and his insides are pinched by cold panic. Drift is already streaking across the patch of thawed and refrozen grass; the little space their living warmth has thawed there in the midst of the waste looks as passionately and finally abandoned as the fresh earth of a grave.

Little Horn is tying them together, using the rope to snug and hold the blankets they have wrapped around themselves, when out of the tattered edge of storm cattle appear, longhorns that swerve away at a stumbling half-trot. After them and among them, a streaming miserable horde, come the whiteface and shorthorns, cows and calves, some steers, a few bulls, with no noise except an occasional desperate blat from a calf, and the clicking of longhorn hoofs and joints carried headlong southward by the wind. Well fleshed and round-bellied no more than a week ago, they stream and flinch past, gaunt ghosts of themselves, and Rusty thinks sullenly, while Little Horn ties the rope tight around him and their four hands tuck the blanket under, that it has been human foolishness that has brought the cattle to this condition. Driven all day by cowboys, and every other night by blizzards, they have eaten hardly anything for days. Left alone, yarding up in the coulees and river bottoms, they could at least have gnawed willows.

He is furious at their violent futile effort, and at Ray Henry for insisting upon it. Inhuman labor, desperate chances, the risk of death itself, for what? For a bunch of cattle who would be better off where their instinct told them to go, drifting with the storm until they found shelter. For owners off in Aberdeen or Toronto or Calgary or Butte who would never come out themselves and risk what they demanded of any cowboy for twenty dollars a month and found.

The tip of his mitt is caught under the rope; he tears it loose, and for a moment Little Horn's barely exposed eyes glint sideways, surprised. Out of the storm behind the last straggling cattle rides Ray Henry, already plastered white. He waves, somebody shouts, the wind tears the sound away and flings it across the prairie, the Clydes jerk sideways, the frozen wheels of the wagon crackle loose and crush through a crested foot-deep drift. The five walkers bunch up to get the protection of the wagon for their faces and upper bodies; the wind under the box and through the spokes tears at their legs as they swing half around and jolt off angling across the storm—northeast, Rusty judges, if the wind is northwest—following the stooped figure of the foreman on the horse. As they pass the corrals, Rusty sees the stained ground humped with carcasses already whitening under the blast of snow and wind.

He huddles his blanket across his chest, clenching and unclenching his numb hands; he crowds close to the others, eager to conform; he plants his feet carefully, clumsily, in the exact footprints of Ed Spurlock, and he tries to keep the rope between them just slack enough so that it does not drag and trip him. His face, unless he carelessly falls behind, is out of the worst lash of the wind; with walking, he has begun to feel his feet again. It seems possible after all—they can walk under these conditions the necessary five or six miles to shelter. He is given confidence by the feel of the rope around his waist, and the occasional tug when Spurlock or someone else up ahead stumbles or lurches, or when he feels Little Horn coming behind. Beside his cheek the wheel pours dry snow, and every turning spoke is a few inches gained toward safety.

Once, as they bounced across the flats, Slippers leaned out and shouted something down to Buck, leading the single-file walkers. An unintelligible word came down the line, the wheels beside them rolled faster, and they were forced into a trot to keep up. Rusty staggered sideways in the broken snow, kept himself from falling under the wheel by a wild shove against the wagon box, lurched, and was yanked forward into step so roughly that it kinked his neck. The line of them jogged, grunting in cadence, trotting awkwardly armless, wrapped in their blankets, beside the ponderous wagon. Eventually Buck shouted up at the seat, and they slowed to a walk, but the run had done them good. The blood was out at their edges and extremities again. Rusty felt it sharp and stinging in his cheeks.

Up ahead, revealed and half covered, and revealed and nearly obscured, moving steadily through the lateral whip and crawl of the storm, went the whitened horse, the humped white figure of Ray Henry. Once when Rusty looked he was down, walking and leading the pony. A few minutes later he was up again. The plain stretched on, interminable. Rusty dropped his head turtle-fashion, wiped an edge of the blanket across his leaking and freezing nose, concentrated on putting his feet precisely into the tracks of Ed Spurlock. Dreamlike and hypnotic, body moved, brain moved, but both sluggishly, barely awake. Life was no more than movement, than dull rhythm. Eyes were aware only of the drooping rope, the alternating feet ahead, and once in a while the glimpse of Ray Henry moving through the blizzard out at the edge of visibility. Walking or riding, he went with the inevitability of a cloud driving across the sky; to look up and find him not there would have been a shock and a dismay. And yet he went ambiguously too, something recognized or remembered from an old charade or pantomime or tableau, Leader or Betrayer, urgent, compulsive, vaguely ominous, so that one hurried to keep him in sight and cursed him for the way he led on, and on.

In the thudding hollows of the skull, deep under the layered blanket, the breath-skimmed sheepskin, inside the stinging whiskered face and the bony globe that rode jolting on the end of the spine, deep in there as secret as the organs at the heart of a flower or a nut inside shell and husk, the brain plodded remotely at a heart's pace or a walking pace, saying words that had been found salutary for men or cattle on a brittle and lonesome night, words that not so much expressed as engendered what the mind felt: sullenness, fear, doubt.

Up ahead the foreman moved steadily, dusky stranger, silent companion, and if he did not "bend upon the snowshoe with a long and limber stride," he had a look as tireless and unstoppable as if he had in fact been that Spirit Hunter, that Walker of the Snow, one of the shapes with which the country deluded frightened men.

The wind had changed, and instead of driving at their legs under the box between the spokes was coming much more from behind them. Rusty felt Little Horn's hand on his back, but when he turned to see what was wanted, Little Horn shook his head at him from under the blanket hood: only a stumble, or the wind hustling him along too fast. The pour of dry snow from the wheel blew on forward instead of sideward into their faces. Except for his hands and his impossible leaky nose, he was not cold. They must have come more than half of the three miles that would bring them to the river, where there would be protection among the willows and under the cutbanks, and where they might even choose to make some sort of shelter of the wagon and the tent—build a big wood fire and thaw out and wait for the storm to blow by. He hoped they would; he did not relish the thought of turning into the wind, even in the more sheltered river valley.

He saw The Walker coming back, bent double, his face turned aside. When he reached them his pony turned tail to wind and Jesse cramped the Clydes around and they stood for a brief conference. It seemed that the wind had not changed. The horses simply wouldn't head across it, and kept swinging. That meant they would hit the river lower down, and have a longer upwind pull to Bates.

Only Ray's eyes showed through the mask-like slot of a felt cap that came clear down around his throat. To Jesse and Slip he whisper-shouted something that Rusty could not hear, and mounted and rode off again. The wagon crunched after him, the segmented ten-footed worm beside it took up its lockstep. Deafened by fur and wool, anesthetized by cold and the monotony of walking, the next-to-last segment, joined to the segments before and behind by a waist of half-inch hard-twist rope, plodded on, thinking its own dim thoughts, which were concerned with cosmic injustice and the ways of God to man.

Why couldn't there be, just at this moment, the lucky loom of an unknown or unexpected cowcamp, the whiff of lignite smoke on the wind? Why, just once, could not rescue come from Heaven, instead of having to be earned foot by foot? He dreamed of how warmth would feel in the face, the lovely stink of four or five shut-in cowboys in a hot shack, and he sucked and sniffed at the drooling of his mouth and nose, a hateful, inescapable oozing that turned to ice in his beard and on his lips.

Head down, he plodded on, one step and then another. Once as he put his foot in the print that Spurlock's foot had just left, he caught the heel of Spurlock's overshoe with his toe, and saw Spurlock fling an irritable snarl over the shoulder. Oh, the hell, he thought. Can't you be decent even when we're like this? The rope tugged tight around him, he hopped to get in step again, walking carefully, left, right, left, right, wiping his leaking nose against the blanket's edge and feeling slick ice there.

Sancta Maria, speed us!
The sun is falling low;
Before us lies the valley
Of the Walker of the Snow!

Later—hours or days, for time whipped and snaked past in unceasing movement like the wind and the trails of drift, and all its proportions were lost—Rusty bumped into Spurlock and an instant later felt Little Horn bump into him in turn. The wagon had stopped, and Ray was back, leading his pony by the bridle. His visor of felt was iron-stiff with ice, so that he pulled it down and craned his neck and lifted his chin to shout over it to Jesse, perched on the high seat beside Slip with the buffalo robe folded up around him under the armpits. Rusty, squinting to see what they were looking at, felt the sticky drag of ice on his lashes as if his eyes were fringed with crickets' legs, and saw that ahead of them the land fell away beyond an edge where the grass was blown bare. Ahead or below, the ground-hugging trails of drift were gone, leaving only air murky as dusk, with fitful swirls and streaks of dark at its bottom which he realized were brush. He dragged at his wet nose. The river.

But the brief, gratified expectation he had that this would be an easier stage lasted no more than two minutes. The hills dipping down to the floodplain were gullied and washed, and drifted deep. Even with Ray riding ahead to try the going, the wheels dropped into holes and hollows, rose over knobs; the wagon canted at perilous angles, groaning and jolting its way slanting, with the wind almost dead behind it. Pulling out wide from the rocking wagon, the men were caught in the open wind and blown along. Rusty saw the Clydes braced back in the breeching, their hairy fetlocks coming up out of the snow rattling with balls of ice, and their muscular haunches bunching under the blankets, and then here came Slip digging out from under the buffalo robe to throw his weight on the brake. Ice against ice, shoe slid on tire and held nothing; the wagon rolled heavily down upon the Clydes, who braced lower, slipping. The walkers jumped aside and then, as the wagon lumbered past them, jumped to the endgate to try to hold it back. Its ponderous weight yanked them along, their dug heels plowed up snow. They could feel it under their hands getting away, they knew it without Jesse's yell that snapped off on the wind above their heads. Jesse rose half to his feet, braced between seat and box. The wagon jackknifed sharply as he swung the Clydes along the sidehill to slow them. The left side dropped down, the right heaved up, and with a neat final motion like the end of a crack-the-whip the wagon tipped over and cast off Slip in a spidery leap down the hillside. Jesse, hanging to the tilted seat to the end, slid off it to land on his feet with the reins in one hand and the lantern in the other. By the time Ray discovered what had happened and rode back, he had unhooked the Clydes and got them quiet. The wagon lay with its load bulging out of the lashed cover, the busy wind already starting to cover it with snow.

Rusty would not have believed that in that wind and cold it was possible to work up a sweat, but he did. It was a blind and furious attack they launched on the tipped wagon, unloading almost everything and carrying it down to more level ground where the abrupt hill aproned off, stacking it there while they floundered back to dig and pry at the jackknifed wheels. Ray hitched on with his saddle horse, they heaved while their held breath burst out of them in grunts and straining curses, until they righted it, and straightened the wheels, and a spoke at a time got them turning; three of them carrying the tongue and the others ready to push or hold back, they angled it down onto leveler and smoother ground.

There they wasted not a second, but hitched up and loaded as if they raced against time. When the muffled-up figure of Spurlock started to heave a saddle up, and slipped and fell flat on its back with the saddle on its chest, Rusty coughed out one abrupt bark of laughter, but no one else laughed. Panguingue and Buck picked the saddle off Spurlock's chest and tossed it aboard, and before Spurlock was back on his feet Little Horn and Buck were starting to tie together the worm of walkers. Up where Jesse and Slip were fussily folding the buffalo robe around and under them it looked bitterly cold, but down where Rusty stood it was better. He could feel his hands all the way, his feet all but the tips of the toes. Where the fur cap covered it, his forehead was damp, and under the ponderous layers of clothing and blanket his body itched a little with warmth. He was winded, and dead tired, and his shoulder ached as if the fierce haul and heave of the unloading and loading had pulled it from its socket, but the dismay of the accident was worked off. They were all right, they would make it yet.

He twisted to help Little Horn tuck the blanket-ends under the rope, and at that moment Spurlock, moving awkwardly in front, put his foot down crooked, reeled against him, landed on his foot and anchored him there, and bore him helplessly over in the drift. If it had been anyone else, Rusty might have laughed, reassured and warmed by work as he was; but since it was Spurlock he rose to one knee anticipating trouble. He was not wrong; the hand he put on Spurlock's arm was knocked off angrily, and through the layers of the muffler the words were savage: ". . . the Christ you're doing!"

The boy's anger blew up instant and hot, and he bounded to his feet freeing his elbows from the blanket. They faced each other, tied together by four feet of rope like gladiators coupled to fight to the death, and then the shadow above them made itself felt and Rusty looked up to see Ray Henry sitting hands-on-horn and looking down on them.

"What's trouble?" the foreman said.

The unintelligible growl that came out of Spurlock's muffled mouth could have told him nothing, but Rusty pulled the collar away from his chin and said passionately, "Look, put me somewhere else in this line! I'm not going to stand for . . ."

"What's trouble?" Ray said again.

"He keeps stumbling around and falling down and then blaming me . . ."

"If he falls down, help him up," Ray croaked, and kneed his frosted pony around and rode off in front. The wheels jerked, the icy axles shrieked, their feet automatically hopped to get in step, and they were walking again. Rusty pulled his chin back inside the collar and went sullenly, furious at the injustice of the rebuke, and alert to make the most of any slightest slip or stumble ahead of him.

Down in the bottoms among the willows the wind was less, and they could bring the horses to turn halfway into it, feeling for the river. But if the wind was less, the snow was deeper; the Clydes floundered belly deep and the wagon box scraped up a great drift that piled up over the doubletree and against the stallions' rumps and finally stopped them dead. They shoveled it away and cleared the Clydes' feet, never quite sure whether or not they would have their brains kicked out. Then they fell into two lines out in front and tramped a way for the horses and the wagon wheels down through smothered rosebushes and between clumps of willow whose bark gleamed red under the hood of snow. Ten feet of it was enough to wind a man; they panted their way ahead, turned to tramp backward and deepen the track, stopped every twenty yards to dig away the snow that the wagon box scooped up. They worked like people fighting a fire, exhausted themselves and stood panting a minute and fell to it again, frenzied for the easy going on the river ice.

The wagon eased over the edge of a bushy bank, the Clydes plunged as Jesse took them over straight on. The front wheels went down, pushing the stallions out onto the ice. Just as Rusty saw them lunging to pull the wagon through, a jerk from behind dragged him over in the drift and the whole line of walkers came down. When they got to their feet there was the wagon on the river.

Getting up watchfully, Rusty thought he felt Spurlock yanking at the rope, and he yanked back harshly. Sunk between the muskrat cap and the muffler, and blindered on both sides by the wings of the mackinaw collar, Spurlock's eyes peered out like the eyes of a fierce animal peering from a crack in the rock, but he turned away without a word, giving Rusty at least the smoldering satisfaction of having yanked last, of having finished something that the other had started.

The cutbank partially shielded them from the wind. Upriver was a straight reach with an irregular streak of clear, blown ice down its center, grading up to shelving drifts against both banks. Drift skated and blew down it like dust down an alley. The last lap of the road to shelter lay before them as smooth as a paved highway.

Ray Henry, leading his pony down the broken bank, stopped by them a moment where they hung panting on the wagon. "Everybody all right?"

They looked at him from among their wrappings.

"Ed?" Ray said.

It seemed to Rusty terribly unjust that particular attention should have been paid to Spurlock rather than to himself. It meant that the foreman still looked upon Spurlock as in the right, himself in the wrong. It meant that he had no concern for the one of his men who was hurt, and might be in trouble. He saw Ray's eyes within the visor that was like the helmet of a hero, and his unhappiness that he had lost prestige and respect drove words to his lips, impulsive and too eager, anything to be recognized and accepted again. He did not care about Spurlock, actually; he was already ashamed of that quarrel. But he wanted Ray Henry to notice him, and so he said, "What do we do now, Ray? Camp here till it's over?"

"Not hardly," Ray said. "The Clydes have had all the fresh air they need."

"How much farther?"

"Three miles, maybe four."

"Do we ride from here?"

The gray, thinking eye examined him from within the helmet of ice-hardened felt. The foreman said, "You reckon you're any more petered than them studs?"

He went stooping and slipping out in front to confer with Jesse and Slip, and Rusty, avoiding Little Horn's eyes and with his back to Spurlock and the others, watched the smothered rosebushes on the bank quiver in a gust. The slow warmth under all his wrappings might have come from the heavy work of getting the wagon through the brush and the drifts, but it might just as well have been shame, and he hated them all for never giving a man a chance, for taking things wrong, for assuming what should not be assumed. He hadn't been wanting to quit, he had asked only for information. Sullenly he waited, resolved to keep his mouth shut and plod it out. Once they got back to the ranch, he could simply leave the job; he was under no obligation to stay at it any longer than he pleased to. Neither Ray nor anyone else could compel a man to stick it through months of this kind of thing, no matter how short-handed the T-Down was. There was sure to be a great change as soon as he announced he was leaving. He could see Ray Henry's face—all their faces. Every man who left, left more for the remaining ones to do. Too late, chaps. Sorry. Ta-ta, gentlemen. Enjoy the winter.

In the river bottom the wind was louder, though he felt it less. The bare willows and the rosebushes, bent like croquet wickets into the drifts, whistled with it, the cutbank boomed it back in hollow eddies, every corner and edge and groove of the valley gave it another tongue. More than out on the flats, even, it echoed with hallucinatory voices, shouts, screams, whistles, moans, jeers. Rusty concentrated on it. He had only been asking a perfectly reasonable question, considering that they were running for their lives and still had an unknown distance to go. Would it be so terrible to climb up and let those big strong horses pull them for a little while along the level ice? Would it, for that matter, be entirely unheard of to sacrifice the Clydes, if necessary, to save eight lives? He asked himself what about a leader who thought more of his horses than of his men.

The blood in his veins was sluggish with cold, his mind was clogged with sullen hatred. Ray, shouting up to Jesse and Slip, and Spurlock, weaving bearlike from one foot to the other, were both part of a nightmare which he loathed and wanted to escape, but the numbness held him and he stood spraddling, squinting from behind the wagon box, hearing the shouts of those ahead torn from their lips and flung streaming down the ice to become part of the headlong illusory wailing that blew and moaned around the river's bends. His mind, groping among images, was as clumsy as his mittened unfeeling hands would have been, trying to pick up a coin from the snow. He thought of old Jesse's friend down by Sheridan, with his frozen conversation, and of how others had explained, not so humorously, the voices that haunted the wind in this country.

> For I saw by the sickly moonlight
> As I followed, bending low,
> That the walking of the stranger
> Left no footmarks on the snow.

The voices of all the lost, all the Indians, *métis*, hunters, Mounted Police, wolfers, cowboys, all the bundled bodies that the spring uncovered and the warming sun released into the stink of final decay; all the starving, freezing, gaunt, and haunted men who had challenged this country and failed; all the ghosts from smallpox-stilled Indian camps, the wandering spirits of warriors killed in their sleep on the borders of the deadly hills; all the skeleton women and children of the starving winters; all the cackling, maddened cannibals; every terrified, lonely, crazed, and pitiful outcry that these plains had ever wrung from human lips, went wailing and moaning over him, mingled with the living shouts of the foreman and the old-timer, and he said, perhaps aloud, remembering the legend of the Crying River, and the voices that rode the wind there as here, *Qu'appelle? Qu'appelle?*

Heartless and inhuman, older than earth and totally alien, as savage and outcast as the windigo, the cannibal spirit, the wind dipped and swept upon them down the river channel, tightening the lightly sweating inner skin with cold and the heart with fear. Rusty watched Ray hump his back and shake off the worst of the blast, saw the arm wave. The wagon rolled again. Ed Spurlock, unready, was pulled sideways a stumbling step or two by the tightening of the rope, and Rusty got one clear look into the brown, puckered eyes. Out of his fear and misery and anger he sneered, "Learn to walk!" But if Spurlock heard he made no sign. In a moment he was only the hooded, blanketed, moving stoop, not human, not anything, that Rusty imitated movement for movement, step for step, plodding up the river after the wagon.

Exhaustion and cold are a kind of idiocy, the mind moves as numbly as the body, the momentary alertness that a breathing spell brings is like the sweat that can be raised under many clothes even in the bitterest weather; when the breathing spell is over and the hard work past, mind and body are all the worse for the brief awakening. The sweaty skin chills, the images that temporary alertness has caught scrape and rasp in the mind like edged ice and cannot be dislodged or thought away or emptied out, but slowly coagulate there.

For Rusty they were the images of fear. No matter how much he tried to tie his mind to the plod-plod-plod of foot after foot, he heard the spirit of that bitter country crying for cold and pain. Under his moving feet the ice passed, now clear, with coin-like bubbles in it, now coated with a pelt of dry smooth snow, now thinly drifted. The world swung slowly, the dry snow under their feet blew straight sideward, then quartered backward; his quickly lifted eyes saw that the right bank had dropped to a bar and the left curved up in a cutbank. The wind lashed his face so that he hunched and huddled the blanket closer, leaving only the slightest hole, and still the wind got in, filled the blanket, threatened to blow it off his back. His eyes were full of water and he wiped them free, terrified that they would freeze shut. With his head bowed clear over, almost to the rope, he stumbled on. Through the slits of sight remaining to him he saw that the drift now was blowing straight backward from Spurlock's feet. The river had swung them directly into the wind. The line of walkers huddled to the left until they were walking bunched behind the feeble protection of the wagon.

The wagon stopped, the line of walkers bumped raggedly to a halt. Rusty had forgotten them: he was surprised to find them there, glaring from the frozen crevices of their clothes. From out in front Ray Henry came looming, a huge indomitable bulk, leading the pony whose bony face was covered with a shell of ice, the hairy ears pounded full of snow, the breast of the blanket sheathed. He unlooped the halter rope and tied it to the endgate, pulled the bridle and hung it on the saddle horn. For a minute he rubbed and worked at the pony's face, turned grunting, and said from inside his visor, "They just can't buck it. We're gonna have to lead 'em." He helped Little Horn pull open the loose, frozen knot in the rope and free himself from the others. "Rusty," he said, "see if you can find a blanket up in the load somewhere."

Rusty found the blanket, the foreman and Little Horn flapped off with it, the walkers huddled back to the wagon, eying the miserable pony which now took half their shelter. After a minute or two the yell came back, they turned, they stirred their stiffened legs and moved their wooden feet. The wind shrieked around the wagon, between the spokes, along the axles and the snow-clogged reach, and Rusty, colder now than at any time since he had awakened half frozen in his blankets, heard the blizzardy bottoms wild with voices. *Qu'appelle? ... Qu'appelle? ... Qu'appelle?*

In an hour, or four hours, or ten minutes, the river blessedly bent rightward, and the wind went screaming and flying above them but touched them only in swoops and gusts. There was a stretch where the inshore drifts let them go close up under the bank, and for a brief time the air was almost still, the snow settling almost gently as on any winter's day, a day to put roses in the cheeks.

Sancta Maria, speed us!

During that brief, numbed lull Spurlock tangled his feet and fell again, pulling over Panguingue ahead of him. Rusty, hopping awkwardly to keep from getting entangled with the sliding, swiveling figures, saw Buck squat and grab the rope to maintain his balance against the drag of the fallen ones. There went the three of them, helplessly dragged along on back or feet, and here came Rusty, a lead-footed dancer, prancing and shouting in their wake until those up ahead heard and they stopped.

Ray was back again. Panguingue and Buck stood up and cleared the rope, but Spurlock sat on the ice with his head down, pawing at his face and heaving his shoulders under the blanket. Rusty stayed back in scorn and contempt, sure that the blame would somehow be pinned on him. He was the proper scapegoat; everything that happened was caused by his awkwardness.

Ray was stooping, shaking Spurlock's shoulder. His hand worked at the muffler around Spurlock's face. Then he straightened up fierce and ready and with so much power left that Rusty moved a step back, astonished. "The lantern!" Ray shouted, and lunged around the line of walkers to reach and take the lantern from Jesse's hand. Back at Spurlock, stooping to hold the lantern directly against the muffler, he said over his shoulder, "Rusty, unhitch yourself and rustle some wood. We're gonna have to stop and thaw out."

The knot was stiff with ice, his fingers like sticks, but he got loose and stumped around in the deep snow breaking dead stalks out of willow clumps. Slip appeared to help him, and Rusty said, pausing a second in his fumbling, "What's the matter with Spurlock?"

"Smotherin'," Slip said. "God damn muffler froze to his whiskers."

"Are we going to camp here?"

"Why?" said Slip in surprise. "Do you *want* to?"

Rusty floundered down the bank with his handful of twigs, watched Panguingue cone them on the ice and souse them with kerosene. The smell cut his nostrils, and he sniffed back the wetness and spat in the snow. It was that drooling that had got Spurlock in trouble. Drool and freeze fast. Dully curious, he watched Ray moving the lantern glass around on the frozen wool, while Buck pulled on the unfrozen ends. Spurlock's head was pulled out of his collar; he looked like a fish on a hook. Then Panguingue found a match and reached across Buck to scratch it on the dry bottom of the lantern. The little cone of sticks exploded in bright flame.

"More," Panguingue said thickly.

Little Horn, who had led the Clydes around in a half circle, was already up over the endgate, unlashing the wagon cover. Stupidly Rusty watched as he loosened it all across the windward side and dropped it in the lee, and then, comprehending, he helped tie it to the spokes to make a windbreak. The fire had burned out its splash of kerosene, and was smoldering in the snow until Panguingue swished it again and it blazed up. "More!" he said. "We need wood."

"In the wagon," Jesse said. "What do you think I chopped all that wood for yesterday?"

He climbed the wheel to burrow into the uncovered load, and his face with its bowed mustaches emerged from under the tangled tent like a walrus at a waterhole and he winked in Rusty's face, handing him out wood two and three sticks at a time. His manner was incredible to the boy. He acted as if they were out on a picnic or a berry-picking and were stopping for lunch. Buck and Ray were holding Spurlock's face close to the little fire and working away at the muffler. The wind, here, was only a noise: they squatted in their bivouac with the fire growing and sputtering in the water of its melting, and they gathered close around it, venturing their faces a little out of their coverings.

Spurlock cursed clearly for the first time, the muffler came loose in Buck's hands. Ray set the lantern aside while Spurlock breathed deeply and passed his hands around on his face.

"Stick her right in," Jesse said. "That's the quickest way to thaw her. Set those weeds on fire."

They sat knee to knee, they put their mittens on sticks of wood in the snow and held stiff red hands in the very flames, they opened collars and exposed smarting faces. Life returned as pain: far down his legs Rusty felt a deep, passionate ache beginning in his feet. He knew from the burn of his cheeks and the chilblain feel of his fingers that he would have some frostbite to doctor. But he loved the snug out-of-the-wind shelter, the fire, even the pain that was beginning now and would get worse. For no matter how they came out, or whether they camped here to wait out the storm or went on after a rest to Bates, which couldn't be more than another mile or two, he would go with a knowledge that warmed him like Jesse's lantern under the robe: it hadn't been *he* that cracked. And what a beautiful and righteous and just thing it was that the one who did crack should be Spurlock! In triumph and justification he looked across the fire at the sagging figure, but he couldn't make the restless reddened eyes hold still. Spurlock hadn't said a word since they released him from the smothering scarf.

A half hour later, when Ray said they must go on, Rusty received the words like a knife in his guts. He had been sitting and secretly willing that they should stay. But he glanced again across the fire and this time caught Ed Spurlock's moving eyes, and the eyes ducked like mice. He told himself that if he was unwilling, Spurlock was scared to death. When they lashed the wagon cover back on and tied themselves together again and hooded the Clydes in the red Hudson's Bay blanket and Little Horn and Ray swung them by the bits and the forlorn night pony stretched his neck and came unwillingly, Rusty had a feeling that the moving line literally tore Spurlock from the side of the fire, now sunk into the crust and sizzling out blackly at the edges in steam and smoke.

The river swung, and the wind got at them. It swung wider, and they were plucked and shoved and blinded so that they walked sideward with their backs to the bar and their faces turned to the fantastic pagoda-roof of snow along the cutbank. In fury and anguish they felt how the river turned them. Like things with an identical electrical charge, their faces bent and flinched away, but in the end there was no evading it. The wagon stopped and started, stopped and started. The feet that by the fire had felt renewed life began to go dead again, the hands were going back to wood, the faces, chafed and chapped and sore, were pulled deep into the wool and fur. Gasping, smelling wet sheepskin and the tallowy smell of muskrat fur, feeling the ice at their very beards and the wind hunting for their throats, they hunched and struggled on.

Rusty, bent like a bow, with every muscle strained to the mindless plod, plod, plod of one foot after the other, and his eyes focused through the blanket's crack on Spurlock's heels, saw the feet turn sideward, the legs go out of sight. Apparently Spurlock had simply sat down, but the rope, tightening on him, pulled him over. Sliding on the ice, hauled after the backward-walking, braced, and shouting Panguingue, he was trying to untie the rope around his waist with his mittened hands.

Again their yells were torn away downwind, voices to blend with the blizzard's crying, or thaw out to haunt hunters or cowboys in some soft spring. They dragged Spurlock a hundred feet before those up in front heard. Then Rusty stood furiously over him and cursed him for his clumsiness and cried for him to get up, but Spurlock, straightening to sit with his arms hung over his knees, neither looked up nor stood up. He mumbled something with his head down.

"Lone," he mumbled, "rest minute."

Rusty's leg twitched: he all but kicked the miserable bundle. Slip and Jesse or both were shouting from the wagon seat, Ray Henry was coming back—for the how many'th time? They were utterly exposed, the wind whistled and the drift blinded them. He dropped his mouth again to Spurlock's ear, shouted again. Panguingue was hauling at Spurlock's armpits. "Can't sit down," he said. "Got to keep him movin'."

Not until then did the understanding grow into Rusty's mind, a slow ache of meaning like the remote feeling in his feet. Spurlock was done. It wasn't just awkwardness, he wasn't just quitting, he was exhausted. The danger they had been running from, a possibility in which Rusty had never thoroughly believed, was right among them. This was how a man died.

His hands found an arm under blanket and coat, and he and Panguingue helped Spurlock's feeble scrambling until they had him on his feet. They held him there, dragged down by his reluctant weight, while Ray peered grimly into his face. "He's played out," Panguingue said, and Rusty said, "Couldn't we put him in the wagon? He can't walk any farther."

Ray said, "Put him in the wagon he'd be froze stiff in twenty minutes." His hands went out to Spurlock's shoulders and he shook him roughly. "Ed! You hear? You got to keep movin'. It's only another mile. Just keep comin'."

"'mall right," Spurlock said. "Just rest minute."

"Not a damn minute," Ray said. "You rest a minute and you're dead."

Spurlock hung between Rusty and Panguingue until they were holding almost his whole weight. "You hear, Ed?" Ray said, glaring from his visor like a hairy animal. "You stop to rest, you're dead. Come on now, stand up and walk."

Somehow he bullied strength into the legs and a glitter of life into the eyes. Then he drove back against the wind to take the bridle of the off horse, and the halting, laborious crawl moved on. But now Rusty and Panguingue had hitched their ropes around and walked one on each side of Ed Spurlock, each with a hand under the rope around his waist to haul him along, and to support him if he started to go down. He came wobbling, and he murmured through the blanket they had wrapped over his whole head, but he came.

Rusty's shoulder ached—he ached all over, in fact, whenever he had any feeling at all—and the strain of half supporting Spurlock twisted his body until he had a stabbing stitch in his side. The hand he kept in Spurlock's waist rope was as unfeeling as an iron hook.

A mile more, Ray said. But the river led them a long time around an exposed loop. He had all he could do to force himself into the blast of snow and wind that faded and luffed only to howl in their faces again more bitterly than ever. When Spurlock, stumbling like a sleepwalker, hung back or sagged, trying to sit down, Rusty felt Panguingue's strength and heard Panguingue's stout cursing. His own face was so stiff that he felt he could not have spoken, even to curse, if he tried; he had lost all feeling in his lips and chin. His inhuman hook dragged at Spurlock's waist rope, he threw his shoulder across to meet Panguingue's when the weight surged too far forward, and he put foot after foot, not merely imbecilic now with cold and exhaustion, but nearly mindless, watching not the feet ahead, for there were none now, with three of them abreast and Buck trailing them behind, but the roll of the broad iron tire with the snow spume hissing from it.

He watched it hypnotically, revolving slowly like the white waste of his mind where a spark of awareness as dim as the consciousness of an angleworm glimmered. His body lived only in its pain and weariness. The white waste on which the wheel moved broke into dark angles, was overspread by blackness that somehow rose and grew, strangely fluid and engulfing, and the air was full of voices wild and desolate and terrible as the sound of hunting wolves. The led pony reared and broke its halter rope and vanished somewhere. Then Rusty felt himself yanked sideward, falling into Spurlock and Panguingue in an encumbered tangle, seeing even as he fell, shocked from his stupor, that the endgate was clear down, the hub drowned in black water that spread across the snow. Kicking crabwise, he fled it on his back, helped by someone hauling on the rope behind, until they stood at the edge of the little shallow rapid and saw Jesse and Slip in the tilted wagon ready to jump, and the round wet heads of stones among the broken ice, and the Clydes struggling, one half down and then up again, Little Horn hanging from the bits, hauled clear of the ice as they plunged. There was a crack like a tree coming down, the stallions plunged and steadied, and then Ray was working back along the broken tongue to get at the singletrees and unhook the tugs and free them.

Ray was standing on the broken tongue and calming the stallions with a hand on each back while he yelled downwind. Rusty pulled at his cap, exposed one brittle ear, and heard the foreman shouting, "Get him on up to the cabin . . . two or three hundred yards . . . right after you."

So with hardly a pause longer than the pause of their falling sideward away from the crunch of ice and the upwelling of water from the broken shell of the rapid, he and Panguingue were walking again, cast free from the rope and supporting Spurlock each with one arm around his shoulders, the other hands locked in front of him. He drooped and wobbled, mumbling and murmuring about rest. He tricked them with sudden lurches to left or right; when he staggered against them his weight was as hard to hold as a falling wall. Twice he toppled them to the ice. Compelled to watch where he walked, Rusty had to let the blanket blow from head and face, and without its protection he flinched and gasped, blinded, and felt the ice forming stickily along his eyelashes, and peered and squinted for the sight of the dugway that would lead them out of the channel and up the cutbank and across a little flat to the final security, so close now and so much more desperately hard to reach with every step.

The river bent, they dragged their burden along, they yielded to his murmurings and to their own exhaustion and let him sag a minute onto the ice, and then hauled and dragged him onto his feet and staggered on. The right bank was low and brushy; the wind came across it so that they leaned and fought across its whipping edge. Rusty freed his left hand and scoured the wrist of the mitten across his eyes and looked into the blast for the slant of the dugway, and saw nothing but the very throat of the blizzard. It was more than muscle and will could endure; panic was alive in his insides again. Even a hundred yards was too much; they could fall and die before the others could overtake them, right here within a few rods of safety. He gasped and sucked at his drooling lip, lost his hold on Panguingue's hand, felt with anguish how Spurlock slid away and went down.

Somehow they got him up again; somehow they struggled another hundred feet along the ice, and now a cutbank curving into a left-hand bend cut off some of the wind, and Rusty heard Panguingue grunt and felt the veer and stagger as he turned in toward the bank. Rusty still could not see it, but starting up, slipping, he put a hand down to stay himself and felt the dugway. Strengthless, they leaned into the bank; Spurlock tried to lie back; they held him with difficulty, and lifting the blanket to look into his face Rusty saw his eyes frozen wholly shut with teardrops of ice on the lashes. Above the dark beard the cheekbones were dead white.

When they tried to move him again, he sagged back against the bank and gave them his limp arms to haul at, and their combined strength was not enough to get him onto his feet, much less to start him up the steep dugway. They tried to drag him and stopped exhausted after six feet. The glare of uncertainty, fear, helplessness, was in Panguingue's glimmer of eyes and teeth. Rusty understood him well enough. Leave him? The others would soon come along. But if they didn't come in a few minutes he would be dead. Again they lifted and hauled at Spurlock, got him halfway, and felt him slip and go comfortably down again. Panguingue let go. "We better try to get up to the cabin. Schulz might be there."

"Suppose he isn't?"

He heard the forlorn, hopeless sound of Panguingue's snuffing. The face looked at him, bearded clear to the eyes.

"You go," Rusty said. "I'll wait here with him."

A snuffle, a momentary look, and Panguingue ducked away, scrambling with hands and feet, to disappear over the dugway edge.

For a while Rusty lay beside Spurlock on the slope, his blanket huddled over to cover both their faces, and simply waited, without mind or thought, no longer afraid, not hopeful, not even aware or sentient, but simply waiting while the gasp of breath and hammer of heart labored toward some slowing-point. He could not feel his feet at all; his hands were clubs of wood. Driven inward from its frontiers, his life concentrated itself in his chest where heart and lungs struggled.

A little later there was a stage in which his consciousness hung above him, like the consciousness in a dream where one is both actor and observer, and saw him lying there, numb already nearly to the knees, nearly to the elbows, nose and lips and forehead and the tender sockets of the eyes gone feelingless, ears as impersonal as paper ears pinned to his head. What he saw was essentially a corpse huddling over another corpse. He recognized the fact without surprise or alarm. This was the way it ended, this was the way they would be found.

Under the blanket's hood was a darkness and stillness. He felt how absurd it was, really. Absurd for men to chase around an arctic prairie wearing themselves and their cattle to death. Absurd. Take a rest, now, and . . .

Coming? Who? *Qu'appelle?* Old wolf, old walker of the snow, old windigo, *qu'appelle?* He smiled. It was a joke between them.

He heard now neither the wind nor the dry rustle of his mind. Inside the blanket the air was still, red-dusky, not cold. But as he moved to make his legs more comfortable the hillside toppled, a dull anguish of unwilling sensation spread in his throat, and he struggled back up, straightening the elbow that had given way and let him fall across Spurlock's up-jutting face. A powder flash of terror lighted up his whole head. The imprint of Spurlock's chin, unyielding as stone, ached in his Adam's apple. The face of a corpse—his too? But it was not his own pain so much as the appalling rigidity of Spurlock's jaw that shocked him. The man was dying, if not dead. Something had to be done, he couldn't just wait for help from Panguingue or the others.

His hands clutched and shook the stiffening bundle, the unfeeling hooks tried to close, to lift. "Ed! Ed, come on! We're almost there, man! Get up, you can't lie here. Only a little way farther. Ed! *Ed!* You hear? God damn it, Ed, get up! Come on, move!"

His eyes were full of catastrophic tears; he dashed them away with a fold of the blanket and threw a look up the dugway and gulped a burning throatful of the wind. He heard the voices wail and howl around the eaves of the riverbank, and he bent and slapped and pounded and tugged, screaming at the clownish, bearded, ice-eyed, and white-cheekboned face that turned and whimpered under his attack.

Gasping, he stopped a moment, threw another look upward. The top of the bank was less than thirty feet above him. Beyond that, within two hundred feet, should be the cabin. Five minutes, no more than ten even on hands and knees. He looked in anguish for the outfit, possibly coming up the river ice, and saw only trails of drift vanishing around the bend. The boys rendering their fantastic duty to the horses could not possibly come in time. And Panguingue must have found the shack deserted or he would have been back by now. Was he stopping to build a fire, or was he too exhausted to come back? Or was he lying in the snow himself, somewhere between the cutbank and the cabin?

"Ed! Wake up! Get up and walk! It's only a little way!"

Hopeless; inert and hopeless. He could not help the tears, though he knew they would be his blindness and his death. "Please, Ed! Please, come on!"

In a clumsy frenzy he hauled and yanked and dragged; his frantic strength skidded Spurlock a yard or two up the dugway, and when Spurlock began mumblingly to resist with arms and legs, Rusty attacked him with three times more fury and by slaps and kicks and blows reinforced his resistance until, miraculously, Spurlock was on his feet. With hooks and shoulder Rusty helped him, braced him, shoved him upward, moved him a step, and another; and crying encouragement, panting, winded and dead-armed and dead-legged, forced the man foot by foot up the dugway path until he felt the ground level off and the wind fling itself full against them.

They toppled and almost fell. Spurlock sagged and started to sit down and Rusty barely managed to hold him. He could not see more than a bleared half-light—no objects at all. His tears were already ice, his lashes stitched together, and he could make no move to clear his sight without letting Spurlock slip away, probably for the last time. Savagely he rasped his face across the snow-slick wool of Spurlock's blanketed shoulder; with what little vision he could gain he glared straight into the wind for the dark wall or icicled eaves that would be the cabin. The wind drove down his throat; his shouting was strangled and obliterated; it was like trying to look and shout up a waterfall. The wilderness howled at him in all its voices. He was brought to a full stop, sightless, breathless, deafened, and with no strength to move and barely enough to stand, not enough—frantically not enough—to hold the weight of Ed Spurlock that despite every effort he could make slid away and down.

With a groan Rusty let him go. Both hands rose to rub the wristlets of his mittens across his sealed eyes. Pain stabbed through his eyeballs as if he had run across them with sandpaper, but he broke the threads of ice that stitched him shut, and looked again into the gray and howling wind, saw a square darkness, a loom of shadow in the murk, and thought in wonder, My God, we've been right against the shack all the time, and then the darkness moved and the wind's voice fell from whine and howl to a doglike barking, and Panguingue was there shouting in his face.

Relief was such pure bliss to him that he was rendered imbecilic by it, and stood mouth open and cheeks stretched to force open his eyes, watching Panguingue try to pull Spurlock erect. He loved Panguingue, the stoutest and decentest and bravest and most dependable man alive. Merely his presence brought not only hope but assurance. It would be no trouble now. And even while he was bending to help he heard the unmistakable dig and clump of the Clydes behind him, and turned to see them clear the dugway with tennis balls of ice rattling in their fetlocks and Jesse hanging to the lines behind them, and then the others—one, then another, then another, leading the pony.

What had been impossible was suddenly easy, was nothing. Among them they hoisted Spurlock to his feet. Rusty felt an arm around him, the urge of someone else's undiminished strength helping him along through a thigh-deep drift that gave way abruptly to clear ground. His head sounded with hollow kickings and poundings and with one last defeated howl of wind, and he saw icicles under the shack's eaves like yard-long teeth, and the wind stopped, the noises fell, the light through his sticky eyelids darkened, his nostrils filled with smells of mice, kerosene, sheepskins, ham rind, sardines, and a delirious tropical odor of cinnamon and cloves like his mother's spice cupboard, and someone steered him and turned him and pushed on his shoulders, and Ray Henry's whisper said, "O.K., kid, take a load off your feet." He felt safety with his very buttocks as he eased himself down on the rustly hay-stuffed tick of a bunk.

. . .

Later he sat with his aching feet in a dishpan of snow and water, and when the pain in his hands swelled until it seemed the fingers would split like sausages, he stooped and numbed the ache into bearability in the same dishpan. His eyes were inflamed and sore; in each cheek a spot throbbed with such violence that he thought the pulse must be visible in the skin like a twitching nerve. His ears were swollen red-hot fungi, his nose that had run and drooled incontinently all the way through the blizzard was now so stuffed and swollen that he gurgled for air. He knew how he looked by looking at Little Horn, who had got wet to the knees when the Clydes went through the rapid, and who sat now on an apple box with first one foot and then the other in a bucket of snow. Little Horn's skin showed like a flaming sunburn through his reddish beard. He had innocent blue eyes like Jesse's, and the same blunt chin. When he was twenty years older he would look a good deal like Jesse—they were members of the same tribe. Now he lifted one tallowy foot from the deep snowprint in the pail and set it tenderly on the floor and lifted the other into its place, and looked across at Rusty with his mild ironic eye and shook his head in acknowledgment of something.

Ray and Jesse were squatting by the bunk against the side wall where Spurlock lay. Each had a blotched foot in his hands, each was massaging it and sousing it with snow. At the head of the bunk Buck worked on Spurlock's hands. Spurlock's fiery face looked straight upward; his teeth were set; he said nothing. Back by the door Slip and Panguingue had just finished washing each other's faces with snow. All of them, emerged from their cumbersome wrappings, looked disheveled as corpses dredged from a river. Rusty marveled at their bony hairless feet, their red hands, their vulnerable throats. They were making a good deal of talkative noise, their skins were full of the happiness of rescue, and not yet quite full of pain.

Little Horn looked at Panguingue's wet face. He said to Rusty, "Ain't that the way it goes? Of all the people that might of froze their feet and got a good wash out of it, who is the one God damn boy in the outfit without even a frozen toe but old Pan?"

355

Jesse said from the end of Spurlock's bunk, "Cold couldn't get through that crust."

"B.S.," Panguingue said. "I'm just tougher than you. And besides, I froze my face damn good."

"Snow washed some of the protective layer off," Little Horn said. "No, more I think of it, more I think you shouldn't make any mistake and wash them feet till spring, Pan. We'll need somebody around to do the chores while we get well."

"Hey, by God," Panguingue said. "How about my face?"

"Just leave it go. A little proud flesh would improve it."

"B.S.," said Slip, in imitation of Panguingue's growl, and he and Panguingue threatened each other with pans of snow. From the other bunk Ray Henry said, "Feelin' 'em yet?"

"You're damn right," Ed Spurlock said through his teeth.

"Better let 'em set in the water for a while," Ray said. "The slower they come back the better." He stood up, looking at Rusty. "Rusty, you needin' that dishpan for a while?"

"No, take it." He moved his feet carefully out onto the dirty board floor, and the foreman shoved the pan under Spurlock's dangling feet. Standing over Rusty, burly, matted-haired, grave-eyed, totally enigmatic to the boy but restored to his position of authority and respect, he said, "How you doin'? Feelin' yours?"

"Enough," Rusty said. He raised his head a little. "What's the cure for frostbite?"

"Whiskey," Jesse said from beside Spurlock.

"Fine," said Little Horn. "Just what we ain't got."

"If we had some rocks we could have some rock and rye," Slip said. "If we had some rye."

"No particular cure," Ray said to Rusty. "Thaw it out slow, keep away from heat, little arnica if you get sores, cut it out if you get gangrene. And wait."

"How long?"

"Depends how bad you are. You and Little Horn, maybe a week, ten days. Ed maybe two-three weeks. It's the hands and feet that lay you up."

"What do we do, stay here till we're well?"

"I expect we'll cobble up that tongue and beat it for the ranch soon as it clears off."

"Vacation with pay," Little Horn said. "Peach pies. Whiskey every hour, while Panguingue does the chores. I tell you, Rusty, there's no life like a cowboy's."

But Rusty was thinking of the two weeks they had just gone through, and of the cattle that had gone streaming miserably downwind from the Horse Camp corrals, the gaunt exhausted horses that had hung around the tent and wagon until the wind literally blew them away. "What about the calves?" he asked. "And what about the horses?"

"Horses we'll have to round up, some of them anyway. They'll winter out all right, but we need work ponies."

"You mean—ride out there and hunt through all that country and drive them on back to the ranch?"

"Uh-huh."

"I tell you," Little Horn said, and lifted his left foot out of the bucket and raised his right tenderly in, "there's no business like the cow business to make a man healthy and active. There's hardly a job you can work at that'll keep you more in the open air."

Rusty smelled the coffee that Jesse had put on the fire as soon as he got it going. He saw the flaw of moisture the spout cast on the stovepipe, and he moved his pain-distended hands cautiously, cradling them in his lap. The shack's growing warmth burned in his cheeks. Over on the other side of the stove Slippers' face, purple in the bare patches, black where the beard grew, brooded with its eyes on the floor. This was the leathery little man who would ride out to bring the ponies back across sixty miles of rough country. And maybe one or two others—maybe himself—with him. The very notion, at that moment, moved the boy to something like awe.

"What about the calves?" he said.

For the first time expression—disgust? anger? ironic resignation?—flickered across Ray's chapped, bearded mouth. "The calves. Well, the ones that ain't dead by the time this one blows out may find some willows to gnaw in a coulee, and if we get a chinook they'll have feed and come through all right. If we don't get a chinook the wolves are gonna be very fat by spring."

"But we aren't going to try rounding them up again."

Ray turned away with the flicker widening momentarily on his mouth. "I wouldn't worry about it," he said.

"Don't be impatient," Little Horn said, and hissed sharply as he moved his foot and bumped the pail. He set the heel on the floor and looked at the swollen toes, looked at his sausage-like fingers, shook his head. On the bunk Spurlock raised one foot from the dishpan. "Wait a minute," Jesse said. "Got enough of that footbath for a while?"

He helped the legs with their rolled-up pants to straighten out in the bunk. In the silence that came down as the pain of returning blood preoccupied them Rusty heard the undiminished wind shriek along the icicled eaves of the shack and swoop away. Smoke puffed out around the rings of the stove lids, lay there for a minute like fat white circular worms, and was sucked in again. Shaggy as cavemen, weather-beaten and battered, they huddled back against the walls and away from the stove and contemplated each in his own way the discomforts of the outraged flesh. Each retired within his skinful of pain and weariness, and among them Rusty Cullen, as weary as any, as full of pain as any—pain enough to fill him to the chin and make him lock his jaw for fear of whimpering. He made note that none whimpered, not even Spurlock; the worst was an occasional querulous growl when one moved too fast. Jesse, the oldtimer, the knowing one, Nestor and patriarch, unfrozen except for a touch on the fingers and ears, moved between them in stockinged feet and flipped the coffeepot lid with the edge of his palm, saving his tender fingertips, and looked in. The mystic smells of brotherhood were strong in the shack. The stove lids puffed out worms of smoke once more, and once more sucked them inward. The wind went over and around them, the ancient implacable wind, and tore away balked and shrill.

The Rusty Cullen who sat among them was a different boy, outside and inside, from the one who had set out with them two weeks before. He thought that he knew enough not to want to distinguish himself by heroic deeds: singlehanded walks to the North Pole, incredible journeys, rescues, what not. Given his way, he did not think that he would ever want to do anything alone again, not in this country. Even a trip to the privy was something a man might want to take in company.

The notion insinuated itself into his head, not for the first time, that his sticking with Spurlock after Panguingue left was an act of special excellence, that the others must look upon him with a new respect because of it. But the tempting thought did not stand up under the examination he gave it. Special excellence? Why hadn't anyone praised him for it, then? He knew why: because it was what any of them would have done. To have done less would have been cowardice and disgrace. It was probably a step in the making of a cowhand when he learned that what would pass for heroics in a softer world was only chores around here.

Around him he heard the hiss of air drawn between clenched teeth, he saw the careful, excruciating slowness of hands and feet being moved in search of more comfortable positions, he saw and smelled and felt how he was indistinguishable from the other seven. His greenness did not show, was perhaps not quite so green as it had been. And he did not take it ill, but understood it as a muffled acceptance of acknowledgment, when Spurlock sniffed thickly and said to the sagging springs above his nose, "Is that coffee I smell, Jesse, or is it only fawncy?"